# FROM THE GROUND UP

## Mennonite Contributions to
## International Peacebuilding

Edited by

CYNTHIA SAMPSON

JOHN PAUL LEDERACH

OXFORD

UNIVERSITY PRESS

2000

# OXFORD
UNIVERSITY PRESS

Oxford   New York
Athens   Auckland   Bangkok   Bogotá   Buenos Aires   Calcutta
Cape Town   Chennai   Dar es Salaam   Delhi   Florence   Hong Kong   Istanbul
Karachi   Kuala Lumpur   Madrid   Melbourne   Mexico City   Mumbai
Nairobi   Paris   São Paulo   Singapore   Taipei   Tokyo   Toronto   Warsaw

and associated companies in
Berlin   Ibadan

Copyright © 2000 by Eastern Mennonite University

Published by Oxford University Press, Inc.
198 Madison Avenue, New York, New York 10016

Oxford is a registered trademark of Oxford University Press

Library of Congress Cataloging-in-Publication Data
From the ground up : Mennonite contributions to international
peacebuilding / edited by
Cynthia Sampson and John Paul Lederach.
p.   cm.
Includes bibliographical references and index.
ISBN 0-19-513642-X
1. Peace—Religious aspects—Mennonites—Case studies.
2. Mennonites—Doctrines—History.
I. Sampson, Cynthia.   II. Lederach, John Paul.
BX8128.P4.F76   2000
261.8'73'088287—dc21        99-044848

1  3  5  7  9  8  6  4  2
Printed in the United States of America
on acid-free paper

# Preface

D URING THE 1980S AND 1990S, the literature on conflict resolution and peacebuilding grew exponentially. But within that literature, there have been a number of important gaps. One certainly is the sparsity of materials that assume a legitimate connection between spirituality and pragmatic international peacebuilding. A second is the limited case material documenting the full range of peacebuilding activity by religious actors. This volume fits both of these categories and responds to yet a third gap: more formal and explicit documentation of the work of Mennonite-supported practitioners of international peacebuilding.

Within the arena of track two, or unofficial diplomacy, the Mennonites' sister peace church, the Society of Friends, or Quakers, has generally provided more documentation of that community's important work in international conciliation and mediation. While Mennonite practitioners have a theological tradition of pacifism dating from the sixteenth-century Reformation and broad-based contemporary international experience in relief, development, and conflict transformation activity, the stories of such initiatives have rarely been disseminated outside of Mennonite circles, much less been formally documented, studied, and analyzed. One reason for this may be the breadth of activity, which neither conforms with a single methodological approach to peacebuilding nor operates exclusively within one level of society. Another reason may be a tendency on the part of Mennonites not to document their peace activities using the analytical approaches of social science.

With this book of reflections, case studies, and analytical chapters, we begin to fill that gap. We are indebted to our funders for making the volume possible: the U.S. Institute of Peace, which provided the initial grant, the World Conference on Religion and Peace through a grant from the Rockfeller Foundation, and the Mennonite Central Committee.

Our approach is to begin by providing a set of essays by Mennonite or Mennonite-supported practitioners that document their approaches and specific experiences in international peacebuilding. The lead essay, written by a Mennonite historian, provides a historical overview of the emergence and work of the Mennonite Conciliation Service, International Conciliation Service, and Christian Peacemaker Teams. This will provide a context for understanding the institutional motivations and support for conciliation and other peacebuilding work within Mennonite circles. It is followed by two chapters written by the two Mennonite practitioners with the longest and broadest range of experience, and they reflect across the different contexts in which they have been active. These are followed by a somewhat representative set of case studies, which cover diverse geographic locations, levels of application, and peacebuilding approaches. The case study authors have sought to identify some of the dilemmas they faced and the philosophical and strategic underpinnings of the choices they made in pursuing their work.

Finally, to provide an independent assessment of the body of work represented by the case materials, four non-Mennonite scholars have written analytical chapters from four perspectives: the cultural, conflict resolution, and spiritual dimensions of the work, as well as the assessments of local parties who have been partners in or in some way beneficiaries of Mennonite initiatives.

Two meetings of the authors were held as part of the research process. The first came at the beginning of the project and established guidelines for the work to follow. The second meeting provided an opportunity for the case study authors to present drafts of their chapters and for Mennonite and non-Mennonite authors alike to question, draw out, analyze, and compare the different experiences represented. Both meetings provided additional insights into the subject at hand, and these, too, were considered part of the pool of data from which the non-Mennonite analysts could draw.

A note to the reader: We have not thought it advisable to attempt to impose terminological conformity on the authors, particularly those writing the four analytical chapters, who represent different disciplines and institutions and somewhat different ideological frameworks. We have, however, asked the authors to signal for the reader the ways in which they are using key terms, such as *peacemaking* and *peacebuilding*, *conflict resolution* and *conflict transformation*, *conciliation* and *mediation*.

In parallel with the checks and balances inherent in our research design, we, the two editors, also represent the two sets of authors in this volume. One of us is a Mennonite peacebuilding practitioner, the other a non-Mennonite scholar. We hope this combination of perspectives in the chapters that follow will provide a distinctive blend of individual insight and independent analysis, which will enliven the record even as it illuminates it.

*Arlington, Virginia*                                                          C. S.
*Harrisonburg, Virginia*                                                    J. P. L.
*January 2000*

# Contents

# Contributors

BONNIE BERGEY works for Ten Thousand Villages, a nonprofit fair-trade organization that markets third world handicrafts. She formerly held a joint appointment as Somalia/Somaliland Representative for Eastern Mennonite Missions and the Mennonite Central Committee from 1990 to 1995. She also formerly served with EMM in Tanzania. She holds a master of arts in peace studies at Associated Mennonite Biblical Seminary.

JOSEPH CAMPBELL is assistant director of The Mediation Network for Northern Ireland, with support from the Mennonite Central Committee and Mennonite Board of Missions. He formerly worked as a secondary school teacher and as youth director of the Belfast YMCA, where he pioneered in conducting programs for both Protestant and Catholic youth. Mr. Campbell is an elder in the Presbyterian church. He is working on a master of arts in conflict transformation at Eastern Mennonite University.

MARK CHUPP is project manager at the Center for Neighborhood Development at Cleveland State University. He formerly founded a violence prevention agency in Elkhart, Indiana, directed a victim-offender reconciliation program, and directed the Mennonite Central Committee's Conflict Transformation and Mediation Project for Central America. He has initiated alternatives-to-violence projects in the United States and internationally. He holds a master of social work degree from the University of Michigan and is completing a Ph.D. in social welfare from Case Western Reserve University.

RICARDO ESQUIVIA is director of the Centro Cristiano para Justicia, Paz y Acción Noviolenta, Justapaz, of the Colombian Mennonite church. He has thirty years' experience in promoting human rights and nonviolence education and action. He is cofounder of the Colombian Community Justice and Conflict Treatment Network and of the Coalition for Conscientious Objection. Mr. Esquivia is also a member of the National Peace Council. He is a law graduate of the Universidad Externado de Colombia with a specialization in human rights from the Escuela Superior de Administracion Pública of Bogotá.

MARC GOPIN is adjunct assistant professor of diplomacy at the Fletcher School for Law and Diplomacy. He is also a senior associate in the Preventive Diplomacy Program at the Center for Strategic and International Studies, a research fellow in the Sociology Department of Brandeis University, and a practicing rabbi. Rabbi Gopin is the author of *Between Eden and Armageddon: The Future of World Religions, Violence, and Peacemaking* (2000). He holds a Ph.D. in ethics from Brandeis University and was ordained by Yeshiva University.

BARRY HART is an associate of the Institute for Justice and Peacebuilding of Eastern Mennonite University. He spent four and a half years in former Yugoslavia, where he conducted trainings and seminars for teachers and community leaders in trauma awareness, conflict resolution, and prejudice reduction. He also worked to develop ties among religious leaders in Croatia, Bosnia, and Serbia. Dr. Hart has conducted workshops on trauma healing and reconciliation in Liberia and Northern Ireland and among Rwandan Hutu refugees. He holds a Ph.D. in conflict analysis and resolution from George Mason University.

ROBERT HERR and JUDY ZIMMERMAN HERR serve as codirectors of the International Peace Office of the Mennonite Central Committee. They formerly served with MCC in South Africa from 1982 to 1991. During that period, Mr. Herr served as a development projects consultant with the South African Council of Churches/Transkei Council of Churches and then as the acting organizing secretary. Ms. Herr served as the MCC South Africa country representative for nine years; during the last five years, she shared the post with her husband. They also shared the post of MCC Southern Africa regional coordinator for five years.

KATHLEEN KERN is a full-time worker with the Christian Peacemaker Teams, an initiative of the Mennonite churches, Church of the Brethren, and Friends United Meetings. She has served with CPT in Haiti, Palestine, Washington, D.C., Mexico, and South Dakota. Ms. Kern has been a frequent contributor to adult Bible-study curricula since 1988, and she has published numerous books, articles, essays, and columns, including *We Are the Pharisees* (1995) and *When It Hurts to Live* (1994). She holds a master of arts in biblical studies from Colgate Rochester Divinity School.

RON KRAYBILL is associate professor of conflict studies at Eastern Mennonite University, where he also serves as associate director of the Institute for Justice and Peacebuilding. He formerly served as director of training at the Centre for Conflict Resolution in South Africa and as director of the Mennonite Conciliation Service in North America. He holds a Ph.D. in religious studies from the University of Cape Town, South Africa. His doctoral dissertation was "An Anabaptist Paradigm for Conflict Transformation: Critical Reflections on Peacemaking in Zimbabwe" (1996).

JOSEPH LIECHTY has worked in Ireland and Northern Ireland with Mennonite Board of Missions since 1980. Since 1995, he has worked (with Cecilia Clegg) for the Irish School of Ecumenics on Moving Beyond Sectarianism, a six-year research project on religion and conflict in Northern Ireland. He holds a Ph.D. in Irish history from St. Patrick's College, Maynooth. His doctoral dissertation was "Irish Evangelicalism, Trinity College Dublin, and the Mission of the Church of Ireland at the End of the Eighteenth Century" (1987).

JOHN PAUL LEDERACH is professor of conflict studies and sociology and founding director of the Conflict Transformation Program at Eastern Mennonite University. Dr. Lederach has extensive experience as a peacebuilding practitioner, trainer, and consultant throughout Latin America, Africa, and the United States, as well as in the Philippines, Northern Ireland, and the Basque Country. He has pioneered in culturally contextualized, elicitive methods of conflict resolution training and practice. He holds a Ph.D. in sociology from the University of Colorado.

SALLY ENGLE MERRY is the Class of 1949 Professor in Ethics and a professor of anthropology at Wellesley College. She is the author of many articles and books on mediation, law and society, and conflict resolution and is the coeditor (with Neal Milner) of *The Possibility of Popular Justice: A Case Study of American Community Mediation* (1993). Her most recent publication is *Colonizing Hawai'i: The Cultural Power of Law* (2000). She is past president of the Association for Political and Legal Anthropology and of the Law and Society Association. She holds a Ph.D. in anthropology from Brandeis University.

JOSEPH S. MILLER is on the pastoral team of Waterford Mennonite Church in Goshen, Indiana. In 1985–1989 he served as a Mennonite Central Committee volunteer in Budapest, Hungary, where he was the first Westerner permitted by the Communist government to study at the Baptist Theological Seminary. Mr. Miller also formerly served as administrator of the Mennonite Heritage Center, which oversees a museum, historical library, and archives. He holds a master of arts in religious studies from Villanova University.

CHRISTOPHER MITCHELL is the Drucie French Cumbie Professor of Conflict Analysis at the Institute for Conflict Analysis and Resolution of George Mason University. He served as director of the Institute from 1991 to 1994. Among his many publications on conflict resolution and third-party involvement in international disputes is *The Structure of International Conflict* (1981). Dr. Mitchell is also an active conflict resolution practitioner and has worked with conflicts in Europe and Africa. He holds a Ph.D. in international relations from University College, London.

CYNTHIA SAMPSON is president of Peace Discovery Initiatives, an organization that works in religious and interreligious peacebuilding, and an associate of the Institute for Justice and Peacebuilding of Eastern Mennonite University. She is an author and coeditor (with Douglas Johnston) of *Religion: The Missing Dimension of Statecraft* (1994). Ms. Sampson formerly worked with the World Conference on Religion and Peace and as an editor on foreign affairs at the *Christian Science Monitor*. She holds a master's in international affairs from Columbia University.

PAUL STUCKY works with the Centro Cristiano para Justicia, Paz y Acción Noviolenta, Justapaz, of the Colombian Mennonite church, in training and organizing churches and local communities for nonviolent action and conflict transformation. He holds a Ph.D. in psychology from George Peabody College, Nashville, Tennessee.

# Abbreviations

AMBS   Associated Mennonite Biblical Seminary
CPT   Christian Peacemaker Teams
EMM   Eastern Mennonite Missions
EMU   Eastern Mennonite University
ICS   International Conciliation Service
IJP   Institute for Justice and Peacebuilding
MBM   Mennonite Board of Missions
MCC   Mennonite Central Committee
MCS   Mennonite Conciliation Service

# I

## SETTING THE CONTEXT

# One

## A History of the Mennonite Conciliation Service, International Conciliation Service, and Christian Peacemaker Teams

JOSEPH S. MILLER

ARMISTICE DAY 1918 WAS REMEMBERED BY most Americans with pride and joy. The great war was over, and America had triumphed over Germany. But for Mennonite farmer John Schrag and his family, Armistice Day was always remembered with horror. On November 11, 1918, the patriotic citizens of Burrton, Kansas, decided that it was high time to show their Mennonite neighbor John Schrag that holding to the ancient pacifist faith and practice of his Anabaptist/Mennonite ancestors was not acceptable—not in America.

Five cars full of local men drove out to the Schrag farm. They vandalized the farm and dragged Schrag back to town, where they demanded that he purchase war bonds. He refused because he said it would be the same as serving as a soldier. The mob grew ugly and demanded that Schrag salute the American flag and carry the flag at the head of their Armistice Day parade. Schrag quietly and firmly refused to cooperate.

One thing led to another, and soon the flag had fallen on the ground. The crowd was incensed. They poured yellow paint on his head and beard and threw Schrag into the town jail. One of the citizens went for a rope to hang the Mennonite farmer, but Tom Roberts, the head of the local Anti-Horse-Thief Association, mediated the conflict in a very non-Mennonite fashion by pulling his gun and declaring, "If you take this man out of jail, you take him over my dead body" (Juhnke, 1989, pp. 224–225).

World War I, like all periods of war, was a time of sober reflection for the Mennonites in the United States. They had discovered that the American melting pot had turned once again into a crucible, which tested their faith and commitment to being conscientious objectors to war. There was shock and dismay among Mennonites when they realized that their neighbors were woefully unsympathetic to the Mennonites' peace position.

John Schrag's experience that disquieting day in 1918 in central Kansas was deeply rooted in the origins of his Mennonite faith and his church's 400-year history. Mennonite history dates from the Reformation in sixteenth-century Europe. Mennonites were first known by the epithet Anabaptists. Anabaptists believed that only an adult could make the necessary commitment to become a baptized Christian and that the bread and wine of the Lord's Supper were more symbolic of the body and blood of Christ than the state churches of the period taught. The believers' church tradition also practiced from its very beginning a deep commitment to peace and nonviolence—what would later become known as *nonresistance*. Most Anabaptist/Mennonites throughout their history doggedly refused to use a sword or gun in their own or their neighbors' protection. The Anabaptists drew on the words of Jesus in the gospel of Matthew 5:39, when they declared their unwillingness to use violence: "But I say to you, do not resist an evildoer. But if anyone strikes you on the right cheek, turn the other also." During the Reformation, thousands of Anabaptists were put to death by civil and religious leaders without violent resistance in their own defense.

When the Mennonites first settled in Germantown, Pennsylvania, in the late seventeenth century, they had well-developed survival skills, which resulted in sectarianism and quietism. With only a few exceptions, American Mennonites practiced a self-protective withdrawal from the world around them until the mid-twentieth century.

Changes became widespread during World War II, however, and were formulated theologically by John Howard Yoder's call (1954, pp. 1209, 1221[1]) and C. Norman Kraus's appeal (1968, pp. 538–540) for their fellow Mennonites to embrace a theology of involvement. During World War II, Mennonites were stirred from their isolated farming communities. Thousands of young Mennonite men were drafted by the government and then sent by their church across the nation to do alternative service, in lieu of military service. They had powerful moments of epiphany as they experienced the world beyond their sectarian enclaves. Leo Driedger and Donald B. Kraybill catch the spirit of the times when they write:

> Uprooted from rural homesteads, seeking higher education, entering professions and engaging in worldwide service activities, many Mennonites joined the mainstream of social life in the last half of the twentieth century. (1994, p. 15)

Many Mennonite men did their alternative service in Civilian Public Service (CPS) camps, which were under the administration of the Mennonite church. Through an agreement with the Selective Service System, the CPS camps were to engage in "work of national importance" (*Mennonite Encyclopedia*, 1955, p. 604).[2] There was also a concerted effort by the administrators of the CPS camps to introduce the young Mennonite men to the world of arts and letters. Most camps offered college classes, which were taught by the few Mennonites who had advanced academic degrees. CPS men learned much that they could offer their home communities on their return (Hershberger, 1945; see also Derstine, 1946, pp. 190–191).

Most Mennonites had a deep ambivalence about World War II. Many felt that German and Japanese fascism could not go unchallenged. Emotional and spiritual confusion was exacerbated by the fact that the majority of Mennonites were of Germanic background, and large numbers, even in the 1940s, still spoke German dialects in their homes and churches. Mennonites were keenly aware that some neighbors viewed them as slackers because of their conscientious objection to war and their refusal to be drafted into the military.

Reinhold Niebuhr had in 1937 (pp. 1390, 1391) articulated succinctly the criticism Mennonites had been hearing from their non-Mennonite neighbors throughout all of Mennonite history when he asserted that their nonparticipation in war made Mennonites "parasites on the sins of others."[3] Mennonites felt the sting of Niebuhr's indictment and began to see the inconsistency of the church's nonresistance, which at times seemed to value only withdrawal and separation from the larger culture. Mennonites began to seek more meaningful ways of fulfilling their alternative draft service. Many of the Mennonite conscientious objectors (COs) were grateful to be reassigned to what they considered to be more significant work as aides in mental health hospitals (Sareyan, 1994, p. 11).[4]

During World War II, there was for Mennonites an amazing coalescence of their deep and resolute commitment to biblical peace and justice and their intense desire to not be viewed by the larger society as slackers. These two motivating ingredients would push many Mennonites out of their quiet withdrawal and into involvement as active peacemakers.

It is noteworthy that Mennonites serving as COs repeatedly expressed a desire for work of real consequence for the larger community and society. They were not able, in good conscience, to serve in the war effort, but there was a palpable desire throughout the church to contribute constructively to society.

One of the most popular alternative service assignments for young Mennonite men during World War II was as smoke jumpers, fighting forest fires. These COs lived a life that had some of the trappings of military service. There were uniforms, danger, and even the coopted military language of fighting fires. The lucky few who were able to serve as smoke jumpers were only too happy to risk life and limb parachuting out of planes.

The desire to do something meaningful found some drafted Mennonite men and even several Mennonite women volunteering to serve as human subjects in medical research (Braden, 1965, pp. 22–24; see also Keys et al., 1950[5]).

Mennonites quietly noted with appreciation and satisfaction when newspapers and magazines began carrying stories about the important work that COs were doing through their participation in various medical experiments. They could not help but feel some measure of vindication when the *Tribune Journal* in Sioux City, Iowa, declared:

> In any nation at war, it is so customary to glorify deeds of fighting men that it is rather generally assumed there is no other form of heroism than facing danger and death at the fighting front. . . . The role of a CO with the courage of his convictions is particularly unenviable. . . . Considering this situation there seems reason to say a word of commendation for the more than 100 COs who are voluntarily serving as "human guinea pigs." (Sareyan, 1994, pp. 13, 14)

In their search for meaningful work as COs, Mennonites asked for permission to serve as aides and orderlies in the nation's mental health hospitals. In this work, they were shocked by the widespread cruel and inhuman treatment of patients. Young Mennonite men, who had not long before been naive farm boys, began to speak out in protest for the "voiceless" residents of psychiatric institutions (Sareyan, 1994, pp. 66–71). With such advocacy, the spell of Mennonites being the "quiet in the land" was broken.

If Mennonite farmer John Schrag served as the symbol of the Mennonite peace position prior to World War II, young men demanding justice for the voiceless residents of mental health hospitals became the symbol for the Mennonite peace position at the end of World War II. This was something new for American Mennonites and began the church's move away from the earlier teachings of Guy F. Hershberger, one of the denomination's leading writers on peace.

Hershberger had formulated a peace position that said that Christians must do justice but never demand justice: "It is not a demand for justice that the New Testament upholds, but rather an appeal to both parties to deal with each other in the spirit of love" (1946, p. 217). In clarifying his position, Hershberger condemned Gandhi by explaining: "Gandhi's program is not one of nonresistance or peace. It is a form of warfare" (1946, p. 220). By the end of the Second World War, Hershberger's teaching on nonresistance was no longer the single voice within the denomination on how to be a Christian peacemaker.

The shift from quiet separation to a theology of active involvement was furthered by the creation in 1942 of the Peace Section, the rambunctious institutional child of the Mennonite Central Committee (MCC). Formed in 1920, MCC is the relief and service agency that represents the various branches of the Mennonite church. John A. Lapp, executive secretary of MCC's Peace Section, in 1970 reflected that MCC's peace mission had three foci: (1) nurturing peace convictions, (2) staying out of military service, and (3) expanding peacemaking in conflict situations and promoting peace concerns among other Christians (Driedger and Kraybill, 1994, p. 143).

The third phase of Mennonite peacemaking went beyond a willingness to protest against injustice. It called Mennonites to become involved by helping the larger society find reconciliation in what would come to be called "social disasters." During the 1960s and 1970s, Mennonite involvement in domestic and international relief mushroomed. Throughout North America, Mennonites became well known as the people who arrived to give assistance after natural disasters. Their efforts to clean up devastated communities were directed through the Mennonite Disaster Service, which like the Peace Section was a subsidiary of the Mennonite Central Committee.[6]

Mennonites by the hundreds also fanned out across North America and the world teaching, cultivating fields, and dispersing relief goods sent by their fellow church members, who were prospering in North America. The relief and service work done under MCC auspices was enormous considering the size of the church. After World War II, nearly every North American Mennonite extended family had at least one member who had spent several years as an MCC volunteer (Kehler, 1981, pp. 7–10).

Paul L. Peachey was a central figure in setting the tone of post–World War II Mennonite peacemaking. As early as 1951, Peachey was cajoling his fellow Mennonites not to retreat back into their old sectarian nonresistant notions of peace. Peachey called on Mennonites to spread out across the world to preach and to practice peace. Significantly, he told Mennonites that as they traveled the world they would need to be ready to listen and to be in careful dialogue with the various cultures they would encounter (1958, pp. 283–289; see also 1976, pp. 247–258).

Increasingly educated Mennonites with their new mobility wandered the nation and the globe in search of places to do good works. But they also listened to their hosts, and they heard yet another call to mature their practice and understanding of biblical peacemaking. One such MCC relief worker was Hedy Sawadsky, who served as a two-year volunteer in Jordan and Israel in the late 1960s. A Palestinian woman spoke the words to her that would be repeated time and time again to Mennonite volunteers spread across the globe: "Hedy, what you're doing here is fine, but it's Band-Aid work. You came after the war, after the damage was done. Why don't you go home and work for peace and get at the root causes of evil and war?" (Driedger and Kraybill, 1994, p. 137).

Getting at the root causes began to weigh on the hearts of MCC relief workers and administrators and even people sitting in church pews. There was a growing sense that relief and service could not be disconnected from the Mennonites' stated commitment to peacemaking. In 1950, Harold S. Bender, editor of the *Mennonite Quarterly Review*, sowed seeds that would produce fruit much later by proclaiming on the pages of the *Review* that the denomination should do much more for vigorous peacemaking throughout the world. Bender wrote cogently, "It is a way which is aggressive and positive in its attack upon the problems of peace, and not merely passive" (1950, p. 150). After listening and learning from people around the world, one MCCer asked his readers in a church periodical if Mennonites were not actually joining the oppressors when they asked weak and powerless people not to resist their intolerable living conditions (Burrell, 1965, pp. 783–784).

There was an increasing realization that cleaning up and rebuilding after a war, riot, or tornado was important, but a Christian was also called to address systemic conditions that created injustice and violence. Mennonite relief workers were taught by their hosts that it was not enough for relief workers to distribute food and clothing to the starving and homeless. The starving and homeless articulated the need for more than material assistance. Mennonites were asked also to be peacemakers, to work at changing systems and institutions that caused suffering.

Herman Bontrager, an MCC administrator, stated what was becoming axiomatic (1979, pp. 4–8). Christians could no longer allow relief, development, and justice to be in tension because the Bible demanded a creative synthesis. The creation of the Mennonite Conciliation Service (1979), International Conciliation Service (1988), and Christian Peacemaker Teams (1989) were the direct results of an enlarged concept of Mennonite peacemaking, which sought to address the root causes of injustice and violence.

This ability to learn from the people to whom they were offering relief is perhaps rooted in Mennonites' sense of Christian humility, as well as a theology and ecclesiology based on group discernment and a high view of community. They understood that respect for their own families and faith community also meant respecting the systems of community discernment and wisdom of other cultures (Liechty, 1980, pp. 5–31).[7] It was out of this context that these three organizations emerged in the 1970s and 1980s.

## Mennonite Conciliation Service

In 1974, the MCC Peace Section asked three church leaders, Ted Koontz, Harold Regier, and Guy F. Hershberger, to begin a conversation with fellow Mennonites in California regarding a farm labor dispute between farmworkers and owners of fruit farms. Koontz wrote in his March 1974 report that they discovered there had been a great deal of heated disagreement between the United Farm Workers of America, led by Caesar Chavez, and the growers. There had even been a number of occasions of violence.

Ironically, Mennonites were on both sides of the picket line. There were a number of Hispanic Mennonites, who worked as laborers, and there were Mennonites of European descent, who were growers. Both groups of Mennonites stated resolutely that they had not been involved in the violence. Koontz reported that some of the Mennonite growers felt that

> the church should not become involved at all, but should rather limit its work to preaching the gospel. They indicated that up to this point the Mennonite church in the area had not become involved or begun discussions of this issue in the church. (1974, p. 5)

Koontz concludes his report by stating that he felt that the church does have a role to play in such a conflict, but he also admitted uncertainty about how the church could become involved in what some had called a secular problem. He pushed his thinking further by writing:

> My feeling at this point [is that] the larger Mennonite brotherhood could be most helpful by simply encouraging those churches and church members directly involved in looking carefully at this question. I also feel that there might be a role for Christians in the area to explore ways for communication to be opened between the parties in this situation. (1974, p. 11)

Guy F. Hershberger (1974), reflecting an older Mennonite quietism, wrote a separate eleven-page report in which he was more hesitant than Koontz about how the church should be involved in the conflict between farmworkers and growers. Under a section entitled "Personal Views of Guy F. Hershberger," he wrote that the MCC Peace Section should not identify itself with the labor unions that represented the farmworkers. Hershberger failed to caution the Peace Section to also not identify itself with the growers.

That summer, three Hispanic Mennonite leaders, Teodoro Chapa, Jr., Lupe DeLeon, Jr., and Neftali Torres, Jr., traveled to California and wrote a stinging indictment not only of Hershberger but of the whole Mennonite church:

> Obviously MCC suffers economically if it aligns itself with those who do not agree with the growers. This assumption is made recognizing that a great many supporters of MCC are Mennonite growers in California who are opposed to Caesar Chavez and the UFW. (1974, p. 15)

The Hispanic Mennonite church leaders noted that Mennonites in California said nothing when Japanese Americans were sent to concentration camps and that European Mennonites were silent when Adolf Hitler carried out the Holocaust. They concluded by demanding: "The problems that the farmworkers face are problems that we need to address ourselves to as Christians. Some of us have been silent for too long" (1974, p. 16).

In the summer of 1975, Bethel College, a Mennonite school in central Kansas, invited James Laue and Paul Wehr to the campus to lead a workshop on managing conflict. Laue was a sociologist on the faculty of Washington University in St. Louis and director of the Crisis Intervention Center, which was connected with the university. Wehr was also an expert in conflict analysis and had written a book entitled *Conflict Regulation* (1979). Their presentations at the Bethel College workshop helped Mennonites begin to answer the question Ted Koontz had asked in his report on the conflict between farm laborers and growers in California. Koontz was not the only Mennonite asking questions about how Mennonites could become involved in mediation and conciliation. Robert Kreider, a professor of peace studies at Bethel College, and Thomas Lehman, a Bethel chemistry professor, had each thought there should be some kind of system established that would identify and train Mennonites to become involved in mediation and conciliation (Keeney, 1995a).

At the workshop, Laue described models for Christians to be involved in conflict mediation. He outlined the various roles people play in a peacemaking process. Mennonites for the first time were shown by skilled practitioners with specialized experience in conflict and conciliation that it was not enough to enter a conflict situation with only a desire to bring peace. Laue also told his audience that conciliation is never neutral with regard to justice. One could, however, seek to be nonpartisan, he posited (Keeney, 1995a).

A flurry of memos and proposals followed on how Mennonites could become involved in conciliation and mediation of conflicts within the larger culture. As Robert Kreider wrote in a June 9, 1975, memo to Ted Koontz:

> We sense there may be need and receptivity for the services of a panel of persons on tap to intervene, mediate, and provide consultative services in crisis situations—including a variety of conflict skills such as assessment, strategizing, organizing, coalition-formation, negotiation, empowerment, etc. (1975)

Kreider concluded his memo by declaring: "We feel that in this is the germ of something which could be quite significant. It would open avenues for peacemaking which goes [sic] beyond the traditional roles of making statements on issues of war and peace" (1975).

The various streams of interest in conciliation and mediation among Mennonites were finally pulled together when it was agreed that the MCC Peace Section would ask William Keeney, a professor of history and peace studies at Bethel College, to systematically gather information, analyze input, and propose a plan for Mennonites to become involved in mediation and conciliation. Notes Robert Kreider, reflecting twenty years later on the origins of MCS: "No one person or institution can clearly be called the 'source of inspiration' for what would become Mennonite Conciliation Service" (1995). Indeed, the record shows a rather remarkable synergy of ideas among Mennonite peace activists, church leaders, and church institutions and non-Mennonite practitioners like James Laue and Paul Wehr.

It was a propitious moment in North American Mennonite experience. Mennonites, who had earlier been content to live as the "quiet in the land" and to meekly refuse military involvements, had slowly but steadily become convinced that speaking out publicly against war, violence, and injustice was central to their Christian faith. Now they went further to assert that they felt called as a church to be instruments of conciliation, mediation, and transformation (Keeney, 1995a).

But this kind of outward-looking and hopeful peacemaking did not happen overnight. Many of the same issues that had made the years of the Vietnam War a tumultuous period for the larger North American culture had also deeply affected the Mennonite church.

Numerous Mennonites took to the streets in protest of the Vietnam War, and a number of young Mennonite men defied their local draft boards by refusing to register or cooperate with the Selective Service System. Mennonite activists' commitment to justice drew them to the civil rights movement and to the picket lines of the freedom marches. Vincent G. Harding, an African-American Mennonite minister, powerfully proclaimed to his fellow Mennonites as early as 1958 (pp. 597–598) that they could no longer afford to be *die Stillen im Lande* (the quiet in the land). Harding challenged the church to renounce white power, privilege, and seclusion so that they could serve people in need.

So, within a matter of two generations, Mennonite understandings of the Bible's teachings regarding peace and justice moved from the World War I attitude—Mennonite men should meekly and obediently go to the military camps but not carry a gun—to the activism and protest of the 1960s and 1970s. In 1963, Frank H. Epp, a Canadian church leader and editor of the *Canadian Mennonite*, wrote without nuance that Mennonites should practice civil disobedience in desegregation demonstrations: "It is better to break the law and be right than to keep the law and be wrong" (p. 6).

By the late 1970s, Mennonites were approaching biblical peacemaking in at least three different ways. There were those involved in protest and civil disobedience (an important story that is beyond the scope of this paper). Others had begun to serve as mediators and conciliators. Yet there still remained a significant number within the church who continued to embrace the traditional quietism and conscientious objection of the past and demurred at what they considered the new Mennonite activism.

Becoming involved in conciliation and mediation offered Mennonites middle ground between protest and civil disobedience, on the one hand, and traditional quietism, on the other. The conciliation movement allowed many Mennonites a way of working at peacemaking that was considered more socially engaging and less radical.

Mennonites would struggle mightily with themselves, however, to discern when and how to decide which tactic to implement in their efforts to be Christian peacemakers. Perhaps it was especially vexing that there were numerous occasions when the lines were blurred between those who called for activism and those who advocated the tools of conciliation. Even those who held firmly to the earlier paradigm of quietism found themselves at times compromising their quietism (Stoner, 1995b).

Ted Koontz drew the various streams of Mennonite thinking together in a 1976 memo, which outlined the mandate to William Keeney to systematically bring together a rationale and vision for a Mennonite Conciliation Service. About the third phase of Mennonite peacemaking needed for North American Mennonites, Koontz wrote:

> There has been concern that we [Mennonites] have a well-developed theology of peace, but not technical skills in peacemaking. We provide services which hopefully help alleviate conflict and we clean up after disasters and conflicts, but it seems relatively ineffectual at the point where conflicts of various sorts are joined. A similar concern has been felt in a variety of circles and some experience has been generated, but no serious effort has been made to develop a program to work specifically at mediation in conflict situations. (1976)

In the summer of 1976, Keeney circulated a proposal, "Mennonite Conciliation Service: A Theological Rationale (Justification)," to fellow Mennonite college professors and church leaders for their critique. The twenty-two-page document was a major expansion of an earlier proposal for a Mennonite Conciliation Service, which Keeney and Anna Juhnke, both Bethel College professors, had circulated a year earlier after the workshop with Laue and Wehr.

Keeney's proposal drew heavily on the work of Adam Curle, a Quaker conciliator; Gene Sharp, a scholar of nonviolent resistance; James Laue; and a colleague of Laue's, fellow mediator Gerald Cormick. But Keeney also kept asking himself and others how the various ideas put forward by these experts fit into the Mennonite context (1995b). The keynote of the Keeney proposal was for MCC to begin to identity people within the Mennonite church who had some experience with mediation. Further, Keeney proposed that the church should systematically begin to offer advanced training for a number of Mennonite people who had been identified as possessing gifts in conciliation and mediation. He stressed that it was vital for Mennonites to learn the so-phisticated skills necessary for this work (1995b).

The proposal also suggested that Mennonites would offer their services as conciliators and mediators to a broad range of social disputes and conflicts both within and outside the church. Finally, Keeney proposed that MCC hire a full-time staff person to administer the program of the Mennonite Concil-iation Service (MCS) (1976, 1995b).

There was concern throughout the church about the expectations for these identified and trained people, who would become involved in the new MCS. Would these people continue in their regular jobs and professions and be on call from time to time as volunteers? Or would they be full-time professionals in the area of conciliation on staff with MCS? Keeney supported a somewhat more professional model of conciliation than would ultimately be proposed; he suggested the creation of a team of traveling conciliators who would be commissioned to move from place to place as the need arose (1976).

One particularly salient response to the Keeney proposal was from John Stoner, a member of the Brethren in Christ denomination, who was serving as MCC's Peace Section director. Stoner offered three significant points. First, he prophetically called Mennonites to humility in their goals and discussions about conciliation. He frankly noted, "Mennonites have need of a concilia-tion service within our own community—conference, educational institu-tions, missions and service agency disputes" (1976).

Second, Stoner asked, "What is the relationship between working for con-ciliation and working for justice—training for conciliation and training for justice?" (1976). He postulated that "perhaps justice is concerned with truth, while conciliation elevates the concern for amity above a concern for justice" (1976).

Finally, Stoner expressed concern that the new MCS not perpetuate a grow-ing specialization and institutionalization of the work of the church. He wor-ried that a professional class of church workers would in time become distant from the grassroots of the larger church. Stoner wrote:

> To counteract a deleterious trend toward professionalism, I think that a Mennon-ite conciliation service should be designed in such a way as to maximize links with the church—with local congregations—as an integral part of the peace-making task force. (1976)

Stoner concluded his comments by suggesting that MCS could be modeled on the Mennonite Disaster Service (MDS). MDS was dedicated to organizing and directing grassroots Mennonites to help clean up and rebuild after natural disasters, such as hurricanes and tornadoes. "Somewhere here," advised Stoner, "there is some relevance in the MDS model. . . . Hundreds of volun-teers directed by trained leaders—a grassroots phenomenon with skilled lead-ership" (1976).

Urbane Peachey, executive secretary of the MCC Peace Section, responded to the Keeney proposal for a Mennonite Conciliation Service with guarded optimism. Peachey echoed the concern of others when he asked if there were a way to begin MCS so that it would draw on grassroots involvement and not add to the growing Mennonite bureaucracy. Peachey wrote:

> Rather than implementing this from the top, I wish it were possible to allow the conciliation function to emerge more dynamically out of the local environment, experience, and initiative. MDS came into existence that way and for that reason is a much stronger organization. (1976)

Peachey concluded by suggesting that MCS not depend "for its impetus on a director situated in the sterile offices of a church agency or educational institution" (1976).

In March 1977, MCC was ready to move forward and establish a Mennonite Conciliation Service. The outline for the new organization was an amalgamation of the experiences, discussions, and discernment of the previous several years. The new MCS was envisioned as a maturation of Mennonite peacemaking. The Mennonite Disaster Service, which helped organize Mennonites' response to natural disasters, was unapologetically seen as the touchstone for the Mennonite Conciliation Service.

So pervasive was the MDS model in defining the mandate of the new MCS that Lynn Roth, director of U.S. programs for MCC, defined the new Mennonite Conciliation Service as dedicated to working to repair "social disasters" that have occurred (Roth, 1977).

Yet there were significant differences between the work of MDS and the proposed work of MCS. MDS did not need to train grassroots Mennonites in the subtleties of carpentry, plumbing, and other building skills. When there was a natural disaster, the call was sounded for men and women to take time off from their various places of work, to bring their hammers, nail aprons, and saws, and to offer several days of volunteer service.

Show up they did, and with remarkable efficiency they would set to work cleaning up and rebuilding. The skills needed for such MDS work were part of the warp and woof of the majority of the Mennonite folk, who tended to be farmers, carpenters, and plumbers. While still drawing on values that held to the sanctity of life and restoration of relationship, conciliation and mediation also called for specific skills, which grassroots people would need to learn and which, by their very nature, would be significantly more challenging for Mennonites to acquire.

Lynn Roth listed a number of specific areas in which he expected the new MCS to involve Mennonites as peacemakers. These social disasters, he predicted, would include events such as prison riots, confrontation between Vietnam War protesters and "hardhats," difficulties between ethnic groups, and disputes between labor and management. The final area of peacemaking and mediation proposed for the new MCS was within the Mennonite church itself. Roth wrote:

> While most church disputes do not turn violent, they can often be bitter. The Mennonite churches have not always done well in meeting such conflicts. It is possible that dealing with other conflicts may prepare us for working with our own conflicts. (1977)

Ron Kraybill, a Mennonite studying at the Harvard Divinity School, was asked to serve as a short-term staff person for MCS. The Peace Section executive secretary, Urbane Peachey, was the administrative head of MCS and wrote to Kraybill in April 1977, offering him the assignment of "special assistant for Mennonite Conciliation Service." Peachey said they were looking for a person who could help sift through the growing wealth of contacts Mennonites were making with non-Mennonite conciliation work, as well as help create a network of those Mennonites who were already working at conciliation (1977b).

An MCC News Service release dated April 22, 1977, told of how Mennonites had recently become convinced that to be peacemakers included "the positive side of helping to resolve conflicts as well as the negative side of refusing to participate in war." Ron Kraybill's assignment, stated the news release, was to begin educating Mennonites about the importance of conciliation and mediation work.

Peachey himself had earlier met with many people from the field of conciliation, including Tom Colosi of the American Arbitration Association (AAA). They had discussed the possibility of Mennonite interns spending several years with the AAA to learn conciliation skills. Peachey noted, however, that MCC was aware and mindful that AAA's conciliation style would be different from the Mennonites':

> While the AAA is clearly a "professional" arbitration association, I feel that there may be some excellent possibilities of working with them in a way that may be of a resource to us as well as AAA. (1977a)

After several months of work, Kraybill produced a fourteen-page document that further defined the framework for the Mennonite Conciliation Service. Like others, Kraybill noted that there had been a "methodological vacuum" within the church regarding conciliation and mediation. He proposed that Mennonites should find a third way between their earlier passivity and what was viewed at least by most Mennonites as the "strident and secular orientation of current" conciliation and mediation outside the denomination (1977b, p. 1).

There was, Kraybill wrote, a growing new sophistication regarding the theoretical aspects of conflict resolution within the church. Mennonite colleges and seminaries were beginning to teach courses and even establish programs in which students formally studied mediation and conflict management. What was specifically needed, Kraybill argued, was for the various individuals and institutions within the Mennonite constituency who were interested and skilled in working at conciliation to be connected to one another: "If the components were linked and mobilized, Mennonites could be uniquely equipped, beyond their presently somewhat negative approach, to provide active witness to the reconciling power of the Gospel" (1977b, p. 2).

Kraybill did encounter a number of Mennonite leaders who had some serious concerns about the new efforts to work at conciliation and mediation. He reported that the strongest skepticism was coming from Mennonites who work day-by-day in situations of conflict in cities, and have been most effective as "reconcilers" in their work. We must carefully listen to these people because what they are saying has the ring of truth even if it is painful. (1977b, p. 3)

Specifically, the concerns expressed were that Mennonites were still a largely white, middle-class, and rural people, who did not understand what challenges minority and urban people face. One Mennonite leader went so far as to tell Kraybill that Mennonites were part of the problem and must repent rather than send in so-called experts who proposed to manage conflict. Kraybill recorded the challenge by documenting what he heard:

Mennonites are a part of the forces that create conflict. Until Mennonites "face their idols," recognize that they are a part of the "oppressor," and take steps to break out of that role, conciliation efforts would have no integrity and are unacceptable. (1977b, p. 3)

In the formative days of MCS, there continued to be much discussion and uncertainty over whether MCS should be patterned on the AAA model, which some suggested was geared too much toward short-term intervention. Many across the denomination felt that the conciliation model proposed by John Adams of the United Methodist Board of Church and Society was most appropriate. This model assumed that local conciliators, who were community members, would always be more effective than outside experts superimposed on conflict situations. Mennonites, with their deep commitment to extended family and community systems, naturally looked on Adams's proposal with favor. Kraybill wrote to Adams in August 1977, asking for advice on the matter:

What type of conflict ought we be looking at; what methods of intervention? One of the most repeated feedbacks I've gotten to the proposal for a "Mennonite Conciliation Service" is that you can't intervene without a basis for intervention—i.e., long-term day-to-day presence in a community. (1977c)

In the end, Kraybill proposed that Mennonite peacemaking, conciliation, and mediation should be firmly anchored within the grassroots community. He wrote to Keeney, explaining the departure from Keeney's earlier proposal:

The report, as you will discover, takes a tack fundamentally different from your initial projections. I continue to be attracted by your vision, yet have been too deeply touched by the experiences of Vern Miller, Dave Whitermore, John Ventura, Macler Sheperd, John Hess, and others, to feel that a centralized office proffering outside specialists is the way to begin. There is still plenty of leeway in the proposal to set up a more centralized effort if experience over a period of time shows that such a commitment is welcome or needed by those dealing with conflict. (1977d)

The reference by Kraybill to "long-term day-to-day presence in a community" as he searched for an MCS philosophy was significant, because long-term commitment to communities had by the 1970s become the hallmark for all of MCC's work. Organizationally, MCC had an ever-deepening commitment to having its volunteers become, as much as possible and as appropriate, a part of the communities in which they were serving.

When MCC received applications from people seeking domestic or international service assignments, one of the main questions asked by the personnel department was whether the applicants were open and able to learn from their host communities. MCC established a tradition of orientation for all its workers that stressed the importance of being connected to the communities in which they were serving. The volunteers were asked to listen and to wait for their hosts' invitation and direction—no small task for North Americans. Those directing MCC orientations for new volunteers saw as key to the process teaching North American Mennonites not to assume they had answers for others' needs. The orientation and institutional mantra was that North American MCC workers were to patiently wait and to be available for the local community to ask for assistance in the projects they felt were important. There was an implicit and explicit assumption that one's own family and community back home could be trusted. For Mennonites it followed, then, that other people's extended families and communities could also be trusted, and it seemed obvious to Mennonites to turn to those innate systems for models of transforming conflict. The phrase all workers had ringing in their hearts as they traveled to their various places of ministry was "Take time to drink tea with the people!" (Peachey, 1996).

Kraybill felt strongly that MCS needed to work hard to include minority people at all levels. There should be a strong emphasis on mobilizing local resources and people all across North America, rather than establishing a "flying squad of intervenors" (1977b, p. 4). There was a fundamental commitment to trusting local congregations and individuals to actually *become* the Mennonite Conciliation Service. The real task of the MCS leadership, wrote Kraybill, would be to be available to teach, to serve as resource people to local groups, and to help connect grassroots Mennonites as they became involved in conciliation work.

Kraybill pointed out that he had heard time and again that Mennonites must face the unresolved conflicts within their own structures. Mennonite churches, institutional offices, district conferences, and families, Kraybill was reminded, were rife with conflict. One Mennonite leader observed that the MCS proposal was "pretty 'blamed audacious' in light of the track-record of Mennonites in handling our own conflicts" (Ediger, 1977). Kraybill reiterated that the new MCS would need not only to look outside the Mennonite church for its conciliation involvements but must also work at mediation and transformation of conflict within the church (1977b, p. 4).

In the spring of 1978, the MCC Peace Section called together an assembly in Kansas City to test the MCS proposal with the larger church. Particular effort was made to be sure that a wide cross section of Mennonites was present. There was a commitment that minority and urban voices be present and heard at the gathering. This gathering was also an occasion to bring together Mennonite peace activists and those involved in conflict management together.

Urbane Peachey remembered feeling the tension among the various groups gathered:

> The result of the meeting in Kansas City was an agreement on two key points. First, that conciliation and mediation must not side-step issues of justice. Second, for conciliation to have veracity it needed to be something that grows out of and is directed from local grassroots communities. (1996; see also Peachey, 1978)

By the fall of 1979, MCC asked Ron Kraybill to serve as the first MCS director, as a volunteer assignment. Kraybill remembered that his role was not only to travel across North America as a roving professional conciliator and mediator: "I saw my task as calling into life people in various communities who would become skilled as conciliators. I was committed to finding practical and concrete ways for conciliation and mediation to happen" (1995a). In keeping with the earlier vision, Kraybill served both as a student and as a teacher of conciliation skills, as he moved among established practitioners, such as Adams and Laue, the Mennonite community-based conciliation groups, and Mennonite colleges and seminaries.

He thus began forming an MCS nexus that went in two interrelated directions. On the one hand, Kraybill continued learning from well-known and respected experts in the conciliation field who were outside the Mennonite church. These interactions continued to significantly shape the new MCS. The letters and memos of Mennonites involved in the founding of MCS expressed the sense that, even though they were part of a historic peace church, they wanted to be attentive to non-Mennonites with more experience and skill in the area of conciliation.

On the other hand, Kraybill began to help develop a core group of grassroots conciliators and mediators within the church in various Mennonite communities across North America (1977a, p. 3). He also explored the possibility of bringing into the process the seven Mennonite mental health centers scattered across the continent. He proposed that MCC and Mennonite Mental Health Services work together by sponsoring a workshop taught by AAA trainers for Mennonites who were already doing conciliation work or who were interested in doing so. But in the end, the professional model of the mental health hospitals was not compatible with the MCS commitment of depending on grassroots staffing (Kraybill, 1977b; 1995a).

The issue of the level of professionalism of Mennonite conciliation efforts would prove an unending point of discussion and discernment, even to the present day. Kraybill, writing after leading MCS for more than a decade, reported, ironically, how he discovered the Holy Grail of conciliation. He found that the Grail was identifying and building on the unique strengths that each individual brought to his task as a conciliator:

> Finally, I learned that the most effective trainers are those who encourage students to find their own Grail. . . . In the end, teachers who imply they have found the Holy Grail disempower their students. I have found myself motivated by and learning from teachers with a story to tell. (1988, p. 5)

In the early 1980s, Kraybill worked closely with Church of the Brethren national consultant Barbara Date to develop and deliver more standardized training modules for a growing network of historic peace church mediators around the United States. Also during this period, a number of local MCS chapters were formed across North America. These chapters were meant to provide local Mennonite communities and congregations with their own networks of resources and available conciliators. One of the MCS chapters was located in the home state of Mennonite farmer John Schrag, who years earlier had been the victim of mob violence. The local MCS chapter in Kansas had thirty-two people trained and serving as volunteer mediators by the end of the 1980s (Kraybill, 1982).

Another Mennonite population center that was home to an early MCS chapter was Harrisonburg, Virginia. Nancy Good Sider, a consistent advocate for the recruitment and recognition of women in church-based conciliation work, served as the primary MCS contact for this area. Sider continues in MCS leadership today as one of the program's four U.S. regional coordinators and advisers. The Harrisonburg MCS chapter is located in the same community as Eastern Mennonite University, which in 1993 became the home of a master's program in conflict transformation and an associated Institute for Peacebuilding. In a further institutionalization of peacebuilding on the part of the Mennonites, the program brought together Kraybill, Sider, John Paul Lederach, and Barry Hart, among others, as faculty members or associates.

In 1983, Kraybill announced an expansion of MCS because of the continuing call from both Mennonites and non-Mennonites for more training and materials on how to be conciliators. He confessed that as the only staff person, he was not keeping up with the demand for training seminars, workshops, speaking engagements, and longer-term organization of local chapters. Several regional MCS staff people, reported Kraybill, would be appointed to direct MCS work regionally. Local initiative and ownership were again the key to this new aspect of MCS. "No fixed pattern exists to which regional structures must conform," wrote Kraybill. "Options for structure, tasks, and support are diverse, especially since we continue our Akron-based efforts" (1983a, pp. 4–5).

Alice Price, a Mennonite working as an attorney in Colorado, became involved in MCS in 1985; in 1990 she became MCS director. Price systematically began to involve women and people of color both in the staff and in the broader MCS network. In a 1990 document entitled "Future Directions for MCS Network," Price outlined her priorities for MCS. She affirmed what MCS had done in the past but stated that under her direction she planned "to look at ways to broaden and diversify whom we work with, where we work, and on what issues. Particular focus will be increasing racial and ethnic diversity and urban-based resources" (1990a; 1996). Several months after setting this new direction for MCS, Price hired John Chapman to work with program development among urban, low-income, and ethnically diverse communities. Chapman, an African-American man who had earlier served with MCC, continued to live in Philadelphia rather than move to the more rural setting of MCC's headquarters in Lancaster County, Pennsylvania (Price, 1990b).

With Dale Susan Edmonds, an African-American mediation specialist serving on the national staff of the United Church of Christ, Price also organized an important conference in Los Angeles, which addressed the interests and concerns of people of color in relation to church-based conciliation efforts. The Consultation on Cross-Cultural Conflict, which involved forty-five racially and ethnically diverse church leaders and conflict resolution practitioners, proved to be a significant watershed experience in the history of MCS.

During the 1991 conference, an MCC constituent denominational caucus expressed appreciation for the work of MCS and raising awareness of the work of MCS within urban and minority Mennonite and Brethren in Christ churches. The caucus members also urged MCS and the Mennonite church to recognize that, just as in international settings, cultural appropriateness and the adaptation of dominant cultural models were factors in the North American setting as well. Together, it was agreed that MCS would make its mediation training model available to the ethnically diverse Mennonite communities in the United States, while also supporting and learning from other appropriate expressions of conflict resolution grounded in the unique cultures of those communities (Price, 1991). In a follow-up letter to MCC executive secretary John A. Lapp, caucus members called for increased training in mediation for minority people and for MCS materials to be made more available to transcultural communities (Caucus Members, n.d. [1991]).

Also high on the agenda during Price's tenure was the development of training and resource materials for conciliators and denominational staff faced with racial and gender bias in church institutions, as well as inappropriate sexual conduct by church leaders. These efforts to diversify MCS and make its resources more culturally relevant continued through the leadership of the two subsequent MCS directors, Jim Stutzman and Carolyn Shrock-Shenk, and urban staff associate Regina Shands Stoltzfus. They have overseen the expansion of MCS resources and work in urban and ethnically diverse Mennonite constituencies around the United States, and they have maintained a persistent focus on issues of race, gender, and power both in conciliation work and in the broader church.

## International Conciliation Service

In the summer of 1984, Mennonites from across the world gathered in Strasbourg, France, for the Eleventh Mennonite World Conference. The assembly of Mennonites from seventy nations that gathered in the shadow of Strasbourg's famous single-spire cathedral was in many ways a homecoming. The city had been an important place of refuge for Mennonites during the Reformation. Mennonites had held their first conference in the city in 1554 to discuss what it meant to be a Christian as an Anabaptist/Mennonite.

One peacemaking initiative emerged out of the 1984 gathering and another took a significant step toward becoming international. The new initiative was the result of the call by Ronald J. Sider, under the rubric "God's People Reconciling," for Mennonites to form groups of Christians who were willing to physically place themselves as peacemakers between hostile peoples. There was considerable support from those in attendance for Sider's proposal, and it subsequently resulted in the establishment of the Christian Peacemaker Teams (CPT). Sider reminded the thousands of Mennonites of their 450-year history of martyrdom, migration, and missionary proclamation, and he proposed that the God of shalom had been preparing Mennonites for a rendezvous with history:

> The next twenty years will be the most dangerous—and perhaps the most vicious and violent—in human history. If we are ready to embrace the cross, God's reconciling people will profoundly impact the course of world history. (1984a, p. 224)

The second significant peacemaking development at the Strasbourg Assembly was that Mennonites from outside North America had a chance to learn of the work being done by the Mennonite Conciliation Service. Barry Hart, a mediator based in Harrisonburg, Virginia, had written to Ron Kraybill urging MCS to share its story with the international church (Kraybill, 1983b). In Strasbourg, Hart led a workshop describing the MCS philosophy and process for working toward conflict resolution. A number of Mennonites from various European countries asked MCC to help make conciliation training available in Europe (Kraybill, 1985).[8]

As early as 1983, Kraybill and others had been asking if it were possible for MCS to have a ministry that included an international component. The overriding question was whether there were "universals" in conciliation. That same year, John Paul Lederach, a Mennonite graduate student studying conflict resolution under Paul Wehr at the University of Colorado, was discovering through practical experience that mediation and conciliation skills could be cross-cultural—when offered with cultural sensitivity and when sensitively practiced.

Prior to his graduate studies, Lederach had lived and served as a church worker in Spain and therefore brought to his mediation and training work a fluency in Spanish and a sensitivity to culture (1995b). While still a graduate student, he was increasingly sought out to help mediate conflicts involving various Hispanic communities, many of them involving displaced Central Americans, who had traveled north to escape the military conflicts raging throughout Central America.

Lederach had shared his vision of how Mennonites might offer mediation training outside of North America with Urbane Peachey and Ron Kraybill. His sweeping vision proposed that conflict resolution become an integral part of all of MCC's overseas work (Peachey, 1995). There were heartfelt and long discussions within the North American Mennonite community regarding how peacemaking and conciliation training could be done internationally with integrity. Some believed that MCS's typology was not suitable outside of

North America, but others believed that conciliation and mediation were not necessarily bound by North American culture. Those with reservations about an international component to MCS argued that North American Mennonites seeking to teach mediation skills in other cultures would only prove to be disingenuous. Rather than risk adding to people's oppression through inappropriate mediation techniques, argued the concerned skeptics, North American church people needed to find the hurting and disenfranchised of the world and stand with them as they demanded justice.

Some clarity was brought into these discussions when Central American Mennonites, deeply concerned about the increasing conflicts in their region, approached Gerald Schlabach, an MCC worker living in Nicaragua, and requested someone who could teach conflict management skills.

In a discussion among MCC leaders in January 1985, it was felt that there were important conciliation tools and skills that were indeed cross-cultural. With a specific request from MCC's partners in Central America, the organization was prepared to respond. But the North American church leaders also underscored that "a great amount of cross-cultural sensitivity is required here, as in all cross-cultural work" (MCS, 1985). In the area of international relief and development, North Americans had for some years been working with a paradigm they called "appropriate technology." Now, it seemed, Mennonites were ready to work internationally with what essentially became a paradigm of appropriate peacemaking (Darrow and Sarenian, 1993).

Because the MCS approach had always been attentive to empowering local communities to create their own programs, North American Mennonites found that they were distinctly prepared to be a part of conciliation and mediation training and to practice internationally. Within the year, Kraybill and Hart had traveled to various European countries and led workshops on conflict management. Responding to the Central American request, in 1985 MCC asked Lederach to go to Central America as a conflict resolution trainer. Two fundamental reference points were eventually established by MCC as guiding principles in its effort to work at appropriate peacemaking internationally. First, North Americans would wait for invitations from local partners before becoming involved in international conciliation initiatives. Second, the international work would be channeled and administered through MCC's area secretaries, who served as MCC's worldwide regional directors, rather than having MCS looking for international involvements.

North American Mennonites involved in international conciliation were teaching and learning in tandem from the beginning. In writing to an Irish colleague, Kraybill acknowledged that there was a North American flavor to his training and process:

> This is the kind of critical testing which must happen if mediation is going to be of any value in Ireland. We continue to learn and explore ways to teach mediation in a variety of cultures in ways that build on the unique aspects of each culture, rather than trying to bring a model from another culture. (1986)

John Paul Lederach also reported that, through his experience of teaching mediation skills outside of North America, he found that language and culture affect the way people approach conflict (1988b, pp. 10–11; 1988c). In the Latin American context, it was vital, he discovered, to incorporate into the training seminars a variety of culturally appropriate exercises, which were based on the use of language and images.

A direct result of Lederach's training activities in Central America was his subsequent invitation to assist in mediating the often violent conflict between the Nicaraguan government and the Miskito Indians. Shortly after receiving training in mediation skills from Lederach, Moravian church leaders were asked by Miskito leaders to serve as mediators in the conflict. The church leaders in turn asked Lederach to walk with them in their important task as intermediaries.

Lederach says of his first involvement in high-level international mediation that it occurred in part because he was in the right place at the right time—but also that there were important points of connection and trust that had been established much earlier by him and other MCC workers. Trust, language, cultural sensitivity and understanding, and skills in conflict resolution came together in such a way that Lederach was able to play a major role in negotiations between the two warring groups. A great deal was learned by Mennonites through Lederach's involvement. He wrote:

> It's much more complex at the international level. This was way beyond anything I had ever experienced in congregational or environmental disputes. There were internal subdivisions in the Indian groups, plus external factors (e.g., foreign influence). Also, I had never been in a situation where I felt so vulnerable as a mediator, given the personal threats, etc. (1988a, p. 6)

During the months that he was involved in the complex and politically charged mediation between the Nicaraguan government and the Miskito Indians, it was discovered that Lederach and the other mediators were being watched by Contra and CIA operatives. These powerful forces did not want conciliation and peace because they stood to benefit from continued fighting. The forces opposed to the peace process even went so far as to make plans to kidnap Lederach's daughter. Later still, Lederach was warned by an inside source that the CIA had offered $50,000 for the assassination of him and the other mediators (Wenger, 1988, pp. 152–153).

An enigmatic counterpoint to the CIA's machinations against Lederach was the invitation Ron Kraybill received in 1987 from the Foreign Policy Institute of the U.S. State Department to join a small group of nongovernmental organizations for a discussion on conciliation and mediation. Kraybill attempted to explain his invitation to the head of MCC by suggesting that it was because he was "rather outspoken in the community of professional North American mediators concerning the ethics of mediation, especially in situations of injustice and long-term structural inequities" (1987).

After several years of working both domestically and internationally, there was a growing awareness that the administrative structure of MCS was not well suited for its increasing international involvement. By the end of 1988, many within MCC were asking for clarity regarding the relationships among MCC's various North American and international conciliation programs. There was increasing concern that the North American focus of MCS work was losing ground to the rapidly expanding invitations from MCC partners for international involvements. Lederach, then the director of MCS, reported that he was spending one fourth to one-third of his time in international conciliation efforts (1989a).

A formal proposal to establish an International Conciliation Service (ICS) was crafted by Herman Bontrager, who called for Lederach to phase out his MCS role and serve as the first staff person for the emerging International Conciliation Service (1989). It was felt that the new arrangement would allow him to focus on the important research and writing he was doing, as well as facilitate his growing involvement in teaching trainers in a wide variety of countries. Notably, Lederach had developed what he called an "elicitive" approach to training and to development of culturally appropriate conciliation models.

Lederach proposed three areas of focus for the new ICS (1989b). The first would be consulting and intervention, the second, networking and program development, and the third, training and education.

Lederach outlined more specifically his vision for the International Conciliation Service in a document entitled "International Conciliation: A 10-Year Perspective." Perhaps most striking was the level of experience and sophistication in the field of conciliation and mediation that had been achieved in the fifteen-year history of formal involvement of Mennonites. Yet, in spite of the new sophistication, Lederach reaffirmed much of what had been agreed upon fifteen years earlier as the Mennonite way of working at conciliation. Once again, there was a recognition that Mennonites should not limit their efforts to picking up the pieces after destructive conflicts. He urged Mennonites to also use their energies, contacts, and resources to transform the root causes of violence and conflict (1990). North American Mennonites were themselves surprised by the amazing depth of worldwide friendships that had developed over the nearly seventy years of MCC's relief and development work. They were also surprised to discover that they were often some of the most trusted outside partners in many countries throughout the world.

Growing out of his experience working in Central America, Lederach proposed that MCC designate a percentage of its relief and humanitarian funding to be directed toward specific peacemaking work:

> Over the next 10 years, let us be more intentional about linking peacemaking with our more traditional relief efforts. Many times relief is necessitated by regional conflict and little is solved in the long run by providing relief without working at peace. . . . We need to communicate both with our constituency and host country partners our commitment to linking relief and development with peacemaking. (1990, p. 5)

Lederach drew on the Hebrew scripture of Psalm 85 when he urged Mennonites to join others around the world in creating a space where truth and mercy, justice and peace could meet. The kind of peacemaking needed in the 1990s, he proposed, was that which helps provide space for the voiceless to be heard. He envisioned ICS as dedicated to creating places where enemies could meet and where diverse and opposing concerns and interests could converge. He gathered together in one sentence his vision for how to be peacemakers:

> MCC recognizes the need for a holistic response to human conflict, that addresses the immediate human suffering, the root problems engendering the destructive cycle of violence, and the creation of space where problems can be seriously dealt with in a way that respects human life. (1990, p. 60)

The kinds of holy spaces that Lederach wanted to help create would be singular, he said, because the church can be a unique institution in conflictive circumstances. Ideally, the church does not enter troubled situations

> in order to capture a political space, but rather to bring our concern for human well-being to create a new and hopefully transforming space in the midst of human conflict. Creating such space happens through and with people. Thus, we have an explicit preference for grounded, contextualized initiatives that support and empower rather than replace people from the conflictive setting who can act as transforming agents within their own context. (1990, p. 40)

Peace Section director John Stoner responded to the Lederach proposal by affirming the importance of North Americans working from the grassroots with people who can serve to help improve their own communities and countries. He observed that North American church workers were by definition outsiders and, for the most part, short term. Stoner had earlier stressed the importance of justice when he critiqued the Keeney and Kraybill proposals for a Mennonite Conciliation Service. Stoner again argued for the centrality of seeking justice and strongly affirmed Lederach's attention to justice issues in his ICS proposal. Stoner concluded his comments by offering to help ICS and Christian Peacemaker Teams to connect and work cooperatively (1990).

In 1993, after three years of ICS existence, Bob Herr and Judy Zimmerman Herr, who were serving as cosecretaries of MCC's Peace Office, called for a review of the program. They felt that such a review would help in making decisions about the administrative and programmatic directions of ICS. Ronald E. Yoder, an administrator at the Mennonite Board of Missions in Elkhart, Indiana, was asked to conduct the review. Yoder's extensive study resulted in a thirty-three-page document entitled "Visioning Future Structure for Mennonite International Conciliation Work" (1993).

As a result of the review, it was decided that ICS should serve as a resource through which the various Mennonite and Brethren in Christ international conciliation efforts could consult and communicate. In their final document, which outlines future direction, Bob Herr and Judy Zimmerman Herr wrote that they saw ICS moving in the direction of a "referent organization" (1994).

They envisioned ICS as a consultative body of various Mennonite agencies and institutions involved in conciliation consulting and training internationally. Networking and communication should be the main focus of ICS, with little actual programming and staffing of its own. They expressed a concern that no one institution or organization become too primary in the identity and growing work of ICS. MCC would continue as the locus of ICS administration, but various Mennonite mission boards, service agencies, and colleges would be equal partners in Mennonite and Brethren in Christ conciliation work internationally.

## Christian Peacemaker Teams

Ronald Sider had also been deeply concerned about holy space when he appealed in 1984 to his fellow Mennonites at their world conference in Strasbourg, France, to never again return to their silence and isolation. Using the language of an old-fashioned revival preacher, Sider in part seemed to be answering Reinhold Niebuhr's indictment of Mennonites as being parasites on the sins of soldiers who laid down their lives in their attempts to serve as violent peacemakers. Sider chided Mennonites congregated that summer day in Strasbourg, proclaiming it was spiritually wrong to lapse into passive nonresistance, withdrawal, and isolation and then to call their behavior Christian. He talked about how Jesus had rejected both isolation and accommodation and had lived in a holy, albeit dangerous, space where he was involved in the larger spiritual, political, and economic culture of his day.

Halfway through his homily, Sider told the gathering, with an eye especially upon North Americans and Europeans, that they should be prepared to die by the thousands as they willingly placed themselves in the dangerous but holy space between the weak and the violent. Later that year, he challenged Mennonites to willingly risk their lives doing nonviolent peacemaking in the same way that soldiers risked their lives in combat:

> Those who have believed in peace through the sword have not hesitated to die. Proudly, courageously, they marched off to death. Again and again, they sacrificed bright futures to the tragic illusion that one more righteous crusade would bring peace in their time. For their loved ones, for justice, and for peace they have laid down their lives by the millions. (1984b, p. 900)

Do we have as much courage and faith as those in the military? asked Sider. He proposed that a new, nonviolent peacekeeping force of 100,000 Christians should be assembled, trained, and sent into the middle of violent conflicts to stand peacefully between warring peoples in Central America, Northern Ireland, Poland, Southern Africa, the Middle East, and Afghanistan. Like a hellfire and brimstone evangelist, Sider beseeched the audience to abandon their lukewarm faith because "today is the hour of decision" and to fall on their knees in intercessory prayer and to join a "mighty worldwide peace revival" (1984b, p. 901).

The editor of the *Gospel Herald*, the largest denominational Mennonite magazine, responding favorably to Sider's call for a peace revival, editorialized, "Nothing quite like this has appeared among Mennonites before, as I recall" (Hertzler, 1986, p. 396). Others were also invited to respond to the proposal. Sara Shenk, a seminary graduate student, said of the vision, "I laud Sider for naming our hypocrisy and for sketching out a plan—not to defend our country—but to defend the credibility of Jesus' peace plan, the cross" (1984, 902).

But not all Mennonites were enamored of Sider's call for Christians to become involved in the world's problems. James Hess, a bishop in the Lancaster Conference of the Mennonite Church, scoffed at the idea that Christians have any business blurring the line between church and state. There were plenty of Mennonites who agreed with Hess's traditional dualism and murmured an amen when he responded to Sider's proposal by writing, "His concept of shalom is apparently consistent with that of contemporary Mennonite liberals but, frankly, I cannot embrace it with integrity" (1984, p. 902).

In contrast, Stanley Hauerwas, a friend of Mennonites and a fellow pacifist, responded to the Sider proposal by applauding the challenge to abandon a two-kingdom theology. He further noted that he had always believed that a great disability of pacifism was its tendency to be "lulled into quietism by a pluralist and tolerant society" (1984, p. 902). Hauerwas did raise concern, however, that Sider assumed that modern-day Anabaptists should be shaping history and policy. Christians' highest calling, he argued, was not necessarily to be effective in changing their world, regardless of how much it needed changing:

> Therefore, our task in such a world is to do as [Jesus] did, namely, to be faithful even if we are not able through our faithfulness to affect significantly the course of world history. Once you start looking for effectiveness, it may mean you overlook the necessity of communities learning how to live peaceably even in a violent world. (1984, p. 902)

Several months after the Strasbourg conference, the Council of Moderators and the executive secretaries of the General Conference Mennonite Church, the Mennonite Church, the Brethren in Christ Church, the Mennonite Brethren Church, and the Church of the Brethren in North America met together and discussed Sider's plea for a peace revival. They must have been amazed by the fact that 6,000 people had already written, requesting more information about the proposal. Out of their discussions, a steering committee was formed with the mandate to explore and formulate a proposal for Christian Peacemaker Teams (CPT) (Metzler, 1987, p. 2).

The CPT steering committee hired Gene Stoltzfus, a former MCC program director in the Philippines, as a half-time coordinator in 1987; by 1989 CPT was ready to hold its first training sessions for volunteers. That summer, CPT sent its first volunteer, David Weaver, to the West Bank to observe and document the many deaths of Palestinians involved in the Intifada.

In its relatively short existence, CPT has been increasingly invited into troubled spaces throughout the world. In November 1990, as the United States prepared to declare war on Iraq, a Christian Peacemaker Team went to Baghdad in the hope that a team of nonviolent Americans could, even in the face of massive armies on the move, serve as a witness to all involved that there were genuine alternatives to war. They also hoped to listen and learn from ordinary citizens of Iraq during their visit. But there was a desire to do something even more dramatic than sending one small symbolic team to Iraq. The leaders of the CPT movement kept dreaming of what could have happened if a thousand people had been prepared and ready to literally place themselves in the desert between armies (Stoner, 1992, pp. 1–2). John Stoner reflected:

> I have always wondered what would have been the impact of 1,000 nonviolent American Christians going to the consulate offices of Iraq in Washington, D.C., seeking visas to travel to Iraq to witness for peace. I believe that the human and environmental tragedies of that terrible war might have been changed by such a profound witness of nonviolence. (1995a)

After several years, there was a growing sense that CPT needed two kinds of volunteers and, boldly plagiarizing the language of the military, CPT began recruitment. The first group, the Christian Peacemaker Corps (CPC) would consist of people who would be full-time volunteers, literally ready to go on short notice anywhere in the world where CPT was being invited. These corps members would spend two-thirds of their time traveling and working in places of conflict. When they were not "active," they would be available to speak to their home communities, to offer training, and to work on other community projects.

The second group of CPT members, the CPT Reserve Corps, would be reservists "on call" to join the full-time corps. These part-time volunteers would continue in their regular jobs, but they would be available to serve several weeks a year, including in places of conflict. The on-call members of CPT, like the full-time volunteers, received in-depth training in the spiritual disciplines of nonviolent action, in cross-cultural understanding, and most important, in the biblical teachings of nonviolence, which were the touchstone for CPT.

Training for CPT volunteers has been a mixture of worship services, lectures in theology and international politics, and learning to witness publicly that there are alternatives to violence. Jon Anderson, a writer for the *Chicago Tribune*, clearly was intrigued by CPT training and watched with interest a practical training exercise where CPTers demonstrated against selling war toys at a Toys-R-Us store. "The point of such actions," reported the *Tribune* article, "is not to get arrested or cause damage; it is to mount a kind of teach-in for the larger community, to combat wrongs by making them visible" (Anderson, 1994). The Christian Peacemaker Teams periodical, *Signs of the Times*, reported in 1992 that more than a thousand people had participated in teams, conferences, witnesses, and other CPT-sponsored events (Stoner, 1992, pp. 1–2)

John Stoner, one of the leaders of the CPT movement, said of their efforts:

> Perhaps the most characteristic mode of CPT action can be described as interventions of truth. Communicating and making space for truth where deceit prevails is the work of peacemaking. Where lies prevail, death is present. In places of death, interventions of truth are anticipations of resurrection. For Jesus and for CPT, typical interventions of truth involve travel, talk, and trouble. (1993, p. 15)

Caleb Rosado, writing in *Christianity Today*, asked the burning question: How did America become such a violent nation? He outlined America's long cultural history of preoccupation with guns and an assumption by many Americans that might makes right. Then, Rosado asked, where are there signs of hope that peace and nonviolence are working? One of several places of hope the author cited were Christian Peacemaker Teams:

> Among the Peacemaker Corps' goals—with a foundation of prayer and worship—are networking with other peacemaking groups, escorting people threatened by violence, and training individuals in conflict mediation and nonviolence principles. (1994 pp. 20–25)

Like the Mennonite Conciliation Service and the International Conciliation Service, the Christian Peacemaker Teams work on certain principles, which serve as the touchstone for all their activities. CPT has listed twelve considerations that its leadership uses to decide if a team should be sent into a conflictive situation (1993). Foundational for CPT is the need to be invited in by partner communities and the presence of grassroots initiative and support. Can the supporting Christian communities in North America and Europe understand and bless our involvements? ask CPT leaders. They also ask questions about the communities with which the CPT teams will be involved: "Is there a trusted welcoming body in the crisis setting with whom we can work? Is the area one in which CPT or its supporting denominations have experience and relationships of trust established?" (CPT, 1993).

Daniel Hertzler, the editor of the *Gospel Herald*, saw in the original proposal for CPT something new, and yet, like his fellow Mennonites, he also saw in the vision something very true to character for the faith communities involved (1986). Even in their most insular moments, Mennonite people have not been able to look away from their neighbors' suffering for long.

In every generation, from the most traditional to the most progressive, Mennonites have felt spiritually compelled to reach out a hand, to offer a word of hope, and to get involved in their neighbors' tragedies. Through their encounters with modernity, the more progressive Mennonite denominations have experienced an ever-enlarging world. Once faraway cities and lands, over time, have become the cities and lands not of unknown strangers but of people who are part of the community—the worldwide community. The Mennonite Conciliation Service, International Conciliation Service, and Christian Peacemaker Teams have been three practical grassroots expressions that Mennonites have offered as nonviolent witnesses to their neighbors both near and far.

# Two

## Reflections on Twenty Years
## in Peacebuilding

RON KRAYBILL

REFLECTING ON TWENTY YEARS devoted to the task of building peace raises the question: Is the story my own or that of my community of faith? Central to Mennonite understandings of human life is the conviction that the web of existence is seamless, that individuals dwell in communities that in turn, nurture individuals. The Christian Gospel is "good news" only if it addresses both. Thus, this account conveys both a personal odyssey *and* a communal journey.

## Historical Context

An epochal story from the congregation in which I grew up, Bosslers Mennonite Church near Elizabethtown, Pennsylvania, sets the context regarding what I see as key understandings of many North American Mennonites about peacemaking in the post–World War II era. Families in our church, farmers nearly all, resided on land that appealed to more than the locals. Situated near the Olmstead Air Force Base at Middletown, within easy reach of the Susquehanna River, well removed from dense urban populations, but serviced by an excellent nexus of highways and railways, the gently rolling hills of western Lancaster County more than once caught the eye of military planners. In 1942 and again in 1951, the U.S. Department of War[1] made moves to expand its facilities by expropriating thousands of acres, including the fertile farmlands that families in our church had tilled for generations.[2]

Both efforts came to naught. I grew up on a story told by my grandfather, preacher Martin R. Kraybill, of a day of deliverance in 1942, when a diverse delegation of community representatives traveled to Washington to meet with planners in the Department of War. As the delegation traveled to the capital, locals gathered at the Bosslers meetinghouse to pray. When the delegation returned that evening, its members reported an experience understood by Grandpa and many others as an act of God. The colonel had been unrelenting. The nation was at war, many were making great sacrifices, and this community too must be prepared to do its part. As the visitors were preparing to leave, however, a cable was handed to them with an unexpected message from home. A hush fell over the group as it was read aloud in the presence of the colonel: "Bosslers Mennonite congregation is gathered at church praying right now for your success in keeping our loved homes and farms" (Kraybill 1974, p. 14). After a long pause, the colonel turned to the group with tears in his eyes and told them to go home and "tell the folks there is no intention of taking that land now"[3] (Kraybill 1974, p. 15).

That a recent historical study has shown the actual sequence of events to be more complex than this account only underscores the world-defining role of this "exodus" event (Kraybill, 1974).[4] The story communicated many things to me and others in our community, beliefs that, as in most epochal stories, often resided beneath the level of conscious reflection. I still believe many of these things; others mark early steps on a path along which I and others have moved a substantial distance.

Perhaps the keystone is the understanding that, in the beginning, is God and God's people, not governments. The land was *ours*, we believed, to use for God's purposes. Government was the invader, a vast power driven in large measure by values and forces not at home in the Kingdom of God. The military, in particular, was a threat. Foreign and suspect though government seemed, Mennonites recognized the need for political structures, even though in that era few voted in elections.[5] But, as an institution openly committed to planning for and executing violence as its primary response to conflict, the military stood fundamentally at odds with what we understood as the teaching of Jesus and thus embodied the most fallen dimensions of government.[6]

Alongside an understanding of the military as a particular threat to God's intentions for human life, the story carried another conviction: divine reality may break in at the moment of greatest hopelessness, if God's people stand faithfully and trusting in the face of threat. We knew, to be sure, from our own centuries-old canon of martyrdom that such in-breaking is never assured. Then, too, the prosperity of the twentieth century had introduced a dimension of self-interest, which surely tainted the motives of those going to Washington. Still, we knew in the end that we lived to serve God, not ourselves, and we believed that God would ultimately honor that commitment.

The story communicated other beliefs that I and many Mennonites have now left behind. Among them was the limiting assumption that peacemaking was primarily a matter of refusing to participate in war. Decidedly sectarian in theology and practice well into the 1960s, the majority of Mennonites were content to express their beliefs about peace to the larger society in negative ways during much of the twentieth century. The Mennonite Central Committee (MCC) Peace Section, for example, which until the late 1980s represented the primary institutional expression of Mennonite peace convictions,[7] was established in 1939 in response to the threat of the military draft in World War II. It largely concerned itself for the next several decades with protecting North American Mennonites from conscription.

But the postwar economic boom of the 1950s and 1960s made Mennonites prosperous and ambitious, increasingly connected to the larger American society and therefore more open to conversation with that society. During this time, the civil rights movement was introducing into mass awareness the concept of disciplined application of nonviolence to social and political problems, a concept that appealed to that growing portion of Mennonites who sought a more active way to express their convictions about peace. Equally important, the Vietnam era presented Mennonites for the first time with a need to wrestle with how their understandings of peacemaking differed from those of millions of others who also clamored for peace.

Thus, the decision in 1979 to establish the Mennonite Conciliation Service (MCS) represented the institutional expression of an awareness that had been developing for twenty years: to be peacemakers requires more than decrying violence; it also calls for active effort to remove the barriers that separate human beings.

## Early Personal Steps toward Peacebuilding

My own movement into the field of peacebuilding began in my teenage years in the mid- and late 1960s, as I heard tales of antiwar protests and marches from four older brothers returning home from college. I bade farewell to one brother, who turned in his draft card and left to teach in Swaziland, uncertain if he could ever legally return to the United States. I saw a sister and her husband head for Somalia to teach for three years. I heard and was impressed by accounts of Mennonites sending aid to the North Vietnamese. These experiences aroused my interest in peace.

As a student at Goshen College, a Mennonite liberal arts school in northern Indiana, I sought out possibilities for a career in peace work. The only option for further education seemed to be peace studies, which focused on historical and statistical analyses of war, offering little that seemed relevant to ordinary people and small hope of employment. Discouraged, I decided to explore seminary and enrolled at the Harvard Divinity School (HDS).

There, in my first semester, a radical Presbyterian, a former Baptist minister, and a pair of Methodists put me on the path to my current work. The radical Presbyterian was Bill Yolton, then field education supervisor at HDS, who first told me about the field of conflict resolution. When I described my interest in peace issues, in an early fall interview, Yolton observed that it was now commonplace for pastors to get training in counseling skills through Clinical Pastoral Education. The pastors ought to receive comparable training for responding to conflicts in the communities in which they live, he added, and he encouraged me to seek out an internship with Bill Lincoln of the American Arbitration Association (AAA). Lincoln was head of the Community Disputes Section of AAA in Boston, and he was deeply involved in efforts to build black-white coalitions in response to riots over school desegregation in Boston. A former Baptist minister, he had hoped for assistance from the city's influential religious communities and was disappointed. "Penguins in white" was his vitriolic characterization of Boston-area clergy, who came and stood in the corridors of tense schools, courageous enough to locate themselves on the scene of trouble but frozen with fear and clueless about how to respond further.

By Thanksgiving of that first year of seminary, I knew that I had found my calling, and I decided to use the flexibility offered by Harvard's master's of divinity program to create a self-constructed program in conflict resolution. Alongside standard seminary fare, each semester over the next three years I took a course in the larger university that related somehow to conflict: an introduction to classic peace studies with Karl Deutsch, a course in the social psychology of conflict with Herb Kelman, a seminar on alternative dispute resolution at the law school with Frank Sanders.

One class project involved convening a one-day consultation in late 1976, under the joint auspices of AAA and HDS, to discuss the possibilities of religiously based peacemakers assisting in community conflicts. Yolton guided me to Jim Laue and John Adams, two Methodists who might be called the grandfathers of conflict resolution in the United States.[8] Both came at their own expense to the consultation held at the National Council of Churches in New York.

Flush with the discovery of an approach to peacemaking that seemed relevant to ordinary life, during Thanksgiving break of my first year at Harvard, I was introduced at a wedding shower to Urbane Peachey, head of the MCC Peace Section. I nearly dropped my crackers and cheese when he began describing a proposal, just then under consideration by the Peace Section, to establish a Mennonite Conciliation Service (MCS). This led to an invitation from the Peace Section for me to assist in consultations about this proposal as a summer assignment in 1977, from which point the story is picked up in chapter 1 of this volume.

## Roots of International Interest

My interest in international issues also has roots in the church and family influences of my childhood. Separated though we were from American culture by a rural location, television-free homes, and a profound skepticism of "worldliness," the families at Bosslers Mennonite Church were more connected to the rest of the world than many sophisticated urbanites. In the years of my boyhood, at least half a dozen people from our small congregation lived abroad in mission work. Frequent reports were made about needs in faraway places and offerings were regularly taken to meet them. "Some can go, some can help go, and some can let go," Grandpa Kraybill was fond of repeating from the pulpit about service abroad. Three of my elder siblings spent several years in Africa in development or education work.

I took my second year of college at Dag Hammarskjold College, a short-lived 1970s experiment in international education in Columbia, Maryland.

Living for nine months with forty other students from all over the globe, including a month spent at the United Nations and a month in Japan, fixed in me a lifelong interest in international issues. A year later, I took this a step further by taking a break from college and spending nine months living and working in Germany.

My experiences during the years of work with MCS provided another push toward spending time overseas in peace work. As director of the only religiously based conflict resolution organization at that time, from 1979 to 1988, I interacted extensively with people in the rapidly growing field of conflict resolution. One consequence was that I came to a fuller awareness that peacemaking as I and my community of faith understood it raised profound moral issues, whose full import could not be grasped except in the context of global awareness. Initially, the practical problem-solving focus that then and now provides the common denominator of the field had been highly attractive to me, for it helped me connect my desire to be a peacemaker to everyday problems in ways that neither my religious tradition nor the field of classic peace studies had accomplished. But, increasingly, I realized that my own understanding of peacemaking was rooted in commitments deeper than those of many in the field.

The most sobering and revealing moments for me were the national conflict resolution conferences where, in the heat of competition for recognition and turf, it became apparent that many of the professionals hustling into the field would not or could not practice what they taught. Most memorable for me was the 1986 National Conference on Peacemaking and Conflict Resolution in Denver, Colorado. On one hand, I was stimulated and encouraged by the intense commitment to peaceful resolution of conflicts apparently shared by a body of more than 500 people. But at the same time, it seemed that many of the participants had only a superficial grasp of the concepts to which they so glibly referred. Ideas of "win-win" negotiations and joint problem solving were frequently cited, but it seemed apparent that great competitiveness was at work among those attending. Participants guarded their training materials carefully. Prickliness among competing organizations and individuals became apparent in a number of sessions. I had the feeling that many were more interested in demonstrating their own success than in learning from or genuinely contributing to others'. Perhaps most disconcerting, as an individual, I felt drawn into the spirit of competition and egocentrism. Throughout the conference, I wrestled with my own desires for personal and institutional credit for the work in which my colleagues and I had been engaging.

I was scheduled to address a plenary session of the conference, and I decided to share my experience with the group as the core of my presentation. I confessed the inner pulls of competition and desires for credit and influence I felt, and I observed that it appeared that these pulls were also at work in other attendees. I suggested that conflict resolution is potentially more than a set of techniques, that it can also be a way of being, with much to say about all of life, including the ways in which we function in our private and professional relationships. I closed by suggesting that, as peacemakers, we needed to articulate our "theology of peacemaking," that is, to identify the values underlying our work in conflict resolution, and we needed to work out ways to bring our lives and professional conduct into consistent service of those values.

I said all this with sweaty palms and quaking knees, afraid that I would sound "soft," parochial, and judgmental and that my words might effectively end my ability to work in the larger professional field. Thus I was astonished after the session ended, when many individuals pressed to the front of the crowded auditorium with words of deep gratitude. They too had experienced the struggle I had shared and were disturbed by the dynamics present in the conference. For several years, people continued to approach me in letters, in phone calls, and at conferences to talk further about a theology of conflict resolution. Some worked for religious organizations, but most did not. The majority were simply sensitive and thoughtful professionals working in secular organizations, people who through the course of their work in conflict resolution had come to realize that more was at stake than merely a body of skills and tactics. Most were not sure exactly what else was at stake nor how far it could take them, but they were eager to explore.

Understood as a way of life, conflict resolution enters the terrain of some of the toughest philosophical questions of human existence. To assert, as conflict resolution does, that it is possible for human beings to address significant conflicts without violence contradicts a key assumption on which virtually all political structures of our world are based.[9] It is one thing to make such an assertion in an interpersonal dispute over noisy children or boundary lines in a monocultural, middle-class American suburb. It is quite a different thing to assert it in settings where peoples are separated by ethnic or religious identities and generations of killing, where injustice is a central part of the problem, and where one group holds more economic, political, or military power than another.

As my understanding of conflict resolution as a way of life developed greater clarity, I increasingly felt that integrity and the frontiers of the field required me to spend an extended period of time in a place characterized by deep-rooted, violent conflict and structural injustice. Only if I were willing to make myself in at least a small measure vulnerable to the pain of people in such a setting through daily, long-term exposure to the realities they faced did I feel that I could, with integrity, hold to the conviction that it is possible to work for justice and peace simultaneously.

Then, too, after nine years at the Mennonite Conciliation Service, I felt that it was in the best interests of that growing organization to be headed by a person with a different mixture of strengths and weaknesses than those of the founding director. Although my wife, Meribeth, and I contemplated Northern Ireland, the Middle East, and Korea, South Africa seemed to be the best choice. MCC staff supported this choice, for they had sought for many years to work in that country and had been providing modest financial grants to numerous South African Christian "struggle" organizations. At their suggestion, I contacted a well-known South African Quaker, Professor H. W. van der Merwe, who knew MCC workers in the region and headed the Centre for

Intergroup Studies in Cape Town. Van der Merwe replied that he would be glad to assist if we came and offered a part-time research position.

In the year prior to my departure for South Africa, John Paul Lederach and I began a conversation about the future, which continued over the next several years. Our goal was to define our long-term vision for the ideal institutional base of operations for ourselves and others, who we hoped might join us. The components we wanted were: a setting where people worked collegially as an interactive team, rather than as ambitious individualists; a mix of academic and practitioner work so as to enable a healthy mix of travel and home life, action and reflection; and an opportunity to work closely with religiously based peacemakers, particularly through the far-flung Mennonite network, without being completely defined by a religious institution. From this discussion, sustained via correspondence and my occasional visits to the U.S., as well as Lederach's careful spadework with receptive colleagues at Eastern Mennonite University, emerged what we today call the Conflict Transformation Program and Institute for Justice and Peacebuilding.

For some time, I had thought that unless I was prepared to spend the rest of my life as a traveling trainer, I ought to acquire a Ph.D., so that I could be at least partially based in a university setting, where I could train without living out of a suitcase. This personal desire, bolstered by the conversations with Lederach, fit an unanticipated dimension of the South African explorations. Whereas incoming church workers were carefully screened by the Nationalist government, we were informed, university students attracted little interest. Thus, I applied as a Ph.D. student to the Religious Studies Department at the University of Cape Town.

Still, it seemed unlikely that we would gain entry into South Africa. Mennonites had been routinely denied visas there throughout the 1980s, at least in part because of the extensive interactions between Mennonite development workers and exiled African National Congress (ANC) members in Botswana, Swaziland, and Lesotho. Certain that formal ties to Mennonite structures would be the kiss of death for our mission, I resigned from MCS before applying for a visa. But MCC promised to provide us with a grant to cover travel and settlement costs, plus occasional living grants in South Africa, if needed.

It felt at times like cloak-and-dagger work on behalf of peace, and we joked about being Mennonite undercover agents. The visa application forms sought extensive information about previous employers, church affiliation, and education, and we struggled with how to truthfully complete these without flagging ourselves as "enemy" to computer-assisted South African security agents. When I described our dilemma to Peter Dyck, legendary among Mennonites for his spell binding stories of MCC relief operations in postwar Europe, he chuckled and quoted Scripture. Remember Jesus' words, he advised, "Wise as serpents, harmless as doves." Never lie, always tell the truth he went on. Then, eyes twinkling, he added that we should remember that it isn't always necessary to tell the whole truth! On the visa application form, my last employer became "Conciliation Services," our home congregation, the Community

Mennonite Church of Lancaster, became "Community Church of Lancaster," and so on.

We heard nothing for months after sending in our applications, and our planned departure date of late March 1989 was rapidly approaching. In January, I encountered Don Jacobs, a Mennonite with many years' experience in Africa, who saw part of his current mission as circulating among American evangelicals. Thus Jacobs attended National Prayer Breakfast meetings in Washington, a type of gathering that many Mennonites considered too discomfiting a blend of faith and nationalism to patronize. He advised us to visit the South African ambassador to the U.S., whom he considered a friend from these gatherings. Piet Koornhof was a complex man who had been ousted from a senior cabinet role for being too accommodating to blacks. Yet he still represented the Nationalist government abroad, and he counted himself an evangelical Christian. He received my wife and me warmly at the embassy. When we had laid out our desires to work with van der Merwe and to contribute to peaceful change in South Africa, he nodded in recognition and responded animatedly. If we were friends of van der Merwe, he said, it would be a "sin against the Lord himself" to keep you out of South Africa! At the end of the conversation, he picked up a phone, called the visa section of the South African embassy in New York, and asked that our visas be expedited. Within a week, they arrived.

With a daughter of two and another just a month old, we landed in South Africa in March 1989, in what turned out to be the dying days of the reign of President P. W. Botha. By September, Botha was out of power, felled by a heart attack, and replaced by F. W. de Klerk. On February 2, 1990, de Klerk released Nelson Mandela and unbanned the ANC. Thus, with a precision of timing that for me is difficult to attribute to mere coincidence, we received the priceless gift of being personal witnesses to the South African political transition. We cheered with tens of thousands in Cape Town as we heard Mandela's speech upon his release from prison, and we roared with hundreds of thousands in Pretoria when he was inaugurated as president. Not only did I have the privilege of being an official election monitor, with access to all polling stations, but having acquired permanent residents status in South Africa, Meribeth and I were able to vote. Between these landmark events, we rode the roller coaster of do-or-die national negotiations. Along with our South African friends, one week we were filled with hope from unexpected breakthroughs, the next we were brokenhearted and fearful, as violence repeatedly erupted and stalled talks.

Most satisfying of all, during the years when the future of the nation hung in the balance, I was able to work alongside hundreds of South Africans as they desperately labored to establish what eventually came to be called a "culture of negotiation," so as to enable a peaceful transition to democracy. When we arrived, "negotiation" was virtually a swear word, for it implied willingness to compromise with the devil. But as the transition advanced, in the face of mountainous skepticism within the black majority, who had lived with decades of dirty tricks from the Nationalists, people began to recognize that indeed their future might be determined across a bargaining table rather than beneath the barrel of a gun. This meant that bargaining skills were increasingly seen as a tool for constructing the future, a tool required not only by national-level politicians but also at local and regional levels, where new structures would have to be created. From about mid-1990 onward, people with conflict resolution skills could no longer meet the demand for training workshops. Everybody seemed to want them, from white Nationalist party members of Parliament, on the one hand, to radical Pan Africanist Congress youth groups on the other, with local, regional, and national ANC organizers and progressive police officers somewhere in the middle.

Although my first love was mediation, it seemed clear that training should be my primary area of focus. For most of our six and one half years in South Africa, I served as director of training at the Centre for Intergroup Studies, renamed the Centre for Conflict Resolution in 1994. Initially, I conducted most of the trainings myself, but as our staff expanded I trained assistants, and by 1993 much of the training was being done by others. This freed me to work on special projects, including efforts to introduce journalists to the concepts and skills of conflict resolution; to train election monitors in conflict resolution skills; to train police officers in conflict resolution skills; and to introduce conflict resolution and public participation processes into development planning under the new government.

## Themes in Peace Work

Twenty years of experience and reflection with colleagues have brought a number of themes into focus in my understanding of how to work for peace. At the level of fundamental purpose, I have come to see the most important goal of peacebuilding work is to support and empower local facilitators of healing, not to seek major healing roles for outsiders. Healing, of course, is the hoped-for result, but if our vision is to introduce a new way of living and being to the world, which for me it is, we must focus on setting in motion processes that do not depend on external peacebuilders in order to be sustained.

Early in my work with the Mennonite Conciliation Service, I met with John A. Lapp, the incoming executive secretary of the Mennonite Central Committee. The goal of my efforts should be to work myself out of a job, he commented. I understood him to mean that mediators should seek timely withdrawal from conflict situations so as to encourage parties to develop their own means of working out differences. It seemed like good advice, and I sought to follow it. As requests for mediation increased, however, I realized that it might call for a deeper forfeiture than I had first understood. As a peace activist, I should seek to avoid entirely becoming the mediator and instead aim to mobilize others as mediators. Thus, I shifted my priority to training mediators.

But as demand for MCS workshops increased, it became apparent that a still deeper level of relinquishment was required. The impossibility of training all the people who wanted and needed peacebuilding skills was rapidly growing apparent. Rather than training mediators, I ought to be training trainers. I began pulling away from doing training workshops myself and sought to focus my priorities around developing others as trainers and pushing them into the limelight in workshops.

Even this focus eventually proved too narrow. The greatest requirement of peacebuilders in our world is for more than training skills, it is for a broad and courageous vision of possibilities widely dismissed as utopian and for a capacity to mobilize practically with others in *living out* that vision. Thus, I have come more recently to seek to move beyond mere training of trainers. The task, as I see it now, is to be an ally to those with a vision for healing, who are present in every society and situation of conflict, to support them in finding ways to bring their dreams for creating institutions and networks of peacebuilders in their own context into practical expression.

Perhaps it goes without saying that this progression of letting go does not fit all situations. I still mediate, train, and train trainers, because I enjoy these activities and because I need to keep my skills sharp at all levels. Nevertheless, I find it a useful guiding principle that peace workers ought to seek to empower others to do the work of peacebuilding and that this often requires us to let go of doing things we are good at and enjoy, to make room for others. Of course, this is difficult. Mediating and training satisfy deep personal needs for recognition and involvement. Every stage of letting go has for me come at some personal cost. Yet, having made the move to withdraw from the limelight of one sphere of operation, I have consistently found that different but even more satisfying rewards await in other spheres.

I have shifted, then, from an early focus on peacemaking as "doing events" (mediating or training) to "transforming and empowering people." Leaving MCS was an important turning point for me in this shift, for it gave me a chance to step back from something in which I held deep personal investment. When I ask myself now what really endured from those nine years of intense labor, it is clear that it was not the number of mediations and trainings conducted nor the gratitude of conflictants in a successful mediation. What continues to leave ever-broadening circles of impact are the activities of a handful of people who heard and responded to a personal call to peacebuilding, due in part to their involvements with MCS.

This raises a second and related theme, the complexity of empowering others. It is easy to fall into patterns in which the activities of professional peace workers empower themselves more than anyone else. The South African experience was particularly illuminating because, for the first time, I resided on the receiving end of overseas largesse. The number of offers to do workshops from foreign trainers was an eye-opening experience. My response shifted from initial openness to skepticism and then to eventual irritation with having to constantly field queries from people eager to contribute to the South African transition.

Our greatest limitation as an evolving South African conflict resolution center was not a lack of knowledge about conflict and training but rather a lack of funding for infrastructure to do things we already knew how to do. After a few experiments, I realized that even workshops conducted "for free" by overseas trainers cost us heavily in precious organizational capacity. Why should we tie up our staff organizing workshops for overseas visitors when South African trainers were already underutilized because of a lack of organizing capacity?

It also soon became evident that in the inescapable mix of motivations driving overseas conflict resolution organizations that sought to work in South Africa, self-interest heavily outshadowed commitment to South African needs. Few funders were prepared to simply fork over money to American trainers to junket abroad; they wanted evidence that U.S. trainers were seriously desired overseas. That meant that in order for their $1,000-per-trainer-per-day proposals to stand any chance of getting funded, overseas organizations needed relationships with South African organizations, like our Centre for Conflict Resolution. Years of watching the overseas organizations maneuver, exaggerate, and, in at least one case, lie to win the support of South African organizations for their training expeditions made me a deep skeptic of my own kind: conflict resolution trainers abroad.

Had foreign trainers been our deepest need, the enthusiasm among the foreigners for workshops would have been less onerous. But, in South Africa, what conflict resolution people needed most was not foreign trainers. They needed funds for infrastructure and for personnel to do things already well illuminated by hard-won South African experience. Much was contributed, I am sure, by the foreign trainers, but I believe much more would have been contributed had the money that went into their training and travel budgets been allocated instead to the hiring of South Africans.

Another dimension of the empowerment question is the length of commitment and the location of peace workers. Short-term visitors are powerfully driven to provide answers, for they feel pressure to contribute something tangible, and they rarely have sufficient understanding of the local scene to grasp the complexity of the situation. It takes time to discover how ignorant one really is! If peace workers view their involvement as a long-term one, it is easier to avoid the temptation to offer foreign solutions. Living locally is, of course, an enormous asset as well, for it not only enables far greater understanding, it signals commitment. We were surprised at how much it meant to some South Africans that we bought a house in Cape Town. We learned that a South African speaking to a North American group of conflict resolution practitioners commented that if they wanted to work in South Africa, they should do what the Kraybills had done, buy a house and stay for a while!

In South Africa, I came to appreciate that a great portion of the reality experienced by people locked in deep-rooted conflict has to do with fear and suffering. To have credibility in the eyes of such people, peace workers need to be connected to that reality in visible ways. This realization has moved the concepts of vulnerability and solidarity with people in conflict into a place of prominence in my thinking about peacebuilding.

On the other hand, I have also learned that the picture is more ambiguous than the above paragraphs suggest. Several years ago, I spent a week in Thailand, under MCC auspices, with the goal of fostering reflection about Thai approaches to conflict. Long-term MCC staff worked with several Thai partner organizations, which set up meetings in villages so local people could speak of the conflicts they experienced and how they dealt with them. We heard deeply moving stories of painful, embittering conflicts, mostly unresolved. In a culture where public displays of emotion are unusual, storytellers often wept as they spoke. Driving home one day, the Thai pastor who had set up several such meetings and accompanied us expressed surprise at the experience. Although he had known these people for years, he had never heard many of the stories told to us that day.

Sometimes, people will say things to visiting outsiders that they might never say to people who are close to them, because it would be unacceptable to do so. Similarly, I realized that six years with a South African organization was at times a handicap, for this made me a potential competitor in the eyes of some South African organizations. Outside resource persons depart, leaving locals to move into leadership, whereas people living in-country raise the threat of displacing locals.

The key, I have come to feel, is the commitment of visiting peace workers to give priority to local resource people whenever they are available. Being a resource person, after all, is highly empowering to self, for it enhances one's visibility, credibility, and experience, not to mention financial status. Thus, being a resource person is an asset that peacebuilders ought never to horde. A question I ask in evaluating an invitation to work away from home is whether there are local people who could do the task I contemplate doing. Such a question may appear so obvious as to be trivial, but in South Africa it seemed that few overseas trainers asked it. It seemed rather that they reasoned: if an opportunity to train comes your way, grab it. The ethics of modern competitive professionalism take such reasoning for granted. But if our deepest commitment is to call people broadly to work for peace, I believe that we must consider all training activities in light of their impact on the empowerment of locally based peacebuilders.

Another major theme for me has been pedagogy, for I have come to believe that currently accepted teaching methods constitute one of the many obstacles to constructive human responses to conflict. Small children are driven irresistibly by instinct to learn, but by the time they finish formal schooling, most have come to hate it. This ought to alert us that something is terribly wrong with accepted understandings of pedagogy. I believe much of that wrongness has to do with what Paulo Freire calls the "banking" method of teaching, in which it is assumed that a few people wealthy in knowledge, teachers, possess what others need. Students are poor in knowledge, and the challenge of learning is to transfer knowledge from rich to poor. Any difficulties in making this transfer are seen as reflecting personal inadequacies in the student, who is repeatedly goaded by criticism, negative comparison to peers, and threats for failure to try harder. Of course, a small percentage of students thrive in such a setting. But I am convinced that years of struggling to survive in school environments that fundamentally de-valued their own existing knowledge and ideas, and which daily fed fears of failure, has left most adults deeply uncon-fident about learning, especially when it happens in any setting resembling a classroom.

Pedagogy is further complicated by the legacy of colonialism in a multicul-tural world. Conflict and appropriate responses are of course culturally rooted. What works in one place may be disastrous in another. This means that efforts to develop peacebuilding skills must build on local insights, not inject pre-scriptions from other places. But trainings outside one's culture in ways that truly accomplish this is extremely difficult, for although few colonial political structures survive, their impact on global consciousness remains pervasive.

When I am honest, I must admit that there is a part of me that thinks I know what others need to know, that my way is better. This is not entirely bad. If I didn't believe this, after all, I wouldn't be interested in spending a lifetime trying to educate others about alternatives to violence. But a healthy vision for a different world is one thing; cultural chauvinism is another. For their part, when they are honest, I suspect that many people in countries with a history of being dominated politically and economically by others would admit that a sense of inadequacy or inferiority lingers. The places where I most consistently encounter expectations from workshop participants that I, the "teacher," bring "answers" and should deliver them are in post-colonial settings. Deep-rooted conflict, of course, makes things even worse, for it fur-ther erodes the confidence of people affected in the value of their own cultural resources. No person who is committed to the empowerment of others—above all no American, whose cultural glitz dominates the imagination of the world's youth through mass media—and who packs a bag to "train" overseas can ignore these realities. Falling unawares into disempowering exchanges is dis-mayingly easy, and only constant vigilance can mitigate it.

In 1985, I was invited by long-term MCC workers in Ireland to do medi-ation training in Belfast and Dublin. I taught mediation as I had been teaching it for several years in North America: a four-stage model for structuring face-to-face discussions. Concerned about cultural issues, I was at pains to stress that this approach may not fit in all cultures and that it would need to be adapted to their context. In 1996, I heard a presentation by Brendan McAl-lister, director of The Mediation Network for Northern Ireland. Their network had had its beginning in 1985, he said, when I had led a workshop in Belfast. My chest swelled for I had not realized that this active network traced its roots so directly to my workshops. But later in his presentation, McAllister provided additional information. For the first several years, he said, the network floun-dered, for their responses to conflict seemed ineffective. In 1991, John Paul Lederach came and led a workshop, assisting them to look at Irish ways of responding to conflicts. Thereafter, McAllister said, they gave themselves permission to adapt the model of mediation they had been using. From that point on their efforts began to have more impact.

While I accept credit, then, for providing an important impetus to get the Mediation Network established, I must also acknowledge that my inability to create a learning experience that truly empowered the Irish to acknowledge and build on their own culture may have handicapped their efforts for six years of precious time. Fortunately, MCC's commitment to long-term peacebuilding ensured that this initial gap was corrected as Lederach later brought an approach that reflected more experience in training cross-culturally. I realized how confident and mature The Mediation Network for Northern Ireland had become by 1999 when, in planning for another workshop that I would be teaching in Belfast, the Irish specifically suggested that I ignore cultural issues. They were looking for fresh ideas, they said, and I should teach whatever I knew. They would sort out what worked in the Irish context and what did not.

The South African experience also illuminated for me the connections among empowerment, cultural issues, and long-term perspective. In desperation at the rapidly rising tide of violence sweeping the country during the political transition, the South African political parties agreed to erect a massive national structure, the National Peace Accord, to respond to the violence. Heavy pressure existed for immediate results, and one key strategy chosen was to quickly field as many trainers as possible. Along with many others, including a substantial number of overseas trainers, I booked my calendar full of trainings.

But when I look now at the training materials that I and others worked from, there is little evidence that they were grounded in South African experiences. In our haste to get something going, we grabbed the training materials available to us, and these were based almost entirely on American and European experiences. I would like to think that in the oral, experiential part of our workshops some of us took South African experience and culture more seriously than the written materials would suggest, but I suspect that even here, we fell short. Developing responses to conflict that truly correspond to local culture is a slow, multi-stage task that requires several years to unfold. Haste and short-term horizons in peacebuilding almost inescapably lead to overreliance on external resources and undervaluation of local ones.

Finally, a theme that has slowly worked its way to a central place in my consciousness as a peace worker is *community*. Peacebuilding in the ways called for above places enormous demands on peace workers. To seek to make all training decisions, for example, in light of their impact on the empowerment of others may be an impossible goal for an individual peace worker who faces the demands of supporting a family. As the majority of people who seek to earn a living as specialists in constructive responses to conflict discover, our world does not yet value the skills of consensus building sufficiently to make steady income-generating work in the field easy to acquire. For the individual practitioner who has already made personal sacrifices to pursue a risky career option, peacebuilding as understood here may be impossible. One friend, a gifted and deeply ethical trainer who is struggling to establish a niche in the field, lamented that if the requirements of peacebuilding are too demanding, the temptation to give up and shift to a secure profession becomes overwhelming.

The truth is that I could not have done the things I have been doing for the last twenty years had I been a solo practitioner. I depended at every step on the emotional and spiritual support, counsel, connections, and, by no means least of all, the financial largesse of a network of people scattered worldwide. This support has made it possible to be guided by a set of ethical standards, indeed a vision for what might be accomplished in human affairs, in a world whose fundamental structures erode empowerment for peace. Peacebuilding as here described is only possible, then, as it is grounded in a community of people who share a common vision of reality and who are prepared to work actively, indeed, self-sacrificingly, to extend that reality to others.

Perhaps more important than any of the above, my community of faith gives me a framework for recognizing and responding to the deep, spiritual issues that the work of peacebuilding raises for all who attempt it. The biggest obstacle to peacebuilding efforts, I have gradually come to see, is not the feistiness of the warring parties, but rather the inability of those working for peace to live by the values they teach. Conflict resolution organizations vie for recognition, turf, and resources and are unable to cooperate in ways that would enhance one another's efforts. Leaders of these organizations horde personal credit, opportunities, and control for themselves, which deserve to be shared with colleagues. At root these are matters of the spirit and heart, but they have inescapably practical consequences, for the one thing required by the practice of peacebuilding is an abundance of genuinely good relationships, and wherever the cravings of ego rule, relationships flounder.

A healthy community of faith provides tools for the never-ending task of working with these spiritual issues, and the Mennonite community provides such for me. Like any authentic commitment to community, I find this commitment painful, costly, even infuriating at times. Yet I cannot shake the conviction that it is from this place that I am called to operate, that more than any other place it enables me to engage in peace work as I have come to understand it and thereby to live in the service of God. Surely, life-giving approaches to making peace can come from a variety of communities and visions for human life. But only as peacebuilders root themselves in such communities and visions can we offer true alternatives to the life-destroying visions that currently govern our world.

# Three

## Journey from Resolution to
## Transformative Peacebuilding

JOHN PAUL LEDERACH

"So, WHERE WILL YOU GO when the revolution comes?" The question was posed by a middle-aged Angolan activist and university student to a much younger student, the son of a future president of Portugal. It was the kind of dinner-table conversation I heard often in 1976 at the David Livingstone residence located in Brussels, Belgium. In my early twenties, I was doing several years of voluntary service with the Mennonite Central Committee (MCC) in a housing project that brought together some thirty university students from nearly as many countries, mostly from Africa. The residence, as the question and the interaction that ensued indicated, was an exciting mix of cultures, peoples, and perspectives. The only thing we all had in common was our foreign status. For me, it represented the first experience of working with people and conflict internationally.

Almost twenty-five years later, I find myself reflecting back on the journey that led me to an orientation toward conflict transformation and peacebuilding. During this period, I have worked in more than twenty-five countries, at virtually every level of society, providing training or consulting with or offering direct support to peacebuilding efforts. I now realize that my early work and thinking emerged principally out of the intermixing of three tributaries of ideas: the Mennonite theological discourse on pacifism, the social-change orientation of active nonviolence, and the practical perspectives proposed by the conflict resolution field. I have always considered myself a practitioner more than a theoretician. Where theory has emerged, it has done so through short, intensive bursts of writing in which I reflected on recent experiences. I have always been reluctant to call it *theory*.

While it is the wide variety of activities at so many different levels and in diverse contexts that has ultimately shaped my analytical contributions, I would like to reflect on three specific experiences that mark important evolutions in my thinking and practice. These experiences, I believe, both reflect and have contributed to Mennonite international peacebuilding work in recent years. They are: efforts in the mid-1980s to develop conflict resolution training in Central America; involvement in the late 1980s in a conciliation effort between the Sandinista government of Nicaragua and the East Coast resistance movement known as YATAMA; and participation in the design of peacebuilding initiatives during the crisis and collapse of the state of Somalia in the early 1990s.

## Training in Central America

When I first was invited by MCC to develop a pilot training course in conflict resolution for grassroots leadership in Central America, my primary concern was how to adapt what I had learned in Spain and North America to a new context. I soon discovered that adaptation was an inadequate framework for the task at hand. While seven years in Europe had provided me with language and cultural adaptation skills, they had not prepared me for the context shift I would experience in the Central American setting over the intensive years of involvement in training during the mid-1980s. This shift involved at least four factors. First, I was working with the diversity of peoples across the region, ranging from indigenous groups in Panama, the East Coast of Nicaragua, and Guatemala to the Mestizo and Ladino populations. Second, I was confronted with the interesting and ever-evolving nuance of language-in-context. Third, I was mainly working with grassroots and often poor rural people. Finally, the region was beset by at least four wars, which spilled across borders and provided the subtext for many of our workshops. The context shift posed the challenge of how to develop an appropriate approach to training in facing conflict, while working in a multiethnic, multilingual setting shaped by overt and structural violence.

I found that my conflict resolution training was too narrow, often out of context, and presumptuous. It was narrow because much of what I had learned about "training" was reductionist. In the North American context, we tended to understand training as revolving mostly around skills for communication and conducting face-to-face mediation sessions, assuming relatively equal partners with a common cultural and educational basis. It was out of context inasmuch as the reductionist process had made assumptions from a North American setting about the needs of workshop recipients for constructive transformation and the best means of responding to those needs. It was presumptuous because the combination of these two factors created a training methodology that removed the power of framing the questions, defining the needs, and naming the processes from the hands of the participants. Bumping up against this reality and self-realization led to a reshaping not only of content but, more important, of training methodology. As I have described in more detail in one of my books, through this experience I moved away from relying on a prescriptive, transfer approach to training and toward the development of an elicitive, discovery-based methodology of learning and practice (1995c).

Sensitivity within MCC to these issues was readily apparent long before I developed the workshops, as is well documented by Miller in chapter 1. The ethos of volunteer work at MCC emphasized a stance of listen and learn rather than one of providing answers. I came wanting to be culturally sensitive in my work. Sensitivity at least provides an attitude of learning. The real test comes, however, through the fire of on-the-ground relationships and work, where we face the challenge of how much we are willing to move away from our preconceived notions of approaches and answers. I found this to be a painful and slow process filled with failures, some successes, and a lot of experiments. As I look back, I can see that my Central American experiences gave rise to three broad, interrelated orientations, which have subsequently shaped my conciliation work.

The first involves moving toward a *contextualization* of theory and practice. I understand contextualization to be an orientation, perhaps more accurately a bias, toward beginning by finding out how conflict and appropriate responses for constructively responding to conflict are understood and rooted in the social realities of the setting—as perceived, experienced, and created by the people in that setting. Context, then, rather than conciliation techniques and methods, is the starting point for defining conciliation work.

Second, this calls for a seedbed *understanding of culture*, as well as of conflict. Culture is not seen as an obstacle to be overcome by innovative conciliation practices. Culture is understood to be the soil in which conflict-handling mechanisms sprout and take root. I found that I was increasingly less concerned about being sensitive and adapting my model to the culture and more interested in developing the lenses that help elucidate the resources available for constructive conciliation and peacebuilding within the culture and context.

Third, these two ideas are oriented toward a process of *empowerment* in which training is better understood as capacity building. In the Central American context, the words "to be able" (*soy capaz*), "power" (*poder, puedo*), and "training" (*capacitación*) are all linked. They relate to the idea of moving from "I cannot" to "I can," a process that Paolo Freire would call *conscientization* (1970). Such a process suggests that learning both about conflict and how to respond to it involves developing the awareness of self-in-context and the recognition that responses lie within the people and their context. Responses are then subsequently submitted to a constant evaluative process of reflection and action. Most important, at a personal level, I found that this redefined my understanding of the trainer's role away from expert-in-content and toward accompaniment-in-discovery. In other words, this orientation represented not merely a shift in methodology but also a change in the nature of the relationship between me and the people I hoped to teach.

Thus, the training challenges of Central America moved me from a rhetoric of cultural sensitivity toward an orientation rooted in the centrality of context, culture, and empowerment. While this reorientation was initiated in the area of training methodology, it has since created a set of lenses through which I view my broader conciliation practice at all levels. It suggests that conciliation is about transformation, which emanates from within the person, context, and culture, rather than a preconceived notion of change, which is defined and transferred in from outside.

## Conciliation in the East Coast of Nicaragua

My first contact with Nicaragua came in the middle of the 1980s' war through a pilot workshop I conducted with East Coast Moravian church leaders, who had been displaced to Managua. I could never have imagined that this early, somewhat bumbling attempt at training would translate itself, several years later, into intense, close, and deep relationships and the formation of a team that would work together for more than four years on a conciliation process aimed at bringing together Costeño resistance leaders and the Sandinista government. It was the first time I had worked directly with high-level, high-stakes negotiations in the context of ending a war and building a sustainable reconciliation. I played a support role to the Conciliation Commission, which was made up of church leaders from the East Coast and Managua.

For several years, this became my primary focus and activity. The experience affected and changed every aspect of my life, from personal to family to professional. As I look back, two things stand out that merit discussion here: my increased appreciation for complexity and a growing understanding of the cost of peacemaking.

### Complexity

As a mediator with experience in a variety of conflicts, I was well aware that developing a conciliation process is a complex matter. The intermediary activity that the Conciliation Commission undertook during the latter half of the 1980s increased that appreciation tenfold. I began to understand complexity in more specific ways. Three aspects of the peace process lie behind this growth of vision and understanding.

First, the sheer task of networking provided a whole new appreciation of complexity with regard to the primary and secondary actors in the conflict. The East Coast movement had numerous divisions located in four countries; we dealt with several branches of the Sandinista government; we were obliged to find creative ways to work with neighboring and often hostile governmental officials and bureaucracies; we were faced with outside, often invisible actors, who were not interested in a successful YATAMA-Sandinista negotiation, namely, those people connected to the Nicaraguan resistance (Contras) and their supporters in the CIA; and, finally, we were constantly aware of the broader civilian population in the East Coast, which at times felt greatly marginalized in the process of formal negotiations. I gained a much greater appreciation for the web of relationships that affect protracted conflict purely from the standpoint of actors (1994).

Second, complexity meant working across the levels of the society, both vertically and horizontally. As a commission, we initially functioned through informal networks of contacts and activities. Then, when the formal negotiations began, the Conciliation Commission was officially appointed by the sides to the conflict, YATAMA and the Sandinista government, to carry out the roles of conciliator, facilitator, and overall supporter of the process. One week, we found ourselves working intensely in a Managua hotel, where diplomatic protocol, official representatives, and formal processes of negotiations and agreements carried the day. The following week, we would find ourselves with leaders from both sides, traveling into East Coast riverways and villages to conduct local-level discussions about the peace process.

I was always struck by how different each of those realities felt. The formal process had to deal with political issues, detailed negotiations, protocols, and visibility under the constant eye of the press. The village discussions felt much more direct and organic to the conflict. Accusations would fly as those who were returning met with those who had chosen to stay, or people from different sides who had experienced the war locally met together, with all the pain and fear such an encounter entails.

Through the Moravian church and the Protestant relief organization Comíte Evangelíco Pro Ayuda Al Desarollo (CEPAD) (the two institutions that made up the Conciliation Commission), we were linked to activity at both the top and the grassroots levels and at the same time to all sides in the conflict. Consequently, my understanding over the years has sharpened in reference to the uniqueness and interdependence of each level of work and the need to develop and sustain many relationships across the divide in the conflict. This experience eventually translated into the pyramid of actors and approaches to peacebuilding, which has provided an important lens for understanding the complexity and levels of work in divided societies (1997, p. 39). Further, the experiences at the grassroots level, in working with some early training for local peace commissions, helped flesh out for me the centrality of relationship building in processes of reconciliation. My vision of reconciliation was increasingly rooted in the idea of rebuilding relationships at personal and societal levels. On the one hand, while complexity suggested a comprehensive and operational view of action across the levels, interdependence could only be understood in practical terms as it was embedded in relationship. Reconciliation as relationship building was therefore central to peacebuilding before, during, and after negotiations.

Third and most perplexing to me was the understanding of complexity as it related to time, particularly in this instance to simultaneity, that is, to multiple things taking place at the same time. When I went to Central America, I often used the language of conflict management. Since the Nicaragua experience, I have dropped all references to "management," which seems to connote the ability to control or channel. The reality of protracted, armed conflict is the mix of many actors, at many levels, all engaging in activity at the same time. I felt like a conflict chaser more than a manager—like the proverbial dog that barks at the car that just went by.

I found that our team could rarely plan and anticipate the evolution of events or the changing perceptions of people. This pushed us in several directions. We discovered that there was no ripe moment for resolution that was somehow discernible by objective criteria or even one that could be fabricated. Instead, we understood ripeness to be a function of relationships and availability. As Adam Curle once commented, you must just keep going to the door and knocking (1990).

We were in no position to control the process and therefore, out of necessity, needed to rely on a broad network of relationships. Control of the process would imply that one was able to create a single channel for the process development and thereby create a mechanism for gatekeeping on decision making and the flow of activity. We were obligated to operate with a complex-web approach to process and reconciliation, which at many points was frustrating. In retrospect I can see, however, that a complex-web approach may in fact be an important component of sustainability. The recent history of peace accords has taught us that while we may desire to control a process of building peace, where that has happened the process has been too centralized and defined by too few actors and, as such, is ultimately not sustainable as it enlarges to involve more people.

## Cost of Peacemaking

A second major area of learning and growth that emerged from the Nicaraguan experience was related to the impact of violence on our personal and family lives. Not one of us on the commission was spared the hands of violence in physical or psychological terms. For me, this involved threats of violence against my family; death threats against me personally; physical beating, detentions, and interrogations; and accusations that ranged from drug-running charges to spying for the Sandinistas, on one side, to being a "dog of the CIA," on the other. As one Miskito commented during the swirl of these events, "You are one of us now" (Lederach 1992, p. 12).

What it felt like to be one of them was to have a life of constant suspicion, a subconsciousness filled with fear, and a sense of powerlessness that emerged mostly from not knowing exactly from whom or from which direction the threat was coming. It was this mix of structural and overt violence that left me feeling vulnerable and, at times, unsure of the next steps. At the same time, it seemed that the only way through such feelings was to emulate my colleagues on the commission, who usually had it twice as bad as I did, with no option for leaving. They chose to embrace the vulnerability as a resource rather than as a pitfall, linking it, as the Moravians would say, to the way of the lamb.[1]

While my own faith tradition shares this theology of the lamb—Jesus as an example of a suffering servant, who chooses obedience and respect for life over political power or personal defense—it was only in this context that I understood vicariously what it meant to share a table in the presence of my enemies (Psalm 23). To embrace vulnerability meant embarking on a real journey toward sustaining a relationship with the enemy. It was a time of personal transformation, sustained only by close community and prayer.

In the long run, what has remained with me over the years is a much deeper appreciation of the depth of feelings of suspicion, anger, and vulnerability that

I meet time and again among people in settings of protracted, violent conflict. These feelings often translate into deep-seated animosities, exaggerated suspicions, hard-line positions, and volatility. At early stages of my career, I held much more idealistic views of the potential for change and the seeking of peace in response to such feelings. The Nicaraguan experience created a more deeply engraved understanding of the reality of violence, powerlessness, anger, and fear.

## Somali Crisis

In the early 1990s, I began to work more closely with situations in the Horn of Africa, particularly in Somalia. This work was conducted, in the early stages, through the Horn of Africa Project at Conrad Grebel College, a Mennonite institution in Waterloo, Ontario. It then continued with a Somali-initiated network known as the Ergada, which is still active among Somalis in the diaspora. Later, I worked extensively with the overall program design of the Somalia initiatives of the Life and Peace Institute (LPI) in Uppsala, Sweden, and with Bonnie Bergey in the MCC work in Somalia (see ch. 10 in this volume).

This was my first in-depth introduction into what are now referred to as "complex emergencies." Somalia of the late 1980s to early 1990s was a country experiencing the collapse of its central government, spreading subclan warfare, and a famine produced by the war and drought. It was a crisis that seized the attention of the international community and media and eventually led to massive international responses in humanitarian assistance, mediation, and peacekeeping. It also, however, raised many questions about the nature of conflict, state building, and reconciliation. Working from the perspective of nongovernmental organizations (NGOs), such as LPI and MCC, while simultaneously working with a consulting group providing advice to the U.N. peacekeeping (UNOSOM) efforts, my thinking sharpened on the need for peacebuilding to develop both a comprehensive view of the work and a strategic infrastructure to support it.

### Comprehensiveness

My various experiences in Central America had already caused me to think in more comprehensive terms about the levels of work and interdependence of actors in peacebuilding. This became much more specific in the Somali situation. After numerous visits to the country and after working extensively with the creative thinking of the members of the Ergada, I realized clearly that a classic, diplomatically based process of identifying top-level leaders to negotiate a peace was unrealistic in what it could deliver and that it might, in fact, be counterproductive. Particularly within the circles of Somali intellectuals in the Ergada, we began for the first time to differentiate between top-down and bottom-up approaches to peacebuilding in Somalia.

The top-down approach was pursued by any number of foreign governments, high-profile leaders, and multilateral organizations, including the United Nations. This approach sought to establish a negotiating process among key faction leaders. The concern we found consistently lay with the dilemmas such a process posed in the Somali context. Top-down assumed leaders could be found who actually represented the groups they said they did. It assumed a hierarchy of power by which those same leaders could deliver on promises made. It assumed clearly identified groups in the conflict. It assumed there would be a state to govern—with normal functions and instruments of power—once an agreement was reached. In fact, precious few, if any, of these conditions existed. Clan and subclan affiliations were ephemeral. Representation was never clear-cut. Power was diffuse and rarely hierarchical with regard to delivering on agreements. The central state structure had completely collapsed. Time and again, a high-level negotiating process proved unable to deliver either sustainable agreements or peace throughout the country.

Bottom-up approaches were suggested based on the more contextualized mechanisms by which interclan fighting had traditionally been handled. These included elders' conferences, as well as the involvement of women's associations and other members of the civil society, such as intellectuals, businesspeople, traders, and artists, particularly poets. This approach relied on the analysis that the centralized state had collapsed and that the country had de facto returned to more informal and traditional methods for relating. Fighting in the conflict often took place in the context of local subclan relationships and traditional demands, and thus local responses were needed. True representation and participation were in great demand, thus calling for local-level initiatives where such representation could be identified. The few existing cross-clan mechanisms were almost all related to various networks within the civil society, particularly among women. In this analysis, there was a need to rebuild from the bottom with a focus on local, participatory activities based on an accepted method for assessing due representation. These were the kinds of initiatives that we in LPI and MCC began to support.

The bottom-up approach, however, faced the serious challenge of how to translate its activities into something that moved beyond good intentions, which were extremely localized. Top-down seemed to lend itself to the manipulation of leaders for personal gain and the possible reconstruction of state structures, which appeared to have little long-term viability. I returned once again to a concern for a comprehensive approach that understood the uniqueness and linkages of the different levels involved. It was here that I first visualized the pyramid in graphic form. Building from both the Nicaraguan and Somali dilemmas of watching the simultaneity of top- and grassroots-level peacebuilding initiatives take place in isolation from one another, I added the component that moved toward seeking a strategic infrastructure.

### Strategic Infrastructure

The concept of building a strategic infrastructure for peace was advanced by the Somali experience through two specific dilemmas: How to link the top and grassroots levels? How to respond to the immediate crisis of famine and devastation and yet create the conditions necessary to sustain the desired change over the longer term?

The response to the first dilemma came in part through watching the evolution of elders' conferences held in the northwest region, in what became the independently declared Somaliland. Through supporting and working with the leaders conducting the elders' conferences and through reading first-hand accounts, it seemed that the local conferences were capable of working with local-level conflicts. But they only became strategic to the degree that they were supported by and coordinated with people who could help create conferences at the next level up, in other words, at the cross-clan level and, ultimately, at the level of Grand Elders' conferences, at which representative elders coming from all the subclans met together. What was necessary, therefore, was a set of middle-range actors to create the links, support the activity, and eventually host and facilitate the larger and more encompassing conferences.

In other words, if one relied exclusively on the highest level of actor, the peace process often was not able to translate itself downward in the society with a sense of broad-based support and the potential for implementation. On the other hand, if the process remained completely local, it was often incapable of generating change beyond local concerns. The "middle-out" idea, adding an intermediate level in the pyramid, emerged as a way of locating a set of actors that was able to link vertically (up and down the society through one or another form of network) and horizontally (across the lines of division in the conflict).

In the case of the Grand Elders' Conference in Borama, a city in northwest Somaliland, this was achieved by convening elders who emerged as the designated representatives in the local processes, with innovative logistical support provided by a web of Somali NGOs. Interestingly, the main lesson in this process for outsiders was that the appropriate role for them to play was to provide a bit of cash for rice and transport and otherwise stay out. In fact, perhaps our most useful role was to make the case to other outsiders to allow time and space for local traditions to come into play.

The lesson with regard to infrastructure was to look for those people and networks in situ that have a capacity to create linkages and support initiatives over time. In that respect, the elders' conferences and women's associations in Somalia were analogous to the Conciliation Commission made up of religious leaders in Nicaragua. Both sets of actors represented a middle-out approach to longer-term work; neither included high-level political or faction leaders nor people locked exclusively into localized work. Both sets had the ability to articulate their purposes and initiatives upward, downward, and across the levels and lines of division in the society. As such, they helped create the components of a strategic infrastructure.

The response to the second dilemma in building a strategic infrastructure—how to relate a crisis orientation to longer-term transformation—was a new way of thinking about time. Most of the people responding to the Somali case thought in terms of the immediate crisis and the need to alleviate human suffering of vast proportions. Two things struck me as I interacted with both the humanitarian organizations providing food, medicine, and shelter and the intermediary people from the United Nations and other countries. First, both communities had a finely developed capacity to think of strategies for accomplishing immediate goals, be they the delivery of food or the accomplishment of a cease-fire. Internationally, we have honed our capacity to think in short time blocks in humanitarian crises. Second, neither community had well-developed capacities for thinking in the middle to long term with reference to sustaining peacebuilding. Responses were driven by the crisis not by a strategy for achieving changes in the present that would create the conditions desired and needed to build a sustainable peace and that would not recreate the causes of the current conflict. For the most part, middle- and long-range thinking was seen as contradictory to the demands of "crisis thinking."

The Somali situation pushed me to recognize that we must be able to think in longer blocks of time in settings of protracted conflict. I went so far as to suggest that it may take as long to climb back out of a conflict as it did for the conflict to build up to its worst, most divided moment. This means we must be able to articulate a long-term vision, what Elise Boulding calls "imaging the future," which calls for a capacity to think in generations. We must also be able to think about how to operationalize the vision in terms of the design of social change or what I call "decade thinking." Both of these capacities, then, would inform us about how our current decisions on the crisis are linked to the direction in which we hope to go.

I was also struck by the need to frame the questions about peacebuilding in Somalia as a dilemma rather than as a contradiction. How do we respond to the humanitarian crisis in the immediate term *and* build the infrastructure necessary for creating the change that will move the situation toward sustainable peace? In other words, we must find ways to link different communities of thought and action—disaster management, humanitarian assistance, and crisis mediation, for example, with conflict prevention, conflict transformation, reconciliation, and sustainable development—rather than letting them operate competitively or potentially at cross purposes. In this way, we can envision how the different time frames provide legitimate space for each concern along a continuum from immediate response to strategic change, rather than pitting them against one another. As in the case of middle-range actors in the pyramid, what emerged as crucial for building a strategic infrastructure was an intermediate time frame that linked the immediate and long-term time horizons. The middle-range time frame is the five-to-ten-year block represented by the training and social-change design components.

In sum, the Somali experience linked for me the earlier awareness about contextualization, complexity, and empowerment with an emerging framework for thinking more comprehensively and strategically about the design of peacebulding work. It nudged me toward the articulation of theory, as ambiguous and uncertain as that enterprise may be. My practical experiences in training and in the direct support of conciliation initiatives came together in the publication of two books in 1995 (1995c; 1997 [rev.]), which represented my foray into the world of theory building.

## Conclusions

The path toward transformation and peacebuilding has been a journey toward an understanding that the work of conflict transformation and reconciliation involves both the termination of something undesired—violent conflict—and the building of something desired. It is about change *and* construction. A transformative peacebuilding approach draws upon several key ideas.

First, relationship is central. Both conflict and reconciliation are embedded in relationships. We resolve issues, but we reconcile people. Violent conflict creates a spiral of destructive transformation of relationships. Reconciliation involves creating a space in which the relationship can rebuild or build through a constructive transformation. What matters most in a long-term peacebuilding process is how we address the nature and perception of our relational interdependence.

Interdependence, in turn, requires an understanding of complexity and comprehensiveness as we approach peacebuilding and conflict transformation. Developing a recognition of relational interdependence—across the lines of conflict and the levels of society—is perhaps the single most important goal we undertake in settings of deep-rooted conflict. It provides a set of lenses and a long-term, lifetime perspective, which sharpens and informs short-term decisions.

Lifetime perspectives underscore the goal of sustainability. If we take seriously the idea of sustainable peace and reconciliation in settings of protracted conflict, we must then take up the challenge of being deeply aware of the depth of animosity, anger, and suspicion present, while simultaneously creating the space for articulating a vision of what is desired. For a peace process to be rooted in the present reality and to create a realistic vision for going forward will require the tools of contextualization and empowerment. To move from the reality of devastation to a shared future will require both a design for transformation and the building of an infrastructure to make such transformation possible.

Here the journey comes full circle. Conflict transformation is about change and developing the tools of change. Peacebuilding is about the construction of a vision and developing the design that guides the construction. Both must be built with tools and materials that come out of the realities and relationships that people know and experience in their daily lives. This is building the house of peace—from the ground up.

# II

## MENNONITE PEACEBUILDING IN PRACTICE

# Four

## Building Peace in South Africa
### A Case Study of Mennonite Program

ROBERT HERR
JUDY ZIMMERMAN HERR

IT WAS 1983, the beginning of what would later be known as a decade of decisive and bitter struggle in South Africa. We were visiting a rural African, Presbyterian church. Representing a North American church agency to people in a rural homeland of the then-pariah South Africa was a dicey task. Mennonites in North America were sometimes unsure about our being there. International friends noted the ethical dilemma our presence posed. "We are hurt by the ostracism of the world," said a South African friend, in contrast, "especially by the churches. We didn't ask for this oppression; it was thrust upon us. It's as if we find ourselves on the cross. Please do not say, as did Jesus' tormentors, 'save yourself.' Rather, come and suffer and agonize with us" (Mcoteli, 1983).

This advice on work in South Africa during the years of bloody struggle appeared straightforward enough. However, the advice of a local activist friend and African National Congress (ANC) operative was also part of our reflection. "If I ever need to flee South Africa and go into exile in Lesotho or some other place, I would probably feel compelled to tell Mennonites to do the same. But as long as I am here, struggling in this context, I want you here working with me" (Tapscott, 1983).

The presence of an international Christian peace agency in a context of intense political and social injustice suggests moral compromise. There are no easy paths through the dilemmas that present themselves. Our experience in South Africa was like that. We worked, we made friends, and we occasionally shared in the suffering and pain that fell on so many of our colleagues and friends. It was only because we were there that we could experience these dilemmas up close.

We took up this work in South Africa because we believe that the Christian church, if it is to be relevant to people struggling for justice, must have an international face. This is obviously the case anywhere, but we had come to know many South African Christians and valued their friendships. Our presence as people from the outside added an international dimension to the Christian witness in that context.

The story of South Africa's long struggle for justice is well known. The Mennonite place in that story spans three decades, decades that we now know were decisive. Obviously, Mennonite work in South Africa is not a highly visible part of this story. We went there to support and to accompany people working for change. But our work there is illustrative of the way Mennonites have worked for peace in many other locations.

Mennonite work in South Africa shifted with the changes in the South African struggle, and so the story is one that moves from advocacy for victims of apartheid to support for nonviolent struggle to resourcing for reconciliation. This work also looked especially to the local Christian church. Identification with the church—and especially the church at the grassroots of society—was the umbrella under which individual Mennonites worked. The grassroots nature of this work was less by design, at least initially, than because of restrictions on work permits, visas, and travel. It meant that through the crucial years of struggle, our perspective was influenced by rural, poorer persons, far from the centers of power. Over time, this was a powerful force in determining the way Mennonite workers connected to life in South Africa.

Throughout the three decades surveyed here, Mennonites lived in tension between the disengaged macro-level analysis of South Africa and an engaged, on-the-ground struggle for survival. Because the struggle against apartheid was an international issue, outside comment was plentiful. Questions about economic sanctions or relating to Afrikaners, which sometimes appeared simple from the outside looked mixed from within the country. We struggled to know when we were compromising too much. To complicate things further, from within local church institutions, we saw firsthand the power struggles and corruption that could destabilize the anti-apartheid movement. Although the large issues of justice and injustice were clear, the path to justice through local reality often seemed less so.

Our telling of the story of Mennonite work in South Africa will follow the events in that country over three decades. These decades have been decisive ones for the country as it moved from quiet repression through growing struggle and into a negotiated end to minority rule.

## 1970s: Rebirth of "the Struggle"

"Ultimately what will occur in South Africa is a revolution, a radical change from the current situation to some alternative," summarized one participant at the 1978 Mennonite Central Committee Peace Theology Colloquium, which was called to review the nature of a Mennonite peacebuilding presence in South Africa (Rempel, 1978). During the 1970s, "the Struggle" in South Africa gained world attention. Would it be cataclysmic and bloody, or evolutionary? Should one become involved internally, or work from outside the country? How should one determine when efforts were being coopted by the authorities and when they were making an authentic contribution to liberation?

Mennonite agencies sponsored fact-finding and study visits in the late 1960s and early 1970s. Learning about the depth of South African racial division and oppression is evident in reports, seminars, and symposiums. Questions about initiating a Mennonite program were debated. Is peaceful change possible? Will it be enhanced or retarded by the presence of outsiders who profess a commitment to finding peaceful responses to oppression? Is peace and reconciliation even a valid or welcomed goal, or is this a time for confrontation and revolution? Consensus was seldom reached, but by the end of the 1970s, the first placement of personnel was made in the rural, "independent" homeland of the Transkei. During this decade, the discussion moved from analysis and review on the part of North American church agencies to resident Mennonite workers and an internal program committed to justice. With an imprecise understanding of the implications, Mennonites had joined the Struggle.

At the beginning of the 1970s, internal South African resistance to apartheid appeared all but defeated. The liberation movements had taken up residence outside the country. Resistance leaders were either in exile or in prison. It was a time of discouragement and repression. Because things were quiet—and the international climate for investment good—the economy grew, as did government attempts to entrench the apartheid system.

The 1950s and 1960s had seen the growth and codification of apartheid as a political philosophy and as a governing system, albeit one accompanied by growing resistance. The African National Congress took the lead during the 1950s with campaigns of nonviolent resistance. But the authorities increased their efforts at repression. In 1961, at a nonviolent march in the small town of Sharpeville, police opened fire on unarmed demonstrators. Sixty-three people were killed.

The Sharpeville massacre was a turning point in the resistance. In response, the ANC and other groups adopted a new strategy of sabotage and violent resistance. Within two years, the government had outlawed all leading resistance organizations. Prominent leaders fled into exile or were imprisoned. Nelson Mandela, arrested in 1963, was given a life sentence. The loss of central leadership and the banning of organizations meant that average people were left without political focus or channels for action. Opposition to apartheid was muted for much of the 1960s and early 1970s.

In 1972, with the establishment of what became known as the Black People's Convention and the rise of a new leader, Steve Biko, the Struggle again began to take shape as an effective internal force for change. Although its start was feeble and focused on grassroots organization without outside support, it laid the groundwork for the rebirth of a struggle that would in the end dismantle the system of apartheid. Biko reflected both the reality of the era and a philosophy of ground-up self-reliance, called Black Consciousness, in the frequently repeated slogan, "Black man, you are on your own." The suggestion was that this is not only reality, but the way to liberation.

Because of growing involvement in the civil rights movement in the United States, American Mennonites in the 1960s were increasingly aware of the injustice taking place in South Africa. In 1967, a Mennonite leader visited but found little likelihood that Mennonite involvement would be welcomed. The regime was not interested in outsiders, especially from pacifist church organizations. In 1968, a Mennonite program was started in Botswana and soon after that in Swaziland. Interest in responding to injustice in South Africa from the perspective of peace and reconciliation was always a part of the agenda. The phrase "a window on South Africa" appeared frequently in Mennonite Central Committee (MCC) reports during this time.

A substantive study of South African dynamics was carried out between November 1971 and May 1972 by James Juhnke, then the Mennonite program director in Botswana. The written reports from this study formed a benchmark for ongoing Mennonite thinking about involvement in South Africa.

Juhnke's first report focused on the status of conscientious objection in South Africa. "Your Bible will not protect you from bullets," he quotes a judge saying in December 1971, while sentencing a nineteen-year-old to jail for objecting to military service (1972a, p. 1). Conscientious objection was then a small movement in South Africa. Only about fifty of the 28,000 conscripts would take this stand. But it indicated the beginning of something that, during the 1980s, would become a much larger movement, with national-level organization.

Juhnke's reports included sections on white politics, on public security, on North American businesses in South Africa, and on the rise of the Black Consciousness movement as an attempt to reestablish a political movement for black liberation (1972b, pp. 49–53).

Some felt that Mennonites should come to South Africa with the open intention of helping, building, and reconciling. But, if efforts were successful, they could serve to contribute toward making a basically unjust system more palatable. One commentator wrote:

> If we assist in agricultural development in the homelands, we contribute [to] entrenching the government's policy of establishing separate reserves for the blacks. If we provide social services for the urban blacks, we help to streamline a policy which keeps racial groups separate and apart. Presence would be facilitated by the very government which legislates separation. (Juhnke, 1972b, p. 50)

This early process of study concluded with the goal of pursuing program in three basic areas. The first was to consider placing a "peace missioner" with the South African Council of Churches (SACC) in Johannesburg. Because of Mennonite interest in peace and peacemaking, such an assignment would engage the churches in a dialogue about justice and reconciliation. A second goal was to place secondary school teachers in selected institutions that were identified as places where especially creative work was going on in preparing for the future of South Africa. The third was to become engaged in rural or agricultural work in the Transkei. The local SACC program was especially interested in having Mennonite participation in programs in that area, which had begun in the newly burgeoning self-sufficiency initiatives that grew out of the Black Consciousness movement.

It was quickly recognized, however, that even if Mennonites could find places to be involved redemptively in South Africa, there remained an over-riding practical problem. Would Mennonites be allowed in at all? Would the South African government grant visas to Mennonite workers, and on what conditions? The South African government was putting growing pressure on progressive churches that opposed apartheid. The fears proved accurate when visas were denied on two successive attempts to place a Mennonite peace missioner in Johannesburg.

The year 1976 was a crucial one in South African history. The Soweto uprising of black high school and primary school pupils set a spark to the growing self-awareness nurtured in Black Consciousness. When the govern-ment said that all South African students would need to learn Afrikaans and be taught some courses in Afrikaans, many students said no. *Asingeni* became the rallying cry throughout the country. *Asingeni*, "we will not go in," signified a growing resolve to stand up to this imposition of apartheid. Primarily young students initiated this reaction, and it touched off widespread anarchy in Af-rican urban areas. The government, caught off guard, responded by banning youth leaders, shooting into crowds, and generally increasing the authority of police in black urban areas.

In 1976, Biko was killed while being held in prison. The death of such a popular black leader only added fuel to the rising anger among young black students. That year also witnessed the first official "independence" for a South African homeland. The Transkei had gained a level of self-rule in 1963, and on October 26, 1976, the territory gained further autonomy for local affairs. In the eyes of South African diplomats, the Transkei was now an independent country. "Diplomatic" relations were established with South Africa, the only country to recognize the separate status of this territory.

Early in 1976, an invitation came from the Umtata, Transkei, office of the SACC (called the Transkei Council of Churches), asking Mennonites to send a consultant for rural agricultural and community projects. This again opened the possibility of work in South Africa.

In February 1978, Ray Brubacher, then MCC's Africa secretary, visited the Transkei and helped finalize plans for the placing of Mennonite personnel in Umtata (1978). The official assignment was to be a development consultant to local Council of Churches programs. Additional hopes from MCC focused on maintaining linkage with the growing conscientious objector movement in South Africa and developing other contacts that would enable further peace and reconciliation work. With "independence" in the Transkei in 1976, legal residence for work in South Africa became a possibility. Reported Bru-bacher:

> I feel that the church in Transkei has called us to come and strive for justice by identifying with the oppressed. "Identifying" means as much direct, personal "standing with" as possible. While a specific assignment like a rural development officer with the SACC may be important, it is more important to realize that this

is an avenue through which we can "identify with" and "stand with" our Christian
brothers and sisters. (1978, pp. 5–6)

Early in the decade, discussions had focused on understanding the context.
In 1978, discussions were about how to make ground-level connections that
would respond to the Struggle. Suggestions included "adopting" banned persons for visitation and support, working with conscientious objectors, and
being sensitive to the needs of refugees. Mennonite programs in Botswana
and Swaziland helped to establish schools for the large number of students
that fled into exile following the 1976 Soweto uprising.

Late in 1978, Tim and Suzanne Lind took up residence in Umtata. Over
the course of three years, their contacts with movements and people grew.
They quickly became involved in providing support for South Africa's fledg-
ling Conscientious Objector Support Groups, providing not only some financial help but also books on peace theology and publicity for those who were
imprisoned. Mennonite encouragement for this young movement was important at its beginning and contributed to a reputation of interest in peace in
South Africa.

Daily work with rural economic and community development programs
cemented the connection with the SACC. Also, within the first year, Tim
Lind became involved with the SACC's Dependents' Conference, a program
of support for the dependents of political prisoners. Because the number of
political prisoners continued to grow following the 1976 disturbances, the
work of the Dependents' Conference rapidly expanded. During the 1970s, as
the apartheid regime continued to work out its grand vision of separate areas
for the different racial groups, the SACC initiated the Relocations Project to
document the movement of people in this consolidation of racial groups.
MCC provided support to this project in the Eastern Cape region.

In addition to the presence of Mennonite workers and the programs they
could support via their work in Umtata, MCC began a long association with
the SACC Justice and Reconciliation Department. This association began in
the late 1970s with MCC sponsorship of speakers to conferences and workshops and expanded to supporting a field worker for communities facing relocation. The trust that was developed via this association, as well as the
ground-level work in development and social service in Umtata, provided a
foundation for subsequent Mennonite peacemaking work. Two Peacemaker
Seminars sponsored by MCC took place in Swaziland at the end of the decade.
These week-long training meetings involved many SACC staff and other
church workers and helped to establish a Mennonite reputation among South
African churches.

The 1970s had begun with Mennonites discussing, from a great distance,
the ethics and practicality of program relationships with South African
churches and communities. The decade ended with resident MCC workers
established in a rural homeland. This base provided not only the initial ground
for peacemaking work but the chance to gain a perspective on life in South
Africa from the point of view of an oppressed and marginalized people. From

this base, relationships and friendships grew, and subsequent work in peace and reconciliation became possible.

## 1980s: Growing Resistance and Bloody Repression

In mid-1982, after MCC service in Malawi and graduate studies in Pittsburgh, we arrived in South Africa to pick up the work Tim and Suzanne Lind had left the year before. We would end up staying until 1991. The sign in the airport in Johannesburg read, "Welcome to South Africa."

After a day of rest from our travels, it was time to begin orientation to work, and a fellow Council of Churches worker, Ezra Sigwela, began the process. As Bob and Ezra were chatting and looking at the morning paper, into the office walked several men in dark suits. They took Ezra away with them and placed him in detention. Ezra was not released until six months later. The intervening months were our "welcome" to South Africa.

The weeks following Ezra's detention were filled with meetings—with church leaders in town, with local journalists, with police and government officials to determine where Ezra was being held. We learned quickly about the forces of repression in South Africa. We learned to recognize the special cars that often parked in front of our house. When Bob was assaulted on the street on the same night that the chair of the council had his house searched by police, we pondered the connection. We learned to take care when talking on the phone and to suspect strangers who seemed too friendly. We learned how to document detentions and which lawyers would be helpful. We learned how to get in contact with Amnesty International (AI).

Probably largely because of the pressure of AI letters from around the world, four months after his detention, Ezra's status was changed from detainee to awaiting-trial prisoner. He was charged with furthering the aims of the banned ANC and with helping fugitives leave the country. He could now receive visitors, and we made trips to the local prison once a week. Finally, a lengthy and sensational trial led to Ezra's release. This was only the first of many incidents of coworkers being detained or harassed. Apartheid repression was never far away.

The 1980s were decisive in ending apartheid and minority rule in South Africa. While a more removed perspective might point to an economic downturn aided by sanctions and to the personality of F. W. de Klerk as crucial in the move toward negotiations for a change of government, those inside South Africa remember the growth of popular protest and boycotts. Discussions about what peace means and whether and when violence can be justified preoccupied many of the churches. This was a decade of struggle and repression but also a time for the first glimmers of solid change.

During the 1980s, the Mennonite presence in South Africa grew with the addition of village-level development workers in the Transkei and of Bible teachers with African Independent churches. But for the majority of the decade, Mennonite involvement with the larger struggle against apartheid centered around the backwater homeland territory of the Transkei. Visa restrictions limited Mennonite workers' travel and movement in South Africa. Against our will, our perspective on South Africa's struggles was from the periphery.

Because of these restrictions, much Mennonite involvement with South Africa in the 1980s consisted of the funding of specialized programs. For the entire decade, MCC funded a staff position in the Justice and Reconciliation Department of the SACC. Initially, this field worker related to communities facing forced relocation. Later, Mennonite funding supported the salary of the director of Justice and Reconciliation, who coordinated a network of local field workers throughout the country. Mennonites also gave some support to the Dependents' Conference program for families of political prisoners.

In 1984, the International Fellowship of Reconciliation decided to open a South African office and to employ a staff person. MCC shared in funding this position for first one and later two workers, who led trainings in nonviolent tactics for change and worked actively in the fight against military conscription. Miscellaneous grants went to special projects, including some support for communities resisting forced removal.

Travel restrictions hampered some involvements in South Africa and caused a redoubling of efforts to find other channels for relationships. We were eager to have knowledge of African, black theology in South Africa grow in North American Mennonite circles, and we pursued a variety of exchanges between the Federal Theological Seminary in Pietermaritzburg (a training institution of the Anglican, Presbyterian, and Methodist churches) and the Associated Mennonite Biblical Seminary in Indiana.

While building connections to black churches in South Africa, we also sought ways to build bridges between our white South African friends and colleagues and these black partners. Our history of relating to conscientious objector groups put us in touch with university-aged white youth. With the help of a Christian student group, we offered opportunities for white students to spend a year with an MCC program in the neighboring countries of Botswana, Lesotho, or Swaziland. The hope was that a step outside South African society would give young persons a larger view—and the freedom to see a new reality. Although there was support and enthusiasm for these experiences, the growing struggle within the country increasingly preoccupied student groups, and time "outside" became difficult.

The early 1980s were a time of seething quiet in South Africa. Several African homelands had been granted "independence" while others, in refusing this status, continued their operations within the structures of the Pretoria government. The pace of forcefully removing small settlements of African people from areas declared for whites only picked up. Stricter influx-control laws removed South African citizenship from people assigned to the "independent" homelands, making some who had lived and worked all their lives in urban South Africa into foreigners. As outrageous as these policies seemed, in subtle ways they achieved a level of success. In 1985, a young eighteen-year-old South African soldier, AWOL from his regiment, appeared at our doorstep frantically looking for help. His home was in Johannesburg, and this was his first visit to a black homeland. One of his first comments to us was, "I didn't know there were so many black people in South Africa."[1]

Already in 1983, the government had begun to feel the pressure for change in a real way, and it attempted to introduce a new constitution. This 1983 constitution became a new rallying cry for mobilizing grassroots resistance throughout the country. Among other provisions, it set up three chambers in the legislature, one each for whites, Indians, and "Coloureds" (persons of mixed race), but veto power was retained by the white chamber only. Community groups that had their roots in the Black Consciousness movement joined with the growing trade unions in opposition, and together they formed the United Democratic Front to oppose the constitution. Rallies were repressed, and in the larger urban centers people took to the streets. These events released a widespread spirit of resistance that could no longer be contained.

Throughout the decade, the pattern of rising protest met by stronger repressive measures repeated itself. Beginning in 1984, boycotts spread across the country. Growing unrest led to deployment of the army in the black townships, which provided a new focus for the growing protests. By early 1985, rumor was that certain areas were "ungovernable" and that police and the army were afraid to enter. Finally, in June 1986, the government declared a state of emergency for the entire country. Thousands were detained in large, sweeping police actions, and strict censorship was imposed on newspapers.

As Mennonite workers in a rural homeland, we connected frequently with this growing violence. People running from police attention came to the Transkei as a place to hide or in hope of getting to political asylum across the border in Lesotho. At times, we provided shelter or, on occasion, a way out. Work at the Council of Churches involved listening to the stories, taking depositions on police brutality and torture, and getting stories and statistics to organizations like Amnesty International. The violence came especially close when police raided a nearby university and beat and detained many of the students. A South African colleague who worked in a rural health project was killed by a death squad rumored to be associated with the security police. Though we helped plan the funeral, police restrictions prevented our attendance. Even local pastors and members of the family were threatened and intimidated.

The state of emergency that began in 1986 did in some ways suppress activities in South Africa. Protests continued, as did detentions and killings, but these could often not be reported, and so the impression from a distance was that the situation had stabilized.

One sign of coming change, however, was the growing refusal of South African activists to go into exile. Earlier, repression had caused many to flee to neighboring areas to join opposition groups in exile. But, in the late 1980s, few were eager to do so. "The end is near," one friend asserted. "These are the kicks of a dying horse. I want to be here to see it" (Seremane, 1989).

Throughout the 1980s, the churches in South Africa struggled with the question of violence. Because the majority of church members were black and suffering under apartheid, the church was a natural channel for speaking out against this injustice. The banning of political organizations often made church organizations the only vehicles for expressing opposition to apartheid.

The social climate in South Africa throughout much of the 1980s made advocating a pacifist stance difficult, even within the churches. The apartheid government had coopted words like *reconciliation* and *peace* to mean not protesting against apartheid injustice, or a quiet acceptance of the status quo. Even though most of the protests and actions against apartheid were, in fact, nonviolent, black persons involved in this resistance, including those within the churches, often made a point of saying that there was a place for justified violence in the Struggle.

In one conversation with black church leaders, we talked about nonviolence as a means to reconciliation. One pastor lashed out angrily, criticizing whites who had used violence for years against blacks, while blacks had tried to use reason and peaceful protest. Now, when blacks had taken up violent means in desperation, he suggested, it was too late for whites in the church to talk about peace, nonviolence, and reconciliation. Later, in a personal discussion, he elaborated on this by saying:

> My quarrel isn't with the Mennonites. My quarrel is with the churches that are suddenly changing their minds. After years of talking about just wars, when blacks want to fight they suddenly turn around and want to talk about peace. With you Mennonites, pacifism has integrity. You have talked about peace for years, and have on occasion suffered for it. (Ngcobo, 1985)

In early 1989, a weekend seminar sponsored by the SACC's Justice and Reconciliation Department and the Transformation Resource Centre was held in the country of Lesotho, just across the border from South Africa. The gathering of around forty people, church leaders and pastors from a variety of South African churches, was funded by the MCC South Africa program. The gathering struggled with ways to be peacemakers in the current situation in South Africa. Stories of peaceful transformation and of the power of nonviolence, especially from the Philippines, where a nonviolent people's protest had recently toppled dictator Ferdinand Marcos, were powerful. Participants came away feeling empowered to find nonviolent ways to challenge apartheid.

The week after this seminar, a meeting of church representatives in Johannesburg picked up the theme. The churches formed the Standing for the Truth Campaign, an effort to speak out and protest injustice in nonviolent ways. Frank Chikane, general secretary of the SACC, claimed that it was time to move beyond the endless debate about whether or not the churches can sanction the use of violence to end apartheid. As churches, they would not in any case take up arms; that was not their role. But what they could do was to work nonviolently for change. The combination of Chikane's call and the experiences of those who had attended the seminar in Lesotho led to a heightened commitment on the part of most of the churches of South Africa to publicly advocate peaceful methods to end apartheid.

The growing violence and confrontation of the 1980s in South Africa caught world attention. As the decade progressed, campaigns for comprehensive sanctions grew in Europe and North America. As resident workers, we strove to find new ways to respond to an increasingly disintegrating South African society. Our vantage point in a black homeland area and our experiences in community development work taught us to walk cautiously as outsiders. What kind of help could Mennonites provide that would both respond to the violence that was growing throughout the country and strengthen our friends and colleagues, especially those working in local churches?

One answer to these questions was the Servanthood Sabbaticals program. Servanthood Sabbaticals began in 1986 and over a period of five years enabled church workers to spend short periods of time outside South Africa. Those taking part were all Justice and Reconciliation field workers for the South African Council of Churches. These were front-line persons who worked at responding to violence in their neighborhoods. Many had been in detention and had been targets of police brutality. They were constantly on call when violence or community disturbances erupted. Many had conducted delicate negotiations between police or army officials and angry demonstrators.

The Servanthood Sabbaticals program allowed them a chance to take a break. Together with their spouses, they spent from six to eight weeks in a Mennonite community in North America or Europe, with time to speak to persons there about their lives in South Africa but also with significant time to rest and reflect. The goal was to forge links of understanding between Mennonite communities and South African church workers but also, and more important, to allow persons who were under a great deal of stress a chance to rest in a place where they did not need to feel under pressure. Implementing the program, however, was not always easy as passports for international travel were difficult for black South Africans to obtain. Participants were nervous up to the moment they boarded the plane, fearing that police would prevent them from traveling.

Servanthood Sabbaticals did not reach a large number of people, but the chances it gave key persons under great strain to have a brief rest were seen as significant by the churches. These church workers were peacemakers working on the front line of conciliation and conflict resolution, and they were also advocates for a new and fair society. They provided a fundamental example of how to start down the path of bringing these two strands together.

A constant from the beginning of Mennonite involvement in South Africa had been work in rural development, which brought its own set of struggles and issues. These villages had long been part of the system of migratory labor, an ingrained pattern in which able-bodied men, and often women, went to the cities or the mines around Johannesburg for wage employment. Village life was carried on by women, older men, and children. Trying to make this life more sustainable was difficult when those in their most productive years were absent.

In addition, in a number of cases, the villages themselves were collections of people who had been moved from other locations because of South Africa's consolidation of black living areas. Such groupings of people, though they lived in proximity and were now called a village, had few village traditions. They were often not ready to trust one another and work together as a community.

The presence of white North American Mennonites in rural, black villages in South Africa was noticed. Local authorities were often suspicious, and the Mennonite workers' motivations were questioned. On occasion, workers were accused of being spies or of working for the banned liberation movements. The positive side of this practice was the witness to a different way of being together as people. In a setting where relationships across racial lines were usually those of master and servant, whites living at the level of poor black villagers could be an important statement of a different way.

The 1980s was not an easy time for Mennonite workers in South Africa. Travel and relationship building in South Africa was difficult, and the upheaval in the larger society also made its way into the Mennonite workers' personal lives. Security police questioned who we were and what we were about. At one point, we personally were threatened with deportation. Friends and coworkers were imprisoned, tortured, killed. In 1986, the entire Umtata-based staff of the Council of Churches, including one Mennonite worker, was imprisoned for several weeks.

The fact that Mennonites were present through this time did much to establish credibility with churches and partners in South Africa. Mennonites were known as an outside group that did not run away when things got rough and as people who were willing to stay and identify with the local residents in their struggle. Being there in person meant that our unpopular stand against violence, even in the struggle for justice, had a chance to gain a hearing.

In mid-1989, Ron and Meribeth Kraybill arrived in Cape Town, South Africa. Ron had significant experience in conflict resolution, including ten years' leadership of the Mennonite Conciliation Service in the United States. He had come to South Africa to serve as director of training for the Centre for Intergroup Studies at the University of Cape Town.

Activists who were involved in the struggle against apartheid, including progressive church leaders, had mixed feelings about the center. Because it was based at a white university and included people who had working relationships with the National Party government, the center was often written off by black church workers.

As the new director of training for the Centre for Intergroup Studies, Kraybill needed to make contact with a wide variety of groups and persons, including anti-apartheid leaders. He recalls the suspicion with which he was greeted in offices like that of the Council of Churches when he introduced himself initially as coming from the Centre for Intergroup Studies. But the wary looks changed when he mentioned that he was a Mennonite. Kraybill told us:

South Africa was so polarized at that time that every institution had a political identity. I felt limited by the Centre's identity, but Mennonite connections helped broaden my base of contacts across those lines. This identity was a gift, which literally opened doors. (Kraybill, 1995b)

## 1990s: Peacebuilding

The 1980s were a decade of confrontation, suspicion, and mistrust. The movements for liberation were growing but under constant pressure and surveillance. Infiltration and the ever-present police informers provided fertile breeding grounds for hostility and confrontation. And for good reason. Although there was an almost universal belief that change was coming, no one could be sure whether that change would be this year or in ten years.

Ron Kraybill recalls an early workshop he was invited to do with young activists in the Eastern Cape region:

As I entered the room, the air was thick with suspicion. For the first hour, I was not allowed to proceed at all with what I had been invited to do. "Who sent you here? Whom do you represent? Who pays you to do this work?" The questions were intense and fast. I had the impression that any misstep would end my usefulness to them for that meeting. Finally, after a prolonged inquisition, one participant said, "Well, let's get on with the workshop." (Kraybill, 1995b)

With this, the atmosphere turned, and the evening progressed. Kraybill's, participation was accepted.

The 1980s ended with suspicion and division. But at the same time, new openings were apparent. During 1989, business and lower-level government leaders began making openly publicized trips to Lusaka, Zambia, to talk with the leaders of the liberation groups in exile. "Negotiations" became less than a dirty word, as the ANC indicated some openness to talking with the government.

On February 2, 1990, in his speech opening Parliament, President F. W. de Klerk announced that all opposition organizations would be unbanned, that political prisoners would be freed, and that the government would begin negotiating with the opposition groups for an end to apartheid and a new constitution that included the right of all South Africans to vote. Two weeks later, Nelson Mandela walked to freedom after twenty-seven years in prison. A joyful population hailed the beginning of the "New South Africa."

The events of February 1990 and the months that followed were certainly dramatic and exciting for those who had struggled through the difficult and violent days of the previous decades. But a reversal of direction for a society is never easy or smooth. The latter months of 1990 and the years that followed were among the most violent in South Africa's history. Some of the violence appeared random, though much was instigated by covert agencies of the apartheid government or of groups threatened by change. Clashes between rival black parties also took place, as they struggled for power in the developing political structures. Throughout these years, however, negotiations continued among the National Party and the former liberation groups, now opposition parties, to decide on the course of a transition to a new constitution.

The opening up of South African society meant a change in the role of the church and, especially, of church agencies such as the SACC, which had been a primary partner for the Mennonite presence in South Africa. When the political actors that opposed apartheid were banned, the church was one of the few channels for African expression and one of the few channels through which outside donor money could flow without being compromised. But once the African National Congress and Pan Africanist Congress could exist openly, money to care for political prisoners, for example, could go to them rather than through the church channels. The Council of Churches needed to restructure, which proved to be an extremely painful and difficult process.

During the long years of repression, leaders were needed with skills in confrontation and speaking courageously to power. But such skills do not always lend themselves to consensus building and constructive activity. When the apartheid enemy, which had unified those struggling against it, fell away, conflicts within organizations became apparent. Churches and community groups across South Africa faced these problems after the big changes of early 1990. At its annual conference in 1990, the Institute for Contextual Theology, which had led in the formation of a "prophetic theology" against apartheid, asked the question: "What do we do with our theology of confrontation?"

In late 1990, a historic gathering took place near Johannesburg at a town called Rustenburg. Here, for the first time, a meeting was held that included representatives from all of South Africa's churches—mainline (the so-called English-speaking churches, members of the SACC), evangelical, pentecostal, African Independent, and Dutch Reformed. The goal was to talk together about how they as churches should work at reconciliation in the changing political situation. Mennonites Ron Kraybill from Cape Town and Harold Miller, representing the All Africa Conference of Churches, based in Nairobi, were present at the meeting.

Early in the gathering, a white Dutch Reformed pastor, Willie Jonkers, stood up in tears and asked forgiveness for the way in which his church had supported and justified the practice of apartheid and for the activities of the National Party government. Archbishop Desmond Tutu, speaking for black Christians, responded with a word of forgiveness. Many were moved and excited by this interchange. But some black church representatives had different reactions. They were cynical and angry at Archbishop Tutu for so easily offering forgiveness. To them, this looked like a familiar pattern—whites apologized, but nothing substantial changed.

The churches in South Africa struggled in the 1990s with the questions of forgiveness and reconciliation. Some talked of the need for restitution before there could be real reconciliation. Others spoke of a theology of vengeance, which would answer the wrongs that had been done. The question of a truth commission to deal on a national level with crimes and violations of human rights was a part of this debate. The Rustenburg conference set a tone for church deliberations in the new decade.

Mennonites working in the region were also thinking about the shape of their involvements in the new situation in South Africa. It seemed that the problems Mennonites had experienced with visas would be easing, so that we could consider new locations for work. In addition, a number of churches and related groups had begun thinking about how they might work toward reconciliation in communities at a time when negotiations were going on among the political players.

In March 1991, we met with some of our historic partners, including the South African Council of Churches, representatives of the Methodist Order of Peacemakers, and the staff of the Wilgespruit Fellowship Centre, an interchurch ministry in the Johannesburg area. Wilgespruit was the one group that had done actual program thinking and had a structure to welcome Mennonite involvement. But all those we talked with were strong in their encouragement for more Mennonite involvement. We were told that Mennonites had credibility because of our long involvement in South Africa. Mennonites were known as peace people, and these skills were especially needed. We were affirmed for having stood with the churches when they needed to confront injustice. Now they needed new skills—to negotiate and to find ways to live together in peace.

The Wilgespruit director, Dale White, was especially pointed in his call for our involvement. "We have a window of opportunity now," he said. "In about four years' time, we'll have elections. The years between now and then are crucial in building a culture of goodwill in this country. This is when we need peacemaking skills on all levels, to prevent fracturing and to learn to live together" (1991).

The pace of change did not let up. By the time elections were held in 1994, several more Mennonite workers had come to participate in South Africa's peaceful transition. In 1992, MCC opened its first official agency office in Durban, with Peter and Leona Penner, who had worked with MCC in Zambia, Swaziland, and Canada, becoming the first MCC South Africa country representatives to reside officially in South Africa. At the end of 1993, Carl and Carolyn Stauffer moved to Johannesburg. Carl, who had worked in Virginia as a pastor, social worker, and community mediator, became a staff member for the Letsema Conflict Transformation Program of the Wilgespruit Fellowship Centre. With elections poised to take place early the next year, these placements proved to be timely and well situated to participate in both elections monitoring training and peace monitoring.

The Penners served as observers at locations where violence was occurring and at polling stations during the days of the election. Following the election, Leona Penner reflected:

> Right now I feel somewhat drained but quietly exuberant. It's as though I've participated in a birth, a birth which included a lengthy labor involving major heart-stopping complications; a birth which required expert handling so that life

could be born instead of death; a birth which required miracles of grace and peace at opportune moments throughout the labor; a birth which at last brought forth a new child, highly vulnerable and dripping with the blood which seemingly had to be shed. (1994, p. 1)

Following the election, Carl Stauffer's work with other trainers in the negotiation program picked up, with mediation training workshops in many different settings. These included Johannesburg civil servants, members of the police force, and the "civics" (local community organizations formed as a part of the resistance to apartheid) in surrounding townships. In a report to MCC, he commented that interpersonal tensions in post-apartheid South Africa made each workshop a unique experience in which he and his coworkers had to recreate their mediation tools and techniques to fit the needs of that situation (n.d. [1995]). Peace in South Africa was on its way, but there was still much that needed work.

Mennonite involvement in South Africa in support of training programs in conciliation and mediation was enhanced by Ron Kraybill's work at the Centre for Intergroup Studies (now renamed the Centre for Conflict Resolution). Between 1989 and 1995, the mood of the society changed from one of suspicion about negotiations to one of openly seeking skills at all levels. Kraybill worked with the churches' Empowering for Reconciliation with Justice (ERJ) effort and was a senior consultant for the National Peace Secretariat, the body responsible for implementing the National Peace Accords. These activities were fundamental in laying a foundation of skills and traditions for the peaceful resolution of social tension and conflict.

Kraybill and other colleagues from the Centre for Conflict Resolution assisted in the training and coordinating of monitors for the 1994 national election and in beginning the training of police officers in communication and nonviolent conflict resolution skills. Kraybill had arrived at a time when receptivity to the notion of negotiation was opening up in South Africa. Because he came from the outside and did not have a history in the country, he was perceived as someone without an ax to grind. Consequently, he was able to share his skills across the spectrum of positions in that deeply divided society.

In 1995, Mennonites had an opportunity to take peacemaking work to an even more significant level through the work of Dr. Karl and Evelyn Bartsch. During the 1990s, in South Africa and in other places where traumatic scarring had left its mark on people, it became evident that a peacemaking process needs to be accompanied by work at emotional healing and restoration. Two organizations in the Natal region of South Africa, the Vuleka Trust and the Diakonia Council of Churches, approached Mennonites for assistance in initiating a program to foster recovery from the psychological trauma inflicted during the years of struggle and change. The Bartsches brought to this effort their experience as clinical psychologist and psychiatric social worker, respectively, in North American community and academic settings. From 1995 to 1997, they conducted workshops and training seminars for caregivers who

Table 1. Mennonite Agencies Supporting Workers in
South Africa, 1978–1996

| | |
|---|---|
| Mennonite Central Committee (MCC) | 22 workers |
| Africa Inter-Mennonite Mission (AIMM) | 3 workers |
| Eastern Mennonite Missions (EMM) | 1 worker |
| Independently Supported Mennonites | 2 workers |

carried community leadership responsibilities. These workshops and seminars involved pastors, school teachers, and community leaders and resulted in the publishing of *Stress and Healing: A Manual for Caregivers* (Bartsch and Bartsch, 1997). The manual was published in both Zulu and English and, subsequently, was translated into Spanish and French. Its continued use reflects an ongoing contribution to peace in South Africa.

The extensive history of Mennonite work in South Africa served as a backdrop to the more recent work in conciliation training and trauma recovery and shaped its orientation. Mennonite orientation and rooting in rural village realities provided a cultural undergirding for those workers who lived in urban settings. This rural and church perspective also brought to the fore connections between conflict resolution, trauma recovery, and questions of rural development.

The constant during the three decades of Mennonite work in South Africa has been this peripheral, rural base. While this account focuses on the peacemaking dimensions, Mennonite workers also dealt with questions of rural empowerment and village-level development (see table 1). In a situation where people have been pushed onto marginal land and where migratory labor takes the strongest and most able members away from the communities to the cities, working at sustainable rural living can itself be a statement of protest. Questions of land tenure and of the use of church-owned land also become questions of justice. Work with African Independent churches in leadership training established relationships with many who were at the bottom of the South African social ladder. The everyday experiences in these arenas grounded Mennonite work in South Africa throughout the 1970s, 1980s, and 1990s.

## Conclusion

Peacemaking in a context of intense injustice always raises ethical dilemmas. It is easy to appear to be papering over the status quo of injustice in order to have a limited peace. Mennonites have at times been accused of doing this in theology—of valuing peace above justice and so acquiescing to injustice.

Conventional wisdom suggests there is a tension between taking sides in a situation of injustice and remaining impartial and so able to mediate the conflict. Our experience, on the other hand, leads to the conclusion that a commitment to living in a context softens the apparently irreconcilable opposition between advocacy and mediation. The need to make a choice between these options may appear clear from outside a situation. But from within, for people in the midst of a struggle, work must always include concern for both of these strategies.

Our survey of Mennonite work in South Africa illustrates some answers to this dilemma. In a situation of acute injustice, efforts must be directed first at empowerment of people. When the power balance is seriously skewed, one must identify with the disempowered. As a point of first effort, peacemakers need to seek out those marginalized persons of society.

Mennonite work with churches in South Africa was a way to do this. The churches during the 1970s and 1980s were the one place in which black South Africans could consistently hope to express their resistance and a place where they could organize for change. Overtly political groups and community organizations were always under threat and easily suppressed. Working through the churches was a way Mennonite workers could both stand with those most oppressed and contribute to the development of an orderly and organized program for the future.

But this identification with the marginalized must also be combined with a conviction about the humanity of all people. Living within a context of malignant injustice is one way to understand the almost endless human diversity in such a situation. The lines of injustice seldom run neatly between groups that appear divided. Life within any human society is much too complex for such neat constructs. Peacemaking that hopes to produce results must be close enough to the actual injustice to openly relate to people across the chasms that popularly define a conflict. Mennonites were identified by government authorities, correctly, as opposed to their policies of apartheid. But living within this context also afforded us the opportunity to develop relationships with all categories of people in South Africa, including the white Afrikaner community.

Because of questions about being coopted by the apartheid system, the Mennonite work in South Africa was undertaken slowly and with more than the usual deliberation, including consultation with Mennonite theologians and ethicists. But long-term Mennonite commitment over the decades of struggle gave us the opportunity to participate in the constructive work of building a peaceful society. The history of a Mennonite presence committed to the people, traditions, and cultures of South Africa can serve as the foundation for further involvement in peacemaking work with church partners in that country.

# Five

## Mennonites and Conflict in Northern Ireland, 1970–1998

JOSEPH LIECHTY

BEGINNING IN THE EARLY 1970s, the first Mennonite connections with Ireland were occasional, brief, and limited to a few people, mostly North Americans. Mennonite colleges sent groups to study literature and conflict; Mennonite scholars and administrators visited Ireland to speak and learn. While these visits were not designed to initiate Mennonite institutional involvement, one of them did have that unintended effect.

In 1972, a group of Mennonite Board of Missions (MBM) workers meeting in Dublin accepted an invitation from the Belfast Bible College to speak on Mennonite themes, including peace witness. One of their more skeptical auditors was Mike Garde, a dynamic young Irishman from County Cork, who was doing a degree at the college. On reflection, however, Garde found himself persuaded by what he had heard, and he became increasingly and passionately committed to Mennonite perspectives. From then on, more and more Mennonite visitors met Garde, and from these visits and relationships and from reflection centered in the emerging London Mennonite Fellowship, a vision for Mennonite witness in Ireland began to emerge. This finally took concrete form when Garde returned to Dublin as an employee of MBM and the Mennonite Central Committee (MCC) in 1978. The next year, North American Mennonites Paul and Dawn Ruth Nelson joined Garde, and when my wife, Linda, and I and our baby daughter, Anna, followed in 1980, the initial team of Mennonite workers was complete.

## Background and Assumptions

From the beginning, we knew our work would involve a peace witness. Lacking any natural, historic ties to Ireland, Mennonite interest in Ireland had much to do with the onset of violence in Northern Ireland in the late 1960s, and every person and institution involved in forming a vision for Mennonite work there understood peacemaking as an integral part of Christian faith. When pressing the case for biblical pacifism, members of the London Mennonite Fellowship repeatedly met the skeptical question: How can such pacifism be relevant in Northern Ireland? Work in Ireland was meant to address that question. Despite this solid commitment to peace, however, a combination of forces meant that peace work in Northern Ireland was initiated slowly and took a relatively low priority until at least 1986.

The low priority given to peace work was partly accidental: Plans simply did not work out as intended. Early efforts to recruit a peace-education specialist, for example, were unsuccessful. Failure to fill the post did not, however, indicate a lack of real commitment to peace. It revealed instead an assumption about the relationship of peace and church: Peace is the work and mark of Christian communities, whose calling it is to proclaim peace, to work for peace, and, above all, to live peace. In this way of thinking, a person focused specifically on peace education would be of benefit but hardly essential.

This understanding of church and peace was shared by everyone involved in shaping Mennonite work in Ireland. Garde in particular worked hard at securing joint MBM and MCC participation in Ireland. While both agencies involved both church and peace in their work, it is probably fair to say that MBM emphasized church and MCC peace. Their relatively unusual collaboration in Ireland symbolized the fundamental unity between Christian community and peace concerns.

Thinking about Mennonites in Ireland had included some speculation about whether this might involve an Irish Mennonite church, in other words, a network of Mennonite communities. No one thought this was necessary, and yet no one ruled out the possibility. Most probably leaned away from the idea. In sketching out the first rationale for Mennonite work in Ireland, in 1976, Alan Kreider, an MBM worker in London, simply did not commit himself. He did propose, however, that

> ... Mennonite witness in Ireland must be rooted in the life of *at least one worshipping community*. A "disembodied" verbal witness has its place, but it is only a partial place. We will not really get our message across unless we live it. (1976)

This would be a peacemaking community, proclaiming the gospel of peace, working in the Irish peace movement, and dramatizing peace, Kreider hoped, through the common and reconciled life of "people of diverse and ostensibly antagonistic origins"—Catholic and Protestant, Northern and Southern, Irish and English. On this, he spoke for all concerned, including those of us in the United States hoping to come to Ireland. When we later read drafts of the same ideas, we heard them as a stirring call to action, drawing us to Ireland. These were common yet profound truths, derived from our Mennonite tradition, we believed, yet universally valid.

From the beginning, those planning work in Ireland argued that such a community was best located in Dublin, even though the violence was almost exclusively in Northern Ireland. The most important reason to favor Dublin, wrote Kreider in that first vision statement, was that Mennonite witness would naturally revolve around Mike Garde as an Irishman and initiator. Being from the Republic, Garde naturally leaned toward Dublin as a base of operations, although he was strongly committed to work in the North, as well. Worker safety was another issue: "Civil war is near," wrote Kreider (1976). It was a valid concern. The 1975 death toll had been the third highest since "the Troubles" began in 1969; 1976 would be still more violent, and the killing seemed set to spiral. No one could have foreseen that in 1977 the death toll would plummet and, in the years after, rarely rise to even one-third the average death rate in 1972–1976 (Flackes and Elliott, 1989, p. 411). In any case, Dublin appeared to be a workable base for peace work in Northern Ireland.

> To a very real extent Ireland is a unit. There is real commonality across the borders, and Irishmen south and north of the dividing line know and care a great deal about events on the other side. Thus a Mennonite involvement in the Republic would have ramifications for the situation in the North. And Ireland is geographically small enough that Mennonite personnel in the south could visit the North easily and often. (Kreider, 1976)

Hindsight reveals that this statement, while true, should have been considered in tension with other truths. If Ireland is a unit, it is also deeply divided; the "real commonality" has usually been trumped by real difference; Irish people south of the border (95 percent Catholic, 2.5 percent Protestant) do care about what happens in the North, but they have been confused and ambivalent about the conflict there, which has generally led to ignoring the North and wishing it would go away. In the North (58 percent Protestant, 42 percent Catholic), Catholics are also ambivalent, looking to the Republic in some ways, yet angry at the way people in the South have generally ignored them. Among Northern Protestants, interest in the Republic has taken the almost universal form of wariness about what they see as a Catholic-dominated state from which they are intent on remaining separate. In the end, the counter-truths weighed most heavily, and the Dublin Mennonite Community never figured in peace work, as I will explain later.

A final reason for the initial low profile of peace work had to do with the long-term approach Mennonites were taking in Ireland. Again, this was assumed by all concerned, both institutions and individuals. In the early stages, MBM and MCC quickly discounted people interested in Ireland but unable to make long-term commitments.

As with the assumptions about Christian community and peace, the long-term emphasis fit perfectly with some of us hoping to come to Ireland. Beginning in 1977 in Goshen, Indiana, a core group of five, all students in a Mennonite college or seminary, began living together as an intentional Christian community, specifically to explore the possibility of doing international mission or service work together. We had no particular notion about where we wanted to go and eventually considered possibilities on four continents, although we probably did incline toward a Third World location.

Twenty years later, our motivations are not easily reconstructed. We may have been motivated to leave partially because of our feelings about a materialistic, imperialistic America, which we gained growing up in the Vietnam era. We were never conscious of this as a motivation for our plans; however, and our sense of the church as something radically counter, in message and mode of operation, to powerful governments kept us from even considering that five young Americans abroad might be another expression of imperialist America. More positively, we had undoubtedly been influenced by our parents, all of whom had been involved at some point in church-related international or cross-cultural church work at some point, and by our own international experiences, which included Goshen College's Study Service Term.

I would name our primary motivation as youthful yearning—undoubtedly naive but surely heartfelt—to do Something Big for Jesus. We never talked in those terms, but looking back I am struck by an essential and long since unattainable simplicity of motivation, and I cannot put it any other way. Eventually, making our home in another land and working in a broadly missionary capacity came to be our model of Something Big. While Dawn and Paul Nelson had looked forward to this, Linda and I surprised ourselves, as we had been marked by an ill-considered but definite disdain for mission work. Like many other young Mennonites of the time, however, we were admirers of John Howard Yoder, a Mennonite theologian whose brilliant restatements, criticisms, and transformations of traditional Mennonite positions helped Mennonites develop new ways of being in the world. We were influenced by his little booklet on mission, *As You Go* (1961), which advocated a model of small, self-supporting communities emigrating to another culture, integrating themselves into the life of their adopted homeland, and there becoming the nucleus of a congregation. This notion was different enough to help us set aside our prejudices about mission work. We would not just do a term or two of service somewhere, count it as an enriching cultural experience, and settle back in the United States. We would emigrate for the sake of the Gospel. When we heard about the possibility of work in Ireland, that quickly became our preferred location, although we were inadequately qualified for the work anticipated at the time. That MBM and MCC settled for us was one more indication that they were committed to the long haul. We were not in a position to make a quick contribution, so a decision to send us to join Garde was a decision to be patient.

## Vision Meets Reality

Once in place in Dublin in January 1980, patience was surely required, because the clash of vision with reality was mighty and painful. We each suffered our own distress, and in that first two-year term, Linda and I remember accomplishing little more than survival. The restoration of our house stretched on for more than a year, which meant that when our sons Jacob and Aaron were born in May 1980, they came home to a construction site. The five workers, three babies, and up to five short-term residents were crammed into a cold, damp, and filthy environment, which contributed to some disastrous relationships. It soon became apparent that the would-be reconcilers would be the first to require reconciliation. To our credit, we persevered at the task of reconciliation, although it took many years before we were granted anything like healing. Any naive messianic complex was unlikely to survive such a beginning.

Amidst the early tumult, we began to consider how vision might be translated into reality. Over the years, some elements have been discarded, others altered, and a few even fulfilled. At first, however, it seemed all a matter of discarding, including more ideas than space here permits me to detail.

One early and significant casualty was our concept of community, which was firmly, but naively and narrowly, tied to the notion of living under one roof. After a little more than a year, Linda and I moved into a house a few minutes away. This left us feeling at once liberated and a little guilty: Were we settling for the bourgeois nuclear family rather than radical Christian community? Community remained our ideal, but it would no longer involve close proximity.

More substantially, the development of community life eventually revealed that our notions of church and peace required radical rethinking. Given our premise that Christian community is the foundation for peacemaking, community building was an early priority. At first, the core community was MBM/MCC workers and a few others living in the house. Chaotic living conditions and troubled relationships made expanding beyond this base a slow process, but by the spring of 1982, some other Irish people had joined us, and with their strong encouragement, the Dublin Mennonite Community began to take shape.

As the community developed, those of us interested in the North began to discuss our limited Northern involvements and new possibilities in community meetings. When I brought up Northern issues, the response seemed, at first, polite but evasive and, eventually, flatly uninterested. I was puzzled, but finally all became clear: If some of us were interested in the North, that was fine, but most community members saw no reason why Dubliners should concern themselves with issues in Northern Ireland, which they regarded as essentially a foreign country and of little relevance to the community's work and witness. From then on, Northern Ireland would figure in community prayers at times, and those of us involved would occasionally report on what we were doing, but in no practical way did Mennonite peace work flow from a living community.

If our assumptions about the relationship between church and peace took a battering, our commitment to community was not lessened, and a core group of MBM/MCC workers and other Irish people invested themselves selflessly in the community. In 1991, however, the Dublin Mennonite Community decided to stop meeting. To summarize a complicated and painful story, I will say that, by the time we had learned the hard way the things we needed to know, it was too late.

## Forging a New Vision for Peace Work

All these chastening experiences required forging a new vision for peace work or, at least, applying old ideas in new ways. We worked at this in the context of several peace-related involvements. Alan and Eleanor Kreider had been developing Irish contacts, North and South, from the mid-1970s, and they visited from London about once a year. For those of us in Dublin, their visits were pastoral, but they also brought their inimitable and ecumenically accessible brand of Bible teaching—typically on themes of Christian community, discipleship, and peace—to a good range of groups, North and South.

From 1979 to 1983, Dawn Nelson worked for *Dawn*, a magazine that promoted nonviolent change in Irish society, and she also was part of a study group that was looking at ways to implement the insights of the nonviolence theorist Gene Sharp. Mike Garde sometimes traveled north to sell Mennonite books, to lecture, or to visit people, notably prisoners and friends in republican circles, with whom his contacts were then very strong. From 1982, my job description had three elements: to do a Ph.D. in Irish religious history as preparation for contributing to Catholic/Protestant reconciliation and church renewal, to work for the Dublin Mennonite Community, and to visit in Northern Ireland when possible.

For all of us, our Northern Ireland work was done on marginal time. To my frustration, visiting the North always needed to fit around other priorities, and from 1982 to 1987, I made only six to twelve visits per year, sometimes to Belfast and back in a day. Nelson and Garde spent even less time in the North. Even so, we gradually began to formulate a shared analysis of the Irish situation and a vision, now more rooted and informed, for peace work.

While our church and peace concerns did not work out as we had projected, we found our general vision for the relationship of Christian community and peace abundantly confirmed. In the North, we got to know a number of ecumenical communities, most coming from the mainstream ecumenical movement but some of charismatic origin, which were living out in different ways the same vision that had fired us: teaching peace, nurturing peacemakers, and, above all, living and embodying peace. Cornerstone, Corrymeela, Columbanus, and Rostrevor are only the best known communities of a broad movement that has had great staying power and significance far beyond its numbers. From the beginning, we found these communities warmly welcoming of us, and we have occasionally been able to offer modest support. Although our relationships have been of the most informal kind, these reconciliation communities are an important part of the peace movement, which is the context from which we have operated.

In the early years, Garde's church and peace concerns ran alongside a strongly republican political analysis of the conflict in Northern Ireland: British withdrawal from Ireland and an independent, all-Ireland republic is the just political outcome. At one point, he suggested that the Dublin Mennonite Community join Sinn Féin, the political wing of the Irish Republican Army (IRA), and act as a reform-from-within element attempting to create a nonviolent IRA. No one else in the community agreed. I probably was not the only one who thought the idea was crazy, or at least impractical and improbable. Looking back, however, I see behind my dismissal an unacknowledged, implicit assumption I now reject—that the violent have cut themselves off and there is no reasoning with them—and I see behind Garde's idea an assumption I now embrace—that those who practice violence must not be demonized and ignored. After all, how will there be peace if no one talks to the violent? I had no alternative plan for engaging the people who use violence and, if the truth be told, little vision for the importance of doing so. But disagreement about the best political outcome for Ireland was never a great hindrance, because none of us saw any reason why we all needed to agree on this in order to work together.

At least implicitly, involvement with the reconciliation communities brought with it a different, though not completely contradictory, analysis of the Troubles, and this was the understanding I favored. Frank Wright gave this analysis its most sophisticated expression in *Northern Ireland: A Comparative Analysis* (1987), which is one of the most profound scholarly contributions to understanding the Troubles and probably the most original. John Whyte observed, in his survey of the literature on Northern Ireland, that up to the start of the Troubles in the late 1960s, most analysts blamed the Northern Ireland problem on external factors: Nationalists blamed the British, unionists blamed the Irish, Marxists blamed capitalists (1991). The onset of violence brought with it a compensating flood of internal conflict interpretations the focused on the relationship between Northern Catholics and Protestants, and internal explanations have dominated ever since (Whyte, 1991, pp. 194–195, 202–205).

Wright created a new paradigm, which incorporated the best of both internal and external explanations and showed how they were interrelated. According to Wright, conflict in Northern Ireland is of a type generated by ethnic frontier societies. In such situations, one ethnic group (Protestant) is dominant over another (Catholic) and maintains this status by appealing to and identifying with the metropolitan power (London). The dominant party comes to regard the law and the state as not only for them but as their own; the dominated regard the law as their enemy, question or deny the legitimacy of the state, and often appeal to and identify with a rival metropolis (Dublin). These dynamics too often produce chaos on the frontier, and even apparent peace is only the "tranquillity of mutual deterrence." The metropolis and the rival metropolis are ambivalent about their representatives on the frontier: They support and identify with one party, yet they may find that party and its demands a burden at times, and they always fear that violence on the frontier will destabilize metropolitan society or that they will be drawn further than they wish into conflict. Depending on their relationship and aims, the two metropolises may feed conflict on the frontier or dampen it, but extinguishing it is virtually impossible. According to Wright, the usual outcome of conflict in ethnic frontier societies is not peace but mass expulsion of one population, genocide, or endemic conflict.

Applied to Northern Ireland, this model takes seriously at least four sets of relationships: London-Dublin; London–Northern Ireland, with Catholic and Protestant variants; Dublin–Northern Ireland, with Catholic and Protestant variants; and Catholic-Protestant within Northern Ireland. Not only is each relationship important; the four are dynamically interrelated, so that change in one relationship shapes what is possible in the other relationships. Wright judged that in Northern Ireland neither victory for one party nor sharper separation could provide a stable peace. The best hope for peace, perhaps the only hope, lies in reconciliation, and the political form of reconciliation would be an authority "which can be seen to place all peoples in Northern Ireland in a symmetrical relationship toward State power . . . , something approaching a joint sovereignty of Britain and the Irish Republic" (1988, p. 72). Thus, Wright gave his qualified support to the 1985 Anglo-Irish Agreement, which did propose "something approaching" joint sovereignty, as has each of the Anglo-Irish documents since, culminating with the 1998 Good Friday Agreement.

In Wright's model, reconciliation in one of the relationships is linked to and perhaps dependent on reconciliation in the others. Thus, the British and Irish governments may agree on the kind of political structures they would like to see in place for Northern Ireland, and they may apply a degree of coercion, but they cannot simply impose them by force. Successful political structures will require an element of at least grudging acceptance, and for this to happen Northern Catholics must grant the British government some trust, Northern Protestants must do the same for Dublin, and Protestants and Catholics must do the same for each other. Without this minimal trust, the forces generated by the old antagonisms can erode or explode any political structures based solely on agreement between London and Dublin.

Thus, viewed within Wright's framework, a little ecumenical community in Belfast, preaching peace, sustaining peacemakers, and, above all, embodying peace by reconciling members from antagonistic groups, is significant as a symbol of and contribution to the kind of public order necessary to accept and vivify new political structures. Furthermore, until the tide of violence and chaos recedes enough that these new political structures can gain a purchase, such a community also has a more profound significance, deeper than politics and preceding politics. "None of us can be innocent of a violence that is everywhere," said Wright. "Only repentance for it and witness to faith in the unity of humankind in any way tends to belittle its coercive pressures" (1987, p. 289). This Wright had learned from his involvement with the Northern Ireland reconciliation communities and other people of like mind:

> I couldn't have written these lines from any other experience than that of meeting many who in their lives refused the siren call of effectiveness, did not embrace reasons for violence with which they were amply provoked, and who practice their faith by living risks in order that that part of humanity they come into communication with shall be one. . . . Politics can teach little that this light does not already teach. (Wright, 1987, pp. 289–290)

Wright's model accommodates, links, and respects—even requires—everything from high-level Anglo-Irish negotiation to small, faithful witnesses to the unity of humankind.

Wright's critique of effectiveness, developed in the context of Northern Ireland reconciliation circles, struck a chord that resonated deeply with Mennonite inclinations. In fact, a critique of effectiveness is an all-but-inbred Mennonite legacy: "Our calling is not to be effective but to be faithful," as a common Mennonite mantra puts it. Fundamentally, all service, including peace work, is done in obedience to God and as an offering to God, in whose hands lies final responsibility for effectiveness. In addition to its inherent integrity, such a conviction is natural, I suppose, for a small church with few opportunities to make a big impact, one that is still shaped by a sixteenth-century martyr tradition in which the ultimate choice, and sometimes the only choice, is faithfulness or repudiation. This is in many ways a good legacy, and applied in Ireland, it has led us to take on work that will not yield quick or easily measured results.

My own work has come to focus on sectarianism, which in Irish usage means the complex of problems that derive from religiously rooted ethnic conflict. Most would agree that changing political circumstances will affect sectarianism, but it is so deeply embedded in Northern Ireland society that even the most perfect political settlement would not make it go away, and ongoing sectarianism would retain a capacity to undermine that settlement. Work on sectarianism is therefore vitally necessary. But it is probably the work of generations, so any perspective that can sustain workers for the long haul is potentially valuable.

Viewed in this way, the obvious developments of ordinary politics in the 1980s and 1990s—rolling devolution, the New Ireland Forum, the Anglo-Irish Agreement, the Hume-Adams talks, the Anglo-Irish Joint Declaration, and finally, the Good Friday Agreement—could emerge and sometimes fade, but for me and others working on issues like sectarianism, the necessary work has remained much the same. Even such dramatic, longed-for, and treasured events as the IRA and loyalist cease-fires in 1994 and the Good Friday Agreement in 1998 have not made a fundamental difference in work on sectarianism. They allowed us to work in a more free and hopeful atmosphere, but they have also revealed clearly that the end of violence is not the end of sectarianism or the fulfillment of reconciliation.

If this Mennonite legacy is valuable, it also has its dangers. Wright praises those who refuse "the siren call of effectiveness," but what about those who can scarcely even hear it? Who, if they did hear it, would be more likely to run away from it than toward it? I sometimes think I see among Mennonites inclinations more toward "ineffectiveness is faithful" or "effectiveness is unfaithful," and I fear that many of us might fail to notice an opportunity to be effective if it jumped out and bit us. In his first book on Northern Ireland, political scientist John Darby applied a quote from Arthur Koestler to the Northern situation:

What we need is an active fraternity of pessimists. They will not aim at immediate radical solutions, because they know that these cannot be achieved in the hollow of the historical wave; they will not brandish the surgeon's knife at the social body, because they know that their own instruments are polluted. They will watch with open eyes and without sectarian blinkers for the first sign of the new horizontal movement; when it comes they will assist its birth; but if it does not come in their lifetime, they will not despair. And meantime their chief aim will be to create oases in the interregnum desert. (Darby, 1976, p. 162)

I agree, and Mennonites are ready-made recruits for Koestler's fraternity of pessimistic oasis creators. But having been bequeathed this perspective as a birthright and having lived it all my life, I wish I could point out to Koestler the downside of what he advocates. Too long a stay in the oasis can contract the vision of its residents so that the oasis becomes their comfortable world. They scarcely see beyond it, and what they do see out there in the desert may be regarded with a combination of fear, indifference, and contempt; eyes may become too dull to see "the first sign of the new horizontal movement" and skills may be too neglected to "assist its birth." None of this is necessary, but it is a danger.

Wright offered those engaged in reconciliation work a model in which their work was not an irrelevant sideshow but had real dignity as an essential contribution to the kind of foundation politics that would make political structures workable. In the case of Mennonites in Ireland, my fear would be that the kind of Christian community and peace work toward which we gravitate and which is, properly understood, foundationally political as it contributes to building a society that can live in peace within new political structures, can slide into harmless apoliticism—ineffective ineffectiveness, one might say—unless it stays closely aware of ordinary and generally depressing politics.

But, whatever the dangers, a critique of effectiveness can be a most useful resource for persevering in a situation like Northern Ireland, which can absorb without apparent effect enormous quantities of good intention faithfully applied and where even the long labors of many may not produce results they will ever see.

As Mennonites appropriated simple but developing versions of what would eventually become Wright's ethnic frontier society model, we applied them to evaluating what we were learning through our experiences and friendships. But our practical limitations, especially of time to give to peace work, were just as important in determining our direction. Between theoretical models and practical limitations, however, more coherent strategies and emphases began to emerge.

Fundamentally, Mennonites based their peace work in Northern Ireland on forming a network of relationships and pursuing possibilities that developed from them. Looking back, this model seems to risk making friends for ulterior motives, but I can only say it never felt that way at the time and still does not. At least, this model seemed appropriately contingent—if we did not make friends who thought we might make a contribution, then nothing would happen.

In any case, everything about our circumstances pointed in this direction. We had no high-powered skills, no novel theoretical schemes, no off-the-shelf programs to offer—and even if we had, we were operating on marginal time, so developing independent initiatives was not realistic. In fact, neither did it seem desirable, because almost everywhere our interests and friendships took us, we found interesting, valuable efforts already in place. Far better, then, to see if we could find ways to encourage these than to start new work. We did notice, however, that sometimes the people we met, who seemed to us a natural network of people doing similar work, actually moved in worlds that scarcely intersected. Perhaps we could be a bridge between them. We also found that others who were doing what we admired as brave and creative peace work were for that very reason isolated, embattled, and regarded with suspicion by their own communities. Perhaps we could support and encourage them.

Applying this emerging approach to our stock emphasis on Christian community and peace produced paradoxical results. Concern for church and peace, we soon decided, suggested that we *not* start a Mennonite community in Northern Ireland. Yet, ironically, starting a congregation in the North probably would have been easy enough, with disgruntled evangelicals as a natural constituency. On reflection, however, several factors pushed us in another direction. We were partly influenced by respect for the vitality of the reconciliation communities we were learning to know. We would, if possible, support existing and emerging communities rather than take new initiative. Still more influential was thinking about the bridging role we increasingly understood as an important and distinctive offering. Were we to start even a small Mennonite community in heavily churched Northern Ireland, we would immediately be regarded as competition, however limited, and our connecting, encouraging role would be hampered, if not impossible.

This new approach was not what we had foreseen, but it has become a dominant approach to missiology among Mennonites. This approach was initiated in West Africa, where for many years Mennonite mission work has deliberately eschewed starting Mennonite congregations, concentrating instead on offering resources to local churches, especially independent churches, in whatever ways possible. Applied to Northern Ireland, the same approach has continued to seem exactly right.

The one element of our original vision that emerged intact, even enhanced, was the importance of long-term commitment. Everything confirmed this approach. One crucial confirmation was that we liked Ireland, and it soon became a genuine and mostly comfortable second home. Linda and I became Irish citizens in 1998. The political situation in Northern Ireland was also a powerful force toward a long-term approach. By the time our team of MBM/MCC workers was in place in Dublin in 1980, violence had dragged on for more than a decade. The view was bleak from all quarters, including the general public, politicians, and, perhaps especially, those scholars who thought most deeply about the conflict. In 1976, Richard Rose had set the epigrammatic standard for cynicism born of despair: "Many talk about a solution to Ulster's political problem but few are prepared to say what the problem is. The reason is simple. *The problem is that there is no solution*" (Rose, 1976, p. 139).[1]

Padraig O'Malley (1983), John Whyte (1991), and Frank Wright (1987) have been brilliant interpreters of the Troubles who, while refusing despair, have emphasized difficulties and talked only sparingly of solutions, which they assumed to be distant, if attainable at all.

Political events and scholarly analysis confirmed what we were already disposed to believe: MBM and MCC must be prepared to stay in Ireland for the long haul or get out. Personal contacts reinforced this conclusion, partly because the situation so clearly demanded it but also because of the bad impression left by hit-and-run analysts and other quick-fix artists. As ethnic conflicts go, Northern Ireland is quite convenient for academics, especially those from Britain and North America. Whyte concluded that, on a per capita basis, Northern Ireland was probably "the most heavily researched area on earth" (1991, p. viii). While some of the work has been valuable, other work has left an impression of superficiality and even exploitation.

One of the most striking signs of MBM and MCC's basic commitment to long-term presence concerned the direction of my work. However weighty the disadvantages of sending a lightly skilled twenty-five-year-old to help begin work in a country where Mennonites had not been previously involved, one advantage was the possibility of shaping my training to suit the situation. Because much of identity and conflict in Ireland is framed in terms of history, I proposed to get a Ph.D. in Irish history as preparation for working in the area of reconciliation. Administrators from both agencies supported my decision, even though they would not see results for years.

Neither would I see any immediate results. In times of frustration, however, I found myself taking solace in the example of a few older missionaries. This surprised me, given my initial suspicion of mission, but I was gradually coming to regard myself as a missionary, not merely as a Mennonite in Ireland who happened to be employed by a mission agency. Albert and Lois Buckwalter's work in the Argentine Chaco particularly caught my imagination. In the 1950s, they abandoned a traditional mission compound setup in favor of a much simpler, but risky and hard to evaluate, relationship-based way of working with local Indian groups. While their work might have been superficially judged a failure at points along the way, after thirty years, their success was recognized, in part through their Bible translation work but more subtly and perhaps most profoundly through their contribution to nurturing a faith-based sense of worth among tribes that had internalized society's judgment of them as worthless. This seemed to me a dramatic, lived parable of the centrality of relationship and the value of sticking around.

Sticking around has made sense in Ireland, too. Two of the main pillars of any credibility I have with Irish people have been each passing year I have lived in Ireland and a Ph.D. in Irish history, both of which suggest that I am not on holiday. The history degree, in particular, has also enhanced the credibility of MBM and MCC. Irish people who learn that the agencies supported me to study Irish history recognize these as serious, culturally sensitive organizations committed to the long view.[2]

## From Vision to Application

By 1983, our involvements in Northern Ireland had begun to take on a pattern. The Kreiders continued their annual visits; Dawn Nelson attended occasional meetings; Mike Garde sold books, lectured, and visited people; and I attended meetings, did historical research, and met with friends. My contacts in the North were primarily with the ecumenical reconciliation movement and evangelical Protestants, two scarcely intersecting circles. Early on, Garde had suggested that Mennonites might usefully get involved with Northern evangelicals, who had a style of biblical orientation similar to Mennonites but who participated hardly at all in reconciliation or other sorts of peace work. This immediately caught my imagination and has been a cornerstone of my work ever since.

For better and for worse, religion is a dynamic factor in Northern Ireland, I reasoned, much more so than anywhere else in Western Europe. While measures of religiosity show declining commitment in Northern Ireland, the churches remain strong, and they have a socializing role far greater than any other institution in society (see Morrow, Birrell, Greer, and O'Keeffe, 1991). Within Protestant circles, evangelicalism is a particularly potent force. This is partly a matter of significant numbers, partly a matter of energy and institutions out of proportion with their numbers, and partly a matter of their relationship to Ulster Protestant tradition.

Crucially, evangelical anti-Catholicism, which remains vigorous though not unanimous, is not an evangelical quirk but a continuously maintained inheritance from the center of the Reformation tradition. Especially in the nineteenth and early twentieth centuries, it was a significant force in forging Protestant unity and resistance to the political goals of Catholic nationalism. Therefore, the anti-Catholicism the mainstream now largely rejects as outdated and destructive can be plausibly presented by some evangelical perspectives as faithful to a Reformation inheritance of constant and continuing truth and utility, as Ian Paisley, his church, and his political party have done so effectively from the fundamentalist end of the evangelical continuum. Thus, an anti-Catholicism rooted in Protestant tradition and significantly maintained by evangelicalism remains a major block to Catholic-Protestant reconciliation and to political accommodation.

Visiting in Northern Ireland, I soon discovered a small number of evangelicals discontented with the tradition's religious and political anti-Catholicism and with the otherworldly and quietist approach to the Troubles favored by more respectable evangelicalism. While a few of these people had gathering places, they were scattered for the most part and had no clearly stated alternative to what they were rejecting. This much was clear, however: They were intent on remaining evangelicals and formulating their alternative in evangelical terms. Moreover, some of them had been influenced by Mennonite writings, and they were gratifyingly willing to receive a Mennonite who valued what they were attempting to do.

The emotional costs of their new departure could be high, as far too often their evangelical churches and organizations condemned what they were doing as heretical and destructive, and they were mostly too scattered to give much support to one another. In these circumstances, I soon discovered that one useful thing I could do with my limited visits was to be a sympathetic and supportive conversation partner, bringing a different but complementary perspective and assuring them that they were not crazy. Some of these people found it reassuring that I spoke not only for myself, but I also represented a church tradition in which their emerging viewpoints and strategies were normative, not heretical.

For me and for Mennonite work in Ireland, by far the most important of my new relationships was with Joe Campbell, an evangelical Presbyterian elder then working for the Belfast YMCA. On a visit to Belfast in 1983, I attended a meeting Campbell organized, and after a brief conversation he generously offered a place to stay if I should ever need one. On my next visit, I accepted his invitation to stay with his family, we quickly became friends, and I have been their guest countless times since.

Through my relationship with Campbell, several new Mennonite involvements developed. I was excited by his work and the direction the Belfast YMCA was taking, so I was eager that Mennonites should support this as appropriate. In conversations with Campbell, his administrators, and MBM/MCC administrators over several years, we developed a job description for a Mennonite volunteer with the Y's youth work program, which led, circuitously, to the first Mennonite worker based in Northern Ireland.

A second involvement came more at my own initiative but was taken in consultation with Campbell. At Goshen College, I had been in a Bible study group with Ron Kraybill, who had since become the first director of the Mennonite Conciliation Service. On a visit to the United States in 1982, I asked if he would be willing to lead some mediation training seminars in Ireland, if I found Irish organizations interested in hosting him. Kraybill was eager to explore whether what he was learning was applicable in a wider setting, and I began testing the possibility in Ireland. Kraybill came in 1985 and led two seminars in Dublin and two in Northern Ireland. His work had far-reaching consequences, as Joe Campbell will make clear in his account in chapter 6.

A third involvement was my initiative although pursued with the consent of Campbell and his wife, Janet. I was concerned that the stresses of Campbell's YMCA work were too great to work under indefinitely. It seemed to me that a sabbatical year in which Campbell could get away, reflect on his experience, and learn new skills might be helpful, maybe necessary, if he were to develop and maintain this kind of work over the long haul. In fact, observing others in similarly vital and stressful situations, I wondered if one sabbatical might be the pilot for a more extended program. Working with the Campbells, their many friends in Northern Ireland, MBM and MCC, and my Mennonite contacts in the United States, we organized a sabbatical year at the Associated Mennonite Biblical Seminary (AMBS) in Elkhart, Indiana, for the 1987–1988 school year.

As I continued visiting Northern Ireland, instinct, experience, and reflection gradually distilled into an identifiable personal approach to working there. It revolved around the limitations and possibilities of being a committed outsider.

Before I set foot in Northern Ireland, I had already learned that becoming Irish was not as simple as emigrating to Ireland, a truth illustrated by a clash with a neighbor. Where we lived in Dublin in the 1980s, an older man two doors down was well known as the neighborhood's flaming eccentric. He particularly favored terrorizing the many neighborhood children. Our daughter Anna came in crying one day because he had hit her over the head with a rolled-up newspaper and yelled at her for sitting on the footpath in front of his house as she recovered from a skating mishap. Infuriated, I forgot everything I knew about constructive conflict and charged down to his house, where we roared and shouted at each other. This was predictably unproductive, and as I stamped away, still furious, his parting shot was, "Go back to New York, ya blow-in!"

This incident came to stand as the symbol of something I had realized years before. Given Ireland's ethnic homogeneity, its stable family and social systems, and its entrenched self-understanding as an exporter not importer of people, I could commit myself totally to Ireland, become a citizen, live there for fifty years, and yet still be the blow-in from New York. Being Irish was not a choice for me to make. I soon reorganized my self-understanding around the idea of making the most of being a committed outsider and began habitually to ask questions that are still with me: What are the things I can contribute as an outsider that are more difficult for insiders? What are the things I cannot do and would be wrong to attempt?

People who have been especially helpful and supportive have often seemed to be working with the same notion. Not five minutes after we met, my eventual Ph.D. thesis supervisor, Father Patrick Corish, suggested that the origins of Irish evangelicalism would make a good research topic. It was an important but academically neglected topic, he noted, and it would take advantage of my religious interests and background. It would also take me into the area of religion and conflict, a minefield of emotive issues for anyone but especially difficult for Irish historians, who were likely to find it distasteful and to be suspected by virtue of background of being biased. He could not possibly have given me better counsel.

Working at how to be a useful outsider has been crucial to being involved in Northern Ireland. Without consciously setting out to do so, I developed a pattern of relating. Whenever I was in a new setting, I listened and said nothing until someone asked me who I was and what I thought, however long that might take. The Irish being fairly gregarious, it was rare to make it through an entire meeting before someone engaged me. Once the initiative was theirs—and I maintained a healthy listening-to-talking ratio—I was almost always generously received. In recent years, however, I am more and more invited to take initiatives that blur the insider/outsider distinction, which presents new complications along with new opportunities. How best to be an outsider seems unlikely ever to settle into a simple formula.

## Consolidating a Program

No single point clearly defines the movement from tentative explorations to consolidating a considered program of involvement in peace work. However, a 1986 report on Mennonite work in Ireland marked the beginning of a transition, and many of the key elements were in place by 1988.

By the mid-1980s, MBM/MCC administrators were eager to evaluate the direction of Mennonite work in Ireland, including the peace work. They invited Atlee and Winnie Beechy, a recently retired couple with long experience in MCC and peace work in North America and internationally, to conduct the review in 1985. In some ways, the Beechy report, issued early in 1986, involved nothing new, as the Beechys strongly affirmed the direction implicit in our Northern involvements.

One new departure, however, concerned responsibility for developing work in Northern Ireland, as MBM and MCC now asked Garde and me to function as Northern Ireland consultants. In 1986, he and I drafted a wide-ranging rationale and strategy for Mennonite work in the North in which we foresaw the development of a "witness council" of local people, who would advise on Mennonite work, as was the case in several other places where MBM and MCC worked (Liechty and Garde, 1986).

In time, we would invite a group of about ten men and women, Catholics and Protestants from North and South, to advise us on the kind of work we ought to be doing. This group gathered informally in 1989 and formally from 1990, calling itself the Support Body for Mennonite Witness in Ireland and meeting twice a year ever since. Their counsel, in matters ranging from shaping vision through sorting out details, has been invaluable, and MBM and MCC have done a good job of honoring their commitment to take no initiatives and accept no requests for involvement without first consulting the Support Body. In the end, Mennonite work in Ireland has in its own way come to involve the life of a community, but the community is not a specific fellowship, Mennonite or otherwise. It is a community of Irish friends and co-workers developed over many years. Though nothing like what we had once anticipated, it continues to seem exactly right.

In response to the 1986 Beechy report, Garde and I proposed to divide responsibilities. Although neither emphasis would be exclusive, he would focus on the political realm and republican circles, and I would concentrate on the churches, especially on the ecumenical reconciliation movement, the radical evangelicals, and the connection between them. In choosing these emphases, we did not attempt to identify some hypothetical real essence of the conflict to which we would then devote our energies. We recognized that the

Northern Ireland problem was multifaceted and that the facets were linked. Our chosen facets were no more important than a number of others, but we judged them to be important in their own right and part of a larger whole; we were drawn to them by inclination, conviction, and relationship; and they seemed to present particular opportunities for a Mennonite contribution.

Garde had intended that his work in the North would lessen as mine increased. The shift was quicker and more complete, however, than any of us had anticipated, because his opportunities to work in the area of new religious movements, an interest that had been developing since 1979, began to increase dramatically. Fortunately, Joe Campbell was becoming more involved with us, and the amazing and expanding breadth of his work helped to restore balance. In mid-1988, Joe and Janet Campbell returned from their sabbatical year, refreshed and with some new skills. They gradually became more and more a part of the Mennonite workers' team. In 1990, MBM and MCC recognized Campbell's increasing involvement by asking him to serve as a quarter-time coordinator of Mennonite work in Ireland, which he accepted. Campbell's work, with Scripture Union until 1995 and now with The Mediation Network for Northern Ireland, has been exactly in line with the direction of Mennonite involvements, and both employers have seen his work for Mennonites as compatible with their own (see ch. 6.)

Another compensation for Garde's diminished involvement was that we began to develop a variety of more short-term, specific assignments in the North, which always built on some variation of peace and church themes. In 1987, David Moser, a recent Goshen College graduate, became the first Mennonite worker in Northern Ireland, and he spent three years as a youth worker for the 174 Trust, an evangelical-run social services organization working in a particularly violence-torn area of north Belfast. Moser did excellent work in difficult circumstances, and since then we have been well served by seven short-term workers.

Other involvements have included only occasional Mennonite personnel in Ireland or none at all. Mediation has been the most important, and Joe Campbell will tell that story in chapter 6. In addition, in 1989, we began New Perspectives, a program designed to give able young people at risk of paramilitary involvement a year in North America to gain new skills, options, and perspectives. This was the brain child of Jonathan Jordan, a Northern Ireland native who was briefly a member of the Dublin Mennonite Community and a resident in the United States from 1985. Two people participated in this program. The first experience was a success, but the second was a disaster, cut short after a couple of months. We reluctantly gave up the program, realizing that it required more time and resources than we were able to give.

Another occasional program, much less ambitious, was to follow the Campbell sabbatical model. In 1991, Ann Dixon, a young evangelical involved in reconciliation work, spent several months on a study and rest leave in the United States. Derek and Arlene Poole, formerly leaders in the Greenfield Community Church in Portadown, County Armagh, and their family spent the 1995–1996 academic year at AMBS in Indiana, while Bill and Ina Ruth

Breckbill, a retired Mennonite pastoral couple from Indiana, spent a year providing pastoral assistance for the Greenfield congregation, an arrangement made possible by collaboration among Greenfield and five Mennonite congregations in northern Indiana. Since the family's return, Derek Poole has taken up work with the vital evangelical organization Evangelical Contribution on Northern Ireland (ECONI).

At the time of the Beechy report in 1986, my own work was about to take a major shift, from orientation to application. I finished my Ph.D. in 1987 and left almost immediately with my family for a sabbatical year in North America. Returning in 1988, my new job description was to use what I had learned about Irish history and affairs to work for Catholic-Protestant reconciliation and church renewal.

As I started working, Linda and I were also making a decision about where we should be located. I had long been drawn to Belfast, and the North looked like the logical place to be based for my work. Unsettled after a year's absence, Linda was also open to considering a move. But this was not a private decision, so MBM/MCC asked Harold and Elizabeth Bauman, American Mennonites then serving as a pastoral couple with the Dublin Mennonite Community, to test the implications of our moving North. Talking to Mennonite contacts in the North, the Baumans found the idea favorably received, provided I had suitable work, and a research fellowship with the Institute of Irish Studies at Queen's University, Belfast, looked a likely possibility. But most members of the Dublin Mennonite Community did not like the idea for two main reasons: First, the community did not feel settled enough to do without founding members, and second, if we moved North, we would be a solitary Mennonite family, so peace witness would not flow from the life of a community.

The first reason I respected but did not find conclusive. The second reason I railed against: My peace-related work did not directly relate to the Dublin community, while in the North I would be part of a community, broadly defined, of Christians working for peace. I did not, however, persuade anyone but myself and a few others, so we finally gave up the idea of moving North. MBM and MCC qualified the decision by saying that the issue could be reopened in a few years, but by that time the family was well settled, and a move would have been most unfair. I am still not sure whether staying in Dublin was right or wrong, but it was certainly the most painful decision I have ever had to accept.

With that decision behind me, I could give my full energies to my new job description. But would anyone be interested? Would anyone invite me to work with them? Would they invite me back a second time? Would word get around and other groups invite me? Part of the committed-outsider role, as I understood it, was to avoid taking initiatives and to define my work around what I was invited to do. I need not be completely passive, of course. I might, for example, send a paper to someone I met who I think might be interested, but if there is no response, I drop it. Or I might try to arrange a meeting with a person I have met who seems to have common interests, but I never push it.

In the first year or so of the new regime, I always had enough work to pull together a presentable quarterly report, but in truth the work was sparse.

Participants in some early seminars must have been bemused by my over-prepared material, although the advantage for me has been that I am still building on work I had the chance to develop carefully in my then-underemployed state. While I have encountered plenty of setbacks and disappointments in my years of applied work since 1988, I have on the whole been invited to take increasing amounts of work of increasing significance. Somewhere along the way, I crossed a threshold from accepting every scrap of work offered to needing to make choices.

Most of my work has centered on some aspect of sectarianism. But, if the theme has been consistent, the pursuit of it has involved many and frequently shifting approaches. My purposes and methods are sometimes academic, sometimes pastoral, often a mix. I am, first, a historian and, second, an amateur theologian, but I increasingly find myself drawing from other disciplines as I am able. While most of my closest coworkers are Christians, they represent diverse perspectives. I work by means of university courses, public lectures, popular and scholarly writing, preaching, seminars, workshops, study groups, consultations, conferences, conversations. My audiences include the general public, students, scholars, and sometimes a specific secular group, but I often work with some Christian group, whether Catholic, ecumenical, mainstream Protestant, evangelical, charismatic, or other.

Lacking a single, consistent Irish institutional base before I began working for the Irish School of Ecumenics in 1995, I was utterly dependent on a small group of friends and advocates, drawn from a network of relationships developed over many years, who directed work my way. Some of these people, whom I came to regard as my guardian angels, were in positions of authority from the time we became friends, but most became vastly more influential, to my great benefit. For many years, my work opportunities were heavily dependent on my friends' successes, and this remains true to some extent.

The variety of my work has mostly seemed a privilege. Occasionally, however, I feel that variety is really a code word for incoherence, and the yearning for a simple answer to the question "What do you do?" becomes almost palpable. I have many friends who understand exactly what I am doing and support it fully, but others are at least a little mystified. One friend, while sharing my delight at a recent appointment was, I discovered, seeing the value of it rather differently than I. For me, the assignment was significant because it allowed me to pursue the theme of sectarianism more systematically than before. My friend was happy for me because it was something like a real job: almost full time for three years, a recognized institution, proper stationery.

Driven by the longing to do one thing well rather than many things more or less competently and by a desire to have a clear and settled place in Irish society, I have twice accepted invitations to apply for full-time history lecturing posts at Maynooth. Both times I came second, which left me with a real sense of loss and regret, wondering what might have been. But I felt simultaneous and at least equal relief. Despite the inherent uncertainties, I value the peculiar mix of involvements that now engage me, and any ordinary job would mean dropping many of them. Even if the coherence of my work is not always externally apparent, internal coherence is the only kind that finally matters, I reason, and more ordinarily employed friends assure me that an institution is by no means a guarantor of such coherence. Mostly, I convince myself.

My efforts at self-persuasion draw on a number of resources. A crucial one is a consistent awareness of being part of something larger: of Mennonite work in Ireland, of the circle of Irish reconciliation workers, of the broader movement of those working for peace, of international Mennonite work, of the global Mennonite family, of the Mennonite tradition, and, ultimately, of God's purposes. A steady sense of meaningful work shared with others and rooted in God's desire for the world is no small compensation for an irregular job profile. Relationships with MBM and MCC have not been ceaseless sweetness and light, but on the whole, I cannot seriously imagine better, more supportive employers. MBM has a large network of prayer partners, who commit themselves to staying informed about and praying for different international situations and for Mennonite workers. A number of supporting congregations in North America have taken a particular interest in our work, some for many years. Though getting a Ph.D. in Irish history is not every Mennonite's idea of mission work, whenever I have explained my work and the logic behind it in North American church settings, I have received only warm support. Finally, there is that Mennonite wariness about bowing before the idol of effectiveness, a spiritual habit that is a limited, possibly dangerous, but still valuable resource.

I do have rough and subjective ways of evaluating whether my work is at least broadly on track, although these are more tests of breadth of acquaintance than of effectiveness. What is the range of my friends and contacts? Who is inviting me to work? What is the significance of the work? Am I getting a steady flow of invitations? As long as a good variety of individuals and groups are regularly inviting me to do meaningful work, I am content to keep at it, believing that the necessary changes in the Northern Ireland situation will involve many people working for a long time.

# Six

## Partnering with Mennonites
## in Northern Ireland

JOSEPH CAMPBELL

MEETING MENNONITES WAS FOR ME an oasis in the dry and barren desert. A Presbyterian from birth and elder in my local congregation, this "new" denomination came into my frame of reference in casual conversation in 1980 with a colleague who was working with youth on urban justice issues in England. He had visited the London Mennonite Centre and counted among his friends Alan and Eleanor Kreider. He spoke of a quality of community life, worship where justice and peace issues were not on the edge but central, and a people who took Jesus' call to peacemakers as a serious call for today. To say I was interested would be an understatement. I read John Howard Yoder's *Politics of Jesus* (1972), and I knew then I had to learn more about this church.

At that point in my life, I was youth director of the Belfast YMCA, at that time a mainly Protestant and evangelical youth organization. I was responsible for running a social education and recreation program for several hundred youth in the sixteen to twenty-five age group, mostly from low-income inner city backgrounds, with a healthy mix of male and female, Catholic and Protestant. Young people with regular jobs were the exception, as the youth often came from neighborhoods where over 70 percent of the people were on welfare. Few experiences in my life had prepared me for the hopeless injustice faced by those youth. I understood in stark terms the connection between social deprivation and political violence. Many of the young people I worked with had lives outside the YMCA in the junior ranks of paramilitary organizations on both sides of our divided society. I started skills training, work programs, and a small woodwork shop in order to give hope to some, and while these had a measure of success, the surface was barely scratched. The pathway of school failure, unemployment, social deprivation, and political violence is a well-worn one in Northern Ireland. As I had been a teacher in a large Belfast secondary school, the injustice of it all was overwhelming.

The other element for me in my work in the Y was getting to work alongside Catholics who took faith seriously. Schools then, and largely now, were either Catholic or Protestant. Mine had been Protestant with only Protestant teachers. My training as an engineer in the Belfast Shipyard had brought only occasional contact with Catholics in an almost exclusively Protestant work-force. I had been raised in a divided extended family; my grandfather, a Prot-estant, was brave enough at the turn of the century to marry a Catholic woman, have eleven children, and raise them male Catholic and female Prot-estant. (It was the custom of the time to raise the children of the opposite gender in the tradition of each parent.) This division was largely ignored and rarely spoken about within my family. But it has given me a sensitivity to and awareness of both sides, something for which, at the beginning of a new century, I am grateful.

The twin factors of working for justice plus a growing awareness of faithful Catholics wanting to talk with God as I did were the seedbed in which my growing interest in the Mennonite church took root.

In 1982, I met Mike Garde, a Mennonite worker from Dublin, though not in Ireland but England, where I was taking part in a Christian Arts Festival. I learned more about Mennonites, and within a few months I met Joe Liechty, then other members of the Dublin Mennonite Community. I did not know it then, but Liechty was to become a supporter, confidant, and adviser as I moved beyond my much-too-narrow evangelical confines to meet with and value those who had made the journey to peacemaking from the ecumenical and Catholic sectors of the church in Ireland.

Ron Kraybill was one of a number of Mennonite church workers whom Liechty brought to Belfast for short visits. In 1985, Kraybill ran a three-hour workshop on conflict skills for my team of YMCA youth workers. That eve-ning lives with me still as I remember what, at the time, was a new approach to interpersonal conflict. Biblically based and practical, the workshop ener-gized me and made me hungry for more. In addition to running another, two-day, workshop on mediation in Dublin, Kraybill ran a session at the Corry-meela Reconciliation Centre and presented the members with a Mennonite Central Committee (MCC) Peace Library, a set of MCC-recommended read-ing materials. Those first short workshops in conflict and mediation sowed the seeds among a diverse group of grassroots community workers and peace ac-tivists, which led in 1990 to the founding of The Mediation Network for Northern Ireland in Belfast and a mediation service in Dublin.

Barry Hart, supported by the Mennonite Board of Missions (MBM), came for almost a year in 1986 and, working mainly from a Dublin base, he built on what Kraybill had begun. Deepening the experience of many of the previous groups in Belfast and Dublin, Hart ran many two-, three-, and five-day courses, as well as training-the-trainer events. Mediation was taking root in Northern Ireland within a community that was experiencing some horrendously violent acts. Here was a sign of hope, a new way of resolving conflict "not by fright or flight but by insight," as we have since phrased it in the Mediation Network. With Hart's advice and contacts in the United States, three people, two from Belfast and one from Dublin, spent ten days with Ray Shonholtz at the Community Boards in California for further training.

In all of those early contacts in Northern Ireland, it was terribly important that Mennonite expertise and thinking should be carefully focused on people working for peace and reconciliation in both communities. To lean too much in favor of one community over the other, even though one may be more receptive than the other, would be for Mennonites to be colonized by one side and to be discredited and finished as a bridge between the two.

After eleven years of tough, front-line, cross-community youth work in Belfast, I was close to a breakdown, and no new opportunity for work was opening up. MBM and MCC provided financial support, as did friends in our home community, and we also used our personal savings for a ten-month sabbatical for my wife, Janet, our three children, and me, so that I could study at the Associated Mennonite Biblical Seminary (AMBS) in Elkhart, Indiana. This model of sabbaticals for hard-pressed peace workers in Ireland has become an important feature of Mennonite witness in support of Irish peace efforts. Four others have benefited from this support in the past eight years.

Attending AMBS classes, reading in the excellent library, and being part of a Mennonite congregation and small group within the congregation was refreshing and energizing. I gained valuable theological underpinnings for the justice and peace work I had been involved in with only scant support from the evangelical community at home. We experienced church as a community with God's people responsible to and for one another. I trained as a victim-offender mediator and mediated six cases for the local Victim-Offender Reconciliation Program office. I also had six days of training in mediation skills with John Paul Lederach and Ron Kraybill. In all of this, our family felt cared for, supported, and loved by Mennonite people. Yet at no time did we feel our own Presbyterian tradition was devalued, nor was there any pressure whatsoever to join the Mennonite church nor to start one in Northern Ireland. The only expectation was that we return to Ireland with our new skills, insights, and energy and work faithfully for peace and reconciliation. This we were happy to do in May 1988.

The question of starting a Mennonite church in Northern Ireland has had less to do with theology and Alan Kreider's "disembodied verbal witness" perspective and more to do with Mennonite neutrality and desire for acceptance from both sides of a very divided society. From an Irish perspective, an important advantage Mennonites have is precisely having no history in Ireland. Being unknown does cause initial interest—at least one cannot be pigeonholed like everyone else! But because Joe and Linda Liechty and their family have stayed the course in Ireland for nineteen years, Joe can speak with enough inside knowledge to make his outsider perspective creditable. To begin a church in the North would threaten those churches already established and suggest other reasons for being in Ireland than supporting Irish peace work. Even in recent years, as increasing numbers from within the evangelical tradition have become disillusioned with most of what is on offer in local congregations, it still does not seem appropriate for Mennonites to add to the already extensive array of church traditions in Northern Ireland.

Those people in Belfast trained by Ron Kraybill and Barry Hart began to run three-day training courses in mediation for community workers, probation and police officers, and others whose work would release them for the time necessary. This small group of committed people had three issues to face.

First, the model being taught and materials being used were essentially American, and the relatively inexperienced local trainers gave little or no recognition to the informal methods of conflict resolution work already operating in Irish society. In a word, the programs were prescriptive in nature.

Second, the assumption was that people in dispute would be prepared to sit down together with two mediators and work for a resolution. Yet, despite an informal referral service that operated in the late 1980s and early 1990s, few cases got to a formal hearing. Irish people find it difficult to speak with and face directly those with whom they disagree.

Finally, in spite of these first two factors, the demand for training was beyond the capacity of the volunteers to provide it.

Funding was granted from government and various trusts to appoint staff to the new Mediation Network. A director, Brendan McAllister, and an administrator, Clare McCormick, were appointed in 1992, with the early aim of enabling people to handle their differences in a positive way by:

- developing appropriate models of dispute resolution specific to the culture of Northern Ireland
- helping people to identify and develop their skills in handling differences
- promoting the positive values of conflict

The Mediation Network proposed to pursue these by:

- piloting a conflict resolution service
- creating a pool of trained mediators
- running a public information campaign
- developing resource materials for use by the public

At this point, the Mediation Network was largely focusing on the training of trainers and volunteers and on providing a mediation service for neighborhood disputes. I served as a regular trainer and volunteer mediator. Having returned from our sabbatical, I was also employed as a trainer of youth workers by Scripture Union, a leading evangelical organization. I began to work on justice and reconciliation themes, applying the tools of mediation. From being ambivalent on these issues, Scripture Union has since become much more proactive and continues to identify with and provide opportunity for evangelical Christians to apply biblical understandings and faith to our divided society.

MBM and MCC were becoming increasingly aware of political and religious sensitivities in Ireland and especially in Northern Ireland. As Mennonite witness expanded, the opportunity for mistakes also increased. In order to minimize the risk, a Support Body for Mennonite Witness in Ireland was established in 1989 to guide MBM and MCC in their work and the setting of priorities. The group is made up of Protestant and Catholic, lay and ordained, from the North and South of Ireland. Both Mennonite agencies are committed to testing any new involvements and initiatives with the Support Body, and consequently Mennonite witness in Ireland has a sense of ownership by Irish people.

From working only on neighborhood disputes, the Mediation Network began to develop programs in four additional key areas of Northern Ireland life: political affairs, justice, family and child care, and the churches. John Paul Lederach made his first visit to Ireland in 1992. In an inspiring address to a hundred peace activists, he opened the debate on culturally appropriate models of mediation. His experience of political mediation in other countries gave insights into how mediation might be applied in Ireland. This first visit was a model of what became for several years an annual seven-day consultation with the Mediation Network, in which he would normally meet with Director McAllister and me, as assistant director, for one day of briefing and then conduct a two-day training for mediation volunteers, using an elicitive model of training. Also held were one-day workshops in Ireland's top security prison for politically motivated prisoners, a public meeting to an invited audience of policymakers in the public sector, a meeting with political leaders and government officials, and a final session for debriefing and reflection for Mediation Network staff.

Hidden within these visits is the style of Mennonite witness in Ireland, which is deeply sensitive to the local situation and aware that in a long, protracted conflict there already are local people with experience and skill in peacemaking who need to be respected, affirmed, and supported. The question always uppermost in the minds of the North Americans is: How can Mennonites best support Irish peace efforts? Respected, experienced peacemakers like Lederach can, however, open up access to high-level actors, upon which staff at the Mediation Network can then build. Short seminars with the four different factions in prison can provide the framework for regular work over the months and years of a long sentence.

In 1994, after careers in pastoring, teaching, and marriage therapy, Naomi and John Lederach, parents of John Paul, joined the staff of the Mediation Network for three years as MCC volunteers. In the rapid growth of this small organization, they have established systems, helped with training, especially within the churches and family programs, and have been a supportive presence to the staff and an increasing number of others working for change in Irish society.

I joined the Mediation Network staff as training officer in 1995, having been increasingly involved as a volunteer trainer and prison worker for several years. At the same time, the Northern Ireland Probation Service seconded a worker to develop the justice program.

One personal struggle for me over the years of involvement with the Mediation Network has been the work with police officers. Several years ago, these heavily armed forces of the state asked for help in developing mediation skills training for their recruits. This has expanded into a much broader program of eight days and evenings of community awareness training for police officers. Some 93 percent of their 13,000 members are from the Protestant tradition with a strong law-and-order ethos.

My pacifist beliefs have been challenged and stretched through this work. The obvious institutional dangers of colluding with such a powerful system are obvious, as are the personal dangers, since those who support the forces of the state in any way have been seen by the Irish Republican Army as legitimate targets. Many people over the years have paid the ultimate price. With the Mediation Network's increasing involvement in political mediation, shortly after the 1994 cease-fires by the paramilitary forces on both sides, we took the decision to make our work with the police more public. We concluded that it was better that people understand from us what we were doing and why than to have it leak out with our being accidentally or deliberately misunderstood by republican groups. This transparency is now an important cornerstone in our mediation work. We talk to all sides and make that known to all sides.

In our development of mediation practice for political work in Ireland, we have identified four goals:

1. Facilitate communication. To be trusted to carry a message where trust has broken down is not only a responsibility but an honor.
2. Improve understanding. In a deeply divided community, one side's understanding of the other is at best poor, at worst warped.
3. Support creative thinking. Our access to MCC's International Conciliation Service has enabled us to learn from other conflicts and to explore paths other than the well-worn ones.
4. Explore accommodations. We help individuals and groups to take the first tentative steps toward a more inclusive way of thinking and acting.

In all our mediation, we work only with the agenda of the participants. Irish people are wary of mediators bearing solutions. Almost all of our political mediation is what we call intermediation, where we serve as a formal go-between. McAllister and I also work as comediators, a Protestant and a Catholic together, so that we can be a balance to each other and yet have both mediators bring their finely tuned knowledge of their own side.

One example of our work was in July 1995, forty miles west of Belfast, where a standoff had developed between some 5,000 Protestant demonstrators and several hundred police officers. A march by a local Orange Order of Protestants had been blocked by police from going through a Catholic neighborhood. Within hours, a call went out and was responded to by thousands of supporters, who tested the police lines. The police responded with plastic bullets, shields, and riot equipment.

Twenty-four hours into the standoff, the Mediation Network was called in to work between the Protestant marchers and the residents of the Catholic neighborhood. Our work lasted sixteen hours and included the police as participants when we neared an accommodation. The solution, after forty hours of deadlock, allowed a small silent march, without bands and with only one flag, to proceed through the contested road with the permission of the residents, who claimed their right to display their antimarch banners and posters. Only a thin line of nonriot police officers was needed to separate the two groups. For Northern Ireland, this was the first formal recognition of mediation as a way of resolving community disputes.

The Mediation Network now has a practitioners register of more than fifty trained mediators who are regularly engaged in practice. In addition, a team of ten sessional trainers are involved with the eight core staff from the Network. Programs have been developed in the housing, education, and public and private sectors of Northern Ireland society.

# Seven

## Creating Space for Peace
### *The Central American Peace Portfolio*

MARK CHUPP

THE ESCUIPULAS II PEACE ACCORD, signed in August 1987 by all of Central America's presidents, provided the impetus for major shifts throughout Central America, especially in the Nicaraguan conflict. The accord included a cease-fire covering all armed conflicts in the region, steps toward free elections and pluralistic democracy in each country, amnesty for all irregular forces fighting against their own governments in the region, the end of all types of government aid to such forces, and an agreement that these forces could not use a base in one country to attack the government of another Central American country. The Mennonite Central Committee (MCC) actively engaged in a number of peacemaking efforts that gave flesh to the accords.

Central America drifted through uncharted waters. The persistent winds of the Cold War were waning. Years of armed conflict were coming to an end. What would peace look like? How would those who had turned into hardened enemies somehow live together again in the same country?

These questions plagued Nicaragua in 1990. It was a year filled with dramatic events. Internationally monitored elections were held. On February 26, Violeta Chamorro and the UNO Coalition emerged as victors over the Sandinistas, stunning the nation and the world. Cease-fire agreements were carried out on both the Northern and Southern fronts of the Contras, the U.S.–supported Nicaraguan forces that had waged war against the Sandinista regime throughout the 1980s. The agreements included their demobilization and return to civilian life. Incoming President Chamorro maintained her campaign promise by beginning her term on April 25 with the dissolution of military conscription. Her commitment to retain Sandinista comandante Humberto Ortega as minister of defense, however, shocked the United States, her supporters in the country, and Nicaraguans living in exile in Miami.

What was happening during this dramatic year among common folks? A rather insignificant encounter demonstrates the changes occurring at this level. Earlier, in late 1989, the United Nations had facilitated an accord between the Contra forces and the Sandinista government. In mid-1990, the last of the Southern Front kept its promise and demobilized its forces. Under U.N. instructions, several thousand Contra soldiers traveled down from the mountains to the small village of Yolaina, outside of Nueva Guinea in southeastern Nicaragua. They excitedly shot their rifles into the air, feeling that sense of power one last time before turning over their weapons.

According to plan, three Soviet-made Sandinista Armed Forces attack helicopters swooped over the hills, landing amidst the armed Contras. As quickly as they touched down, soldiers swarmed the rear of the helicopter to receive their promised civilian clothing, boots, seeds for planting, and farming tools. What more tangible sign could there be that the war was coming to an end?

Meanwhile, an even greater symbol of the transformation that was occurring inside the hearts of Nicaraguans was taking place at the front of the helicopter. Members of the Zonal Peace Commission followed several Contra comandantes, who approached the head of one of the helicopters. As the pilot, a Sandinista captain, opened his window, his eyes met those of a Contra comandante. In their exchange, the Contra comandante recognized the identification numbers on the helicopter and began taunting the pilot. He asked the pilot if he was the one who had earlier flown missions over them in this same helicopter, firing from the nose gun. The pilot laughed nervously, acknowledging that he, indeed, was the one who had been trying to kill them. The pilot then asked if they were the same forces that had fired up at him as he flew over. The comandante laughed, pointing to an inch-deep indentation in the steel frame just below the pilot's window, and said, "Yes, and it looks like we almost got you here."

As these former enemies continued, their laughter gave way to a profound encounter. Their initial teasing opened a space for true dialogue. Before long, they talked about which part of the country had been home to them before the war. They realized both had been simple rural farmers. Their eyes met, and the comandante concluded, "In the end, I guess we're all still a bunch of Nicaraguan peasants. That fact hasn't changed even after all the fighting."

I witnessed this exchange, moved by the small yet profound inner change taking place in the lives of common Nicaraguans. I was also moved by the local peacemakers at my side who were, in part, responsible for making the demobilization possible. These, too, were simple peasants who, along with priests and pastors, had formed local peace commissions. As a foreigner, I counted it a privilege to accompany these peacemakers and to be present at such a historic event.

I had come to Nicaragua at the end of 1989 from Costa Rica, where I had been living for the previous two years. My assignment with the MCC Peace Portfolio Project consisted of promoting a network throughout Central America of those working at conflict resolution. I had worked for a number of years in the United States, directing a victim-offender reconciliation program and later coordinating a community organizing project for urban youth. Coming to Central America provided me the opportunity to learn from another culture and to integrate the techniques of conflict resolution with broader efforts at social change. After a year of language and cultural study and a year giving workshops throughout Central America, I was now ready to dedicate myself to a specific project.

Ann and Jim Hershberger, MCC Nicaragua country representatives, invited me and my family to move to Nicaragua to accompany the Nueva Guinea peace commissions during the electoral campaign and potential demobilization of the Contras. MCC had been working closely with the Comité Evangélico Pro Ayuda Al Desarrollo (CEPAD), an evangelical coalition with more than ten years' experience in providing relief and development throughout the country. In region 5, southeastern Nicaragua, CEPAD provided much of the logistical and organizational support to dozens of local peace commissions centered around Nueva Guinea. Together, they proposed establishing a Christian Peacemaker Team (CPT) in this area. The team was to provide an international presence, to accompany and support the peace process being carried out by the local peace commissions. Rather than bring CPT personnel from North America, who might require months of preparation, they invited us to relocate. We had already been in Nicaragua on several occasions and were familiar with the political and social situation. Sharon Shumaker, my wife, would work as a family therapist among women in the community and network among those working with people traumatized by the war.

This project would further the Peace Portfolio's goal of developing a regional network of peacemakers. From its beginning, the project had sought to cultivate relations across borders, to promote a cross-fertilization of effective methods, and to disseminate news of successful peacemaking on an international level.

## MCC Peace Portfolio Project

Dating back to the devastating 1976 Guatemalan earthquake, the Mennonite Central Committee had had a permanent presence in the region. Prior to that, MCC had sent material aid and temporary relief workers to specific areas that had been damaged by hurricanes, earthquakes, or other natural disasters. From the start, MCC attempted to partner with local churches and other indigenous organizations. In Honduras, for example, MCC first provided financial support to the Honduran Mennonite church as it began a program for the large number of refugees in the country. In 1984, MCC initiated a more permanent presence to support the Honduran Mennonite church as it established a Social Action Commission.[1] By the mid-1980s, MCC personnel were in every Central American country. Increasingly, MCC workers found themselves engaged in development work, which confronted the complexities of the regional and local conflicts. Attending to someone with a gunshot wound, for example, might incriminate an MCC worker as a guerrilla supporter or as an unofficial arm of the state, depending on who was shot and in what context.

The Mennonite churches in each country grew out of the efforts of Mennonite mission agencies dating back to the 1950s. The first-generation

Mennonites increasingly sought to connect Anabaptist/Mennonite history and theology to their current wartorn realities. At the annual gathering of Central American Mennonite leaders, known as CAMCA, they spoke of the need for a more concerted effort at peacemaking. Faced with the challenge of responding to these complexities, MCC set out in 1984 to establish a more direct effort to apply Anabaptist theology and practice to the Central American context. Doing community development work could not be separated from the clear political and military realities of the region. While the impetus came from the region, MCC leaders in North America supported it. In 1984, the MCC board of directors adopted a Declaration on Central America.

Through these close relationships with regional Mennonite partners and other nonviolent activists from the region, MCC opened a Central American Peace Portfolio in 1985. In part, the Peace Portfolio gave MCC an organizational structure for focusing and concentrating the many existing peacemaking efforts. Cosponsored by the Honduran Mennonite church, the Peace Portfolio emerged as a natural outgrowth of ten years of service by MCC in the region. Gerald Schlabach, an MCC worker in Nicaragua, articulated the initial concept of the Peace Portfolio around the experiences of Central American peacemakers in Nicaragua and the broader region.

The first annual plan of the Peace Portfolio outlined the philosophy, organizational vision, and program objectives. Under Schlabach's leadership, the Peace Portfolio carried with it thirteen assumptions. Among them, MCC needed to "show the first fruits of the justice we seek between nations by seeking the counsel and partnership of our Central American brothers and sisters." MCC must "listen attentively to others, especially fellow Christians, who view differently than we the relation of means and ends in the achieving of justice." The document also reflected the balance that MCC workers sought in offering knowledge, resources, and services, while admittedly being outsiders "having at least as much to learn about nonviolence as they have to share." The project attempted to revive a vision of Anabaptism that "offers to nonviolent popular movements a particular methodology for social change based in the resources and example of covenanted community and its servanthood" (Schlabach, 1984, pp. 1–2).

MCC recognized that its contribution would be modest but at the same time wanted to make a long-range contribution. The Peace Portfolio offered the mechanism for making nonviolent alternatives known to groups and leaders working for social change, even if these groups continued to hold open the possibility of armed means of resolving conflict. Within the nonviolent alternatives MCC presented, there was a clear bias, however cautiously it was communicated:

> In the peaceful resolution of conflict, dialogue, mediation and negotiation are preferred and should receive priority in projects of skills development. But we should also be open to and explore strategies of nonviolent resistance to oppression, since from a disadvantaged position the poor need ways to organize, survive

and assert their case if dialogue and negotiation are to have meaning. (Schlabach, 1984, p. 2)

The Peace Portfolio personnel, along with their local partners, were to network and meet together on a regular basis to share resources, provide moral support to one another, and coordinate regional planning. Program objectives anticipated providing resources, constructing forums for reflection, and supporting grassroots institutions. The ambitious plan also outlined research projects for later publication, training in conflict resolution and mediation skills, and the encouragement of specific peace efforts, such as the Moravian church's efforts at reconciliation in Nicaragua. Throughout the plan, MCC carried a responsibility to reflect back to North America the challenges facing Christians in the region and the challenges that injustices placed on Mennonites' praxis of peace. Indeed, "reverse mission" was a concept referred to often: Mennonites would take the story back to the United States in an effort to promote First-World changes that would positively affect Central America.

Throughout the history of the Peace Portfolio, there has been a commitment to resource and to accompany regional peacemakers at various levels of society. Rather than serve as "lone rangers" who ride into town one day, wipe out a conflict, and are gone the next, Peace Portfolio workers centered their work on a commitment to building long-term relationships with local peacemakers. The covenanted community served as the base of operations. Decisions were not made in isolation. What role to play emerged through persistent dialogue with trusted partners, at the invitation of those most directly involved in any given situation. More often than not, the role of the MCCer was one of supporting a front-line peacemaker. Neither Schlabach nor any of the Peace Portfolio coordinators who followed him dictated program priorities.

In practice, MCC placed workers in each of the Central American countries for a minimum term of three years. Many of the Peace Portfolio workers drew on previous MCC experience in Latin America. From Susan Classen (1992), who served as a health worker in guerrilla-held territory in El Salvador, to Luke Schrock-Hurst, who worked with conscientious objectors from Nicaragua and Honduras, Mennonites from North America dedicated some of their most productive years to aiding Central Americans in their struggle for peace. Networking efforts included regional correspondence, training seminars, itinerant specialists throughout the region, and conferences on specific topics, such as conscientious objection to military service.

The Peace Portfolio team worked at overcoming the artificial barriers that war had created among Central American countries. Rather than develop annual plans for each country, one joint Peace Portfolio Program plan emerged after consulting with partners in each of the countries. In addition, the Peace Portfolio coordinator called regional meetings of the team to further coordinate efforts and to maximize the networking and mutual support across borders.

## Nicaragua: Great Opportunities, Great Challenges

Peace Portfolio workers faced some of their greatest challenges in Nicaragua, both at the highest levels of government negotiations during the fighting and at the grassroots at the end of the Contra war. Defining their roles at both levels required discernment and advice from local partners and the MCC team. While not all Peace Portfolio assignments concerned conflict mediation, these two examples illustrate many of the challenges faced by all personnel. The first example involves high-level negotiations between the Miskito Indians of the Atlantic Coast and the Nicaraguan national government; the second involves the role of local peace commissions in southeast Nicaragua in mediating between Contra forces and the Sandinista Army and government.

Beginning in 1982, leaders of the Moravian church and the evangelical alliance CEPAD initiated contact with high-level leaders from the Sandinista government and the Miskito Indians regarding the growing tensions on the East Coast of Nicaragua. They persistently pursued peace over the next few years, creating safe forums for leaders to meet in private settings outside of Nicaragua and, in time, being constituted as a Conciliation Commission. Eventually, MCC joined the efforts by providing financial resources and consultation.

As a regional trainer on conflict resolution and mediation, John Paul Lederach had traveled to Nicaragua on numerous occasions to give seminars and to meet with Nicaraguans involved in peacemaking activities. This work came at the invitation of the MCC Nicaragua program staff and their primary partners—two Mennonite church conferences and CEPAD.

Through these initial contacts, Lederach became aware of the ongoing peace efforts between the East Coast indigenous groups and the Sandinista government. CEPAD leader Gustavo Parajón and Moravian church leaders Andy Shogreen and Norman Bent were pivotal in making these talks effective. Not only was Parajón the director of an organization with programs throughout the country, but he was also a member of the National Reconciliation Commission, established according to the Escuipulas II Peace Accord. Bent and Shogreen were Nicaraguans from the Moravian church, the most influential church among the indigenous peoples of the East Coast. Lederach expressed an interest in supporting the peacemaking efforts and was eventually invited to join the Conciliation Commission as the only non-Nicaraguan member. In the end, the team mediated three significant sets of talks in 1987–1988 among East Coast indigenous groups, led by Brooklyn Rivera, and a government delegation, led by Minister of the Interior Tomas Borge.[2]

Lederach provided several critical elements needed on the conciliation team: a thorough knowledge of conflict resolution strategies, the ability to cross borders easily between Nicaragua and his home base in Costa Rica, and the willingness to devote significant time and energy in support of the process. Many Contra and East Coast indigenous leaders were living in exile in Costa Rica and could not travel to Nicaragua. Likewise, the flood of Nicaraguan refugees had led the Costa Rican government to tighten its border, making it difficult for Nicaraguan political leaders or peacemakers to pass freely into Costa Rica for negotiations. Indeed, much of Lederach's energy focused on the logistics of making meetings possible—preparing exit visas, receiving and delivering documents, purchasing tickets, and setting up meeting sites. Through these more mundane tasks, he gained trust with each party and increased his credibility in making things happen.

Members of the Conciliation Commission committed enormous time and energy to negotiating with each party simply to get them to come together face to face. Their long-term relationships with the parties, their groundedness in the Nicaraguan experience, and their credibility as Christians committed to reconciliation created a space for true dialogue, which was absent in more public processes. While the three major mediations did not yield a final agreement, the basic framework and trust established created the basis for a later agreement facilitated by former U.S. president Jimmy Carter just prior to the Nicaraguan national election in 1989 (Pilarte, 1989).

Lederach's expertise in conflict resolution proved invaluable as the Conciliation Commission planned the mediation sessions. Simple matters of where to meet, what agenda to discuss, and who would attend all had serious implications. While the other commission members provided the long-standing trusting relationships that crossed political boundaries, Lederach provided expertise that helped maintain integrity in the process. At times, for example, the Conciliation Commission had to discern when to continue talks and when to separate the parties, as the atmosphere became tense and tempers rose.

The other major role in promoting peace at this high level involved finances. MCC, CEPAD, and the Moravian church drew on connections to international funding sources to cover all the costs of the mediation sessions. As Christian organizations, these groups could request funds without the taint of political favoritism. In a country facing extreme economic difficulties, the financing of airfares, meals, and lodging proved to be a significant contribution to the peace process. As we will see, this was also true for grassroots peacemaking efforts among the local peace commissions, the second example of the Peace Portfolio Project in Nicaragua.

The Nueva Guinea peace commissions played a major peacemaking role in this conflicted area of southeastern Nicaragua (region 5), simultaneously paralleling high-level peacemaking efforts. The first commission formed on its own, prior to the signing of the Escuipulas II agreement in 1987. Catholic and evangelical clergy and lay leaders came together to respond to the violence and suffering resulting from the Contra war. The first commission began with a mission to create an opening for dialogue. In October 1988, twenty-two members traveled into the hills for five days, seeking out the Southern Front of the Nicaraguan Resistance—the Contras—in order to engage them as fellow human beings, loved by God. They traveled unarmed, preaching reconciliation. When they eventually came across a group of Contras in El Jícaro, three commanding officers accused them of being Sandinista spies worthy of execution. They talked with their accusers in a small Catholic chapel from two o'clock in the afternoon until the early morning hours. Their message was unapologetically Christian, and they felt they gained their credibility through the church's legitimate identity as a respecter of all life. It was their faith, not techniques, that provided the inroads and that sustained them over time (Jeffrey, 1989).

The emerging vision from this first commission was to stand between the Contras and Sandinistas, to create a space where dialogue could take place. By 1989 there were thirty-three local commissions operating in this remote area of Nicaragua, many in areas under the control of Contra forces. Commission members included illiterate peasant farmers, former Contras, clergy, and lay church leaders. Their coming from the most common walks of life in the area increased their effectiveness. They knew the people, the issues, and the adversities of life, all factors that helped them establish credibility.

The commissions developed an effective organizational structure. A Zonal Commission in Nueva Guinea served as the hub to the many grassroots commissions. Headed by Antonio Vivas, a Central American mission pastor, the Zonal Commission included a private farmer, a Catholic priest, a Delegate of the Word, a Red Cross representative, and Arcenio Castellón, the CEPAD local director. The Zonal Commission related to a regional commission, based in Juigalpa, which provided the necessary connections to the National Reconciliation Commission, Managua, and the national scene.

In the 1989 annual report, the Nueva Guinea Zonal Peace Commission cited nine major activities (Zonal Peace Commission, 1990). These activities represented six distinct peacemaking functions.

*Information network.* Given the lack of telephone communication and a highly polarized media, the two-way information network created by the Zonal Peace Commission was vital to communication among Nueva Guinea, Juigalpa, and Managua.

*Assemblies and public forums.* Semiannual peace commission assemblies and public gatherings provided unique nonpartisan forums for education, dialogue, and communicating breakthroughs in negotiations.

*Human rights work.* The commissions investigated alleged human rights violations, traveling to the site of the incident, where they would interview the various parties, search for evidence, and then summarize their findings in a written report. A similar process took place if someone was reportedly being jailed without just cause. The commissions facilitated safe-conduct passes for Contras seeking amnesty and helped reintegrate the soldiers into civilian life. By 1990, local commissions had facilitated the amnesty of more than 150 Contras.

*Consolation and pastoral care.* The majority of commission members were Catholic or Protestant clergy or lay leaders. They would listen for extended periods to people who had experienced loss, acknowledging the atrocities of war and conveying some sense of public outrage over the human loss. Commission members would normally pray and read Scriptures before leaving such a situation.

*Voice for those without a voice.* The commission members also heard petitions from displaced families needing shelter or food, received complaints about government neglect or injustices, and recorded human rights violations. They then channeled the concerns to the appropriate body.

*Mediation and negotiation.* Many comandantes of the Southern Front felt left out of the peace process, which focused primarily on the larger Contra forces in northern Nicaragua. They were distrustful of any agreements, and in general refused to be "bought off by some demobilization scheme" (Halcon, 1990, p. 1). The Zonal Peace Commission provided shuttle diplomacy between comandantes and government officials. The commission would obtain authorization from the Sandinista Army to enter a particular conflictive area on a given day. In the preceding hours, the army would withdraw from that area to allow the Contra force to come down from the mountains as planned. The commission would travel to the area, hold talks, and, upon returning, provide a detailed report to the Sandinista Army and political leaders. This process provided reliable communication between the warring parties, as well as the perspective of a third party. It helped establish sufficient trust and confidence in the region for national elections and demobilization of the Contras. Even after the Sandinista defeat in the February 1990 elections, these negotiations continued as leaders of the Southern Front felt abandoned by leaders of the Northern Front and equally distrustful of newly elected President Violeta Chamorro.

Sometimes this mediation role occurred by happenstance. Traveling at dusk to Juigalpa on March 15, 1990, Contra Comandante Aguila and his troops confronted the Zonal Peace Commission as it attempted to cross the Rama River. Fortunately, the comandante recognized a Peace Commission member and prevented the normal looting that took place in such after-dark encounters. After an informal exchange of the latest information, the Contra forces allowed the Peace Commission to proceed toward Juigalpa. Less than a kilometer later, the commission encountered a squadron of the Sandinista army traveling toward the same bridge where the Contras were located. Over the next hour, the Peace Commission was able to convince the army squadron to not proceed until the commission was able to persuade the Contras to back away from the bridge. In the end, they saved many lives by averting a battle between two military leaders highly sought after by the opposing sides.

## Role of the MCC Peace Portfolio Worker

I had the unique opportunity to work alongside members of local peace commissions who were risking their lives to forge real peace in a country divided by war. While others witnessed the signing of peace accords orchestrated by the United Nations in capital cities, I walked alongside those who made peace a reality in the very communities most affected by the war. Concrete talks were taking place about what disarming and demobilizing the Southern Front of the Nicaraguan Resistance would mean in practical terms for Contra soldiers, their families, and the surrounding population.

Sitting outside the Juigalpa Municipal Building on a warm March evening in 1990, I felt it a privilege to be present at such a historic time in Nicaragua. This dusty city had doubled in population due to the Contra war, as rural farmers from across southeastern Nicaragua moved to the interior to avoid the violence. Now, after the Escuipulas II Peace Accords and several optimistic talks between the Contra leaders and the Nicaraguan government, the end of the war seemed more than just a dream.

As the sun went down, I was pleased to accompany members of the Nueva Guinea Zonal Peace Commission, who had requested an emergency meeting with regional leaders of the newly elected government and the army. In order for the Southern Front of the Contra forces to disarm, clear assurances needed to be granted soon. The Zonal Peace Commission had just traveled into the mountains to meet with Contra comandante Frijol. From this meeting, it was clear that the lack of reliable communication, coupled with purposeful disinformation campaigns, was creating enough uncertainty among the more than 5,000 Contras that they had no intention of disarming. The Zonal Peace Commission created bridges among the various parties to make disarmament promises a reality.

As privileged as I felt, however, I also was keenly aware that I was sitting outside the municipal building on the steps, while the important discussion took place inside. I asked myself if this was why I had moved my family from Costa Rica—so that I could sit outside important meetings. Part of me recognized the rightness of a U.S. citizen not being allowed into such a delicate discussion. But, at the same time, I wanted a greater role. I wanted to be able to say I was there and maybe even that I was crucial in the peacemaking process that was unfolding in 1990. I was not satisfied being on the outside; I felt powerless and insignificant.

Much like Lederach at the high-level negotiations, my role was primarily to support the Nicaraguan peacemakers. Members of the Zonal Commission did not have formal training in conflict resolution and mediation. My expertise in conflict transformation skills and methods complemented their expertise on the region. They were the decision makers and key facilitators of the process.

At the request of the Zonal Commission, I offered training in conflict resolution and mediation to members of the Zonal Commission and local commissions in Nueva Guinea. This training provided experienced peacemakers the opportunity to sit back and reflect on their work. Working from their own case studies, I was amazed at the similarities in their methodologies with those advocated by North American mediators. Beyond specific skills, participants also provided in-depth reflections on the challenges of being mediators in a highly polarized conflict. This, too, echoed some of the state-of-the-art discussions taking place internationally. The training affirmed them and their home-grown approach.

Beyond training, my involvement pertained to accompaniment, a concept promoted throughout the region by the Mennonite Central Committee. To accompany, or walk alongside, our Central American brothers and sisters meant to support them while not taking over or playing too large a role as an outsider. The intensive orientation that all MCC personnel go through stressed this concept over and over again. It was based on a theology of presence. Accordingly, one serves by being present with those who are to be served, by sitting where they sit, and by experiencing firsthand what they have experienced. Only then is one able to minister, which takes the form of support and the encouragement of a collective response by those suffering. This type of role requires discipline, patience, and an inner conviction that if we have done our job well, we will not receive credit. Indeed, those involved will say they did it themselves. While I believed this, I struggled within, not knowing whether I was actually contributing or simply tagging along. I easily learned as much as I offered, another expectation instilled by MCC orientation, but this only added to my inner questions.

A major part of this accompaniment involved observing, listening, and reflecting. When I was present in significant encounters, I seldom spoke. My role as an observer served the commission members, who would later turn to me during our debriefing sessions. Without leadership responsibilities, I could focus on listening. My perspective as a specialist in conflict transformation, as someone outside the culture, also offered a vantage point they did not have.

Walking on footpaths for several hours one afternoon following a meeting with a comandante in the mountains, I offered my observations of the formal meeting. While Peace Commission members had concentrated on the content of the dialogue, my observations focused as much on the process. I reflected on the implicit messages being conveyed through the encounter and the emotional pulse of the Contra forces. I also reported on separate conversations I had initiated with lower-ranking soldiers on the periphery of the meeting. These conversations provided at least a sample of views of the common soldiers, to see, for example, if they were as committed to maintaining the armed struggle as their commanding officer reported.

Another aspect to accompaniment involved offering moral support to Peace Commission members. Their work was exhausting, involved personal risks and sacrifices, and yielded too few success stories. Commission members were frequently accused of being partial or of actually acting on behalf of one side in the conflict. They needed a safe space to express their own doubts, frustrations, and fatigue. While I experienced and felt many of the same frustrations, I became an outlet for them to vent and a source of support.

I spent the greatest percentage of my time with the commissions in planning and debriefing sessions. These sessions followed a patterned format. The session began with the commission members reporting on the latest news, rumors, and requests they had received. This provided the sociopolitical context, or *coyuntura*. Following this debriefing, someone would lead the group in biblical reflection and prayer. The texts flowed from, and interacted with, the context that had just been set. The Bible study and prayer informed the group as it created an agenda and set the priorities for what needed to be addressed. In these settings, I felt like a team member, equally sharing my thoughts and observations. While it was always clear that they were the decision makers, I freely offered suggestions or asked questions that might eventually be drawn upon in the final decision. My assistance took the form of helping to prepare the agenda for meetings and in suggesting a series of "what ifs" that needed to be considered.

Such a low-key role departed markedly from my previous leadership roles in North America. Journaling on March 29, 1990, I questioned what my purpose was in being in Nicaragua. I arrived at three goals: "to learn from the peace process; [to] communicate to North Americans the role of the peace commissions; and to support the commissions in their work, through helping with logistics, training on mediation, and assisting the planning and evaluation process." I needed to somehow guard against asserting myself for personal gain (Chupp, 1990). To make sure I was being accountable to my limited role in a foreign culture, I wrote the following cautions in this same journal entry:

1. Wait for an opportune time to share my observations, agenda suggestions, etc.
2. If I do speak in meetings, it is better not to share it as a personal concern, but rather as something I see that flows from the group.
3. Do not wait forever, take initiative, but do it as an offer and wait for them to pick up on it.
4. Always give credit and allegiance to the commission leaders and CEPAD personnel, and in that order.
5. Come prepared and ready to share something that I feel they could use.
6. Do not try to interpret the political situation—they understand it better.
7. Share from my cultural experience, not as if I were a Nicaraguan. (Chupp, 1990)

I referred to these points in the following months. Gradually, I realized my presence alone was a sustaining force for commission members. I did not need to prove myself. I began to accept my role as standing with those who stood between enemies.

Lederach also faced challenges related to the accompaniment role in the high-level negotiations. He provided critical support to the Nicaraguans who were the primary mediators, even while being confounded by his role. Lederach spent countless hours facilitating communication, working on logistics, and holding loose ends together prior to face-to-face meetings. At the same time, he often felt powerless and out of the loop as a foreigner who was not a primary mediator nor formally affiliated with one of the powerful players in the conflict. Writing in a report to MCC, Lederach reflected on a meeting in which he felt he had perhaps pushed too hard, "We are always at the edge with both sides, pushing in order to understand better and to get clarity and flexibility" (Lederach, 1987, p. 3). Being on the edge made Lederach's role so vital as a process consultant but also made it most difficult.

In addition to supporting the accompaniment role, MCC also provided direct financial support to the work. As was true with the high-level negotiations, MCC provided food, material aid, financial contributions, and supplies to CEPAD and other nongovernmental organizations. This support helped make possible the work of the peace commissions, which relied in part on this support to function. Since these shipments came through indirect channels, recipients seldom made the connection to MCC, which was the way MCC would have it—to be supportive behind the scenes. Some outsiders were critical of material aid distributed through local peace commissions, feeling it provided an improper motivation for members to be involved. But without this type of support, physical constraints would have hamstrung the peace efforts even further.

## Challenges and Dilemmas

Peace Portfolio workers brought a variety of peacemaking skills to their diverse assignments. The insights they gained, however, were similar across time, position, and geography. Drawing on the range of Nicaraguan experiences, here are some of the major challenges and dilemmas faced:

1. Being a peacemaker requires standing in the middle, a vulnerable position where attacks to your credibility can come from all sides. My identity and allegiances became a topic of discussion as we engaged in an important negotiation with a Contra comandante. Traveling with three regional peace commission members to a remote border crossing over the San Juan River into Costa Rica, I was not prepared for the grilling given me by José Guerrero, also known as Comandante Navegante, chief of the High Command of the Southern Front of the Nicaraguan Resistance. He singled me out, took me aside to answer his questions one on one. In his barrage of questions, he asked who I had voted for in past elections, my position on U.S. aid to the Contras, and my political party affiliation. Fearing how he would respond to my liberal leanings, I concentrated on his questions about my personal upbringing, highlighting my affiliation with the Mennonite church. I also tied my identity to MCC and CEPAD, groups known for providing nonpartisan support in the name of Christ to those in need. While I wanted to focus on my role as a mediator and as a representative of the MCC Peace Portfolio, the comandante insisted on direct answers to his personal questions. I returned to the hotel room convinced I had jeopardized our mission.

In recounting the experience to the other members of the team, they shared their own discomfort from similar experiences. They were frequently accused by both sides of being aligned with the other side. Rather than feeling singled out, I realized I was now initiated. I had gone through the same personal challenge that all of the peace commission members had faced as they began their work.

Being neutral in a polarized setting is not possible. I also recognized that part of my discomfort came from being singled out, having to stand alone, apart from the community in which my identity is enveloped. My responses were both an attempt to avoid giving Comandante Navegante personal answers he did not want to hear and an attempt to place my identity in the context of my faith community and trusted friends in the Zonal Commission.

2. Out of my desire not to lead but to support the front-line peacemakers, local partners were not always aware of my strengths and what I could contribute. While we related as friends, I was never convinced the commission members knew my leadership strengths and expertise as a mediator. Playing the support role requires a different type of assertiveness than that of a leader. I was accustomed to being in a more central role as a trainer and mediator.

Even in offering training, I chose an elicitive approach, where the participants reflected on their own indigenous styles of managing conflict. While I affirmed them for the effective methods they had developed, it diminished my image as an expert. I avoided presenting lengthy discourses on conflict theory and elaborate models of conflict resolution. The advantage of this approach, of course, is that it reinforces their leadership and abilities. In the end, however, I wonder whether they would have benefited from my own experiences and knowledge, which I never adequately shared.

A few years later, I had the opportunity to work with the Programa de Capacitación y Apoyo para las Comisiones Municipales de Reconstrucción (PROCAP), a comprehensive peacemaking program in postwar El Salvador. There, I served as lead trainer to a group of Salvadorans, who then critiqued the training before adapting it, as they prepared to train community leaders. Under this model, I felt the freedom to exercise more leadership and to draw upon my hard-won experiences in the United States, Nicaragua, and other countries. I combined the elicitive approach with a participatory learning approach from the Quaker Alternatives to Violence Project.[3] This appeared to strike a better balance.

3. Being a foreigner, especially a U.S. citizen, inevitably comes with a special status, at times leading to exclusion and at times leading to inclusion. While my U.S. citizenship put me outside on the steps during some key negotiation sessions, at other times it put me on center stage. I sometimes felt that my foreign status was used as a drawing card to increase the appeal of an event. In the assemblies of all the local commissions, I was asked to join other presenters seated on the stage. My presentation was usually brief, but it seemingly served to signal to the participants that this was a special event. I was uncomfortable with both special inclusion and exclusion. Ideally, I thought, I should become one of the people, and then I would not receive any special treatment. In reality, however, I recognize that my special treatment was precisely because I had a unique contribution to make.

In the case of the high-level negotiations between the East Coast Indian groups and the Nicaraguan government, Lederach was the only member of the Conciliation Commission not allowed to sit at the table. While physically in the room, he literally sat behind a curtain, where he could hear the proceedings but not see or influence them. While understanding the purpose of such decisions, the inner struggle to know one's role and limitations is at times confusing. After working for years at fitting in and adapting to a foreign culture, there is real disappointment in recognizing that, at a certain level, you will always be an outsider. For many Mennonites, this is especially difficult as we have intentionally downplayed the power and status that comes with being a U.S. citizen. Opting for a different type of power, we are satisfied by empowering others. To be excluded, then, reminds one all over again that you are still a U.S. citizen, a fact that cannot be denied or dismissed as irrelevant.

Not being from the culture but living and breathing it so intensely did provide key advantages. We were able to see things from a different vantage point. We could recognize certain cultural styles and methodologies for resolving conflict, which were assumed and therefore not within the conscious awareness of those from Nicaragua. Being an informed and trusted outsider with a thorough knowledge of mediation and other conflict resolution strategies did enable a significant contribution, albeit all informal one.

4. Having the ability to leave a situation separates you from others who stand in the middle. My commitment to the peacemaking effort in Nicaragua was 100 percent while I was there. At the same time, I had choices available to me and relationships beyond Nicaragua that meant I would not be there over the long haul. Looking back, I realize that most Nicaraguans were grateful for the contribution I and other internationals made and willingly invested in the relationship, knowing it might yield few returns before we left.

At a much deeper level, the ability to leave means the risks I take and the dangers I encounter are always lessened by the possibility of pulling up stakes. For the Nicaraguan peacemakers, any threats to their safety or future security might mean major life changes, long-term disruption, or death. For John Paul Lederach, threats to his family in Costa Rica resulted in a major upheaval in the family, but it was a turmoil that was largely eliminated when they moved back to the United States. For my family, the prolonged intestinal infection that threatened the health of my one-year-old son frightened all of us. But, when we moved back to Costa Rica to receive specialized medical care, the threat diminished rather quickly. I will never forget Antonio Vivas' words to me when I reported our decision to leave Juigalpa for the sake of my son. He said:

> You are fortunate. Many of our people can only pray that God will work a miracle when faced with such a sick child. They are forced to wait in the absence of medical care. Your choice to leave the commission is a hard one, but be thankful you have a choice. May God be with you. (Vivas, 1990)

5. A major dilemma for both the high-level Conciliation Commission and the Nueva Guinea peace commissions pertained to the relative lack of international status held by the members. We did not enjoy the same access and ease of mobility characteristic of better-known international mediators. At the same time, the Nicaraguans' long-term commitment as residents provided them an edge that high-profile mediators from a distance are not able to maintain. Being fluent in Spanish and living in the region, we could understand many of the nuances of the conflict. Unlike outsiders who came for short stays, we enjoyed on-the-ground support from our faith communities. This became critical for the future of the work, as members received death

threats and suffered physical violence as a result of their peacemaking efforts. Lederach and I relied heavily on being able to process our involvement back in Managua with other members of the MCC team.


## Conflict Transformation

My work with the Nicaraguan peace commissions transformed my view of conflict mediation. I learned that neutrality is rarely possible and often not desirable in mediation. The local commissions were effective because their members were known, not because they were outside neutrals. Their legitimacy rested on the identity of the Christian church as a nonpartisan institution engaged in promoting peace based on the value of all life as sacred. The fact that they had diverse theologies and political leanings collectively provided credibility with Contras, Sandinistas, and rural farmers. The peace commission members demonstrated their consistent respect for all people by making great personal sacrifices to help those caught up in violence.

Beyond mediation, conflict transformation involves creating space for dialogue to take place. At times, this means standing beside one party as an advocate for its rights. At other times, it means speaking out and asserting a position that you know might not be popular. Building trusting relationships with all parties is essential to creating the space where conflict can be transformed. As the trust is established and the space opens, the peacemaker is able to serve as a bridge between enemies. The power of mediation techniques is only realized when trust and space are established. What occurs outside the formal process is as important to peace as the mediation session itself.

Conflict transformation is fundamentally a spiritual process. The peace commissions recognized this and were unapologetic about their faith in a higher power, a power they believed helped create a space between enemies. Their pastoral ways broke through where no one else had—among fellow Nicaraguans who had learned to hate each other enough to kill. The indigenous approach the commissions developed centered on creating a safe space for true dialogue to take place. From the start, they trusted in God to lead and protect them. They drew on their faith and familiarity with the region to make connections and establish their credibility. Community members and potential new peace commission members responded by trusting in the commissions, thereby opening up a small space for dialogue in polarized communities filled with fear and intimidation. This led to links with the primary players in the conflict who became receptive to the peace commissions' efforts. As trust grew, the peace commissions created a space for dialogue between the warring parties themselves. In so doing, the commissioners were always guided by spiritual resources, such as prayer and the Bible, which transcended the limited perspectives of those caught up in the conflict. They became brokers of trust, where the space they created provided an arena for the Contra leaders and Sandinistas—and the rest of the polarized population—to see each other again as human beings.

International peacemakers can best develop effective roles through this trust-building process. Zooming in from the outside for a short intervention produces limited results. The MCC Peace Portfolio proved to be effective because of its close relationships with local partners and the on-the-ground presence of its workers. There is no substitute for knowing the language and culture. Even with this knowledge, however, international workers are most effective when working in partnership with local peacemakers. After all, the local peacemakers understand best the problems, needs, and long-term implications of any proposed solutions.

At times, mediation is not enough. It is, at best, one of many tools employed by the peacemaker. Advocacy, pastoral care, education, social action, and community development all have a place alongside negotiation and mediation.[4] The local peace commissions were more than mediators. They were peacemakers who continuously analyzed the situations they faced to determine the appropriate response at the moment.

But beyond the changes in my views of mediation, my experience led to a much deeper transformation of who I am and what I believe. The professionalization of U.S. society so often deemphasizes the importance of community and trusting relationships. For peacemakers to move beyond the settlement of specific disputes to the transformation of conflict, we must address the spiritual, relational, material, and emotional needs of those in conflict. I experienced a transformation as I witnessed grassroots peacemakers facilitate this holistic process. The members of these local peace commissions had little formal training and relatively little power. Together as a collective force, however, they were able to intervene from a spiritual center that penetrated the walls created by war. My own strength as a peacemaker in Nicaragna depended less on my technical skills and more on my own spiritual well-being and the support network I had developed with the MCC team and peace commission members.

Transforming conflict requires work at multiple levels but often begins at a personal, inner one. One person makes a shift and it has a ripple effect. As one person makes the shift, the context changes and other like-minded people join together to form a new space in the middle. A few brave individuals affected by the war in southeastern Nicaragua took the first step to say "enough." They joined together to form the first peace commission, committed to not simply dying passively as the war consumed more and more of their communities. This inner shift among the first commission members created a space for peace, where others soon entrusted these peacemakers to engage those directly involved in the conflict.

The conflict is further transformed as the parties in conflict begin to recognize the presence of a third party, often with one side taking the first step to build trust with the peacemakers. The peacemakers' challenge then is to establish trust with the other side before being discredited as aligned with the enemy. In reality, this challenge persists throughout the peacebuilding process. The peace commissions were constantly accused of serving the interests of one side or the other. This was also true in the high-level negotiations. The mediators were accused of being Sandinistas and, therefore, of being aligned with the Nicaraguan government.

The space in the middle provides new opportunities for those in conflict to experience a taste of peace. As they encounter the peacemakers they begin to know again the power of trust, respect, integrity, and nonviolence. Gradually, the trust in the peacemakers creates the possibility for each side to trust the other enough to engage in dialogue. At first the trust is weak and only permits communication through the third party, but eventually it can lead to direct dialogue—an implied if not explicit recognition of the other. Recognition and true dialogue are often the prerequisites to working toward an agreement. When an actual agreement is then reached, it symbolizes a more profound shift that has already taken place.

Yet trust will not be sustained and the space for peace will close up again if the transformation of the conflict does not include changing the structures and systems that contributed to the creation of the conflict. Building peace is a process that often requires a length of time to reach sustainable peace that is comparable to the period of time it took for the conflict to develop. A cease fire and even disarmament represent critical steps toward long-term peace but must be followed by peacebuilding steps that restore relationships, bring healing and forgiveness, and ultimately, establish a more equitable and just society (Lederach, 1997).

The MCC Peace Portfolio participated in a peacemaking process at a critical time in Central America. The transformation process was not complete in Nicaragua, as numerous former Contras rearmed and other paramilitary groups emerged in the early 1990s. Not all previous agreements were fulfilled, suspicion and mistrust continued, and violence even continued to break out from time to time. The peace commissions continued to work at maintaining a space for building a sustainable peace. At their 1994 annual assembly, more than 200 commission members met in Nueva Guinea. Their roster included the listing of eighty-five commissions in the Nueva Guinea and El Rama zones. MCC continued to place workers throughout the country and Central America and to channel resources to the people of Central America.

Creating space for peace is a process best achieved through close collaboration between those in the midst of the conflict and those committed to peace from the outside. The Nicaraguan peacemakers illustrate the knowledge and credibility that comes with being insiders familiar with and affected by the conflict. MCC and its Peace Portfolio Project represent a small testimony to the resources, expertise, and support that outsiders can bring as they commit to following the lead of their indigenous partners. While violence begets violence, creating space for peace also involves a chain reaction, one that appears to be spiraling forward in Nicaragua.

## Eight

### Building Peace from Below and Inside
### *The Mennonite Experience in Colombia*

RICARDO ESQUIVIA
WITH PAUL STUCKY

From the beginning, I have lived and suffered with the conflict in which my country, Colombia, has been immersed, and I have participated in and contributed to the development of the course of action of the Mennonite church in this situation of social upheaval. What follows is a description of the evolution of the active response of the Colombian Mennonite church in the ongoing conflict.

### Providing Refuge and Support in the Midst of Violence

To understand the situation, let us go back to 1956 in Cachipay, Cundinamarca, Colombia. For nine years, from 1947, the General Conference Mennonite Church of the United States and the American Leprosy Mission had been operating a boarding grade school as a support to the healthy children of people with leprosy. This was a project of missionaries from the United States who had moved to this community and settled there with their families.

People with leprosy had been abandoned by a society and by a state that, at that time, had the belief that this was a contagious disease against which society had to be defended. For this reason, the sick were taken, often by force, to a quarantined community called Agua de Dios (Water of God), located approximately three hours' drive west of Bogotá. The children were separated from their families and placed in a state-operated boarding school called Nazaret under miserable conditions.

This was an era in Colombia when the period now known as *la violencia* (the violence), which had begun in 1948, was in full swing. Society had plunged into terror and cruelty. It marked the beginning of a process in which the dominant economic groups, in their struggle for hegemony, began to use the traditional political parties, Liberal and Conservative, to take over the state and use it as a weapon in their struggle. They began to use civil society as a means to carry out their fight, leading to civilians both committing atrocities and being victims of atrocities.

The Catholic church, by far the largest in Colombia, was not exempt from this fight. The Catholic church and the Conservative Party were traditional allies, while the Protestants, a small minority, tended to sympathize with the Liberal Party. The government was Conservative. So it followed that the government and the Catholic church persecuted the Protestants. Pastors and their families were murdered, church buildings were destroyed, and whole families were displaced from their homes as they fled persecution. The state prohibited public schools from accepting children who were not Catholic, and the dead body of a Protestant was not allowed burial in the public cemetery, which was in the hands of the Catholic church.

This situation posed a dilemma for the nascent Mennonite church. Faced with political and religious persecution by the government and the Catholic church, should members highlight their particular Anabaptist identity and commitment to justice and peace? In doing so, they risked friction with and division from their Protestant brothers and sisters of evangelical orientation, who shunned critical political action. Or, should they downplay these distinctions for the sake of unity and a common Protestant front to face the onslaught? They opted for the latter, which was also more consistent with the theological formation of the missionary founders and early leaders of the Mennonite church.

The political violence and religious persecution were aggravated by other forms of violence, which manifested in a high rate of illiteracy, vast numbers of impoverished people without land because of inequitable distribution, and strong discrimination against the black and indigenous communities.

In this context, the boarding school founded by the Mennonites was a haven not only for the healthy children of parents with leprosy but also for the children of Protestant victims of this religious persecution. In this context and growing out of this act of service, the Colombian Mennonite church had its beginning. And it was in this context, in 1956, that I arrived at the Mennonite boarding school in Cachipay, a child rejected by society for being the son of a father with leprosy and additionally discriminated against for being black and poor.

How to respond to embedded and generalized violence was a dilemma for a church led by North American foreigners, whose theological, cultural, and political development did not orient them toward identifying and taking action to address the social causes and forces that fueled this situation. The boarding school was an initial response, through service, to the institutionalized violence against the victims of leprosy and to the political and military violence against Protestants. The Mennonites also initiated health services for the community surrounding the boarding school and started a small project whereby people could acquire housing. They chose to offer refuge and support to the victims of the different forms of violence and to provide them an education based on values of love, solidarity, and fraternity. But, at that point, the root social causes of injustice and their expression were not confronted.

In that period and environment, I met and formed relationships based on a foundation of shared faith and values with many who have become part of a broad community of support for a lifelong work, including Gerald and Mary Hope Stucky, two of the missionary founders of the Mennonite presence in Colombia; Judy, Peter, Paul, and Tim Stucky, their children; Luis Correa and José Chuquín, among many others.

As the children at Cachipay finished grade school and moved to different regions, some of us moved to Bogotá, the capital of the country. With the passing of time, local Mennonite churches were established in nearby towns and in Bogotá.

## Searching for New Responses in a Changing Situation

Following the success of a new treatment for leprosy, the state determined in the early 1960s that it was no longer necessary to isolate those with leprosy. The leprosy colony was opened up, children were permitted to live with their parents once again, and by the mid-1960s, legal and formal discrimination was lifted against those with leprosy and their children. At about the same time, the two major political parties struck a deal to bring an end to the armed warfare between them. The direct and material persecution of the Protestants by the state and the Catholic church lessened. All this had a bearing on the boarding school's reasons for being, and it changed to a day school dedicated to serving the children of the surrounding area.

In spite of the formal changes, social discrimination continued against Protestants, those with leprosy, the poor, and the black and indigenous groups. The violence also changed form, but it remained quite alive and manifest in people's daily lives, poisoning the environment and being fed by the destruction of the values of solidarity and fraternity. "Street," or informal violence, to assert power and to settle all sorts of disputes began to vie with partisan violence for the most number of dead. And although the two major parties agreed to stop the fighting between them, the armed struggle of guerrilla groups with leftist orientations, initiated in the 1950s against the government, gained in strength. The strongest among them was the Revolutionary Armed Forces of Colombia (FARC). Other groups also emerged, including the National Liberation Army (ELN), inspired by the Cuban model.

The proportion of dead from street violence increased over time. By the 1960s, the ratio of murders from street violence to murders from partisan, ideological violence was estimated at fifty-fifty. In the 1990s, an estimated 90 percent of violent deaths were the result of street violence, and only 10 percent were due to drug traffic and struggles for political power.

In the early 1960s, I moved from Cachipay to Bogotá to continue my studies. There, I participated in the founding of two new Mennonite congregations in the city. The vision and theology that oriented the Mennonite church at that time was evangelical, tended toward a separation from political structures and processes, and viewed with distrust anything that appeared as political activism. There was a lack of critical political analysis. The response continued to be one of service, of providing assistance, and was framed within the dilemma of whether to address social conflict and social ills by building a community apart or by direct insertion and action upon that reality.

In effect, the Mennonite church was caught short in its ability to respond to this new reality. Of the young people who had been educated in the values of solidarity and fraternity, some took refuge in a theology of noncritical obedience to the power of the state and an individualistic salvation removed from societal problems, since at that time there were no seminaries in Colombia offering a different vision. Some left the church and dedicated themselves to seeking private economic solutions for themselves within the country, or they went to the United States, as the cultural orientation toward that country presented it as the dreamed-for utopia. Still others, myself among them, feeling confronted by the violent and conflictive social conditions but not finding within the church the tools for analysis and direct action, distanced ourselves from the church and were drawn into the social struggles of the time, which to a great extent were motivated by the revolutionary fervor emerging from Cuba.

Within the larger society, there were also difficulties with traditional postures. During this time, Father Camilo Torres emerged in the Catholic church, challenging the passivity and complicity of that church toward the social and political establishment and toward misery and poverty. He called for more direct action, opening the way for the theology of liberation and with it, for many, for just war. I met and was much impressed by Torres, and I joined with other students in community work with him.

The Cuban Revolution had recently triumphed and begun to impregnate Latin America with its vision. It was a time when Che Guevara fought in Bolivia, the Tupamaros in Uruguay, the MIR in Chile, and the ELN in Colombia. Torres subsequently joined the ELN and was killed. At the same time, the government of the United States went to war in Vietnam. All of this stirring began to touch the Mennonite church in Colombia, in the rest of Latin America, and in the United States, since the church is in society and is affected by what happens in society.

## Turning to the Anabaptist Vision and Example

In time, the exuberance and triumphalism of the armed revolutions of the 1960s were beaten into disillusionment by the brutal military repression of the state establishments. Dictatorships emerged in Brazil, Argentina, Uruguay, and Peru; and in Chile the dream that grew with Allende was smashed by one of the bloodiest military repressions in Latin America.

Our nation and continent were pressed and impressed by the violent social situation. Little by little, groups and leaders were destroyed, victims of the dialectics of war, the very strategy they had chosen. Violent revolutionary action inflamed and justified the repressive reaction of governments, and war that was waged in defense of the human rights and liberties of the people in the end destroyed those rights.

Within this social and ecclesiastical impasse, the Colombian Mennonite church began to turn to the vision of our forerunners, the small group of Anabaptists of the sixteenth century, who also lived in a time of social change and violence. Those Anabaptists' return to the roots of the Gospel and to living consistently with the message of Jesus had led to their being attacked by the Catholic church, by the state, and by most leaders of the Protestant Reformation. Anabaptists were committed to the evangelical meekness of Jesus, to living out a call to faithfulness and responsibility in which the individual's basic rights and beliefs—the antecedents of what today are understood as fundamental human rights, duties, and freedoms—were upheld over and above the concerns of the state. It was a way of life that affirmed a community process, rather than an individualistic one, and a way in which nonviolence was both a means and an end. This Anabaptist vision provided an alternative to a theology that justified the necessity of violence, which in Colombia has been, for many, liberation theology.

In the 1970s, the revolutionary fervor, change, new ideas, concerns, and awakening in Colombia found their complement in the ideas and initiatives of missionaries from North America, who were interested in recovering their Anabaptist roots. The North Americans who came to Colombia had had to face the Vietnam War and the draft, and they had been drinking from the wells of both new ideas and the history of Anabaptism. They encountered some fellow church members in Colombia who were thinking and living similarly.

These missionaries and Colombians began to take steps to contextualize the actions of the church and to situate them in their social reality. They held seminars on Anabaptism, wrote articles, and made efforts to recover Anabaptist history. Although Mennonite congregations continued to be places of encounter and fraternity, for the most part people in the church were neither employing nor seeking an analysis that would promote social and political transformation. A service orientation without a political vision still prevailed. Yet, even without a clear understanding of the link between economic disparity and violence, there was growing recognition of the need for economic solutions for people.

Emerging out of this broadening vision of service, the Colombian Mennonite Foundation for Development (MENCOLDES) was created, funded by the Mennonite Central Committee (MCC) and the Mennonite Economic Development Association (MEDA). MENCOLDES initially focused on promoting economic development through individual initiatives. As it began to acquire a sociopolitical vision, however, MENCOLDES began to experience rejection from the church. Its personnel also isolated themselves, resulting in a largely nominal relationship between MENCOLDES and the rest of the Mennonite church.

The underlying challenge thus became to find a vision and a focus of action that would not alienate and divide but rather strengthen the church's sense of identity and community. MENCOLDES found its way separately, largely independent of a faith community process. This led to MENCOLDES being isolated in its efforts and, for a time, to the church closing itself off from the option of direct action for social change. They were limited in their ability to light each other's way.

The dilemma could be viewed at several levels. On the one hand, there was the question of how to pursue a vision while maintaining dialogue with those who do not share it and being open to reconsidering this vision and action as a fruit of that dialogue. On the other hands, there was the question of how to respond to the urgency demanded by the context while keeping pace with the slower process of congregational discernment.


## Anabaptism as a Resource in the Latin American Context

The seeds of awakening began to germinate and bear fruit, and their Good News began to spread throughout Latin America. The Anabaptist vision was shared among Christians more broadly, and its implications for Latin America were explored. New needs were identified.

From the beginnings of the Mennonite way of addressing social conflict and social needs in Colombia, it had been necessary to merge and integrate influence from abroad with local approaches and priorities—fostering autonomy, respecting and integrating differences, and addressing the power imbalances implicit in partial control of the purse. When the missionaries first came, it was naturally they who determined the course and approach of action. MCC and MEDA were crucial, for example, in determining the initial direction of MENCOLDES.

But, by the late 1980s in the church, a different approach was prevailing, which brought together the needs, concerns, and visions of Latin Americans and North Americans. In persons like Peter Stucky, these came together. Born and reared in Colombia, the son of the original missionaries, he was at one and the same time a person from the North, who represented the new Anabaptist vision, and a Latin American, who was working on this vision in Latin America. The two sources came together in him. And because Stucky had roots and was known in both continents and cultures, the trust (*confianza*) in him built a bridge that linked South-North institutional efforts as well.

Peter Stucky and others in the church recognized the need for a place for people to study and to become formed in the Anabaptist vision; hence the need for a Mennonite seminary. Once the need was identified, it took eight years of gestation for the seminary to be founded in 1989.

At the same time, the Anabaptist interest and awakening were taking place not only in Colombia but in many countries of Latin America. There were many people seeking resources and orientation. Robert Suderman, a Canadian working in Bolivia under the Commission of Overseas Missions (COM) of the General Conference Mennonite Church, began to dream about the creation of a Latin American Anabaptist resource center. When COM circulated the proposal in Latin America, the Colombian Mennonite church immediately offered Colombia as the host country. Following a number of consultations, in November 1989, at a gathering of representatives of the Latin American Mennonite churches in Montevideo, Uruguay, the Latin American Center of Anabaptist Resources (CLARA) was born. Suderman was invited to head both the seminary and CLARA. He subsequently played a key role in the whole process of development of the work for peace of the Mennonite church in Colombia.

## Beginnings of Justapaz

In 1989, the same year that Robert Suderman arrived in Colombia, my wife, Patricia Zapata, our children, and I returned to Bogotá from San Jacinto, a town near the Atlantic Coast in northern Colombia, where we had been working since 1986 in the area of human rights, within the perspective of the Anabaptist vision. We arrived with the intention of working with the church in this same area.

Our work in San Jacinto had benefited from the support of MENCOLDES through Luis Correa, World Vision through José Chuquín, and the Mennonite church through Peter Stucky. The year 1989 brought us all together in Bogotá. It was evident that the *confianza* among us—all of whom had grown up at the Mennonite boarding school in Cachipay—opened doors and served as the cement to bind together the efforts of these institutions.

### Question of Focus

We were faced with a social situation of enormous proportions. The dilemma of whether to specialize and focus efforts in one area or to take a broader approach was to recur again and again. Resources were, and always have been, limited. Seeing much to do and having a broad vision of the work leads to taking on a lot but raises questions of quality, depth of work, and follow-up. In the Colombian culture of the poor, within which the Mennonite church is situated, a frequent solution is the "variety store," which sells a little bit of everything. It is a typical way that poor families get a business started, as there are usually not enough funds to set up a well-stocked specialty business.

What was evolving was a multifaceted presence of the church in the social conflict in Colombia. Initially, the church focused on service through education and economic development, together with study and reflection on the

Anabaptist dimensions of the Christian being. Now, reconciliation and education in nonviolence, conscientious objection to military service, and human rights began to be brought into the mix.

In 1989, we took up work in human rights and conscientious objection. I worked for human rights in Bogotá through World Vision and, supported by MENCOLDES, developed a theology of human rights and a critical sociopolitical vision more in keeping with Anabaptist theology.

We also decided to launch full scale into conscientious objection. Already in 1987, Peter Stucky had started work on this in Colombia and had done all he could to get an invitation for a Spanish lawyer to come to Colombia to speak about conscientious objection. He took the initiative to CEDEC (now CEDECOL), the Colombian Confederation of Evangelical Churches. While initially facing the aloneness of a pioneer, his effort initiated networking and the fostering of a community space wherein these initiatives could take form and evolve.

We took up the contacts Stucky had initiated, establishing a connection with a group called Movimiento por la Vida (Movement for Life) through the Jesuits. With the convening of various interested parties, we organized the Colectivo por la Objeción de Conciencia (Collective for Conscientious Objection) to focus not only on the church but on the broader society.

## Creation of a Justice and Peace Commission

At that point, we had the sense that the Mennonite church was ready to initiate work from within the church itself not only on conscientious objection but on human rights and on the development of a critical sociopolitical vision. At the 1990 annual meeting of the Colombian Mennonite churches, a Justice and Peace Commission was proposed and approved, composed of thirty members, three from each congregation.

The commission immediately took on four human rights projects: in Agua de Dios; in Chipaque, a town near Bogotá; in Girardot, a medium-sized city three hours' travel from Bogotá; and in Bogotá. It supported a young man, Ricardo Torres, who wished to refuse compulsory military service. The commission joined with CLARA and the seminary in offering workshops and courses on conscientious objection, nonviolence, human rights, and Anabaptist theology, among other subjects. The commission also became a space for discussion, analysis, and exploration. Out of multiple conversations came the decision to train people in the churches and to consolidate the work rather than proceeding with isolated efforts. MCC was approached for financial support.

In January 1990, Peter Stucky and I proposed the creation of a center, later called Centro Cristiano para la Justicia, Paz y Acción Noviolenta, Justapaz (Christian Center for Justice, Peace and Nonviolent Action, Justapaz), with the backing of the Mennonite church, and I urged the formation of a Reference Group.

The Reference Group brought together Juvenal Pacheco, Mennonite church president; Luis Correa, director of MENCOLDES; Peter Stucky, executive secretary of the Mennonite church; Noé Gonzalía, pastor of the Teusaquillo Mennonite Congregation; Robert Suderman, director of CLARA and the seminary; Leopoldo Bonilla, overseer of the church; and me. The Reference Group met almost weekly to discuss the idea and to discern the way to proceed. This discernment was a process whereby the community of faith gathered together to analyze the times and situation in the light of the Word of God and the wisdom of the group.

A central dilemma was the definition of the organizational structure. Should Justapaz have a legal status independent of the church, like MENCOLDES? This would give it more autonomy and flexibility but could lead to independent development without mutual accountability. In this, there was the experience with MENCOLDES. There was also the example of strong conflict in Central America between a national Mennonite church and a social institution that grew out of the church but with an independent organizational status. Another alternative was to have an interchurch governing board. This could foster a broader, more ecumenical effort, but another organization with such a structure was seen as being nonfunctional.

As we analyzed the options, we became clear that our work was a work of the church, and so we did not want to be separate from it, in spite of some apparent disadvantages. It was decided that Justapaz would remain a structural part of the Mennonite church, under its direction, and would seek to hire church people, although it would also be able to work with other churches and sectors of society.

This has had the drawbacks of a slower and more involved decision-making process, given that not everyone in the church is of the same mind and also that nonchurch people and organizations at times view us with suspicion because of the "confessional" status of Justapaz. The strength of this option has been that we remained true to our purpose of being a part of the church, and we did not have the problem of developing separately from the church.

I gathered together the ideas and developed a formal proposal for Centro Justapaz, its vision, objectives, by-laws, functions, and name. The proposal was discussed and refined by the Reference Group, then brought to the board of the Mennonite church, which approved it in September 1990.

Justapaz had been given form in faith by a group. We began with four employees. I served as director and was joined by Lucero Fandiño, Caleb Aranguren, and Diana Hurtado. We received financial support from Diakonia, an agency of the Free Churches of Sweden.

An initial issue within Justapaz brought into focus the orientation of the center: Would we permit the influence of a theology of liberation, which I believed would lead us, in the final analysis, to the use of violence, or would we remain within the theological orientation of Anabaptism, which would lead us to social change through nonviolence as a political tool? One staff member was apparently much in sympathy with liberation theology. Following a period of dialogue and discernment, this person chose to leave the team.

## Work of the Church through Justapaz

The conflictive social situation in Colombia was to be addressed through Justapaz in the broad manner that had been evolving. In keeping with this, several programmatic areas were targeted.

### Conscientious Objection

The right to conscientious objection to military service has been central to the work of Justapaz from the beginning. It has included work with churches, young people, and on the legal and political fronts.

*Work within the churches.* Thanks to the financial support of Diakonia, in 1989 and 1990 a strong effort was made to address conscientious objection within the Mennonite congregations and within the churches affiliated under CEDECOL, which had given its formal backing to this focus.

In addition to work in specific congregations, in 1992 we convened a retreat on conscientious objection for young people at Chinauta, near Bogotá; nearly 300 attended, mostly Mennonites. The vigor with which Justapaz approached the churches with this topic began to elicit rejection from some congregations, which felt that Justapaz was swamping their own programming.

Faced with the dilemma of how to promote conscientious objection without disrupting local church programming and also taking into account the skepticism toward the topic on the part of some within the congregations, we changed strategy. We recognized that we could not impose our point of view, but rather we must find the way forward together with the churches and allow interest to develop for what we had to offer.

We suspended the global conscientious objection program in the congregations and switched to approaching each congregation individually, asking members what they wanted and seeking to arrange our programming accordingly. We also began a process of education in nonviolence, offering congregations workshops in Alternatives to Violence (a Quaker-designed program), which contributed to constructive transformation of conflicts within the congregations. This new approach was well received.

*Work for constitutional reform.* At the same time as we worked with the churches, in 1990–1991 we joined with the Collective for Conscientious Objection to launch a campaign to secure conscientious objection as a constitutional right. The campaign was directed at the Constitutional Assembly, which had been convened to overhaul the Colombian Constitution. Meetings, marches, and vigils were held, including a gathering of 250 people at the Teusaquillo Mennonite Church for analysis and discernment of the current sociopolitical situation.

Through CEDECOL, the Christian Union political party was launched. It supported the candidacy of two Protestants to the Constitutional Assembly with the promise that they would support conscientious objection. A national forum was held on the topic "The Country Faces Military Service." There was also abundant media attention. Thus, conscientious objection successfully achieved national attention; it became one of the issues of debate on the new constitution; and the Mennonite church became identified with it.

In the new constitution, which was approved in 1991, Article 18 states that no one will be forced to act against his or her conscience. Although this was taken as a partial victory, the armed forces did not relinquish the compulsory draft. Subsequent court decisions determined that Article 18 did not include military service.

As a next step, we started the Objectors for Peace Program, and together with the Collective for Conscientious Objection, we initiated actions to call attention to and advance the cause of conscientious objection and objectors being pursued by the state. We again carried out vigils, marches, and other civic acts. We launched a campaign to collect one million signatures to bring a citizens' legislative initiative before Congress to enact a law guaranteeing the right to conscientious objection to military service. This campaign continued for two years but was then suspended for lack of resources.

In the course of carrying out actions, on one occasion we were attacked, and it became evident that we needed training in nonviolent direct action. In response to this, in 1995 we held the first weekend workshop on nonviolent direct action, attended by more than thirty people. In time, the Objectors for Peace Program took on as its central focus the Seminary for the Training of Peacemakers.

*Seminary for the Training of Peacemakers.* In accordance with the new constitution, the government had to revise certain aspects of military service, which it did through Law 48 of March 3, 1993. We faced a dilemma. Should we train young men to engage in immediate action and confront the state, or should we be more proactive and take advantage of the gaps in the law to develop a slower, less spectacular educational program?

In an effort to redeem the positive from the negative in the Military Service Law, we took advantage of the provision that specifies that young men enrolled in seminary would be deferred from military service and subsequently exempted. We created a program called the Seminary for the Training of Peacemakers. It was attached to the Mennonite Biblical Seminary and directed to young men of military age who chose to train themselves for peace instead of training for war through military service. This program was not confrontational and did not require that participants publicly declare themselves before the state as conscientious objectors to military service, running the risk of imprisonment. Yet, it provided them a real alternative to military service and made it possible for them to obtain exemption from the military obligation. It was open to all young men, not just those of the church, since the law does not require that they be of a specific creed.

The Seminary for the Training of Peacemakers was coordinated by Ricardo Torres, with the support of Maricely Parada, and is designed with a double emphasis. First, it has a conceptual curriculum, including, the biblical and theological bases of nonviolence; conscientious objection; the mission of the church and human rights; Colombian community, the constitution, and training in community education; social ethics; history, philosophy, and pedagogy of nonviolence; conflict transformation; ecology and the environment; and Colombia and the Christian churches in the current scene. The second emphasis is a concurrent experiential component of community service in which the participants assume a commitment to carry out an alternative civil service on weekends. With this, we seek to apply the theory and to show that conscientious objection is more than just saying "no" to military recruitment. It is a lifestyle, and it recognizes that there are no rights without obligations. It is also a step toward opening the way to an alternative civil service, which in the future, when conscientious objection is legalized, would replace military service.

The Seminary for the Training of peacemakers has not been easy to implement. The legal and academic aspects have been the simplest; but a dilemma that we have faced is that once young men in the program are exempted from military service, their motivation often drops for continuing in community service and nonviolence training. It is a challenge to channel this effort constructively and not be simply a shelter from the draft. Yet, the effects of this program on the lives of the 150 young men who have participated is a testament to its impact.

### Education in Nonviolence and Human Rights

The antecedents of this program included the early human rights work of Justapaz, which had organizational antecedents in the activities of the Justice and Peace Commission in behalf of the rights of those with leprosy in Agua de Dios; in the creation of religious tolerance in Chipaque; in the efforts toward human rights education and consultation with communities where MENCOLDES worked; and in the work of many members of Mennonite congregations. It also built on the work that Patricia Zapata and I had been doing in San Jacinto, Bolivar, before we moved back to Bogotá.

The priority given human rights work is also deeply rooted in my own personal experience. I grew up in an environment of denial of rights, which led me to think that neither I nor my ethnic group had rights. It was when I arrived at the school in Cachipay that I began to see the injustice of that situation. As a way of pursuing those rights and seeking protection from the legal system, I studied law. As an attorney, I discovered that often there is no relation between justice and the law. It was only when I understood what human rights are that I gained an understanding of justice and the importance of promoting and defending these rights in people's struggle for liberation.

From the start of the vision for Justapaz, we have been clear that we should work for human rights. We saw that one of the factors of greatest impact on Colombian society was the violation and denial of human rights and that our churches were not attending sufficiently to them, having been influenced by sectors of the government that argued that to work for human rights was to act like a Communist.

We believe that human rights are more than an academic concern and go beyond the declarations of international organizations. Their fundamental basis is that they are the essential condition for life and the guarantor for the coexistence of human beings on earth. Independent of the ideological, philosophical, or academic conceptualizations about their origin, we see them as a road to life.

We believe that the content of the fundamental rights, duties, and liberties are the minimal conditions for human development with dignity. They are the minimal secular expression of the values of the kingdom of God. Jesus lived and died to show us an abundant life within a liberating search for truth. After almost 2,000 years and after the horrors of World War II, human beings finally understood that in order to survive, they needed a universal code of ethics, which is none other than the reflection of the teachings that Jesus came to share.

We have understood that human rights not only apply to the political struggles of people, but they are essential for the development of the churches, since the sharing of the Gospel is the taking of the Good News to people who suffer, to encourage them in their striving for freedom.

*Solidarity and education.* We have worked for human rights by committing ourselves in behalf of those whose rights are violated; and through biblical and theological study we have strived to show the church congregations how their mission on earth is directly linked to human rights. In this, we have carried out workshops in congregations and for church leaders.

*Workshops in alternatives to violence.* Growing out of our understanding that the means have to be consistent with the end, we have found the need to develop and promote methods of social change that are respectful of human rights and to develop political tools that have human rights as an ethical base. Looking at the experience of the last forty-five years of the Colombian people, we find that violence is not an adequate methodology for dealing with conflicts and promoting social development. The more than 35,000 violent deaths a year show us that we have to find alternatives to violence.

We are convinced that nonviolence is an alternative that works for human rights without violating them. Nonviolence is not only a strategy but a lifestyle, both a means and an end, which can take us to the positive peace of which the Bible speaks.

We are carrying out nonviolence training and formation through the Alternatives to Violence workshops (adapted from the program originally developed by North American Quakers). These workshops serve as an experiential introduction to and comprehension of nonviolence in which participants focus on self-esteem, communication, cooperation, and conflict transformation. Through these workshops, we have been able to do grassroots work within congregations. We have found that, in addition to skill building in nonviolence, the workshops have fostered trust and community and have given an understanding of the relationships among human rights, nonviolence, and the message of Jesus, which can be applied to the participants' own lives and home communities.

### Conflict Analysis and Transformation Program

One of our initial objectives was to work in mediation, with a vision of each congregation as a mediation center, fulfilling the sacred ministry of reconciliation. At the same time, there was interest in the country in dealing with impunity (unpunished crime), which was in part a result of the congestion of the courts. In March 1991, the Colombian government, compelled by the state of violence and impunity in the country, enacted Law 23, the Law for the Decongestion of the Courts. This law states that communities could establish conflict mediation centers and provide mediation services, and it stipulates that agreements reached in these centers have the same weight as a judicial sentence.

To pursue our vision, we sought and received the support of the Mennonite Central Committee. We also invited John Paul Lederach, in 1991, to lead a workshop on conflict transformation for leaders of the Mennonite church. His visit and workshop served to involve more people within the church in the mediation process and to strengthen institutional support for the Justapaz initiative. It also planted the seeds for a working relationship with Eastern Mennonite University, with which Lederach was connected.

*Conflict transformation training and action.* The conjunction of Lederach's visit, Law 23, and the evolving vision within the Mennonite church led to the certainty of the need for a mediation center and of training mediators in the local congregations and communities to provide this service. We understood that it is those who are immersed in a conflict who hold the keys to the way through it, since it is they who know and understand the sociopolitical structures and dynamics of the conflict. Hence, we saw the need to train people from local congregations and communities, even if they were not in the middle of open conflict. They could serve as seeds of reconciliation and prevention and would be able to respond when conflicts erupted, instead of having to rely on people from the outside who, in any event, could only be a support to the transformation process.

Out of this need for training evolved, beginning in 1993, the Curso Permanente (Permanent Course), which, similar to the peacemakers program, combines a theoretical-conceptual dimension with practical ongoing work. A Center for Conflict Analysis and Transformation also evolved and received state approval as a mediation facility in 1994.

The design of the Permanent Course calls for a cycle of workshops each year, with topic areas growing out of the work and needs of the participants, and it also provides a center for mediation services where people can practice.

Participants in the Permanent Course need not necessarily be engaged in formal conflict mediation but may be addressing and promoting transformation of social conflict in any number of ways, including mediation, development, community participation, and education. The Center for Conflict Analysis and Transformation, in addition to being a mediation service within the community, provides a setting for participants in the Permanent Course to obtain practical training experience.

Early approaches in Colombia focused on the conflict resolution techniques of leading North American practitioners. One heard references to the "culture of mediation," and the government treated mediation as almost an end in itself. But, when we analyzed the conflicts of our society in their social and political contexts (*coyuntura*) and in the light of our brief history as a Mennonite church in Colombia, it was clear that conflict had to do with human rights, with justice, with politics. We looked on conflict with the expanded theological vision of our experience. We listened to Lederach and others speak of transformation rather than resolution, and we recognized that the notion of transformation in our country was central in the years of political struggles, armed or unarmed, state or civilian. This notion was present in the work in education for transformation that had been led by people such as Paolo Freire through participatory action-reflection.

Out of our ongoing study and reflection on our own work and reality has evolved the vision for the center and the course as one of building a positive peace through a political process of justice. One challenge has been to integrate action from micro to macro levels, so that even specific micro skills reflect and address the broader context. The vision for this program is to go beyond training mediators, to fostering transformation into a community of peace through justice. Mediation is just one of the strategies for building a peace that is integrated with justice, nonviolence, human rights, and politics.

*Program for Peacebuilding in School Settings.* Beginning in 1992, there was the vision of a program to be carried out for children and youth in the schools. We began to work with Patricia Urueña, Lucero Fandiño, and Gerardo Mecón, three community leaders, in preparing documentation and material for a project in the schools in the city of Girardot. This grew out of an interest on the part of the local Mennonite congregation, responding to the initiative of its pastor, Daniel Vargas, and of the city mayor, in the face of the alarming incidence of violence and death among the youth of that city. At that time, we did not have the resources to give life to this project, yet the idea became the precursor to the Program for Peacebuilding in School Settings, which has been successful since 1994.

Initially, there were no resources for the Program for Peacebuilding in School Settings either. Then, Elizabeth Soto moved to Colombia from Puerto Rico to replace Robert Suderman as director of CLARA. Her husband, Frank Albrecht, brought with him considerable experience in mediation in U.S. public schools. With financial assistance from MCC, a staff of three was put in place, including Albrecht; Lina María Obando, a psychologist and educator;

and Marta Santanilla, a student of community psychology. With these three, we initiated the program in the schools by designing materials and providing direct training and follow-up.

Access to work in schools, like Justapaz's entry into so many settings in this culture, has been through relationships. Work began with two Mennonite primary schools in Cachipay and La Mesa, Cundinamarca. The positive and constructive impact of the program was shared by the director of one of these schools, Guillermo Vargas, with the director of a nearby public school, who in turn shared it with some of her colleagues in other schools. The trust that each of these had with the other, rather than an initial acquaintance with Justapaz, led to requests from larger, better-financed state and private schools. For a small organization like Justapaz, the new requests have necessarily created a tension between responding to opportunities of potentially larger impact and more adequate payment and continuing to serve the church community to which we are committed.

The Program for Peacebuilding in School Settings initially focused on technical training for students in mediation skills. It has become evident, however, that transformation must incorporate broader consideration of justice and rights and engage the different levels and sectors of the school. In the most recent contract with a school, the Colegio Americano of Bogotá, the program is more comprehensively designed to address the entire school structure and involves students as well as teachers, parents, and administrators.

### Networking for Justice and Peace

From its inception, Justapaz has been clear that building peace is not a private effort of particular individuals or of specific groups or peoples. It must represent the combined efforts of the greatest possible number of people, groups, and faith traditions throughout the world.

Bearing in mind that one of the most realistic ways of initiating an endeavor is by starting with what is at hand, and since our effort is based in the Mennonite church, we decided to promote a world network to join efforts among Mennonite churches through acts of witness for justice and peace. We have strived to foster interactions between the churches of the North and South and to convert into something positive the differences in language and culture, which otherwise may appear negative and problematic. We seek to enrich the vision of the world through the multiplicity of cultural experiences.

First steps have been taken to foster a network among the Mennonite churches in more than sixty countries, a network among Latin American Mennonite churches, a network of churches within the Andean region, and a network among the Mennonite churches within Colombia—a vision of a spiral, or concentric circles linking efforts. As part of this networking, we have made contact with congregations in Europe, Africa, Latin America, and North America, a number of which have indicated their desire to participate. We have also been supporting peacebuilding initiatives in Central America through the work of the Mennonite Justice and Peace Commission in Honduras, coordinated by José Perez, Oscar Dueñas, and others; through the work of the Mennonite Justice and Peace Commission in Nicaragua, coordinated by Nicolás Largaespada, Pedro Sarmiento, and others; through KIKOTEN in Guatemala, coordinated by José Luis Azurdia and Olga de Azurdia; through the Mennonite Justice and Peace Commission in Guatemala; and through the Mennonite Justice and Peace Commissions in Panama and Costa Rica.

Our support in Central America is carried out in coordination with MCC, represented by Nathan Zook-Barge and Darryl Yoder-Bontrager. In addition to Central America, we have continued our contacts with the Mennonite churches in the South American nations, especially those of the Andean region.

In addition to networking within the Mennonite churches, we have joined efforts across denominations. We have initiated a special project with the Presbyterian and Lutheran churches of Colombia to actively involve them in the process of building peace. This project has the support of the Latin American Council of Churches. The objective is to train pastors and church leaders in fostering groups of promoters for peacebuilding within their local congregations. These groups will engage the social issues facing their communities and learn by doing, promoting, and discovering the values of the Kingdom of God, using an action-reflection participatory methodology. The training curriculum will address fundamental human rights, duties and problems; justice; politics; conflict; participatory democracy; nonviolence and nonviolent direct action; and the different conceptualizations of peace.

A second network, the Network of Community Justice and Treatment of Conflict, has evolved in Colombia as our efforts have expanded and become linked through the Permanent Course with those of other groups working in the area of mediation. Formed in 1995, this network links public officials, academic institutions, nongovernmental organizations, and citizens working in their communities, as well as people and organizations working at different levels of society, to build a web of working relationships. It currently is made up of eleven organizations from civil society, as well as officials of the Ministry of Justice and the office of the presidency of the republic. Member entities are present in eleven departments (states) of the country and sixty-two counties. They have initiated training of more than 650 community leaders, university students and teachers, and church members. The group has also come together for research on their work, conceptual development, and training and, out of this, seeks clarity on commonalties in conflict transformation that are appropriate to the Colombian culture and situation.

This network has led us into a working relationship with sectors of the state and with other organizations whose visions are different from those of our faith tradition. The risk of conditions being imposed and of being coopted and seduced by the state or other visions is real, and the constructive management of power differences has posed a challenge. Faced with this dilemma, we have found it helpful to take a constructive approach, seeking the potential benefits to the process of working with the state and other organizations. It has been important to come with proposals of our own and to encourage each party, including the state and ourselves, to acknowledge its vantage point and perspective and not gloss over differences for fear of rejection. For us, this has included being clear that we are a church and that we seek to work with and from the community—the grassroots—and that the community should be very much a part of the process. In a politicized context such as ours, differences are deep. For us, it has been important to be consistent with our commitment to be in relation to all, despite pressures to take sides. Finally, it has been crucial to work on strengthening relationships with the persons involved and to foster dialogue and more dialogue.

A third network has linked Justapaz with Eastern Mennonite University in Harrisonburg, Virginia, and with the Nairobi Peace Initiative in Kenya in a design to broaden the vision of conceptualization, training, and action growing out of these centers.

Finally, Justapaz participated in planning the Iberian-American Conference on the Construction of Peace and the Treatment of Conflicts, which was held in October 1996. The planning committee included high officials of the Colombian government and one of the most prestigious and powerful private universities in Colombia. Activities such as this appear to have an almost inevitable centrifugal effect away from the grassroots and community. Given our orientation, we questioned whether we should participate and, if we did, how to engage in the face of such marked power differentials. As with the networking, we found it important to participate, but we clearly defined ourselves, speaking frankly, confronting, and encouraging other participants to similarly acknowledge their perspectives and interests. An important function we were able to provide was to advocate for the community, which was absent in the planning group.

## Justapaz as a Collective Effort

Our work in conflict transformation has evolved over time and has been truly a collective effort. With MCC support, we have been joined by Paul Stucky; we have counted on the able logistical support of Fabiola Clavijo; and we have the participation of a growing number of volunteers. Our decision-making process and our implementation of the decisions and directions have been made possible and enriched by the support and involvement of the entire team. As external demands and opportunities have expanded, we have been continually challenged to balance our response to them with our intention to nurture and build the internal community and to respond to personal and family needs. This has meant striving to preserve time set aside for staff sharing, reflection on the Bible, and prayer. It has also included helping staff members to pursue their academic development.

The larger church body has remained linked and involved through a support committee, through our reports and participation in annual church meetings, and through the active participation of Justapaz staff in local congregations.

## Conclusion

Our current work and vision are the historical accumulation of years of effort, experiential witness, and the community and congregational witness of many persons who have lived, suffered, and grown together on this pilgrimage on this piece of earth called Colombia. Our lives have been a constant struggle against violence with a thousand faces—the denial and violation of legal and fundamental rights, political and religious persecutions, pain, anguish, and, above all, much fear. But this has led us to a life of solidarity, fraternity, and strengthened faith, as we grow in our understanding that in living out the message of Jesus, we receive the strength that will revive the dwindling hopes of a people that has seen its utopias die.

We learn by doing, and we advance by seeking new spaces within the dimension of faith, which make it possible for us to find support and to give support to a community process of peacebuilding, all the while understanding that our goal is the way.

# Nine

## Mennonite Central Committee Efforts in Somalia and Somaliland

JOHN PAUL LEDERACH

SOMALIA REPRESENTS WHAT MIGHT BE considered among the worst-case scenarios of post–Cold War internal conflict. The Somali people have experienced nearly a decade of fighting. The country is flooded with weapons of every kind, mostly supplied by the superpowers during the Cold War. Somaliland was mined to the tune of 1.5 million land mines. For years, Somali president Siad Barre successfully manipulated clanism as a tool to set clans against each other and to keep himself in power. When he fell in January 1991, the opposition movements, based on clan affiliation, turned on one another. Since then, the infrastructure of the country has virtually collapsed, and there has been no functioning vocational government.

In this context, the Mennonite Central Committee (MCC) faced decisions about appropriate activities to undertake. MCC had the benefit of the long-standing program in the country of the Eastern Mennonite Missions (EMM), especially its efforts at education and health. Past Mennonite programs and people—and their relationships with Somalis—have had a remarkable history and still have a place in the minds of many Somalis.

In the early 1990s, both MCC and EMM made decisions to concentrate as much, if not more, on encouraging peace and reconciliation efforts as they did on providing crisis relief and humanitarian assistance in the Somali crisis. These can be outlined in six broad tracks, which point toward several operative principles for the decisions that were made.

## Track 1: Relief and Development

MCC has had involvement in Somalia in various relief and development activities over the years, from refugee camps to agriculture and animal husbandry. By 1989, with the intensification of the war and the questions emerging about program and policy under the falling Barre regime, MCC decided to pull its remaining staff out of the country. Some time later, with EMM, Bonnie Bergey was appointed as representative to Somalia, operating from a

Nairobi base. Her story is included in chapter 10 of this volume. MCC also continued providing aid.

During the period 1991–1995, MCC was involved in a number of select relief and development activities, including food shipments, especially for children in refugee camps over the border in Kenya; a postwar garbage clean-up project in Hargeisa; school kits and textbooks to towns in Somaliland; small grants for development/employment projects for women's groups in Mogadishu; and a repatriation project in the Sanaag/Sool region. A number of these projects were proposed and administered by Somali nongovernmental organizations (NGOs).

In making decisions about projects, MCC personnel made numerous trips to the region. They tried to explicitly link assessment of relief and development needs with the concerns for conflict transformation and reconciliation. It was due to these concerns that decisions were made not to be involved in direct food shipments inside the country nor to rush with the placement of personnel. Further, with these projects, MCC attempted to provide a balance both across regions and with regard to subclans receiving direct benefit. This was an effort to demonstrate a commitment to all Somalis and not just to one region or group. Finally, wherever possible, Somali NGOs and personnel developed and carried out the projects. Time and travel were devoted to meeting with Somali NGOs both across and outside Somalia and Somaliland; this served to build trust with Somalis and to encourage and empower indigenous NGOs in various regions.

## Track 2: Diaspora Somali Peace Initiative

Out of concern for a deeper analysis into the causes of and responses to the Ethiopian famine of the mid-1980s, Conrad Grebel College of Waterloo, Ontario, with MCC support, began the Horn of Africa Project (HAP). From 1987 to 1990, HAP served as a forum to convene African scholars and leaders from across diverse perspectives in the Horn to explore ideas and initiatives about the various internal conflicts, as well as peacemaking possibilities. Efforts were also made to create linkages with other organizations that had common concerns and mandates in the region. In this way, open cooperation in carrying out peace efforts in the Horn emerged among HAP, the Life and Peace Institute (LPI) of Uppsala, Sweden, the Nairobi Peace Initiative of Nairobi, Kenya, and MCC's International Conciliation Service (ICS).

In 1989, a Somali participant at a HAP meeting proposed starting a group focused specifically on Somalia. This led to the formation of the Ergada (Somali Peace and Consultation Committee), a network of concerned Somalis from across clans and regions, most of whom were located in North America. Begun in 1990, well before the collapse of the Barre regime, the full Ergada (fifteen to twenty Somalis) met several times a year and the Steering Committee more frequently. The group has drafted peace proposals; met with U.S.

State Department and U.N. officials; sent delegations to all regions of the country; convened other Somali peace groups; helped initiate similar forums for dialogue among Somalis in Canada (CANERGO), Europe, and the Middle East; and started a communication newsletter, *Ergofax*. Grants and project money have come from Europe, channeled through the LPI, from OXFAM UK, and from MCC.

Several concrete ideas emerged in the Ergada that have had a broader echo. First, members articulated a bottom-up approach to peacemaking in Somalia, and second, from the beginning they have advocated a central role for elders and supporting roles for religious leaders, intellectuals, and women in creating and sustaining peace. This approach was based on the premise that peace-making in Somalia should not concentrate exclusively on the highest level nor rely solely on military and political leaders. It must broaden and build up from the districts and regions if it is to sustain itself over time.

The Ergada proved to be a useful forum for dialogue and exchange. At various times, the members displayed the regional and clan tensions experienced at home. But, although the exile community can often be involved in suggesting approaches and ideas, its role and relationship with those at home remains challenging. Nonetheless, in the Somali case, where so many have fled or left and where divisions are so sharp and extreme, encouraging Somali input and initiatives for peace at any level has been important.

## Track 3: U.N./LPI Resource Group and Consultations

The ongoing cooperation between the Life and Peace Institute and MCC's International Conciliation Service has led to extensive involvement at a number of levels in Somali peace initiatives. To understand this involvement, it is important to trace briefly the outline of the role of the United Nations in Somalia during this period.

For a time following the collapse of the Somali state, the U.N. programs made a decision to leave the country. In late 1990 and into 1991, Security Council deliberations, pushed by a humanitarian concern for the emerging famine, eventually led to the decision to return and to establish the U.N. Operation in Somalia (UNOSOM), which was to coordinate the humanitarian and political affairs of the United Nations. National reconciliation was a primary mandate given to UNOSOM, especially to its Political Affairs Department. Concern for the protection of humanitarian aid and of international personnel led to the placement of peacekeepers and, eventually, to the American-led Operation Restore Hope. In 1992–1993, a series of humanitarian conferences was hosted by the United Nations, primarily in Addis Ababa, which brought together militia and political party leadership. UNOSOM II was created at the culmination of the last conference, with the mandate of humanitarian aid and political reconstruction. In the course of those two years, four successive special envoys headed the U.N. efforts in Somalia: Ambassadors Mohamed Sahnoun, I. Kittani, and Lamsana Kouyate, and Admiral Gordon Howe.

Ambassador Sahnoun wished to initiate his work by consulting broadly with Somalis and Somali experts as to how to proceed both in terms of peacemaking and humanitarian delivery, and, early on, conversations emerged among the LPI, the Swedish government, and members of Sahnoun's team, principally Dr. Leonard Kapungu. These culminated in the Swedish government's agreeing to provide funds for supporting U.N. peace efforts and for broadening the peace process, and it turned to LPI to provide organizational leadership in those efforts. LPI, in turn, requested assistance from ICS in conceptualizing their mandates. Many different initiatives were undertaken, starting in 1991. Among the most important were the following:

1. A resource group of experts on Somalia was convened, which met with UNOSOM leadership, initially with Ambassador Sahnoun and later with the political affairs representatives. The group exchanged viewpoints and wrote reports advising on how to proceed with the peacemaking efforts. The first meeting was with international experts, the second with Somali intellectuals, and two subsequent meetings were held with the two groups together. The primary advice in each instance paralleled the suggestions of the Ergada, namely, to work from the bottom up in constructing the peace process (that is, not to convene national meetings immediately), to broaden the participation in the process, and to proceed using a long-term time frame. Given the turnover of special envoys and the directives about process and time frame emerging from New York, the advice of the resource group was not heeded extensively.

2. As a parallel but supportive effort to the United Nations, LPI moved to implement the advice by broadening the peace process participation and by developing a proposal for a more comprehensive structure for reconciliation. Done in conjunction with MCC, this involved pushing for more participation of elders, religious leaders, intellectuals, and women in the national peace conferences, as well as the holding of supporting local peace conferences and the convening of Somali peace groups to create a coalition movement. LPI has moved to hire Somali liaison officers to work as counterparts with U.N. personnel in developing and implementing peace efforts throughout the country. LPI has also been deeply involved in supporting the ongoing formation of district-level governance councils and in providing local leaders with training. It has also financed research into specific regions to document the local and regional efforts at peacemaking.

Overall, this initiative has placed MCC and ICS in direct contact with key U.N. personnel, national Somali leaders, and a broad spectrum of international organizations. It has provided direct access to the national peace processes. The efforts have been aimed, however, at formulating suggestions and proposals to create broader participation in the peace process, to provide space for Somali peacemaking efforts, and to help create a sustainable infrastructure for reconciliation in the country.

## Track 4: In-Country Conciliation

As a logical consequence of the advice and proposals emerging from the Ergada and from the LPI resource group, MCC sought to support a bottom-up approach to peacemaking wherever that was possible. Essentially, this peacemaking strategy suggested that, in the Somali context, national peace should be built on local and regional efforts at subclan deliberations and reconciliation. This meant enhancing the role of elders, in particular, who have the traditional conflict resolution responsibility at local and regional levels.

In this regard, MCC helped finance peace conferences in various parts of the country. Especially notable was the Grand Elders' Peace Conference in Borama, which brought together people from across Somaliland. Typically, funds were channeled through Somali NGO mechanisms, which were arranged by the elders planning a conference and usually took the form of small cash donations for food and transportation. In such cases, the Somali NGOs were groups that MCC had worked with on other projects, and they provided relationship and context to the funds being channeled for peacemaking. Outside of limited observation and encouragement, MCC personnel have not played any direct role in the deliberations, leaving that to the long-established traditions among Somalis. At various points, they have, however, met with the elders during the convening of the conferences, and they have been given time to speak to the group on two occasions. MCC has consistently attempted to interpret the strategy and to persuade the international community as to the importance of these conferences and the broader approach they represent.

## Track 5: Education and Awareness

As noted, MCC opted in the Somali situation to place primary importance on efforts toward achieving peace and reconciliation. At a time, however, when the news media was portraying sensational and often superficial views of famine, and the international community moved in with military force to protect humanitarian aid deliveries, MCC's position clearly represented a minority voice. This was perhaps compounded by other factors. Delivering food to starving people is a crisis-driven response, which gives the feeling of something concrete being accomplished. Working at reconciliation, the lack of which was the primary cause of the starvation, is a slow, painstaking, and many times ambiguous task, in which one often questions what is being accomplished. Moving with a forceful international response to protect food delivery and to aid the innocent people feels like justice is being served and like a clear demonstration of concern is being made. Moving to encourage Somalis to be involved in resolving Somali problems, providing space for elders and elders' conferences, which sometimes last six months, may seem convoluted and perhaps unresponsive.

All of this points to an important part of the MCC task: providing education and raising awareness about the broader and deeper issues. This has been necessary in a number of directions. First, with MCC's own constituency, it has been important to try to convey the complexities of the situation, the deeper issues that go beyond the media images, as well as the theology and strategies behind the MCC (and larger Mennonite) response. Second, dialogue with fellow relief agencies—many of which called on military protection for humanitarian aid—was important. This afforded a number of opportunities to explore in greater depth the relationships among relief, development, peacemaking, and conflict transformation. Increasingly, the concern for integrating conflict resolution perspectives with the more traditional categories of relief and development is seen as not just a Quaker and Mennonite agenda. Many of the frequent requests to ICS that came from a wide variety of humanitarian NGOs were for advice and consultation on peacemaking, conflict transformation, and training.

## Track 6: Nonviolent Peacekeeping and Disarmament

Among the key issues raised by the internal conflicts in Somalia and the Balkans, to name but two of thirty-five such situations, is that of international military peacekeeping. Increasingly, discussions are emerging in different places about the ethics and effectiveness of international military presence in protracted internal wars. On the one hand, some analysts are calling for a standing U.N. army. On the other, some are advocating the formation of nonviolent peacekeeping initiatives. MCC/ICS has been drawn into a number of these discussions as a result of ongoing conversations with top-level officials (for example, at the United Nations), as well as extensive contact with people at middle and grassroots levels throughout the country. At a more generic level, the MCC Peace Office and ICS have also had opportunities to interact with people at the United Nations and at the U.S. Institute of Peace on nonviolent peacekeeping. For MCC, this issue pinpoints important aspects of faith and strategy.

## Underlying Principles

The following are key principles guiding MCC work, as illustrated by the Somalia case.

*Establish a comprehensive framework and integrated response.* A comprehensive framework suggests that strategies and decisions should be made within a broad scope of reflection, which connects different aspects of the problem. There are at least three concrete aspects that are important to include.

　1. *Acknowledge and be explicit about the connections and dynamics among short- and long-term concerns.* Too often, solutions to conflicts are driven by short-term needs, with little attention paid to longer-term consequences. An inte-

grated strategy requires a long-term perspective for two reasons. First, most armed, internal conflicts are protracted, complex, long-term problems. It is not unrealistic to suggest that it will take about the same length of time to get out of a problem that it took to get into it in the first place, at least in terms of the most recent organization of violence, which is often decades. Second, peacemaking builds less on events than on relationships, and relationships are a long-term investment. Thus, while we will always be faced with making decisions about immediate action, those decisions should be made within a framework oriented to decades and ongoing relationships rather than to months and the demands of immediate events.

2. *Acknowledge and be explicit about the levels of activity within a conflictive situation.* It has become increasingly clear that peacebuilding activity works on at least three levels. The highest level involves very few people (well-known leaders and personalities); its processes are usually highly public, and they tend to focus on cease-fires and political solutions. The middle-range level involves a larger set of people, who may be well known within a given sector, ethnic group, or religious affiliation but who have more room to maneuver in that they are not directly in the limelight. The most populous is the grassroots level, where people often experience the devastation of the conflict and are concerned primarily with daily survival. A comprehensive approach recognizes that sustainable peace builds across the levels of a society and does not rely exclusively on peace trickling down. MCC tends to work by choice at the grassroots level of society, often in coordination with middle-range partner organizations and leaders. This positions MCC to suggest and formulate ways that peacemaking can be undertaken in a more comprehensive manner. In appropriate circumstances, MCC is able to use its insights into context and culture, relationships, and experiences as resources to inform and influence what too often is level exclusivism at the top.

3. *Acknowledge and be explicit about the connections between more traditional relief and development activities and conflict transformation and peacebuilding.* In the evolving post–Cold War era, we cannot rely on a narrow view of our work as humanitarian without an explicit focus on the contexts within which it operates, which more often than not are situations of protracted, armed, internal conflict. In those situations, we must continually pose the questions of how our activities of feeding the hungry are related to the conflicts that produced the hungry.

*Be rooted in the context.* It is crucial that peacemaking efforts emerge from and be connected to the contexts within which the conflicts are raging. This is the fundamental lesson that pushed MCC toward the ideals of sustainable development, appropriate technology, contextualized mission, and popular education. This suggests some important ideas.

1. *Encourage and provide space for peacemaking approaches that emerge from within the setting.* More specifically, we must respect and support indigenous ways of approaching peacemaking, as opposed to relying on transferring or prescribing our ways.

2. *Encourage and provide space for indigenous peacemakers.* We are not primarily about the task of injecting ourselves as peacemakers; we are about the task of supporting and encouraging people from the setting in the process of developing the vision and undertaking this task.

*Build relationships and understanding across the lines of conflict.* While exceedingly complex, this fundamental principle suggests that we are committed to all who are embroiled in the conflict. In the Somali case, this has been a commitment not to neutrality but to relationship with all regions and clans, through which we seek to understand, encourage, and support them in as evenhanded a way as possible. This further suggests that we think strategically about our relationships and that we recognize places where we can make useful connections, particularly within religious circles, that bring healing and understanding. In many instances, such as the Somali case, this can only be done in a quiet and small way, with the aims of promoting trust, respect, and dignity.

*Articulate and advocate alternatives for nonviolent transformation that are consistent with our faith.* For years within Anabaptist discourse, we have engaged in serious debate about the ethics of the use of violence. We have engaged far less in the development of alternatives. To the degree we now see ourselves placed in situations of internal conflicts, in large part because of the call to feed the hungry, clothe the naked, and provide refuge to the homeless, we must raise to equal importance the seeking of alternatives alongside the debate of right and wrong. In the Somali case, for example, this challenges us to develop functional proposals for disarmament of the militias and youth that do not rely on outside military intervention, or proposals for how to provide nonviolent peacekeeping functions, such as protecting innocent populations, without relying on weapons and armed troops.

# Ten

## The "Bottom-Up" Alternative
## in Somali Peacebuilding

BONNIE BERGEY

THE SMALL PLANE HEADED RIGHT into the city of Mogadishu. With the very blue Indian Ocean to the right of the plane and the white, arabesque buildings set among sparse thorny trees and bougainvillea to the left, the plane landed on the edge of the earth. When the door opened, I felt my first blast of the heavy, wet heat that was nearly always a part of Mogadishu's presence. Then began the tight hold on my documents and the attempt to stay calm and unhurried in the midst of seeming chaos—pushing and shoving as if my fellow travelers could not contain the joy and enthusiasm of being home again. Not knowing what would happen, or whether I was capable of doing the work I was assigned to do, I also entered Somalia enthusiastically.

I had agreed to teach English in Mogadishu for three years with Eastern Mennonite Missions. For four months in 1990, I taught English and studied the Somali language, as the Somali state quickly tumbled further into uncertainty. Little did I know that my teaching days would be so short-lived and that I would spend most of my time working at peacebuilding with and among the Somali people. Five months after my arrival, the Siad Barre regime fell.

### Somalia in Collapse

Somalia is one of the world's poorest and least developed countries, with few natural resources. Nomads and seminomads make up about 70 percent of the population, which was estimated in 1995 to be 7.3 million. Significant political turmoil from 1991 to the present has resulted in continuing civil war, with widespread famine and escalating health problems. There has been no formal, widely recognized government since January 1991. Various militia leaders and former military soldiers have continued to fight for power and control. Often referred to as "warlords," these leaders have tried to take political control in almost every region of the former Somalia. Fighting has occurred nearly everywhere.

Most of the international attention focused on two warlords in Mogadishu, General Mohamed Farah Aideed[1] and Ali Mahdi Mohamed. Both were from the same clan, one of Somalia's five major clan families, although from different subclans, and each claimed the right to be president of the defunct nation. Meanwhile, the northwestern land area of the former Republic of Somalia named itself an independent country, the Republic of Somaliland, although at the time of this writing, it had not been recognized as such by the international community. Although Somaliland does have a functioning president, political tensions and clan fighting have occurred in its five regions sporadically since 1994.

Somalia's political troubles were long-standing; the Barre regime had long been accused of severe human rights violations, clan politics, and unusual and unhealthy alliances with other governments. Somalia had spent unprecedented amounts of the country's resources on building up the military. Never at total peace with the boundaries established by European powers, Somalia had earlier had bouts of war with neighboring Ethiopia and Kenya. As a pastoralist, survival-of-the-fittest culture and environment, conflicts over land rights were common. Disputes between neighboring clans arose regularly throughout Somali history, with some more serious than others.

The early 1980s saw significant international focus on and aid for Somalia's drought and poor economy. The country hosted numerous refugees from other countries, and the government learned quickly how to exploit money that was designated for refugees or for other improvements in the society. The 1980s were heavy-handed years in which the government tried to squelch various groups that were working to aid the people and to highlight government abuses. Government reaction took the form of severe bombings in the north and northwest regions and imprisoning or killing persons thought to be a threat to the government.

The ending of the Cold War also made its mark on Somalia with the escalated import of weaponry being discarded from other parts of the world. This made the possibility of more "efficient" warfare in Somalia more imminent. Development and aid became something to be manipulated and abused, as other resources and the economy fell on hard times in the harsh environment. The traditional mechanisms for coping with drought and power abuses further disintegrated and were held hostage to a central military power that could not effectively govern the whole country.

## Mennonite Presence in Somalia

North American Mennonites, through Eastern Mennonite Missions (EMM) and the Mennonite Central Committee (MCC), have been present in Somalia since the 1950s. They are widely remembered for their secondary boarding schools, which educated people from across clan lines, some of whom became the elite of Somali society. Mennonites also built and staffed hospitals, and a bookstore was set up and managed in Mogadishu. MCC worked in the refugee camps hosting nearby Ethiopians and with agricultural projects before the war. A Mennonite man from North America was killed by a religious fanatic in the 1960s, and the story is still widely remembered throughout Somalia. At one time, when all Christian missions were asked to leave if they would not agree to teach the Koran, EMM was the only mission that agreed to the conditions. Although EMM was also asked to leave at a later time, it was the first Christian group invited back in the early 1980s, when international organizations were beginning to be welcomed by the Somalia government.

In 1990, just prior to the collapse of the Barre regime, EMM had nine adults working under contracts with the Ministry of Education or the Ministry of Health. When the fighting escalated into civil war, the others were sent back to the United States or reassigned, while I stayed in Nairobi, Kenya, to try to maintain contact, especially with the long-time Somali friends we had in Mogadishu and outlying areas. I also agreed to keep in touch with the larger international nongovernmental community, which was beginning to show interest in aid to Somalia. It was then that I also began to represent MCC, as it became more likely that some forms of aid and peacebuilding work might be encouraged and sponsored by that agency. From that point on, I was jointly appointed by the two agencies.

From mid-1991 to mid-1995, in giving oversight to other Mennonite personnel working in Somalia or with Somalis in Kenya and in managing various MCC projects from my Nairobi base, I had the opportunity to travel at times from Nairobi into various parts of Somalia, Somaliland, and Djibouti. In total, I spent five years working with the Somali people in East Africa. During this time, there were shorter-term Mennonite workers in various places and capacities. Two women were nurses based in Mogadishu for all of 1993; two men worked in the refugee camps in Kenya for one year; one woman worked with resettlement cases in Nairobi for one year; and several others worked at specific tasks seconded to other organizations working in Somalia.

## Mogadishu Just Prior to the War

For the four months in 1990 that I lived in Mogadishu, tensions were high. I had weighed heavily the known difficulties of working in Somalia, had asked many questions of those who had previously worked in the country, and was aware that there had long been rumors of vast corruption and a possible overthrow of the government. I left the United States knowing that I would encounter difficulties in my work with unpredictable school schedules, students' possible lack of motivation for learning English, and communication barriers. I went knowing that it would be difficult to be a single Christian woman in a strongly patriarchal Muslim society. I went knowing that my protection was not guaranteed by anyone, and that if I should be taken hostage, the agency I represented would not pay ransom for my release.

The day after I arrived, shooting began during a demonstration, and later in the day two embassies were bombed. A month later, Mogadishu's post office was bombed twenty minutes after my coworkers and I left the building. Sporadic shooting came more and more often, and we began to wonder at what point the situation would be uncertain enough to vacate the city. We said that *if* there were ever rounds of gunfire during the daytime, we should probably leave. Then, daytime volleys of gunfire began. Yet we kept staying, hesitant to leave our posts and our friends, who could not leave.

By November, the third month after my arrival, it was becoming more apparent that something was going to happen. There were break-ins throughout the city. Just after I had walked the street one day from one house to another, a driver was shot and killed when armed men took his vehicle. Other days, stones were thrown at me by boys playing football. My night watchman, who carried a knife, insisted on having a second watchman after several men tried to climb the wall into the compound where I lived alone. One evening on my way home, I decided against going to the store to buy some bread. By the time I reached my house, a customer had been held up at the bread store two streets away.

But there were delightful times too. I kept in mind that some of my North American friends had told me to enjoy the exotic side of Mogadishu. It really was a rich cultural paradise. A coworker took me downtown by bus so that I could experience a bus ride. We had tea in one of the tea shops, although these were understood as places for men. I visited both museums in Mogadishu, which now have been looted and destroyed. I visited in a few homes, had wonderful meals of roasted goat, rice, and the sweetest bananas and grapefruit I have ever tasted. Somalia *was* intriguing and exotic, and I was determined to enjoy it to the fullest.

## A Nairobi Base

From Nairobi in 1991, with a continuing desire to learn about the Somali people, I began to fly into Mogadishu for several days at a time. I attached myself to other nongovernmental organizations (NGOs), so that I would have transportation from the airport and a place to stay for the night. At this time, there were no warlords, no United Nations presence, and no government; there was still a semblance of order, even among the clan militias.

That September, I happened to be in Mogadishu when fighting first began between two of the subclans of the Hawiye clan family. Ali Mahdi had declared himself president, but General Aideed felt that he deserved higher status for having toppled Siad Barre's government eight months before. As my driver, another NGO worker, and I turned onto a sandy Mogadishu street, I saw dust fly from gunfire, and we nearly collided with another vehicle in getting to a safe place. For five days, I heard nearly constant machine-gun fire throughout the day and night. I heard bullets sizzle overhead as I ducked and ran to a nearby building to find someone with a radio. I felt the buildings shake as they were hit with artillery, the names of which I have tried not to remember. I heard rocket-propelled grenades rip through the intersection where I was in a car headed for the airport. I heard the deep booms of whatever it was that fell into the school in the distance where displaced people had taken refuge. I took refuge in a hallway with a friend, hoping that we had at least two walls between us and the bullets, some of which came through the windows.

I was unsuccessful in making sense of the mortars, bullets, and rocket-launched grenades exploding around me. This madness of turning against the people of one's own clan for the status of corruptible power in a central government eluded me. This was the beginning of the warlord phenomenon in Somalia.

The other NGO worker and I were hosted by a Somali family during this time. Two of them risked their lives going to find food for us: The food was taken at gun point by fighters, who then fought each other for it. A close Muslim woman friend later began to introduce me to others as "one who has been with us in the war." One of my most vivid images from that time is watching an elderly man running down the middle of the main street, holding a small tree branch as the only protection he could find.

I sometimes felt overprotected when being met at the Mogadishu airport by a vehicle loaded with guns of all sizes and shapes, but there was no unarmed alternative. Most vehicles were hired out with gunmen included. I later learned that keeping the vehicle from being stolen was of crucial importance, and the guns were not necessarily there for my protection. I felt better about their not fighting a gun battle for my protection, but I still frequently prayed that we would not encounter trouble. I was never sure that I could live with the knowledge that someone had been killed transporting me, when I had made the decision to be there.

Still, I always felt better when there were no weapons with me, whether on foot or in a car. Somalis knew immediately if a vehicle was unarmed because the guns were usually visible; I felt less of a threat to the bandits or militias when I was unarmed. I later wrote a poem about feeling like a prisoner of guns after being transported in a U.N. vehicle in Mogadishu. I did not feel protected by the guns; I felt terrorized by the guns.

When I did encounter bandits on the way to a peace meeting in Somaliland in early 1993, I thought my life was abruptly ending. One of the bandits pulled the driver out of our car and tried to drive off into the countryside with us. When he could not get the car started, a gun battle ensued, including the use of a large mounted weapon. As we sat huddled in the car with various guns pointed at us, I felt utterly helpless and without choice. The violation and vulnerability of rape came to me in those moments. I had thoughts such as: *They are going to kill us. This is where my life ends. No, they're not going to kill us or they would have already. My family won't like hearing about this. I might die in this black and green dress.* And boom, the big gun was fired yet again. Still, we were alive.

There is more to this story. Negotiations were taking place in that little town among some of the community leaders and the community's bandits. The community itself seemed to "win" as the bandits stormed off. No one was injured. It was a disgrace to the town that we had been harassed on our way to a major peace meeting in Somaliland. After the bandits drove off, the people who gathered in the streets sang and clapped for us as we continued on our journey. "*Alxamdullila!*" (God be praised!) they said. The strength of those people, that community, was more powerful than the guns. Peace that day was stronger than violence. It was a peace story of Somali people with community rules, religious conviction, integrity, and accountability.

## A Mennonite and a Woman

I began to listen to and believe how Somalis had traditionally kept peace among themselves. I was intrigued by the role of community leaders, elders, and women. I was impressed by the culture's decision making by consensus. And I began to hear how I was perceived in moving among them.

I was seen, first of all, as a Mennonite. Mennonites over the previous forty years had earned credibility with the Somali people. The names of teachers were remembered, and practically everywhere I met Somalis who had attended Mennonite secondary schools or had relatives who had. Somalis were especially grateful for the opportunities to learn English, as English was not widely spoken in Somalia. This gave me an opportunity to connect with a significant number of people, who provided "protection" for me wherever I went. This uncanny protection allowed me to talk about peace, about the past, about the future, about the effects of drug abuse on Somali families, about faith. I was perceived as a "person with religion." I heard that one Muslim sheik had told his friends to work with me because I took religion seriously. Some of the most heartfelt caring for me was expressed in the sentiment that if only I would become Muslim, I would be nearly perfect. Well, I was still a woman.

To my Somali women friends, I was perceived as a friend. I traveled and visited the families of some of them. I believed that women were the keepers of Somali culture and were able to make significant contributions to the peace process. Although most women of Somalia and Somaliland have not received formal education, there are some that have become professors, administrators, even government ministers. These women are determined, strong, empowered. I gained much of my knowledge about the Somali people and their culture through friendly conversations with some of these women.

While being a woman in Somalia is perceived as being less than a man, this was sometimes to my advantage. Being the representative for the Mennonites of North America, I had a position from which to speak out against drug usage and corruption and for community effort and working together. I had many conversations with men regarding the status of women or the importance of protecting my own rights and choices as a single woman. At times, I suspect, I was viewed as an asexual being and was treated much like a man. At other times, I felt sidelined, unimportant, irrelevant to what was happening around me. I worked using intuition as a guide in whether to be assertive and talkative or passive and quiet.

I learned that if the men came to trust me, they were more likely to allow me to spend time with the women. Other times, I was seen as a threat, since I was a Christian visiting with Muslim women. I also faced some harassment from men, who felt that my religion and culture allowed them to treat me with disrespect. North American single women are not generally viewed with high regard. Being as consistent and clear in my intentions as possible allowed trust to build, however, and eventually I earned respect even for taking a stand against common sexual advances. I had been told by North American Mennonites before going to Somalia that it would not be what I said that would be effective and remembered, but how I lived. I was watched.

There were other times when I felt I could not connect with the women or was specifically being kept away from them. I knew many women had no one to listen to their stories. They told the historical events differently from most of the men, with the added perspective of having been overlooked, mistreated, or abused. Women seemed to understand the importance of education for their children in ways many of the men took for granted. Women more readily spoke the truth about the effect that drugs had played in the lives of their families. They took a major role in providing food for their families; they also walked straight and tall while enduring the hardship of their lives. They entertained and cared for me and sometimes encouraged me to speak for them. Many tried to organize themselves as cross-clan communities of women who were working for peace.

Later, in the work of peacebuilding, women hosted clan meetings in their homes, carried information from one side of a conflict to another, and organized marches for women from disputing sides to come together and make a statement for peace. They also were sometimes manipulated by men who wanted to keep them clanist, unfulfilled, uneducated, and without access to resources. Women have probably suffered the most in all regions of Somalia. The high incidences of rape and torture by their own and other clan militias should be unthinkable in the Islamic religion. Only a few women had access to aid dollars and used them to play the war and clan games like the men. The energy of most women, however, was consumed with the daily struggle for food.

## The Qat Specter

The drug trade in Somalia and Somaliland is something I once promised a Somali woman that I would speak up about wherever I could. Almost all male Somalis use what has always been considered a mild narcotic, called qat, khat, or chat. The drug is grown primarily in Ethiopia and Kenya for Somali consumption. Qat used to be chewed only by elders for special occasions or during meetings with hours-long discussions. It was considered a recreational drug.

A positive accomplishment of former President Siad Barre was to make the drug illegal for a number of years. That law was changed in early 1990, however, and qat was selling in huge quantities even before the war. It became a weapon of war as warlords negotiated for quantities to give to the militias each day, and qat started being chewed daily by many more men for much of every afternoon. There is disagreement over whether the drug is habit forming; one study failed to find negative effects.

I began to ask questions, however, about current usage, its cost, its effects on the body, and the effects on the family. Speaking to a person alone nearly always resulted in different answers than when I spoke to men in a group. The effects of qat are said to be clarity of thought, a feeling of power, freedom from feeling hungry and from worrying, and sometimes a feeling of excitement or hyperactivity. But men admitted that with their qat use they were making the women suffer even more. Some said that it helped them forget their desperation for just a little while. A few bold men spoke openly about the evils of qat; some have even been killed in qat fights. A few said proudly they had never chewed it.

Even during the Somali famine of the early 1990s, between $150,000 and $200,000 was reportedly being traded in qat every day. The effects on the family were devastating. Women were forced to hide the little bit of money they made at the market, and sometimes they were beaten and forced to give it to their husbands. Qat profits helped warlords pay their militias and purchase illegal weapons in the international market. Qat generated significant amounts of money, even as Somalis asked for millions of dollars in international aid. I believed that qat was such a major contributing factor to the collapse of Somali society that it could not be talked about openly. I therefore used the credibility and freedom I had as a North American Mennonite to refuse to chew qat myself and to frequently speak out about the connections among the users, their families, their religion, and their society. This was done in some group settings as well as in individual conversations.

## Discovering a Modality for Action

Once established in Nairobi, I milled around various circles, trying to be aware and appropriate and trying to give time for trust to build with Somali contacts both in Nairobi and Mogadishu.

One of my primary functions in representing Eastern Mennonite Missions and the Mennonite Central Committee was to determine how our resources should be allocated. Some thought my sole purpose in having an office in Nairobi was so that I could distribute money to Somali individuals and organizations, for that was what many international organizations did whose workers feared to travel to Somalia. I tried to treat each request for money, projects, or other assistance with respect. I made myself listen to countless stories in my office, and sometimes it was enough just to listen. Other times, I argued with Somalis who were trying to get easy access to aid dollars for suspect motives. Mostly, I advocated the use of nonviolence to face the problems of the former Somalia.

Because I was traveling into the country more often than some of the Somalis who came to see me in Nairobi and was experiencing some of Somalia's violence myself, I could better assess if I were being told the truth about an event or situation. I became known as an advocate for Somalia and Somaliland. I was not interested in setting up meetings and doing projects in Nairobi. I traveled into Somalia often enough that I was assumed to be somewhat knowledgeable about recent events and their implications. Although I never felt I had sufficient knowledge or understanding, I began to act and to take risks with what information I did have.

The Mennonite office became a place to ask not only for money but for medical assistance and study scholarships, or it was a place just to visit, lament, or dream. I tried to focus on personal relationships with these men (and the occasional woman) and tried to be as consistent as possible in listening and giving assistance, attention, and care.

In the midst of my trying to pretend that my life had a schedule and routine, the massive famine of 1992 hit, the fighting continued, and U.N. and U.S. troops entered Somalia. For those of us already on the scene, the challenge was not simply in deciding how to respond to reports of mass starvation but in how to keep asking the broader questions. Should we do our own projects, my Mennonite coworkers and I wondered, or support those of others? How can we maximize communication? We reminded ourselves that we were message carriers and contributors. We needed to keep in touch with the community-level connections. What are the *real* sources of the conflicts in Somalia? we asked. How can we better link to other groups? We knew we must keep working from the belief that Somalis themselves could work at peace among themselves, that they had the keys necessary to bring a lasting peace to the people of Somalia.

During my "exile" in Nairobi, I became interested in encouraging various projects that were in line with the peace focus of EMM and the MCC. I was visited by men and women, young and old, rich and poor, and members of different clans and subclans. Often the request was for funds, so I worked out criteria for how to distribute funds. I became more keen on projects that were cross-clan but area specific, projects that included any minority clans in the area, projects that were done by the Somali people who lived where the project would be done, and projects that seemed realistic relative to what people were already doing in that area. I tried to encourage more of the kinds of projects that I had heard were already being done on a small scale by Somalis for Somalis. In this way, I spent less time on professionally prepared project proposals for professional amounts of dollars, although sometimes I offered proofreading or gave suggestions for rewriting major proposals, which went to the larger donors.

The longer I read about and studied the Somali culture and the more I heard, the more I began to see the connections among Somali NGOs, women working for peace, the people Somalis refer to as the "intellectuals," and the traditional peacemaking processes of the elders.

Elders have long been a part of conflict resolution in Somalia and Somaliland. Some elders become elders because their fathers or grandfathers were elders, and they are assumed to carry the values of and to care for the community as their fathers did. Other times, a man becomes an elder because of his good and fair judgment and integrity. Elders become elders much in the same way that people in the North might become known as upstanding; they are respected persons who have acted with integrity and dignity over a lengthy period of time. Elders are still mostly older men, but they can also be younger men if they are highly regarded and are willing to work with and respect the traditional elder systems.

Traditional systems vary in the degree to which they are actually trusted and utilized in various parts of Somalia and Somaliland. Given that many elders had become corrupt in the former Somalia and had functioned less in their traditional roles over the previous twenty years, they themselves were sometimes doubtful that the traditional systems could work. In other locations, stately, dignified elders were still deeply respected and carrying out the roles of adviser and mediator for their particular clan family and village. Disputes were settled within the level of the lowest common denominator possible. Thus, disputes within the family were settled within the family. Disputes between two families were settled by the elders of the two families, etc.

The women had a unique role in traditional peacemaking because they were often the objects of an agreement between two disputing parties. Women were historically given to cross-clan marriages as a means of assuring that there would be no fighting, as it was expected that they could not in good conscience kill their own kin. A woman did not take on her husband's name and cultural identity but retained the name and clan identification of her father. In this way, women have traditionally gone back and forth between clans with information that has helped to keep peace among the clans. There were also, obviously, negative consequences of using women as trade objects in the way one also traded camels, sheep, and goats to pay debts or to make restitution for wrongs done.

The Somali NGOs have loosely been connected with the intellectuals of the society, and I found that it was the Somali NGOs and intellectuals who knew who the key players were in a given area. I therefore gave them encouragement to work at the peace process by once again advocating the use of elders in a traditional peacebuilding role. Some of the Somali NGOs were willing to do this; others felt that the work was too hard and that I expected too much of their involvement.

I frequently asked questions about what was already happening in the various Somali communities, how this group or that group planned to make community contributions to a proposed project, how even one person could make a difference in the community. I asked many times what personal commitment one had for the good of all the Somali people and how the project would contribute to sustaining peace in the area. I often encouraged a visitor to think, plan, dream, imagine how the peace process could be enhanced by members of women's groups, traditional elders, Somali NGOs, and intellectuals. Sometimes people came back to tell me what they thought might be an avenue to a sustainable peace in their village or area.

Some of the projects for which I provided funding and material aid through the Somali NGOs included school kits that were distributed to various regions; food for 1,200 people repatriating to Somaliland and Somalia from Kenya; food given to a project in the Kenyan refugee camps; school textbooks distributed by cooperating Somali NGOs, elders, and government leaders; a city garbage clean-up (where there were potential land mines in the garbage); and women's income-generating projects. Also, on a smaller basis, health books were distributed to NGOs from the office; individual medical assistance was occasionally given; funds were distributed for small, unrecognized schools operated by Somalis; and connections were made with U.N. agencies on behalf of people trying to learn how the U.N. system could help them find family members, secure protection as a refugee, or get an education for their children. The majority of our efforts with the Somali NGOs, however, were focused on traditional peacemaking processes among and with the elders at the community level.

There was a strong focus and commitment to working at peacebuilding and education as the priority for Mennonite involvement during this time. Mennonites felt that this was their calling; it was what we were known for and what other aid organizations and many Somalis asked of us. This represented a paradigm shift—from the U.N.'s focus on warlords in "peacemaking" to our own encouragement of Somalis to work at peacemaking themselves within Somalia and Somaliland, using traditional, trusted meeting styles. Although few believed initially that the Somali tradition of keeping peace among Somalis could be resurrected and encouraged, the Mennonites worried that the armed humanitarian intervention would one day facilitate the resumption of war, once the troops were withdrawing.

I was insistent that information not be published about how we were working in Somalia and Somaliland if it would jeopardize our future opportunities to work with the Somali people, if lives would be put at risk, if it jeopardized the local peace process, or if it would give the impression of our working only with one clan or clan area of Somalia.

Working in consultation with many different groups, my sources of information were varied. Several international NGOs agreed to work together at peace initiatives, although this was sporadic, and I often felt like a lone voice trying to focus on sustainable peace issues. I attended meetings of the U.N. in Nairobi, Mogadishu, and Addis Ababa and the NGO coordinating and security meetings in Nairobi and Mogadishu. I often did not speak in these meetings and was usually known by only a few workers from other organizations, as international staff changed so frequently. On several of the better-known elders' peace meetings or conferences that were initiated and organized by Somalis themselves, I worked with the Life and Peace Institute (LPI) of Sweden in providing encouragement and support and in sharing information. This working relationship helped me better understand some of the dynamics among Somalis I was meeting in my office.

I also had the consultation of John Paul Lederach and other Mennonites, who helped me in making decisions or in asking appropriate questions for the situation. While Lederach was often called into the situation to work at higher levels than I, my consultation with him eventually brought me into contact with various levels of the peace process as well. Most of my time, however, was spent at the community level. I always felt that I was working as part of a team of people with a common agenda, and I felt strongly affirmed and encouraged in my work by some of my coworkers in the United States, Canada, and Kenya. Still, I made most of the recommendations on my own for action on projects, meetings, and contacts with people. And although I felt sustained by my own faith and that of the broader community of Mennonites to which I was strongly attached, I often felt that I was working very much alone and sometimes was quite sure that I knew absolutely nothing about what I was doing and promoting in peacebuilding. I was afraid at times, but I always knew that there were coworkers who would listen to my fears and still encourage my continued participation and involvement.

## Building Peace from the Bottom Up

Word spread that the Mennonites were working with various clans throughout Somalia and Somaliland, encouraging peace efforts. It did not seem to matter that Mennonites were not present en masse. In fact, we sometimes got credit from Somalis for meetings I knew nothing about or had only heard about!

My asking questions and encouraging the elders who came to the office led to small peace meetings in various places around Somalia. The durations and results of these meetings were beyond my control. Sometimes I received feedback on them, and other times I did not. But I continued to work in the good faith that something positive was happening "out there," and it usually was confirmed to me by members of other clans, who had noted the activity and labeled the efforts as positive. As I had never had any training in mediation, conflict resolution, community development, or project management, I am certain that I missed opportunities others might have taken. But I also may have more authentically believed that the Somali people could work out their own peace because I was sure that I could not manage or engineer the task. It was absolutely clear to me, however, that peacebuilding in Somalia and Somaliland would be extremely complex and therefore would inevitably be a long-term process.

The first major elders' conference that the Mennonites contributed to financially was the Borama Elders' Conference. With assistance from MCC, LPI, and several other aid organizations, this was an attempt to give the traditional approaches to settling conflict some hope and credibility. Our contribution of only $18,000 to this peace conference was increased by several other donors to support a meeting that took place from January to May 1993. These funds from the North American Mennonites, made possible by individual and church contributions in support of the work of MCC worldwide, were few in comparison to U.N. spending, but they contributed significantly to a Somali process involving many Somali people.

The first talk of a peace meeting, to my knowledge, came from a meeting I had in a small Djibouti cafe in September 1992 with two Somalis from a Somali NGO. What happened was typical of how things work in Somali culture. These men talked with me about their dreams for peace in Somaliland, and I encouraged them to plan something creative that, with international assistance, would help to make and sustain the peace. They then talked to others, who talked to others, who talked to others. These two men did not themselves figure prominently in the actual conference, which happened in early 1993, but by that time, many others had come to believe that they could resurrect some of the traditional leadership and ways of settling conflict. It was also widely agreed that the United Nations was not wanted in Somaliland and that aid organizations were focused mostly on Somalia in the south. As Somaliland had seemingly fewer alternatives for making peace, they turned more quickly to the option provided by the traditional roles of elders and of peacebuilding mechanisms in general.

Marv Frey, an MCC administrator, and I attended the first days of the conference and gave our encouragement to the participants to work at the issues in Somali style. While there, we met with elders, women, intellectuals, and Somali NGO representatives. In the meetings themselves, poetry was quoted, the Koran was read, and endless speeches were made.[2] I can only guess that this kind of interaction continued for the next several months. At the end of the conference, a president was selected for Somaliland by the elders. Although this was not an intended outcome, it was one that was agreed upon by the conference attendees, made up largely of elders. This proved not to have been a perfect process, and some of the agreements broke down in Somaliland. People again became discouraged with a centralized governing system. But there continued to be significant elder involvement in local affairs and disputes within the five regions of Somaliland and in ongoing work at peacebuilding.

The second significant elders' conference that was partially financed by MCC was in the eastern part of Somaliland. This area felt it had something unique to offer to the overall peace process because the area was inhabited by five of Somalia's major clan families. It was felt that if they could succeed in working together and respecting one another's grazing lands, it could provide significant hope for addressing cross-clan difficulties in all of Somalia and Somaliland. MCC gave $10,000 toward this effort, which lasted approximately three months. I also attended this meeting of men, where I gave a speech about the need for personal commitment, community support, and long, hard work in order for a peace process to succeed. Later, MCC published the content and agreements from this conference to give access to a broader Somali population. Copies were distributed as people met together. Second and third printings of the report were needed as the document was shared around the regions of Somalia and Somaliland. One person noted that it was the first time he had seen their agreements written down in a way that reflected what actually happened in the meeting. Many were pleased that the report was printed in both the Somali and English languages.

Gradually, groups of elders began to show up at my office to report on how peace meetings were going in a particular area, or certain elders would send greetings from various places inside Somalia. I often wondered if more connections were happening among the elders *because* of my ignorance of the situation. How could I really know what was happening, or who was telling me the truth? I learned to say enough to seem knowledgeable about an area or situation, which, I think, encouraged more truth telling about what was actually happening there. One elder came to my office and said that he had been watching me for many months. (I had only seen him once.) He said that he had observed that I could look in the eye of a person and know if the person were telling the truth. He was, apparently, getting information on exactly who was being helped and how and which people were leaving my office with ideas and which ones with discouragement because I had not given them money. So now, this man (a known elder among his clan) was coming to present his truth to me and to ask for assistance with primary schools.

I even had disgruntled elders come to the office to protest assistance given for a particular meeting, but then later they returned to talk about the meeting's success and how they were now in communication and working together with elders from other subclans or clans. On the second visit, these elders came with a letter of apology, recommended by the clan leader, for having harassed me earlier. The clan leader was embarrassed that his elders might be seen as hindering a peace process with their neighbors. In fact, my office door was open to any who came, and when people questioned how I could know whom to assist, I replied that I was trying to treat each individual the same and to promote the same ideas, regardless of status, motives, or clan.

Working with any Somali person, regardless of clan, region, or religion, was not only a matter of conviction for me, it was a necessary component to staying alive and integrated in Somali culture. I believed that Mennonites could lose significant credibility among Somali people if we looked only at assisting a few marginalized peoples. It was extremely important to be able to show that we were working with multiple clans in various regions. This meant that, because of the limits of my knowledge, projects had to be small enough that I could make a judgment of the situation and distribute assistance appropriately. To focus on only one area with one program would have taken all of my available energy, and the continuity of the Mennonite presence in Somalia and Somaliland could have been significantly hindered for future work and association.

In 1994 and 1995, we gave small financial contributions totaling $25,000 to four more small peace meetings. I did not attend those particular meetings, although I was cordially invited. Because of my unfamiliarity with the regions and the high political tensions at the time, I felt it best for me to remain in the role of encourager rather than to become a potential target for clan tensions and warlord skirmishes over land ownership.

I had individual meetings with persons in my office when at least an additional ten peace meetings were being dreamed about or proposed. Part of my focus was to encourage broader participation in the peace process by other organizations, and even the United Nations if possible, for I was feeling increasingly vulnerable as focus kept coming back to me as a key person supporting and advocating the traditional peace meetings. Some other organizations did assist in small ways; others could not understand the usefulness of such meetings and refused to participate. At least twice I arranged meetings of Somali NGOs from various clan areas, and we met to discuss how to promote the peace process. Mostly, these were opportunities for persons to meet those from other clans and to recognize that some of them were working toward the same goals of peace for all Somali people.

Toward the end of my stay, one of the warlords spoke out against me. I heard that he used me as propaganda to show a particular clan or clans that I was confusing the issue of peace and was meeting with the "wrong" people. He charged that I was helping militias to rearm themselves for attacks on the warlords. Me. A Christian, a pacifist, and a woman. I felt somewhat threatened to hear that I was being discussed among the warlords of Somalia. A Somali woman said that our work was having an effect, otherwise it would not be noticed by the warlords. Still, this news was disconcerting to me, while at the same time it affirmed that Somali people were coming together in ways that were becoming threatening to the larger power struggles. Somali people were beginning more readily to call the bluff of the warlords to the international community.

## Postscript

The conflicts and dilemmas of my experiences in Somalia and Somaliland still rage inside me. The polarizations have no answers. My understanding of commitment, community, relationships, and trust became more central to my own personal processes, more connected to a broader community of faith people, and more committed to nonviolence. I realized that true pacifism could sometimes be a lone voice, a risky voice, a belief in following through with justice, even at my own personal expense. This was the case even when I felt helpless, watching a suffering person and knowing that no immediate help was going to save that particular life. But, it called me to action to be creative in ways that might give courage to others in the struggle for the good life. There were moments when I thought I would die in Somalia. Some of those moments were worth dying for, some were not.

I am sometimes angry about all of the injustices I saw among Somalis and among the international community and the expense of many lives lost. I do not know what to do with the vulnerability and helplessness Somali people have felt as they have watched their children murdered before their eyes, their wives raped, their husbands killed, or their brothers and sisters gunned down.

I have never been so aware of my own transparency and vulnerability as when working among the Somali people. It is said that they look into the eyes of a person for the first time and know whether or not there will be relationship and trust with that person. Apparently, the Mennonites have had some "good eyes" over the years, which has put us more in a position of trust among Somalis than perhaps our small presence has deserved. With such an understanding, however nebulous, there are still creative ways to be a presence, to stand with, and to assist the Somali people.

It has been painful to care. Painful to hear the story of a shopkeeper shot dead while a customer was making a purchase. Painful to watch women selling qat because they have not found another way to feed their children. Painful to hear detailed stories of terror. Painful to hear one by one of the deaths of friends and to try to compare the cost of lives with my own comparatively temporary and seemingly insignificant sacrifices.

I made hard choices in Somalia and Somaliland to love, to be vulnerable, to believe that I did not have the answers for Somali people, and to believe wholeheartedly in presence. Presence is sharing both good times and bad, is walking with those who suffer. Presence without needing to see an outcome of peace or of government. Presence without an outcome of converts. Presence just because we believe in hope and peace. My experience has permeated so many parts of myself. I feel a part of the Somalia/Somaliland story.

I hope that other persons will commit themselves to a time of difficult interaction and vulnerability with a beautifully unique people and culture. I hope that others will hear the language, respect the religion, experience the culture, and will be a presence for peace among the many Somalis who are working for the hope of peace. Most of all, I hope for a lasting peace for the Somali people and that their homes will once again be safe and secure.

## *Eleven*

## Trauma-Healing and Reconciliation Workshops during Liberia's Civil Crisis

BARRY HART

"TRIBAL LIBERIANS LIVED WITH one another *very understandably* before the war."

This statement, made by a Liberian ninth grader,[1] reflects a widely held perception among Liberians about their personal and intergroup relations before the war that began on December 24, 1989. Prior to that time, most members of Liberia's seventeen ethnic groups did live, work, and trade with one another peacefully, and they often married across ethnic lines. Even those from the America-Liberian minority community who stayed after the 1980 coup, which ended 133 years of America-Liberian rule, experienced a certain tolerance and sense of peace before the war. But, as another ninth grader, a member of the Krahn ethnic group, stated:

> Generally the civil war has created some gigantic impact on the lives of the Liberian people. The war has caused some great changes in the minds of the typical Liberian. The Krahn, Mandingo, Gio, and Mano [ethnic groups], who are the major perpetrators of this war, once lived together very happily and inter-married. [Now] the Gio and Mano from Nimba County have become enemies to the Mandingo and Krahn. . . . They look at each other like two different people. (Hart, 1995 p. 192)

War dramatically changed the relationships among those four ethnic groups,[2] as well as among all of the ethnic and religious communities of Liberia. The civil crisis caused divisions among groups based on fear for their survival, victimization, divisive political rhetoric, and myths of differences and boundaries among the groups, whether remembered or newly developed. They quickly came to see the other groups as different and distinct peoples. Trust among groups was lost, and tolerance was replaced by fear and intolerance of the "other." An "us" and "them" dichotomy developed, especially along ethnic lines.

Although these factors were a result of the war, they were not without historical precedent. The traumatization that resulted from the destructive and divisive aspects of the civil conflict was based on sociocultural differences and economic disparity, as well as on political and ethnoclass animosities, which existed from before Liberian statehood in 1847. Threats and wars across ethnic lines were a part of the historical development of the people who were indigenous to or who had settled along West Africa's Grain Coast.

A lengthy explanation of the sociocultural, political, and relational history of Liberia is not appropriate here (see Dunn and Holsoe, 1995; Liebenow, 1987; Sawyer, 1992), but an overview of these factors is important to help explain the war, as well as the trauma-healing and reconciliation work I was involved in with the Christian Health Association of Liberia (CHAL), in response to the war. It will also help clarify the research on threats to ethnic identity that I conducted for my doctoral work and that I draw upon here (1995).

## Factors Leading to Civil Crisis

Even prior to the arrival of freed American slaves as settlers in Liberia, tribal groups[3] along the Grain Coast were frequently at war and enslaved or sold one another into slavery. Groups in one part of the region, because of their numbers and centralized forms of governance, dominated trade and expanded their territory at will, forcing smaller groups to assimilate or move on. The traumatization and threat to identity from the violence and deprivation caused groups to change and adapt. But the "normalcy" of these evolutionary conditions was modified substantially with the arrival of the Americo-Liberians and the American Colonization Society representatives who came with them in the early 1820s.[4] The values and attitudes brought by the settler community threatened ethnic identity at a different level than before and altered the course of relationships among indigenous Liberians by adding a new set of social and political variables to the region. The settlers' symbolic codes, such as those relating to nature, religion, or governance, were clearly not the same as those of the indigenous communities.[5] This led to misinterpretations and regular defensiveness between the new arrivals and the native peoples.

For its part, the Americo-Liberian community was plagued by issues of minority status, perhaps causing them to regard most members of the indigenous community as the enemy. This can be seen both as a psychological need of Americo-Liberians to maintain individual and group identity and as the related need to maintain political and economic power, which is also related to group identity.

This brief overview is inadequate to fully explain Americo-Liberian identity or the Americo-Liberian–indigene relationship. There are many other factors related to history, tradition, culture, prejudice, traumas, and so forth that inform both of these categories. But what this overview does point to is that the settler community recognized the vulnerability of its minority status and used various political, economic, military, and other means to protect it. That this led to a long-term denial of social, economic, and political justice for the indigenous population can be seen in the light of the need for the Americo-

Liberians to protect their core constructs of identity and security. (A similar protective response was taking place among the indigenous groups.) These and subsequent divisions can thus be understood within a survival/identity framework. It is also certain that contextual and situational factors affected ethnic identification as well.

A partial synthesis of the minority and majority groups did take place in Liberia over time. Indigenous persons took on certain Western values and customs, and settlers eventually intermarried and adopted various symbols of indigenous groups. Even so, the divisions remained. The crystallizing and hardening of what were construed as *self* and *nonself* evolved within a social and political system dominated by the minority community. No final relational synthesis could take place when power was used to deprive, or to threaten to deprive, persons of resources, space (misappropriation of indigenous lands, for example), and full political representation.

Other psychological and real-world factors led to further division of Liberia's peoples along ethnic and class lines. These related to Liberia's role in Africa and its responsibility in and fear of decolonization in other African states. (The political center in Monrovia espoused freedom for its neighbors but limited the freedom of its own indigenous population.)

All that seemed to change as time went on was the expansion of political patronage and the creation of an indigenous elite caught, perhaps willingly, in its vortex. The result was a new ethnoclass division and rising discontent among the intelligentsia, which eventually produced a move for the replacement of Americo-Liberian dominance with leadership from the indigenous community. This finally happened with the 1980 coup, but it resulted in further autocratic, even tyrannical, leadership in the person of Master Sergeant Samuel K. Doe.

## War

The invasion of Liberia on Christmas Eve 1989 by Charles Taylor, a Liberian with Americo-Liberian ancestry, and 150 rebel soldiers was staged to replace the "devil" Doe. Politically, the Doe government was inept and clearly corrupt. His attempt to bring indigenous rule to Liberia had been a ten-year failure. Economically and socially, Doe's kleptocracy and tribalistic governance had brought in a new and still more ethnically complicated era. The threat to ethnic identity had taken on a new form with overt animosity and violence leading to fear and traumatization of various ethnic groups.

Coup attempts in 1983 and 1985 and various "democratic" elections had failed to replace the Doe government. Taylor also failed to eliminate Doe, as he had pledged to do with his invasion of Liberia. (That result was, however, accomplished on September 9, 1990, by Prince Johnson, a rebel leader who broke from Taylor.) What Taylor did succeed in doing was to deepen the division and manipulation of the Liberian people.[6] In the quest for political and economic power, he mobilized the Gio and Mano ethnic groups against members of Doe's Krahn group and sympathetic Mandingos. His invasion force soon mushroomed to 5,000–6,000 men and boys. Over the next five years, the war would claim more than 150,000 lives, displace more than half of the country's population, and traumatize a large segment of Liberia's 2.4 million people.

## First Contact

I first arrived in Liberia in June 1991, six months after the initial fighting had stopped. Some 15,000–20,000 people had already died, and the country was divided into two sections: Greater Liberia, approximately 95 percent of the country, which was controlled by rebel leader Charles Taylor, and Monrovia, which was governed by President Amos Sawyer and protected by the West African Peace Keeping Force, known as ECOMOG.

I was a member of a trauma and conflict resolution team sponsored by the Mennonite Central Committee (MCC), the Mennonite Board of Missions (MBM), and the Lutheran church. We were to work with the Christian Health Association of Liberia in war-related trauma and reconciliation work. MBM had sponsored other workers in Liberia prior to the war. Steve and Dorothy Wiebe-Johnson had been sent to Liberia in the summer of 1988 to establish a link with the indigenous churches and to begin Christian education programs. They were joined by health workers Peter and Betty Hamm in October 1989, just before the outbreak of war in December of that year.

Dale Schumm, MBM Asia director and a psychologist, had laid the ground-work for our involvement with a visit to Liberia in early 1990 and a psychosocial assessment prepared for CHAL in 1991. This assessment could not be done in Liberia because of the war, so Schumm met with CHAL representatives in Côte d'Ivoire to develop an action plan for our team. Other MBM workers in Liberia at that time were Juanita Shenk, a nurse, who was there from March to April 1991 to help with the aftermath of war, and Wayne Weaver, a medical doctor, who was in Monrovia from March to June 1991.

MBM's theme regarding the church's mission to the world is "mediating reconciling love for all creation under the rule of God in Christ." In Liberia, this theme would shift dramatically from biblical education and health work to logistical and relief work and, finally, to involvement in trauma healing, bias awareness, mediation training, and reconciliation. The international trauma-healing and reconciliation team that was responsible for this latter shift comprised Dolores Friesen, an MBM-sponsored psychologist and former African missionary, Al Swingle of the Lutheran church, who had spent fifteen years in Liberia as a missionary, and me. My background was in community-based training and conflict resolution work in the United States and Northern Ireland. The local members were CHAL executive director Elizabeth Mulbah, CHAL program manager Marion Subah, and Deanna Isaacson, a long-term Lutheran missionary and CHAL instructor in curative and preventative health care.

Our assignment was to facilitate two one-week workshops in trauma heal-ing, conflict resolution, peace, and reconciliation for participants from various parts of central Liberia. This had come about as a result of a CHAL request to MBM, a member of a U.S.-based CHAL support group, to do some con-sultations and assessment on the emotional, trauma-related, and reconcilia-tion needs of the Liberian people as a result of the devastation of the civil war.[7] During these consultations, which took place in Côte d'Ivoire in 1991, it became clear that large segments of Liberia's population were greatly trau-matized and needed to be helped. Not being able to deal with every trauma case, it was determined that people who were "caregivers" should be the target group to receive training. This group, many of whom were themselves trau-matized, would still be expected to be a resource of courage and strength for the rest of the population. Therefore, religious leaders, medical personnel, and educators, most of whom were members of CHAL before the war, were invited to the workshops. Furthermore, since schools in most parts of Liberia were to open in July, it was decided that our workshops would include teachers.

The first workshops, with more than sixty adults participating—approxi-mately one-half of them teachers—also provided time for children of various ages and needs to participate. The adults were able to make immediate use of their experiences and skills from the workshop in relating to the children. In so doing, they not only began to help the children deal with their trauma, but the adults also gained insight into their own loss and grief.

The workshops brought together men and women from five of Liberia's thirteen counties and its various ethnic groups. Our training team decided that the best way to serve these people was to develop an overall strategy that would draw both on local cultural themes and on biblical understandings.[8] We entitled the workshops Seeds of Growth, using the farming cycle to show the changes that take place from the ashes (symbolizing war) in which Lib-erians plant their rice, through the seasonal changes, necessary work, and nurturing needed to harvest the rice crop (the healing experience).

The first day's theme was Seeds of Loss and Change, and we dealt with war loss, grief, trauma, stress, and how these had changed individuals, groups, and society. On the second day, whose theme was Seeds of Conflict and Forgive-ness, we asked the workshop participants to examine the dangerous and neg-ative aspects of conflict, as well as stating anything about conflict that they saw as an opportunity for growth. We also explored the biblical meaning of forgiveness and how it can overcome anger, hate, and the desire for revenge.

The third day we looked at Seeds of Hope and Healing, and explored the biblical hope and the psychological and spiritual healing that come through recognizing the place that the individual and group (clan or ethnic) can have in the healing cycle.

Seeds of Mediation/Conflict Resolution and Reconciliation was the fourth day's theme. We examined and practiced mediation techniques (which were adapted to the culture) and talked about the spiritual and practical elements of being reconciled to those who have hurt you. We brought children in to tell of their fear and pain from the war and emphasized listening skills and empathic responses in these storytelling encounters. The day ended with a worship service of remembering the dead and reconciliation.

During the final day, the Seeds of Peace and Reconciliation were planted. The two of us who were Mennonite on the training team shared our pilgrimages as members of the peace-church tradition, and our Lutheran colleague confessed his change of understanding concerning peace and his desire to be a Lutheran peacemaker. The workshop participants were encouraged to reflect on what *peace* meant in their own languages. In Kpelle and Mano, we were told, peace means "a settled heart," and in Kissi and Belle it means "a cool heart," one not heated by anger or hatred. In Loma, peace means "the heart lay down," and in Bassa, my favorite, peace means "lack of noise and confusion." The last exercise we did that day was to ask the participants to write in their journals (which they had been keeping all week) the practical next steps they would attempt to take once they returned home—steps to heal, to prevent further chaos, and to begin the long process of reconciliation and building a peaceful society.

The second workshop was similar to the first, but we decided to do more work on bias and prejudice reduction. *Tribalism* (a term used by Liberians), or ethnic differences and animosities, had been significant factors in this war. When we found that the issues of ethnic conflict were regularly referred to throughout the first workshop, we modified the second to address more fully those concerns. At that time, I was struck by the connections among trauma and issues of identity, security, and self-esteem as they relate to ethnic tensions—a connection I wanted to understand and that I eventually made a central part of my research on threats to ethnic identity (discussed below).

With these workshops completed, my American colleagues left, and my new CHAL colleagues and I proceeded, through twenty-seven rebel checkpoints, to Monrovia. There we did another three-day workshop on the same themes. At this time, I first thought about working full time in Liberia. This would come to pass the following year, when I returned for two years as the coordinator of CHAL's Trauma Healing and Reconciliation Program under a joint MBM and MCC mandate.[9]


## Practical and Theoretical Involvement

I had been emotionally moved and challenged by my experience in 1991 and knew that I wanted to return to further understand the Liberian situation, as well as my own responses to a people and place exposed to the destructive forces of war. My interest in these issues was driven by two factors. One was a need to understand why people feel threatened by others—to the extent that they would violently attack other social units to protect or enhance the security of their own. Parenthetically, I wanted to know how this threat manifests itself and if there are ways to help attenuate this threat through trauma awareness/healing and reconciliation processes.

Second, I knew that my training in conflict resolution was rooted in a religious and philosophical base of peace and nonviolent action. This thinking had been deeply challenged in other contexts, such as the conflicts in El Salvador and Nicaragua and, more recently, in Northern Ireland. Liberia would be a place were I would be faced with this challenge practically as well as theoretically. The real-world experience of suffering and injustice, especially the massive loss of life, was soon to move me beyond an intellectualization of war and its resolution.

## Practical Factors

My task was to direct a reconciliation and trauma program for the largest local health organization in Liberia. Before the war, the Christian Health Association of Liberia had been involved in providing, through its member organizations of clinics, hospitals, churches, and schools, a variety of health care services throughout the country. Although these were Christian-based service providers, they did not discriminate in providing care and services to Liberians; all were served, regardless of faith or tradition. Thus, I knew that I would have access to, and be able to work with, not only CHAL members but also other groups with which they interacted.

Furthermore, because CHAL had been highly respected before the war by Liberians, in general, and by political and other leaders, in particular, access to all regions of the country (when fighting had stopped or was at a minimum) and to persons who were now faction leaders in a divided Liberia would be easier.

Finally, I would be working *within* this organization, as a member of a team, for a minimum of two years. Since CHAL had a practice of inviting persons from other countries to be involved with their various programs long term, I would be seen as a part of CHAL—not as someone visiting Liberia but as someone living and working there.

## Theoretical Factors

I was interested in researching the linkages among trauma healing, reconciliation, and threats to ethnic identity. I knew this academic interest could not be separated from my philosophical or practical ones, so I used an action-research methodology oriented toward participant involvement, as well as individual and social change. This hands-on research allowed me to be directly involved with persons who were aware of the research and also were or became aware of their need to change personally, in order to help society change.

The members of our many workshops—pastors, nurses, midwives, schoolteachers, and later, community leaders, village elders, and traditional chiefs—came to understand that what was occurring was both a cooperative and a collaborative approach to contributing to this change. They understood that they would work with me and others at CHAL in practice-oriented activities that would involve them as individuals and as members of their respective ethnic and religious groups in needs identification, conflict resolution problem solving, and planning and implementing decisions.

In workshops (and other settings), participants helped me understand their context and their belief systems or worldviews. The war was explained to me, and I began to be told about the specific human needs that had been abused as a result of the war. Together, we attempted to address these needs and to gain further understanding of one another. Furthermore, the stereotypes I had held started to be dispelled as I listened to the people with whom I was interacting and whom I was growing to respect. In time, some of the misconceptions emerging from my initial assumptions began to shift.

Of course, no philosophy or theology is value free, and my own understandings regarding what was just or unjust, what constituted peace and peacemaking, who God was, or what finally threatened ethnic or other identity in the Liberian context were all colored by my own value and belief systems. Even using a strict elicitive approach to discover what Liberians thought and felt could not fully supplant my own values and beliefs. I understood, though, that by using multiple systems of inquiry and by involving both human science and a personal, faith-based belief system, which approached "questions about the human realm with an openness to its special characteristics" (Polkinghorn, 1983, p. 289), I would be able to discover the direction for my work and the appropriate methods for starting the process.

Although the connections among my interests, theory, faith, and reality were problematic, the theoretical base created and informed by the consciousness or practical awareness of the people, their history, culture, faith, and psychological condition allowed me to begin to interpret the environment in which I found myself. I was attempting to build a bridge between theory and practice, with the help of people who intimately knew this environment. Their awareness of what they wanted, what their aims were, and the process they wanted to develop and pursue to meet their goals was in large part dependent upon this interaction.

## Nonalienating Methodologies

My personal and research interests necessitated the development of nonalienating methodologies that would help CHAL members and other groups (including children) to explore their needs, be empowered to begin to meet those needs, and then act on their own behalf—as individuals but also clearly within and for their various identity groups, since the majority of Liberians, because of their communal experiences, understood their world only in relation to their subclans, clans, or ethnic groups.

I was interested in an elicitive form of interaction that would bring forth understanding of the psychosocial effects of war on workshop participants and also on persons I met through interviews and everyday encounters. Furthermore, I was interested in how their particular faiths defined the war and how the faiths helped the people deal with it. Through structured and unstructured interactions, a practical-theoretical paradigm began to emerge, which helped me critically reflect on my role as a participant and researcher in what I hoped would also be an empowerment process for people in a war environment. This paradigm was always being informed by the Liberians themselves and through a cyclical process was continually being returned to them for analysis and, finally, for application to their individual and corporate lives. Along with others, I attempted to facilitate "returning of knowledge for use to its point of origin" (Warry, 1992, p. 156).

## Western Concepts

Although elicitive methods were key to the development of a theory that was linked directly to practice, I believed from the beginning that certain concepts and practices from Western psychology and conflict resolution theory and practice, as well as from my Mennonite church background regarding faith and peace initiatives, could also apply to Liberia. Some of the psychological, conflict resolution, and religious concepts had been tried in somewhat similar situations, such as the Middle East, Mozambique, South and Central America, and elsewhere, by Mennonites, members of other religious groups, academics, and members of nongovernmental organizations (see, for example, Kolucki, 1996).

Moreover, the Liberian Christians who had invited the original team and asked me to come back to help lead these workshops believed that certain Western techniques had a place in their war-ravaged country—as did Westerners, who the Liberians believed could provide not only expertise but also perspective that they as victims of war might not have. Our 1991 experience had been a significant indicator that this constructive merging could take place (Schumm, 1991).[10] But the challenge was to use the elicitive model to further test ideas brought in from the outside.

Our standard working model was to first ask the participants how they or their elders or chiefs might resolve conflict, attempt to stop prejudice, or heal persons who had been traumatized. Drawing them out on these issues helped increase our understanding of how existing traditional methods or rituals of healing might be applied in the extraordinary crisis in their country (Hope and Timmel, 1984). (The elicitive model was somewhat easier with CHAL members, since many of them had been exposed to the Training for Transformation model, which is a strictly elicitive educational model. This was not the case with others, who were more accustomed to a lecture approach to learning.)[11]

It was at this point that other, more Western concepts would be introduced into the dialogue to see if they could in any way be merged with existing methods. We usually found that they could. This helped us to develop theoretically sound assumptions together, but, more important for the participants, I believe, it gave them the means by which to begin the healing process for themselves and eventually others as they shared their experiences, insights, and skills with members of their churches, schools, families, or ethnic groups.

## Workshops for Change

From 1992 to 1993, I worked with CHAL from a base in Monrovia. Over the course of those two years, my CHAL colleagues and I conducted some fifty trauma-healing and reconciliation workshops of twenty to thirty participants each in locations all over the country.[12] We knew that our workshops would only begin a process of change. Yet the fact that there were so few people in Liberia qualified to deal with trauma, post-traumatic stress reaction, and other psychosocial issues would often cause us to say, "A one-week workshop is better than nothing." We also knew, however, that this might *not* be the case. In working with such difficult issues as stress, trauma, bias/prejudice, and conflict between individuals and groups in what we initially thought was a postwar situation (the war restarted in October 1992[13]), we knew the task would be daunting and our impact in some ways limited.

We were somewhat consoled by the fact that initially we would work with CHAL members, who had experienced much trauma and needed help but who also already had certain helping skills and who worked with groups that could benefit from their experience and the new skills they would learn in our workshops. The workshops were, therefore, designed both to help the wounded individuals and to teach them skills and to provide a model they could pass on to others. This was also the model used in later workshops, in which we worked with people from ethnic groups whose members had fought, tortured, and killed one another.

## Role of Worship in the Workshop

As a Christian organization, we always prayed and sang gospel songs at the beginning of our workshops. There was a rich tradition of song and prayer in Liberia, and it had helped sustain CHAL's members through the most difficult times of the war. (Sometimes all that persons had were their Bibles, hymns, or gospel songs to see them through times of dislocation and hunger.) I fully supported this way of beginning week-long workshops and was truly moved by these experiences, as well as by the fact that CHAL employees met together each morning before the workshops began for singing, Bible study, and prayer. This was part of a community experience that I desired and needed. Throughout my stay in Liberia, I found love and support in this community and consequently found relief from my own experiences of stress and trauma.[14]

The workshops also included a period of Bible study every morning, which was tied to a theme that would be addressed that day, for example, listening, conflict, forgiveness, and reconciliation. I could see that the use of songs, prayer, and Bible study was important to the workshop participants. This practice proved disconcerting for me in later workshops in which adherents of Islam or Liberia's traditional religions were also present. What I witnessed in those multireligious experiences reflected some of the tolerance that had existed among groups before the war—and some of the problems as well.

Since Liberia had been understood to be a Christian nation from its inception, those who were not of the Christian faith accepted this "fact." Or at least they showed graciousness and tolerance and demonstrated those attributes by participating in the rituals of their state and their Christian neighbors. The problematic side was the historical insistence on Christianity and its link to oppressive political structures, which alienated non-Christians. Throughout Liberia's history, these structures relegated Muslims to second-class citizenship and were often used to manipulate the general population of whom approximately 70 percent still practiced traditional religions.

There was a third and more positive interpretation that may have been demonstrated in these multireligious workshops: that persons of the various faith systems believed in a singular God and, therefore, worshiping God through Christian songs and Bible study or through the Islamic prayers that were also offered in mixed workshops was not offensive to members of the other traditions. It may simply have indicated a worldview and cosmology that predated the arrival of both Christianity and Islam to Liberia, that is, an African understanding of a singular extraterrestrial God who could be worshiped through a variety of means. Whatever the case, consciously or unconsciously, the practice of worship seemed to allow a sense of bonding in the workshops and may have lowered certain defensive barriers among peoples of different faiths.

God certainly was an important figure for the majority of our workshop participants, and so God was evoked, praised, or worshiped as a part of the healing process. From this perspective, God transcended religious doctrine and institutional differences.

## Trauma Healing

As a result of our experience with the two 1991 workshops, trauma awareness and trauma healing were the first topics addressed in the new series initiated in 1992. Though not every person was highly stressed or traumatized by the war, great numbers of Liberians were dealing with symptoms of trauma or post-traumatic stress reaction. The war had been widely experienced by Liberians, and it continued for some time, even though there were cease-fires and long periods without fighting (see Hodges, 1991).[15] In the course of our work, a hypothesis regarding trauma as a basis for individual and group healing emerged. It began with the premise that war—and the trauma of war—levels the playing field or creates common ground and power equality among average citizens. It also embraced trauma healing as a relevant process toward increased individual and group emotional health, therefore helping to stabilize members of a society so that they might participate in the rebuilding of that society.

A corollary to this hypothesis was that trauma analysis and healing could be foundational processes in fostering personal and group understanding of identity, its sources, and development. The rationale was that while dealing with trauma individually and in groups, persons would, possibly for the first time, address in depth primordial issues and situational conditions that help determine their identities. Trauma, therefore, could become a window or a means for observing cultural markers, such as name, language, place, cult, food, as well as the sociopolitical factors that help persons (within their identity groups) understand the forces that made them who they are. This window (or insight) should not only provide persons a historical perspective on the development of identity but also open the way for current and even future insight regarding who they want to become.

I soon became aware that workshops that helped persons analyze and process their war trauma provided a unique opportunity for them to explore, psychologically and contextually, the self and the group (and the self vis-à vis the group) in new ways. In addition, I understood that this new self/group knowledge became important for aiding comprehension of the development of self-enhancing and protective stereotyping within and across group boundaries, as well as how certain malignant stereotyping leads to "enemy thinking" and eventually to conflict and acts of violence.

This led to a final element of this hypothesis, which was that the trauma-healing process could help in the attenuation of both perceived and real threats to individual and (ethnic) group identity, when threat perceptions were altered by new information regarding trauma-related fear, stress, and ambiguity. The trauma-healing process, therefore, could start an intra- and intergroup psychic evaluation process that, when coupled with prejudice reduction, conflict resolution problem solving, and genuine reconciliation procedures within and across group boundaries, could potentially eliminate threats to or repair individual and group identities.

Understanding and dealing with the desire for revenge is one case in which the detraumatization process relates directly to the possibility of attenuating or eliminating the threat to identity. One rather extraordinary example of this occurred in a CHAL workshop done in Voinjama in northwestern Liberia. After leading persons through a time of sharing their losses from the war regarding family members, homes, material goods, time, and hope, and hearing their pain, fear, and anger about these experiences, a pastor of a local church asked to tell his story in greater detail. He told of how his parents had had their throats slit in front of him by rebel soldiers and how he so hated those killers that all he could think about was seeking revenge. His anger was such that he felt that this was all there was for him in life, even though his Christian training and values told him something very different. He could not shake this urge or desire for revenge.

The pastor was relieved to discover through the workshop experience that this was a normal response to being traumatized and to the loss and grief felt by someone who had been so severely shocked and angered by such an event. We asked the pastor if he had experienced some of the other symptoms of being traumatized, such as mental numbness, disbelief that his parents were dead, guilt for allowing the killings to happen, or other emotional and physical responses. He indicated that he had and now recognized that he had let the "sun go down on his anger" (Eph. 4:25–26). This anger had turned into an all-encompassing desire to avenge his parents' deaths.

He also became aware that by going through this process of loss and grief, he could eventually come to accept and/or integrate what had happened so that he might move on with his life. By the end of the week and after several rituals of remembering the dead, grieving, and forgiveness or letting go, the pastor was able to say, "Maybe in two years I'll be able to move beyond this particular stage of loss and grief towards acceptance and forgiveness" (Hart, 1995, p. 223). This was a strong and healing statement (and unusual since we know that the process that allows for this realization normally takes much longer). It resulted in further dialogue about this man's parents as those persons who had played a significant role in teaching him his language and about his ethnic group's culture and myths and who in many ways gave him his sense of self, safety, and predictability.

We also discussed those individuals who had murdered his parents—individuals he did not know and probably never would. But he did know the ethnic group to which they belonged, so revenge as he understood it could be against any or all members of that group. In other words, because his sense of belonging and obligation, which he found in family, kin, and ethnic identity, were so shaken by this traumatic event, an entire ethnic group had become responsible for the deaths of his parents. In this way, what was a normal cultural response in Liberia in peaceful times, when one person could represent an entire group, had deadly consequences in times of war and when caught up in postwar feelings of revenge. I also considered this cultural practice to be a critical factor to an understanding of how prejudice and stereotyping helped create tensions that led to violence and war.

## Prejudice and Prejudice Reduction

In the Voinjama and other workshops, we focused rather narrowly on negative judgments made by individuals about ethnic or religious groups. We used the concept of *stereotype*, understood as a preconceived notion and set of exaggerated beliefs about a certain group of people, where all members of that group are seen to have similar attributes, to explore prejudice and to help define it. We elicited definitions of prejudice and added our own. We noted that the fear, antipathy, and misunderstandings involved in prejudice are based on faulty and inflexible generalizations. We further noted that ethnic prejudice, like any prejudice, may be simply felt or expressed, and it may be directed toward an individual or a group in an attempt to disempower the person or group.

Personally, I was interested in how Liberians viewed other Liberians, especially in war, when the dehumanizing and depersonalizing stereotypes caused large numbers of persons in various ethnic groups much pain and suffering. I was convinced that prejudicial hatred and the malignant stereotypes used to fuel it needed special attention in the process of detraumatization and healing of Liberians. Probably my theological and general human sensitivities related to respecting, even loving, others as a first priority played an important role in my deep desire to comprehend and somehow help change the attitudes and behaviors of those caught in enemy thinking.

I strongly believed that a comprehension of the protective shields that individuals and ethnic groups erect through stereotyping, as well as new insights regarding fear and ignorance of both their own groups and others, would aid Liberians in their understanding of what separates groups and what causes or enhances their traumatization when this separation leads to violent conflict.

In a theoretical sense, I understood that this us/them dichotomizing needed to be done to claim independence, to feel different from outgroups and their cultural and institutional realities, and to protect against potential influences that would alter a group's identity. Practically, I had experienced this regarding myself. As an individual, I was always being challenged by my faith to learn how to appreciate and respect differences *and* to remain open to embrace and celebrate those differences—even with those people whose actions I found repugnant.

We discussed the normalcy of feeling and wanting to be different from others, even the necessity of it to allow individuals and groups to establish their own identities and to experience a sense of security. But we also examined this concept as a form of fear of similarity, which when exaggerated by war, denies a common human identity. This was contrasted with the more overt and logical fear of differences or diversity found in explicit threats to or clear attacks on the target's identity, especially where the ultimate threat to identity manifests itself as violent attacks on or attempts to eliminate a group. This behavior, too, is an obvious denial of a common human identity.

This last aspect of threat to ethnic identity (explicit threat) was also explored in a moral and religious sense. Through depersonalization, dehumanizing, and demonizing, a scapegoat is created of the other, so blame can be ascribed to an inferior set of people for problems past, present, and even future. Many workshop participants, because of their trauma or their historical prejudices based on tribal animosity, differences, or feelings of superiority, could initially only make a negative moral evaluation of other ethnic groups. These groups were not only seen as inferior but were perceived to be evil and therefore were supposed to be condemned, shunned, or eliminated.

By beginning to uncover prejudices within themselves and their ethnic groups, participants—aided by an introspective, grieving, trauma-healing process or rituals that centered on their faith—began to shift in their thinking about the other. We reminded them of a traditional adage that says: "You can break the stick but not the bundle." This helped them see that they could be broken as individuals or even as a single ethnic group, if they did not expand their consciousness beyond themselves and their own group to include others. Religiously, we pushed them further with a set of questions that required a spiritual response.

"Who made you a Kru, Vai, Gio, Gola, Krahn, or Grebo person?"

"My Ma, my Pa, my Grandma, my Grandpa," they replied.

But questioned further, "Who made them?"

Their reply was "God" (from a traditional play performed by the Flomo Theatre of Liberia).

## Conflict Analysis and Resolution

My background as a mediator and a student and teacher of conflict analysis and resolution was a major reason for my being in Liberia. I believed these experiences would be useful in the Liberian context, as did the institutions supporting my work and, of course, CHAL. Furthermore, I had helped analyze conflicts in other contexts and was bringing a certain knowledge about methodologies for resolving both short-term and protracted conflicts.

This training and background provided a sensitivity to cultural issues and the need to listen to and learn from locals regarding their understandings about individual and national conflicts and how they perceived these conflicts might be resolved. This style of conflict analysis and resolution also reflects a spiritual concern for people. Being with Liberians, learning from them, showing solidarity and respect is not only at the heart of a scriptural mandate to love your neighbor (Lev. 19:18; Matt. 19:19) but is also a response to a theological understanding that Mennonites and other peace-church members have regarding encouragement and empowerment of others.

Still, I remember saying on leaving Liberia: "After being here for two months, I was sure I understood this conflict. Two years later, I'm much less certain." The lesson for me was and continues to be that there are numerous understandings of any conflict and various interpretations of not only how or why it began but also how it might be ended.

The specific aspects of the CHAL workshops that concentrated on conflict analysis and resolution were seen as part of the overall healing process. We believed it was important to discover how Liberians viewed conflict before the war, as well as under the present conditions. Elicitive methodologies were used to provide definitions of conflict and descriptions of it in regard to loss of life, suffering, destruction, opportunity, land, hope, and so on. But we were also able to draw out of the participants certain opportunities provided by the conflict. Participants noted that conflict can bring change, tolerance, healing, freedom, and even reconciliation. Examples given from personal experience ranged from "seeing my country for the first time" (in traveling through it as a displaced person) to experiencing issues of regionalism and ethnicity both within Liberia and as refugees elsewhere in the West African subregion.

In other words, the war caused Liberians to place themselves in a wider context; they acquired a broader vision about themselves and their groups, as well as about Liberia and national and international identities. The conflict had exposed them to great danger, but it also taught them lessons about themselves and their need to be tolerant of differences and respectful of others who had suffered—and, in some cases, taught them to understand better those who had caused the suffering. In describing and defining their conflicts, the workshop participants began to see beyond themselves and to gain certain insights about the methods of resolving conflict at these different levels. This was, of course, only a beginning in a long and arduous process of resolving a deep-seated, protracted conflict, one that had multiple sources and ever-changing conditions.

## Holistic Methodologies

In teaching skills necessary to resolve conflict, we used a holistic methodology that merged traditional models with concepts of trauma analysis, prejudice reduction, and conflict resolution. Prior to the war, fundamental human and spiritual needs had been met within communities through their churches and mosques and, for the majority of the population, through traditional conflict resolvers or healers. These conflict resolvers and healers followed ancient tenets for restoring persons in conflict to the community and harmonizing relationships there, as well as with the spirit world. I understood a holistic approach to be one that considered individuals but also, more important, the community and what sustains it, for this reflected my own theological community and sense of justice ("right relationship"). I sensed that this approach would provide fertile ground for the work we were doing in the workshops.

I also was aware that there were some problems in general with the traditional models but that the systems of healing and resolving conflicts had also been greatly disrupted by the war. Healers, chiefs, and other traditional problem solvers were unable to practice their craft. No longer in their traditional contexts because of their refugee status, some would never return to resume their precrisis roles. Furthermore, their prewar medicine and methodologies for resolving conflicts within their communities were not geared to the extraordinary level of emotional, psychological, and real-world problems and conflicts caused by the civil crisis.

The system of healing and conflict resolution had been upset by a war that had fundamentally disrupted the system of how individuals and groups related to one another. Healers, in particular, and Liberians, in general, were no longer in their familiar, historical, geographical, and social contexts and as a result were unable to offer or to experience the holistic healing provided in precrisis Liberia. A new paradigm was needed, one that would draw on positive elements of the past and the expertise of knowledgeable healers, while at the same time allowing for the introduction of outside ideas that could be culturally merged with existing healing and conflict resolution models.

What we attempted, then, was a layering of Western models of conflict analysis and resolution onto a traditional grid. This was done with a sensitivity to ways of healing that begin with the human and relational aspects of the conflict in the manner of traditional holistic methods.

## Reconciliation

In both workshops conducted for CHAL constituents and later ones conducted by CHAL for the multiethnic, Monrovia-based organization United Citizens of Nimba County, I included a fourth element along with trauma healing, prejudice reduction, and conflict resolution: reconciliation. My CHAL colleagues and I understood that if there were no reconciliation among ethnic and religious groups, a lid could be put back on a boiling cauldron by way of a peace accord, but the fire of ethnic hatred would be left burning. The result, of course, would be that the cauldron lid would be blown off at some point in the near or distant future.[16]

Reconciliation, according to Lederach, is built on "mechanisms that engage the sides of the conflict with each other as humans-in-relationship" (1997, p. 28). For me, reconciliation seemed to be the key additional factor that needed to be added to trauma healing, prejudice reduction, and conflict resolution to allow for a restoration of humans-in-relationship after the dehumanizing conditions of war. This would help cool down the cauldron and remove the pressure that could lead to future outbreaks of conflict.

I asked workshop participants what reconciliation meant both in the Liberian languages and to themselves as a result of their languages and enculturation. The responses ranged from "unity," "to fix between," "to have one word," to "letting go of revenge freely for wrong sustained," "sacrifice," and "killing the inner pain for peace." Participants also mentioned something I was interested in from religious, social, and political perspectives: "forgiving your enemy."

For a large number of the participants, forgiveness in its more religious (Christian) sense meant to "set the offender free," as God had done to them on a personal basis through the redemptive act of Christ on the cross (Col. 1:14). It meant that, through this act of forgiveness, they could let go of the anger, hatred, and desire for revenge they felt toward the offender(s). I understood this to mean that, in the process of forgiveness, they could gain psychological benefits and freedom and that this could be fostered through a familiar and meaningful spiritual exercise. This spiritual exercise took on several ritualistic forms, such as naming the dead and letting go of hatred. One way to do this was through burning papers on which individuals had written the name of the person or group that had deeply offended or victimized them during the war. Or they would write about their own acts against others and place it on the fire. In addition, prayers were offered up regarding forgiveness, and songs were sung to express God's role in the healing process.

The process begun by these rituals was initiated with the understanding that it was just that, a *process*, which could help persons reflect on and find some comfort around real-world events in their lives. And since psychological and emotional (as well as spiritual) healing and change were the goals in our workshops, I felt that these and other rituals had social and even political consequences for religious and nonreligious people alike. Acts of repentance and forgiveness, essential to reconciliation, can help transform dysfunctional and violent relationships in ways that diplomatic, political, and economically based peace accords can never achieve.

New understandings at the human level are necessary to restore and allow for new understandings of and changes in the human and social condition. The importance of satisfying human needs—from food, water, and shelter to, especially, safety, identity, self-esteem, and recognition—is underscored in this shift of thought and action.

## Postscript

I left Liberia in December 1993. War continued, with the fighting and fractionalization of the country increasing. At the time this chapter was begun, the thirteenth peace accord had been signed between the warring factions— and then broken. After several more cycles of peace accords and renewed fighting, a final agreement was reached in late 1996. Elections were held the following year, bringing the former rebel leader, Charles Taylor, to power as president.

At time of publication, I have recently returned to the United States after four years in another war-ravaged area of the world, the former Yugoslavia, where 250,000 people died, millions were left homeless, and entire regional infrastructures destroyed. My years there made me even more acutely aware of how difficult a healing peace with justice is to achieve.

My optimism about humans changing, drawing strength from their ethnic and religious communities, and finding new meaning in the self and group through the pain and window of trauma and reconciliation remains. But I am also cognizant of the complexities of moving large groups of people through a trauma-healing process so that they may deal with the pain and eventually integrate it and move on with their lives.

In postwar contexts, political rhetoric and economic restructuring too often obscure the awareness and need for individuals, groups, and nations to deal with the deep psychological and spiritual wounds caused by war. Workshops such as the ones I have described will continue to help, but the degree of help may not be sufficient to break the cycle of revenge caused by hatred and fear. Desire for revenge, or the creation of that desire through political manipulation, cannot be addressed without attitudinal and structural changes of major proportions.

# Twelve

## From Haiti to Hebron with a Brief Stop in Washington, D.C.

### *The CPT Experiment*

KATHLEEN KERN

IN 1984, RON SIDER GAVE THE keynote address at the Mennonite World Conference, calling for the Christians of the world to band together and form a Christian peacemaking army that would intervene nonviolently in situations of conflict. He later expanded on this theme:

> Nonviolent resistance to tyrants, oppressors and brutal invaders is not for fools or cowards. It demands courage and daring of the highest order. It requires discipline, training and a willingness to face death. It produces collective pride in the group or society that successfully . . . stands together and overcomes a brutal enemy.
>
> Are there tough, brave volunteers for that kind of costly, demanding battle?
>
> Would the people be there if the Christian church—and people of other faiths as well—called for a vast multiplication of our efforts in nonviolent alternatives to war? Would the scholars and trainees emerge if we doubled and then quadrupled our study and training centers on nonviolence? Would the nonviolent troops be available to be trained by the thousands and then tens of thousands to form disciplined Christian Peacemaker Teams ready to walk into the face of danger and death in loving confrontation of injustice and oppression? (1989, pp. 93–94)

Churches have expressed their objections to militarism by refusing to serve in the armed forces, to purchase war bonds, and in some cases, to pay taxes. In recent years, Mennonites have taken a more active role in challenging the military industrial complex by calling for nuclear disarmament, expressing their opposition to covert warfare by wealthy nations, and exposing the fundamental injustices most societies impose on their poorest members.

Using Sider's speech as a springboard, a group of Mennonite and Church of the Brethren leaders built on these traditions by establishing Christian Peacemaker Teams (CPTs) in 1986. Director Gene Stoltzfus wrote:

> CPT came into being fundamentally because none of the existing [Mennonite] agencies felt called or able to engage in active peacemaking—meaning direct support of nonviolent forms of struggle, activism and public witness. (1996b)

Thus, CPT began as an experimental peacemaking ministry,[1] rooted in traditional Mennonite theology but prepared to take an active approach.[2] Following Christ's example, CPT seeks to promote justice in all relationships and to take practical steps toward loving the enemy as commanded in Scripture. Although it uses mediation techniques at times between parties in conflict, CPT makes a conscious decision to live with victims of institutionalized violence.

In 1990, CPT sent its first delegations to Iraq, in an effort to help prevent the Gulf War, and to the Oka Indian reservation in Quebec to intervene in the standoff between the Mohawks and the Quebec provincial police. As a part of the witness in Iraq, CPT also sponsored Oil Free Sunday in an attempt to connect the faith of the North American churches with the imminent war over oil. Approximately 40 percent of Mennonite and Brethren churches participated in some way.

In April 1992, as the sentencing for the Rodney King trial approached, Mennonite churches in the Los Angeles area requested that CPT send a delegation to south Los Angeles, because the situation there was "about to explode." Stoltzfus explained that it took nearly two months to put a delegation together. After the Los Angeles riots, members of the CPT Steering Committee felt that CPT needed to have a full-time Christian Peacemaker Corps (CPC) ready to move immediately into a conflict situation.[3]

The CPC is made up of both full-time volunteers, who receive stipends similar to those received by volunteers in other Mennonite service agencies, and Reserve Corps members, who volunteer anywhere from two weeks to several months of their time in a given year. In addition to overseeing the CPC and its projects, CPT's office staff puts out a newsletter, trains new volunteers, organizes delegations, runs campaigns,[4] and keeps in touch with CPT's church constituency. The CPT Steering Committee oversees all of the projects and staff working under the CPT umbrella.

I was one of eight members of the first Christian Peacemaker Corps to go through training. My initial desire to join CPT came when I was in my late twenties and living in community with a family from my church. Most of my friends in college had done some sort of voluntary service after graduating, and I had a sense of not having paid my dues. (I had gone to seminary after college and then worked for five years with an agency that ran group homes for developmentally disabled adults.)

From the time I was a small child, the idea of confronting violence had intrigued me. Since it did not appear that I would have a family of my own in the near future, I decided to look into venues where not having a family would be an advantage. CPT seemed an ideal option.

I believe, along with Sider, that until people are willing to take the same risks for peace that soldiers are willing to take for violent solutions, people will choose violence first as a method of resolving conflict. I believe that God expects us to take the same risks for truth and justice that the prophets and Jesus took. I am in a position to do that as a single member who is part of a supportive faith community.

My experience as a full-time volunteer for CPT has led me to the coastal city of Jeremie in Haiti and to the West Bank city of Hebron. I also participated in a six-week exploration project in Washington, D.C., which eventually grew into the Project on Urban Peacemaking. Because Haiti and Hebron occupied the majority of my time, I will focus on those projects but will draw on the experiences of the Washington team for some comparative insights.

## Haiti

In 1990, in closely monitored elections, an overwhelming majority of the Haitian people chose Jean Bertrand Aristide to be their president. After serving in office for seven months, he was overthrown in a coup d'etat, led by the man he appointed to head the Haitian military, Raoul Cedras. In July 1993, the U.S.–brokered Governors Island Accords, signed by both Aristide and Cedras, specified that Cedras would step down at the end of October 1993. In return, Aristide agreed to refrain from criticizing U.S. policy and to encourage Haitians not to flee the country.

When the date arrived for Aristide to return, U.S. president Bill Clinton ordered the warship *Harlan County* to set the stage for the return. But when hundreds of armed paramilitary thugs greeted the *Harlan County* at the dock, Clinton ordered the ship to pull away—to the astonishment of almost everyone.[5]

From July to October 1993, CPT had joined with a coalition of organizations that operated under the title Cry for Justice.[6] The stated purpose of Cry for Justice was to send teams to different areas of Haiti to provide a violence-deterring, human rights–monitoring presence. In September, when Dante Caputo pulled the Organization of American States (OAS) human rights monitors from Haiti because he deemed the situation too dangerous for them, the need for international observer teams became even more desperate.

The deadline of October 30, 1993, came, but Aristide did not. It seemed as though the United States had lost interest in restoring Aristide to power. Cry for Justice disbanded. But at the invitation of the parish of St. Helene and its priest in the western seaport town of Jeremie, CPT stayed on.

*Daily routine.* Initially, the team in St. Helene began every morning with devotions[7] and a meeting, although at times this morning meeting was more or less abandoned (depending on the predispositions of the team). The team would then separate and go visiting throughout the community of St. Helene. We accumulated a great deal of information about military and paramilitary activity this way and would make a point of visiting the areas in which this activity was occurring.

When Haitians in Jeremie told us about significant human rights abuses, we wrote reports and sent them to our project coordinators in Port-au-Prince, who in turn disseminated them to various human rights agencies. Eventually, people began coming to us with stories of human rights abuses that they wanted documented.

We generally spent the afternoon in language study or reading. A coworker and I often went downtown to hold babies—many of them abandoned by their parents, who could no longer feed them—at the Missionaries of Charity. I saw about one baby a week die there.

In the late afternoon and early evening, we would again make rounds. When we needed to talk to members of the St. Helene parish or to friends from the democratic underground (or when they needed to talk to us), the meetings tended to be at night. Lacking electricity for the greater part of the time we were there, we tended to turn in early if we had no meetings scheduled, although sometimes we played cards, sang, or shelled peanuts for our cook to make peanut butter.

### Highlights

Dramatic episodes in Jeremie happened infrequently.[8] As the United States belatedly tightened the embargo on Haiti, we saw instead the long slow starvation of the people among whom we worked. However, two highlights of the CPT experience in Jeremie that I witnessed were the *bat teneb* and the demonstration after the U.S. military arrived in Haiti in September 1994.

*Bat teneb.* At noon on February 7, 1994, the bells of the downtown cathedral in Jeremie began to chime as usual, but they were soon drowned out by the noise of dozens of people banging on pots, pans, and the tin roofs of their houses.

That morning, our interpreter had told us that people would be participating in a *bat teneb*—or "beating away the shadows"—all across Haiti that day.

*Bat teneb* has a long tradition in Haiti as a sign of social protest. On this particular day, the people of Haiti were calling for President Jean Bertrand Aristide's return. This February 7 marked the third anniversary of Aristide's inauguration. Because of the September 1991 coup d'etat, he had spent the last two Februarys in exile.

Several of us from CPT decided to walk through the neighborhood and see how many people would pick up their pots. We felt slightly disappointed that the entire action lasted for a minute or less.

*So much for social protest,* I thought. *This isn't going to make much of an impression.*

I was wrong. Two hours later, I saw ten heavily armed soldiers gathering outside the rectory compound. I quickly joined the other three people on our team and approached the heavy metal gate. As we did so, a soldier with grenades hanging from his belt dashed to the side, SWAT-team style, and covered us (three women and one man, all unarmed) with his automatic rifle. The soldier who seemed to be in charge told us someone had reported that several Haitians had been standing on the roof of the rectory, banging drums and generally disturbing the peace.

"What is the purpose of the people who were making that noise?" the interrogating soldier asked. "Are you satisfied with what they did?"

"It is not for us to be satisfied or dissatisfied with what they did," replied the member of our team most fluent in Creole. He then pointed out that no one in the neighborhood seemed disturbed by the noise. After further dialogue, the military person said, "Give a message to the people who made this noise. If they do this again, they will be arrested, and you will be arrested, too."

*Demonstration.* On September 30, 1994, Haitians organized nationwide demonstrations to commemorate the 5,000 people murdered for political reasons since the 1991 coup. Patrols of soldiers from the U.S. Special Forces began to come up to the rectory several times a day, asking for St. Helene's priest (who was living in the archbishop's house at the time because of death threats). When we finally learned that they wanted to talk to the priest about the demonstration, we told them that he was not in charge of organizing it, but we could introduce them to the people who were.

Someone from the rectory ran to fetch the demonstration's organizers from St. Helene. Obviously expecting to meet resistance, the officer in charge began the conversation by explaining why it was important for everyone to work together. The St. Helene organizers assured the military men that they had things under control.

Not satisfied, the commander began to explain the things that could happen if the St. Helene people were not more forthcoming about certain details, such as the route of the demonstration.

"Oh," said one of the leaders of the parish. "You want to know the route. We're going to start in the church, make a right, go down the road until we reach . . ."

Everyone visibly relaxed. The organizers began describing how they were going to monitor the parade to ensure that no violence would occur.

The American officers, for their part, began telling the St. Helene people that the Haitian military had informed them that the people of St. Helene were going to engage in indiscriminate killing and looting during the demonstration.

Everyone laughed. Then the church choir director said, "Well, we wanted to dump the [cement slab upon which the army and paramilitary units had performed ritual sacrifices] into the ocean. Is that looting? And we wanted to do the same to the one in the FRAPH[9] compound."

Thus began a twenty-minute discussion over whether dumping the slab on the wharf into the sea and destroying the slab in the FRAPH compound constituted looting. The Americans were about evenly divided in their thinking. Finally, the organizers from St. Helene and the military agreed that the one on the wharf was fair game and the one in the FRAPH compound was not.

Of all the major population centers in Haiti, Jeremie alone had a demonstration on September 30 in which no one got hurt.

## Hebron

Hebron is a city of about 120,000 Palestinians in the midst of whom live 450 Israeli settlers. It is also home to the Il-Ibrahimi mosque, where legend has it that Abraham, Sarah, Rebekah, Isaac, Jacob, and Leah are buried.[10] In 1929, an Arab mob, with the encouragement of the British colonial occupiers, attacked the Jewish Quarter, established in the sixteenth century by Jews fleeing the Inquisition in Spain.[11] At least sixty-seven men, women, and children were hacked to death, and many more were wounded. Nearly 400 were saved by their Muslim neighbors,[12] but the massacre still looms large in the collective memories of both Jews and Muslims in Hebron and it still affects current interactions between the two groups.

Because the patriarchs and matriarchs are purportedly buried in Hebron and because there had once been a thriving Jewish Quarter there, when Israel's settlement policy began to take root in the 1970s, the Hebron area became a special target for the right-wing religious adherents of Gush Emunim.[13]

Kiryat Arba, the oldest settlement in the West Bank, was founded in 1970 by Rabbi Moshe Levinger. He and a band of armed supporters took over the only hotel in Hebron and refused to leave. To appease them, the army gave them an old soldiers' camp on the outskirts of Hebron. Gradually, settlements moved inside the city center under the protection of the Israeli military, despite the protest of the local Palestinian inhabitants. In 1980, six yeshiva students in Hebron were killed by a militant wing of the Palestine Liberation Organization (PLO). The Israeli military response was swift, and two more settlements appeared in the city center.

Relations between the settlers and Palestinians continued to deteriorate throughout the period of the Intifada, culminating with the February 1994 massacre in the Il-Ibrahimi mosque. Official reports of the massacre stated that settler Baruch Goldstein, a medical doctor from Brooklyn, New York, began spraying Muslim men and boys with bullets at 5:30 in the morning on the last Friday of Ramadan. Thirty-nine worshipers died in the mosque.[14] The Israeli Defense Force (IDF) shot an equal number in the demonstrations that followed. The army put all Palestinians in Hebron under curfew for two months, while allowing the settlers to roam the streets freely. By the time our Christian Peacemaker Team arrived there a year later, people expressed as much bitterness about the collective punishment imposed upon them as they did about the massacre.

*Daily routine.* In contrast to the norm in Jeremie, our days had a way of becoming very full in Hebron, even when we did not schedule things. We began every morning with devotions in the park in front of the mosque.[15] When we finished our formal prayers and singing, we would pick up trash, fix broken benches in the park, or play with local children. Afterward, we would separate and visit people. Usually, some of us stopped in to see some journalist friends to pick up the news; others would visit friends or families living near settlements in the city. When there was free time, we would write reports and press releases in the afternoon, go visiting in the late afternoon and early evening, and write more in the evening. Every Saturday, we spent the afternoon and early evening on Dubboya Street to serve as a violence-deterring presence, as hundreds of settlers from all over the West Bank converged on Hebron.[16] We tried to spend as much time as possible in those places on the street where attacks against people and property had occurred; we took notes, recording conversations we had with settlers on the street.

### Highlights

I find it difficult to choose the most important events that happened while I was in Hebron. I have selected the following three because to some extent they enhanced our credibility with Palestinians and with Israeli peace and human rights advocates in Jerusalem. They also helped us facilitate contacts between Hebronites and sympathetic Israelis from the Jerusalem and Tel Aviv areas.

*The water truck incident.* One of the families with whom we became closest was the Abu Khalil family.[17] Their property lies between the settlement of Tel Rumeida and an army soldier camp, both of which have, in effect, put them under a sort of siege for the last decade. One day, we stopped to see Rishad Abu Khalil in the tea shop that he runs. He told us that his cistern had run dry and that he had been unable to take a shower for more than a week.

The settlements between Bethlehem and Hebron consume most of the water supply in the summer. Consequently, people in Hebron who live on the high ground do not get running water because there is not enough pressure in the pipes. They must buy their water from the municipality or from private sources.

Rishad told us, however, that the municipality had decided to stop delivering water to people who lived near settlements, because it had had one too many windshields broken by settlers throwing rocks. We contacted the municipality and told the people there that we would accompany the water trucks it sent out.

As it happened, a female teammate and I were out of town when the two men on the team got the call that a water truck was ready to go immediately. They dropped everything and walked with the water truck through the settlement of Tel Rumeida. Soldiers at the checkpoints detained them both. Our team's leader tried to explain to the officer interrogating him that Rishad had been without water for more than a week.

"But why do you care?" the officer asked. "Why are you doing this?"

The team leader told the officer that if he had been in Germany during the time of the Third Reich, he would have done the same thing on behalf of the Jews.

"Are you calling me a Nazi?" the officer demanded.

The two men were later told that they were being held on charges of entering a closed military zone and calling soldiers Nazis.

Israeli friends from the Jerusalem-based Hebron Solidarity Committee (HSC) called to tell us that they, too, had been arrested for saying statements nearly identical to the one made about the Third Reich. I was touched although a little surprised by their concern. I did not realize the impact this remark would eventually have.

The official IDF report on the incident said that the two CPTers had called the soldiers Nazis and "cursed them in every known language." In the following weeks, if settlers saw us having friendly conversations with soldiers, they would draw them aside, and we would hear them telling the soldiers that we were the ones who had called soldiers Nazis. (That is, we would hear the Hebrew word, *Naziim* and would surmise what the settlers were saying.)

Three positive things happened as a result of the water truck incident:

- A lawyer in the Society of St. Yves in Jerusalem volunteered to represent us. She and her legal staff also eventually provided free legal help to several of the families in Hebron that we knew.
- A *Washington Post* reporter (Lancaster, 1995, p. A16) came to spend the day with us (one member of the team was from Washington, and the reporter's editor told him to work the local angle). While talking to a settler in Tel Rumeida, the reporter dispelled some rumors that had been circulating about a team member being a Hamas activist,[18] and the sporadic death threats that the team had been receiving stopped.
- The subsequent publicity drew both Israeli and international attention to the water shortage in Hebron. The mainstream Israeli public expressed outrage when they saw footage of the settlements in the West Bank with swimming pools and well-watered lawns and then learned that Palestinians in Hebron did not have enough water for drinking and washing. Prime Minister Yitzhak Rabin sent a fact-finding mission to Hebron to determine the extent of the water problem, even though the West Bank cities had been complaining for years of water shortages.

*Opening the gates of Hebron University.* On July 22, 1995, our team and members of the HSC responded to an invitation to open the gates of Hebron University.[19] The military had kept them closed since the beginning of the Intifada, even though the university does not stand near a settlement, checkpoint, or road that the military frequently uses. Students either had to climb the front gate or walk nearly ten minutes out of their way to come in through the service entrance.

Using sledgehammers, our group and members of the HSC began to attack the gates to the applause of students and faculty. After about an hour, the Israeli military appeared and arrested three members from our group and one member from the HSC for refusing to leave a closed military zone.

The group spent the night in jail. The police took the women to Abu Kabeer prison and our team's leader to the Russian compound, where he spent the night in a cell next to some Hebron settler youth, who had been arrested for assaulting a police officer the day before.

An Israeli friend posted bond, and the authorities dropped the matter. Students and faculty gave us a reception at the university, and we later went to talk to the captain in the IDF who had been in charge of the arrests. We told him what we had done in Haiti and why we were in Hebron. We asked why the army wanted the gate closed. He smiled tolerantly and said essentially that it was for security reasons that we could not understand. He also told us that representatives of the university had been in dialogue with the Israeli Civil Administration and that we had ruined the negotiations.[20]

We explained that we were pacifists and would stand between him and an assailant to protect him, which impressed him. When we told him we would stand between a soldier pointing a gun and the other person, he frowned, and said, "You understand I will have to arrest you if you do this." We said we understood.

*The attack.* On September 30, 1995, just hours before I was scheduled to leave the country, a teammate and I arrived early for our regular Saturday afternoon presence on Dubboya Street. The streets outside the settlement of Beit Hadassah seemed to be swarming with settlers. My teammate heard noises and shouting coming from around the corner and went to investigate. She called to me to follow her. Some settler teenagers were throwing bottles at people in the marketplace. As I turned to walk in her direction, I heard people further up the street calling, "Kathy! Don't go. They are coming," and reversed my course.

As I walked toward the people who had called, I looked behind and saw about twenty men, ranging in age from mid-twenties to early forties, walking purposefully up the street. I continued walking toward the lower Tel Rumeida checkpoint. Suddenly, what seemed like a battle cry went up behind me, and I heard the men running. Someone yanked at the red-checked *keffiyah* I had tied to my backpack.[21] I kept walking. Someone yanked harder, pulling me over onto my back. Several of the men spit on me as I lay on the ground.

The men ran past and began breaking the windows of all the cars standing in the street. I got up and began taking pictures. A very large man turned around and shouted, "No! No pictures!"

I am not sure in what sequence the following events took place. Five or six men ran back toward me and tried to grab my camera. One of the men punched me in the ear and knocked me to the ground, but I maintained my grip on the camera. As the men dragged me around on the ground by my camera strap, I noticed that the checkpoint at Beit Hadassah had no soldiers in it. I decided to begin screaming in order to attract attention.

By the time my teammate came back, I was on my feet again and told her they were trying to take my camera. She snapped a picture of my chief assailant and then joined me in trying to retain the camera. We both went down on the ground again. Eventually, the same man who had hit me stomped on her hand, and we lost my camera.

The man ran toward the settlement of Beit Hadassah holding the camera high above his head. As his friends ran with him, laughing and cheering, the scene reminded me of high school athletes running with the football after making a touchdown.

As a result of the attack, we had larger numbers of Israelis and internationals from the Jerusalem and Tel Aviv area come down and participate with the team in the Saturday afternoon Dubboya Street presence.[22] Increased contact with the police in Hebron also helped increase the level of respect and understanding between us and the officers.

## Key Dilemmas and Decisions

CPT is an ongoing experiment in nonviolent direct action. All experiences and actions serve to educate subsequent team members about approaches that work well and others that do not. Some issues and dilemmas that have arisen in the course of this educational process include the following.

### Partisanship

The prime directive for CPT intervention in a conflict situation is that we go only where we have received invitations from local peace and justice advocates. Since the people who issue the invitations are usually from a disenfranchised faction, we open ourselves up to charges of partisanship.[23] Criticisms in this area were mild when we were in Haiti. They came mostly from people who did not want Aristide to return to power. In Washington, no one accused the team of not giving a local slumlord a fair shake.[24]

In Hebron, however, partisanship became a serious issue. Criticisms we received in this regard were sometimes nasty, for example, "You Mennonites and Quakers have always been anti-Semitic." More often, though, they came from thoughtful Jews and Christians who told us we did not fairly represent Israeli mainstream reality in our press releases.

I have not fully sorted out all the dilemmas that come with living among and working with Palestinians in the occupied territories. One of the things that made the issue in Hebron more bewildering for us than it had been in Haiti is that there are far more than two sides to this conflict.[25] We occasionally worked with the HSC—an Israeli group that used rhetoric far more inflammatory than ours when speaking about the settlers. Within Hebron Palestinian society, we sometimes found ourselves caught between the interests of secular and fundamentalist Muslims. The rift between the Palestinian Authority and its Palestinian critics sometimes made us feel caught in the middle.

We used to tell the settlers that we stood with whomever was on the receiving end of the gun barrel. If we saw someone attacking them, we said, we would intervene to protect them. It was not a completely satisfactory answer to the charge of partisanship. Ideally, we would have received invitations from both Palestinian and Israeli groups, but as there were not Israeli groups living in Hebron at the time,[26] we felt we had to respond to the real need that Hebronites had for an international violence-deterring, human rights–monitoring presence.

How can we continue to speak the truth of what we see and yet remain open and sympathetic to people who disapprove of our efforts?

### Solidarity versus Nonviolence

Related to the issue of partisanship in our peacemaking efforts is the issue of how our solidarity with the oppressed at times comes into tension with our commitment to nonviolence.

CPT requires an invitation from "local peacemakers" before entering a conflict situation, but it has construed the term rather loosely. Neither our Haitian nor our Hebronite hosts were pacifists in the technical definition of the term. In both cases, however, they had made a practical decision that using violence to address their grievances would only bring more violence down on their community.

The priority of the people in St. Helene was how they could best be protected not how they could best serve as a model for the effectiveness of nonviolent direct action. When the news came that the American Special Forces would arrive in Jeremie within the week, one of the people with whom we had worked expressed the hope that the U.S. military might establish a command post in St. Helene. When we asked the priest who had invited us whether we should tell the American soldiers to leave their guns behind when entering the church, he said he had no problems with soldiers bearing guns in church as long as they used the guns to protect rather than to oppress people. We felt deflated when we heard these things, because all along the people of St. Helene had told us that our unarmed presence had effectively deterred violence within the community. Yet none of us felt comfortable questioning the wishes of people who had borne political oppression and death threats with grace for three years.

### Solidarity versus Reconciliation

Solidarity issues also conflicted at times with the reconciling model used in Mennonite conciliation circles. Our Haitian friends told us not to talk to the military or to certain Americans in Jeremie who they thought were CIA agents. In Hebron, we came in the wake of a woman who had actively tried to promote settler-Palestinian dialogue with the result that both factions came to view her as ridiculous or even sinister. In both Haitian and Palestinian societies, collaborators have caused a lot of damage, so we went to great lengths to avoid appearing as collaborators.

As a result, we found it difficult to take opportunities to speak with soldiers and paramilitary personnel in Haiti and with settlers in Hebron. The fact that these "oppressor" factions did not want to speak to us either made it too easy not to pursue a reconciling course.

The dilemma thus becomes: When do we separate ourselves from solidarity movements and adopt a reconciling stance? What are the ways in which CPT is *not* a solidarity movement?

### Relationships with the Military

Our experiences with Haitian, American, and Israeli soldiers or police varied widely, so I will discuss these contacts separately.

*Haiti.* I felt a strange elation when I saw the first U.S. military helicopters come to scout likely places to land around Jeremie. I really understood why the people were dancing, singing, and waving leafy branches to celebrate. I wanted to celebrate with them. My reaction disturbed me, and my confusion grew as our team had many emotional discussions over our relationship with the U.S. military.

Our four-person team at the time held four distinct opinions as to how or whether such a relationship should proceed. One felt we should have nothing to do with the soldiers, given the history of U.S. military intervention in Latin America and the Caribbean. Any contact at all with them would diminish our peace witness, she thought. Another felt that we should avoid the U.S. military and make it clear to our Haitian friends that we viewed U.S. militarism as a truly evil institution. However, she treated individual GIs who happened to pass by cordially. Another felt that since our Haitian friends had asked us to serve as translators and liaisons for them with the military, it would show a lack of solidarity with them if we refused to do so. I felt that the more contact we had with the U.S. military, the better able we would be to serve as peace witnesses to the soldiers and the more information we would be able to gather about their intentions. They also spoke English, and since I was the weakest member of the team when it came to speaking and under-standing Creole, I felt that communicating with soldiers was something I could do.

I felt good about the translation work we did on behalf of the people of St. Helene for the U.S. military. I was frankly grateful that the U.S. soldiers took pains to place themselves between the Haitian military and the demonstrators during the September 30 commemoration of the victims of the coup.

Through it all, however, I never forgot that the members of the U.S. Special Forces whom we met had been trained as disciplined and efficient killers. In no way could one term the demonstration on September 30 "nonviolent," given that every soldier carried about sixty pounds of weaponry and ammu-nition. If the organizers of St. Helene had not been so well organized and had not monitored the march so carefully, armed paramilitary could have infil-trated the march and instigated violence. The American soldiers would likely have shot those whom they viewed as perpetrators with little deliberation, as they did elsewhere.

My impression is also based on witnessing a FRAPH member attempt to ride his motorcycle through the crowd. Three soldiers assumed firing positions, and I heard the click of the safety catches on their guns being released before the motorcyclist put his hands up and walked his bike away.

I also saw the potential for abuse of power as the U.S. military remained in Haiti. To us, it seemed as though the Americans responded more quickly to the complaints of the military and paramilitaries against ordinary citizens than they did to the complaints of ordinary citizens against the military and para-militaries. We had no illusions that they felt any feelings of solidarity with those who had suffered oppression, and we saw how easily they could be manipulated by the oppressors.

*Hebron.* Relating to the Israeli soldiers in Hebron felt different than relating to American soldiers. Even though the Israeli soldiers assaulted Palestinians probably as frequently as settlers did, they did not seem to have the same ideological drive. It was easier for us to empathize with them. We made a special effort to remain on good terms because the settlers in Hebron would tell the soldiers we did not like them.[27] Once, however, a soldier, after having been "warned" about us by one of the settlers, made a point of being even more friendly to us. We had encounters with other soldiers who, it seemed to me, were trying hard not to like us, but we could usually wear them down with our relentless friendliness.

Perhaps a more difficult issue in Hebron was our relationship with the Israeli police.[28] A couple of times when we received verbal threats or had stones and eggs thrown at us, Palestinian friends wanted us to make complaints at the police station. Some of the team felt that to do so would show reliance on the power of the gun. We had chosen to put ourselves at risk as witnesses that unarmed peacemaking presences have the power to change unjust social structures.[29] In addition, we were concerned that we might receive special treatment or that complaining might backfire, causing the IDF to evacuate us forcibly from Hebron "for our own safety."

We will continue to struggle with the question of whether we responded appropriately to the military personnel we met in Haiti and Hebron. Did serving as translators for our Haitian friends also make us collaborators with the American soldiers? Even though we clearly stated our pacifist convictions to the U.S. Special Forces, did our relationship with them facilitate their continuing delusion that guns are the most effective way of solving problems? By filing complaints at the police station in Hebron, were we somehow supporting a corrupt system?

When Palestine suffered under the Roman occupation, Jesus still reached out to the centurion who asked for his help in healing his servant. There is no record, however, that Jesus collaborated with the Roman military, and we know that it was the Roman military that tortured him to death. Did we respond to the U.S. and Israeli soldiers as Jesus would have? What is the correct mixture of truth telling, confrontation, and kindness that we need to employ when talking with the military?

### Economic Dilemmas

When I analyze why I found the work in Hebron easier than the work in Haiti, two major issues come to mind: language[30] and the economic situation. In Haiti, we had running water, a cool breezy rectory on the hill, and enough to eat while many of the people in St. Helene starved or died for lack of basic medical attention. In Hebron, our standard of living was essentially the same as those of our neighbors.

Much has been said and written about the damage that aid and development organizations have done to Haiti.[31] There is not the space to review that debate here. Almost everyone who ever worked with the Jeremie team agreed that the most stressful aspect of the work was turning down requests for food, money, or gifts. I am not exaggerating when I say we did this nearly fifty times a day. I came to dread the morning and evening walks through the village; there are only so many polite ways of turning someone down. Sometimes people we did not know would ask us for money and became overtly hostile when we turned them down. We came to expect that most people who sought out relationships with us did so for economic reasons.

CPT has a policy against giving handouts, based on the collective wisdom and experience of Mennonite aid and development workers over the last few decades. I came to appreciate the reason for this when people violated the policy. Those who did were thereafter targeted as the white people one could get something from and were mercilessly manipulated. I did and still do believe that the policy is a good one because of the dependency on foreign aid that internationals have created in Haiti. I also respected the opinion of our primary Haitian contacts in Port-au-Prince, who told us that giving such handouts would dilute our peace witness. In particular, they told us never to give things to children, because people in the Haitian democratic movements did not want to create another generation of beggars.

On the other hand, Haitian culture is a generous, gift-giving one. It is common for Haitians to ask one another for things too, and generosity is a highly prized social trait. Since I perceive myself as a generous person in my own culture, it was difficult for me to be accused of stinginess. In the face of so much starvation and suffering, it seemed inadequate to say, in effect, "I am giving you the gift of my presence."

Of the six months that I spent in Haiti, I do not think a day passed when I did not think of Matthew 25:44–46:

> Then they also will answer, "Lord, when was it that we saw you hungry or thirsty or a stranger or naked or sick or in prison, and did not take care of you?" Then he will answer them, "Truly I tell you, just as you did not do it to one of the least of these, you did not do it to me."

*Talking to the Media*

Three of the four Christian Peacemaker Corps objectives relate to talking about our experiences and promoting the cause of nonviolent direct action.[32] Most cultures assume that violence at certain times and at certain places is acceptable and necessary. CPT wants to challenge that assumption. Because the world does not consider it news when people work for peace, part of CPT's work is to make it "news."

The dilemma that arises from all this attention to the media is that at times I feel I am being self-promotional. One of the important aspects of my faith is striving for humility, and it is hard to do that when writing reports of what the teams are doing. I was keenly aware of how attention became focused on me when I recounted my attack in Hebron. I did not want to appear like I was soliciting pity or admiration, but I thought trying to appear like it was no big deal almost made me seem more conceited. Public witnesses, such as the opening of the university gates, can sometimes focus more attention on CPT than on the problem. On the other hand, as with the case of the water truck in Hebron, they can do precisely the reverse. We found that once several members of our team had been arrested, new doors opened for us within the Palestinian community. Doing jail time apparently marked us as people to be trusted.

How can peacemakers demonstrate nonviolence in action and tell people about it without seeming self-aggrandizing?


## Summary and Analysis

CPT director Gene Stoltzfus has stated:

> I believe there is a core thesis in CPT, namely, that long-term conflict resolution needs to incorporate confrontation (read nonviolence), and acknowledgment of power imbalance, and the need therefore to help shore up one side and thereby work for balance (read justice). The long-term strategy is not to eliminate conflict but rather to develop skills for solving conflict without killing (read guns). (1996a)

That being said, I believe that CPT is more similar to the Mennonite conflict resolution efforts described in the other chapters than it is different. Well over half of the time spent in Haiti, Hebron, and Washington involved visiting with local grassroots people and building relationships with them. We expended much more emotional energy in both Haiti and Hebron on cultural sensitivity issues than we ever did confronting violence.[33] Our broad view of peacebuilding roles included tending to babies at the Missionaries of Charity in Jeremie, teaching English classes, which had a way of turning into nonviolent strategy classes, in Hebron, and rebuilding houses that the Israeli army had destroyed. We later found out thirdhand that these activities had contributed significantly to the levels of trust extended to us by people in both communities. In setting up the projects in each of the three locations, we researched the history of community initiatives to confront violence and identified the most effective contemporary initiatives dealing with this violence. A large part of our work involved seeking to integrate the current peace and justice efforts of local and international, church and secular organizations. We have viewed ourselves as complementing the aid and development work carried on by the Mennonites and by the Church of the Brethren over the last several decades. Finally, CPT has sought to integrate the work in Haiti, Hebron, and Washington, D.C., into the prayer lives of Canadian and American congregations.

Two areas, however, serve to set CPT apart from traditional Mennonite conflict resolution efforts.

*Commitment to long-term perspectives.* CPT is sensitive to the charge of "parachuting" into conflict situations, doing some kind of public witness, and then leaving.

While I believe the long-term approach is preferable to a quick-fix approach (and we see ourselves as embedded in long-term strategies for social change), Mennonites will always be faced with the "What would you do if Hitler. . . ." question. To me and to other pacifists, it is obvious that the questions the world ought to ask are: What could have happened that would have prevented the Nazis from taking power? What are some danger signals that we need to monitor if we want to prevent Nazi-like people from taking control of a society?

In the end, people want to know how they can give up militarism and still be secure in the event of unprovoked violent assault. Christian Peacemaker Teams would like to demonstrate that there are nonviolent ways of intervening in crisis situations without resorting to the use of arms. We have a dream that some day, instead of sending in the military to Haiti or Bosnia, governments will choose to send in, first, unarmed peacemakers, who are well trained and in sufficiently large numbers.

Interestingly, in light of this discussion, the projects in Haiti, Hebron, and Washington, D.C., went on in some form for more than two years. At time of publication, the Hebron project continues, with a primary emphasis on preventing the demolition of Palestinian homes by the Israeli military. We have also had a project in Chiapas, Mexico, since 1998, and we are working on a series of ongoing projects with native communities in Ontario and South Dakota. The Haiti project closed in 1995, and the Washington project in 1996. As time passes, the original goal of CPT to intervene for two weeks to three months at a time seems to be undergoing a shift toward longer-term projects.

*Focus on reconciliation.* The people of St. Helene did not want to have dialogue with the Haitian military and paramilitary groups and vice versa. The Palestinians in Hebron did not want to engage in dialogue with the settlers in Hebron and vice versa. There was a real human need in both cases for a violence-deterring, human rights–monitoring presence.

In Hebron, we helped Palestinians make connections with Israelis in the peace movement—connections that would not otherwise have been made. We traded on our credibility with our Palestinian friends when we asked them to welcome Israeli peace and human rights workers during the Saturday afternoon presence on Dubboya Street. They initially viewed the Israelis, even human rights workers from B'tselem, with mistrust and suspicion. Knowing how much effort it took to promote dialogue between Hebronites and sympathetic Israelis, however, I find it mind-boggling to think about promoting dialogue between Hebronites and settlers, especially since there is little impetus in either of these groups to engage in dialogue.[34]

In the case of Washington, D.C., the team took the risk of inviting people living in a crack house to one of the neighborhood meetings organized to close down the crack house. While the neighbors initially viewed the crack house residents with suspicion and fear, when they found out that these residents were as angry at the slumlord as the neighbors were, the neighbors began strategizing with the crack house residents. Neighbors participated in finding homes for the residents, and some stored the belongings of the residents as they searched for new places to live.

## Conclusion

As I have contemplated the CPT vision and how it relates to the work of reconciliation, the metaphor that comes to mind is that CPT serves as a guest in the house of the disenfranchised. Rather than building our own house between the houses of the two groups in conflict, we accept invitations to live with the oppressed. Within that role, we find ourselves better able than our hosts to greet the oppressors at the door. Using active nonviolence as a means of communication, we confront and engage those in power, making it clear that we will (a) tell the truth about what we see them doing, (b) physically lay down our lives to prevent their harming our hosts, and (c) treat them—the oppressors—with the respect and love to which they are entitled as children of God.

Our position as guests also helps deter violence on the part of our hosts and their extended family. They know that we have already recognized, by moving in with them, that they suffer from overt or institutional violence. They know that our biblical understanding tells us that God has a bias for the poor and oppressed. They know we will treat their stories with the attention they deserve. By preventing violence against our hosts, we help diminish the anger and the trapped feelings, which can lead to retribution on their part. By respecting them, we in turn engender respect for our own nonviolent position and open channels for the teaching and discussion of nonviolent strategy.

We know from Jesus' example that standing with the oppressed does not mean participating in actions that violate the radical command to love the enemy. Should our hosts resort to attacking their oppressor, we have the option of leaving their house or of confronting the attack with nonviolent direct action. If possible, we would continue to suggest nonviolent ways to confront and to respond to institutionalized evil. We may at times leave the house of our hosts to visit the oppressors in their house to listen as actively as possible to their fears and concerns. We can take the opportunity to communicate to these people that their lives are precious in our eyes, because God loves them. Ideally, we can then communicate some of the oppressors' humanity to our hosts when we return to their house, and by doing so we lay the groundwork for future mediation efforts. But in the end, we will always return to their house.

# III

## ANALYSIS OF MENNONITE PEACEBUILDING

## Thirteen

## Mennonite Peacebuilding and Conflict Transformation

### A Cultural Analysis

SALLY ENGLE MERRY

Howdoes the mennonite approach to peacebuilding and conflict transformation differ from other forms of conflict resolution? Although it shares many features of process and structure with other forms of domestic and international conflict resolution, there is a distinctive culture to Mennonite mediation and peacebuilding. I have long thought that conflict resolution processes take shape within particular cultural frameworks, which define the nature of personhood, community, conflict, and social justice. The chapters in this book provide rich evidence of the wide variety of Mennonite mediation and peacebuilding initiatives in international settings, but they also indicate that there are underlying similarities in the cultural frameworks that inform them. This chapter endeavors to describe the fundamental concepts and practices embedded in Mennonite peacebuilding as revealed in the accounts in this book. It also describes the dilemmas and contradictions inherent in the Mennonite approach to peacebuilding.

These practices grow out of a long Mennonite spiritual tradition and history. Mennonite religious faith, conceptions of community, and theories of social justice shape the practices of Mennonite peacebuilding. The religious foundation of the process affects standards of success and effectiveness, modes of entering into conflict situations, notions of the speed of conflict resolution, and assessments of the importance of building relationships or negotiating settlements. One critical difference between those parts of Mennonite peacebuilding that rely on mediation and secular versions of mediation is the continuing commitment of Mennonite mediators to leave control of the process in the hands of the parties.

This chapter is my effort, as an anthropologist, to develop a cultural analysis of a set of practices and beliefs surrounding Mennonite mediation and peacebuilding. I base my analysis on the chapters in the current volume that were written by Mennonite practitioners, John Paul Lederach's book on building peace (1997), and a two-day workshop and discussion among both the Mennonite and non-Mennonite authors of this book. As for any anthropologist, my unfamiliarity with the subject is both a strength and a weakness. The novel aspects of Mennonite peacebuilding practice allow me to see things that those grounded in the process might take for granted and not recognize. On the other hand, this newness also means that there is a danger that I will get it wrong. This is my best effort to draw pattern and meaning from the fascinating stories in this book, but I cannot claim any expertise in Mennonite theology nor that I have presented an analysis that is definitive and authoritative.

I bring to this cultural analysis almost twenty years of research on mediation, particularly community dispute resolution, in the United States. I have studied secular and individual-focused mediation programs, including both community and court-connected processes. As I analyze Mennonite peacebuilding, I use U.S. community dispute resolution as a point of comparison. Comparison is an important part of theory building in the field of conflict resolution, for differences in philosophy, visions of social justice, and images of the power and control exercised by the third party shape conflict resolution processes in significant ways and need to be examined. This book contributes to expanding and complicating our understanding of conflict resolution, and it emphasizes the extent to which the surrounding cultural context defines conflict resolution practice and shapes its outcomes.

I am not entirely an outsider to the world of Mennonite peacebuilding. The third perspective I bring to this project, beyond that of anthropology and conflict resolution, is my own background as a Quaker, a closely related peace church. I expected that this background would help me understand the religious aspects of Mennonite peacebuilding practice. I also expected that Mennonite mediation would be more or less like other forms of community mediation with a more strongly religious commitment. But, when I walked into the conference room as we prepared this volume, I found myself confronted with a very different way of understanding conflict resolution, one that was deeply religious and quite different from most secular versions.

Indeed, in the discussion of the case studies, I felt like an outsider, a welcomed and appreciated outsider but nevertheless outside an amazingly close-knit world that stretches across the continents. As the contributors spoke, they kept tripping across past connections with one another in the same schools, colleges, seminaries, mission agencies—connections through farm and academic communities in Pennsylvania, Virginia, Indiana. I told the group that I thought I might have some insight about Mennonite peacebuilding because I was a Quaker, because I had grown up in Philadelphia and experienced a similar network that stretched among selected high schools and colleges, communities, and parts of the world. No, everyone told me quickly, Quakers do not operate quite the same as Mennonites. Quakers sometimes negotiate with the powerful, the people on the top, the key leaders, as well as working with grassroots groups. We primarily emphasize the grassroots. I came to see that a fundamental part of Mennonite practice is focusing on grassroots and midlevel leaders and activities.

After two days spent listening to these remarkable peacebuilders and reading and rereading the drafts of their stories, I am convinced that there are some significant differences between Mennonites and Quakers as peacebuilders and that there are much larger differences between what Mennonite mediators and secular community mediators do. Here is a distinctive conflict resolution practice, imbued with powerful spiritual beliefs and highly specific techniques of intervention, which are shaped by this spiritual framework.

## Key Terms

I have struggled with the terminology to use in this chapter. Although the field of peacebuilding and conflict transformation has a wide range of terminology, I will use the term *conflict transformation* to describe the broadest range of activities used in reshaping conflicts, *conflict resolution* as the process by which particular conflict situations are moved into a less confrontational mode, and *peacebuilding* as the set of approaches that facilitates conflict transformation. *Mediation* is a subset of peacebuilding, referring to third-party interventions to promote conflict resolution. *Peacemaking* is used by some scholars and practitioners to more narrowly describe interventions that use a third-party model, but I will use it as roughly parallel to peacebuilding.

I will begin by defining several of these key terms, which emerged again and again among the Mennonites, using as much as possible the language of the authors themselves. I will then describe several fundamental principles underlying Mennonite peacebuilding, although these principles were never articulated in precisely this way. Instead, they come out of my own cultural analysis, from looking at a series of descriptions or accounts of action and then abstracting from them the underlying rules of practice. Finally, I raise a few dilemmas that confront the practitioners of Mennonite mediation and peacebuilding.

### Peacebuilding

It appears that the core concepts have themselves been changing and developing as the notion of a peace mission has developed within the Mennonite church, a process described in Joe Miller's chapter. Experience with peacebuilding, in turn, has refined these concepts and practices.

*Peacebuilding* and *peacemaking* are the core terms, of course, and are often used interchangeably. Much of the activity described in these chapters as peacebuilding consists of making connections or building relationships among people who are antagonistic and working to replace this hostility with trust. Bergey, for example, worked with women in Somalia because they were often married across the warring social groups called clans and were able to communicate between clans. Peacebuilding often builds on existing institutions or existing authorities and expertise, such as the peace commissions in Nicaragua described by Chupp. It refers to the long-term construction of relationships among ordinary people, as well as negotiations among leaders.

Peacebuilding refers also to a broad range of social justice work related to poverty and development. As Kern says, peacemaking "in Mennonite circles" includes "relief and development work, education, pursuit of social justice, advocacy-oriented nonviolent direct action, and intermediary work in mediation and reconciliation" (ch. 12, n. 1). Many of the writers describe a wide range of education and development functions they performed, as well as more explicit efforts to contain conflicts, such as trauma-healing workshops in Liberia (Hart) and conflict resolution training in South Africa (Kraybill).

Peacebuilding has a strongly spiritual meaning. Liechty says that the Christian community is his foundation for peacebuilding, and most other writers emphasize that a worshiping community is essential for defining the broad visions of peacebuilding and providing both material and spiritual support. The goal, for some, is not measured by effectiveness but by faith: "Our calling is not to be effective but to be faithful," a common Mennonite mantra, according to Liechty. Peace work, he says, is an offering to God, who is responsible for its effectiveness.

## Witness

One of the most fundamental and commonly used terms is *witness*, which is similar to standing with, accompaniment, and presence. This is a term that defines the core of many of the cases in this book. One aspect of witness is standing with or being there for people facing dangerous or threatening situations. Another is in the area of testimony, expressing support or solidarity. The goal of the Mennonites in South Africa, for example, was to identify with and stand with the oppressed Christian brothers and sisters, to locate themselves in the same position of vulnerability and fear as those with whom they were working. The Herrs refer to a ministry of "presence," of "standing with" in South Africa. In a number of the conflicts described in this book, remaining affiliated with particular groups exposed the peaceworkers themselves to considerable danger.

## Presence

*Presence* means "sharing both good times and bad, . . . walking with those who suffer," in Bergey's words. She values "presence just because I am called to faithfulness by a God who is faithful and because I believe in hope" (ch. 10). Presence is, then, an act of faith regardless of whether or not it produces peace or converts. Much of the peacebuilding efforts described in these case studies is that of presence, or standing with, in situations of persecution, danger, and violence. The Christian Peacemaker Teams explicitly emphasize presence, as in Haiti and in Hebron (Kern). Since these teams are a recent development growing out of decades of international peacebuilding practice, their creation involved an explicit articulation of many of the underlying ideas of this practice. Thus, in its formation, the CPT brought a higher profile to these practices.

## Vulnerability

Closely related to the notion of presence is that of *vulnerability*. One aspect of this concept is standing with, or being close to, those in a state of fear, suspicion, and anger toward others. It is based on the biblical notion of God making himself vulnerable in the form of a man. This concept emphasizes the importance of risking danger and pain to stand with those who are oppressed or in fear, even putting oneself between violence and those facing the risk of violence. The peace worker experiences this vulnerability in the process of standing with others. In Chupp's words, his role was "standing with those who stood between enemies." Many of the stories include descriptions of the peace worker in danger, such as Bergey in Somalia, Lederach in Central America, the Herrs in South Africa. Christian Peacemaker Teams, again articulating the process more explicitly than other groups, grew out of a challenge to expose workers for peace to risks that were parallel to those of soldiers in war (Kern). Some peace workers did depart from dangerous conflict situations, but they also felt some anguish about using their status as Americans or foreigners to leave situations that others could not.

But not all peace workers face personal danger. One can also express vulnerability by making oneself open to others, by not using professional status or citizenship in a powerful nation to shield oneself. This is a concept connected to ideas of humility, servanthood, and discipleship. The theological basis for the notion of servanthood is the example of Jesus, taking up the cross, walking with and embracing humanity. Mennonite peacebuilders emphasize those parts of the Bible that focus on the oppressed and the vulnerable. Jesus provides the model of loving, compassionate, nonretaliatory confrontation with one's enemies, even at great personal risk. For some writers, this is a faith commitment, regardless of its impact (Liechty). Lederach refers to the theology of the lamb, which emphasizes Jesus as the suffering servant who chooses obedience and respect for life over political power or personal defense. In many ways, this is an approach to peacebuilding that appears passive but covertly is powerful and subversive. By supporting the powerless through quiet but persistent approaches, forms of conflict transformation can take place that might not occur through more overt and confrontational techniques.

## Discernment

The term *discernment* is used with reference to particular ways of gaining knowledge and making decisions. It seems to describe knowing and deciding at the same time. Community discernment takes place on the basis of knowledge shared by the community. Since the community holds greater wisdom than any individual, the process of discernment is a deliberation in which the community seeks a decision on the basis of its collective knowledge. As Kraybill observes, since no individual can know the divine will with certainty, only decisions subjected to a critical collective scrutiny can reflect divine intention with any confidence. Moreover, community decisions guard against making decisions on the basis of individual arrogance or ignorance. Esquivia describes a moment of discernment as "a process whereby the community of faith gathered together to analyze the times and situation in the light of the Word of God and the wisdom of the group" (ch. 8). The faith community is, consequently, important for decision making and planning as well as for support. The faith community is a presence both in the international site, which peacebuilders typically enter through existing networks of Mennonites, and back home, where home congregations pray for and pay for peace missionaries with the understanding that the missionaries are their representatives overseas.

### Nonviolence

A commitment to *nonviolence* is the bedrock of the Mennonite peace ministry. All of the above terms describe forms of knowledge, action, and intervention that are based on nonviolence and that seek to transform conflict from violent to nonviolent forms. The practices of mediation and peacebuilding described below all share the intention of providing ways of addressing conflicts nonviolently, although not passively.

## Key Practices

Based on my reading of these case studies, I have distilled the key practices used in Mennonite peacemaking. They describe well the ways of making peace that distinguish the Mennonites from others doing conflict resolution work.

### Not Taking Charge

One of the most distinctive features of Mennonite practice, and the one that sets it apart most dramatically from other forms, is the emphasis on *not taking charge* of mediation and conflict resolution. This is done to empower local leaders and to allow space for others to control the process. Mennonite peacebuilders are constantly on the lookout for local peacebuilders to place in the foreground, to encourage, to facilitate meeting with one another, and to train in useful skills, such as conflict resolution or trauma reduction. They strive to place them in charge while they themselves fade into the background. The scenario Chupp describes of sitting on the municipal building steps while important decisions were being made at a meeting inside is typical. Kraybill similarly moved from mediating to training mediators to training others to train mediators as he sought to step out of the controlling role in South Africa.

The purpose of peacebuilding, Kraybill argues, is to support and encourage facilitators of healing, not to do it oneself or to foster dependence on oneself or other outsiders. Peacebuilding is to promote the fullest development of human capacity in others. It is rooted theologically in respect for human sacredness and pragmatically in decades of development work and efforts to support others in this project. In contrast, most community mediation in the United States, while specifying that the mediator cannot make the final decision, encourages her to set the rules, manage the interaction, draw out the stories of the parties, and press for a settlement. Even though mediators are less powerful than judges, they nevertheless occupy a strong seat at the table in many kinds of mediation practice.

Mennonite practice, on the other hand, seeks to empower others rather than the mediator. Instead of emphasizing the heroic role of the mediator, this practice expects a certain submersion of the self, an eschewing of efforts to formulate an immediate, tangible result. In the authors' discussion for this book, one of the contributors referred to the process as "bumbling": listening, being creative and innovative, remaining vulnerable, making space for others to take control over their own lives. This contrasts with models of intervention that emphasize mastery and accomplishment. The Mennonite approach thus runs counter to dominant North American cultural themes of individualism, success, and being sure to get the credit for personal achievement. As Kraybill points out, the ethics of Mennonite practice also differ from those of modern competitive professionalism, which seeks to develop and sell a service, an approach that has become increasingly dominant within the U.S. mediation movement.

Not taking charge means a deliberate effort to avoid power, to resist taking it when it is offered, to sidestep the role of the educated professional telling social subordinates how to do things in favor of empowering local leadership. To do this while still making skills and knowledge available is a difficult project. As Chupp noted, he held back, offering less direct advice, instruction, and training than he could have, in order to avoid imposing his own ideas and agendas. Lederach describes his change from viewing his training role as providing expertise to one of accompanying discovery.

Not taking charge is also a way of respecting the culture of the groups in conflict. Within Mennonite peacebuilding, there is a deep commitment to recognizing and incorporating the culture of the setting rather than importing models developed in Washington or Wisconsin into Mogadishu or Monrovia. Mennonite training enterprises are highly sensitive to cultural differences, and trainers are quite committed to reframing their models for local situations and getting advice from local people about how to do this. The ideal process is to understand the nature of local peacemaking processes and build on those, rather than to start by introducing any process from outside. Campbell, for example, emphasizes that the initial mediation material he received from the United States in Northern Ireland was not appropriate for the Irish context but could be adapted. Lederach describes his efforts to locate middle-level leaders and provide them support in Somalia at the same time as he tried to protect them from undue interference from outside people. Kraybill notes that in South Africa, outsiders are quick to come and offer skills workshops without engaging in this cultural tailoring process, an observation Liechty also makes about Northern Ireland. In Liberia, the trauma workshops included discussions of local words for peace and reconciliation. It is, of course, always debatable to what extent a model developed in one society can be transferred to another, even with some tailoring; many fundamental assumptions and features of process will inevitably remain from the society that invented it.

### Being There for a Long Time

A second distinctive feature of Mennonite mediation is the commitment to long-term involvement in the conflict situation. This is related to the emphasis on learning the language and culture, on developing workshops and trainings out of local languages and practices, on building relationships and serving as bridges, all of which require an investment of time. It is related to the commitment of presence, to "being there" as a Mennonite religious community, and to the political practice of standing with the vulnerable and oppressed.

This long-term involvement has two aspects. First, it presumes that the generation of a conflict and its resolution both take place over a long period of time. Lederach points out that using a time frame of twenty to forty years rather than a shorter time frame changes the understanding of peacebuilding. Interventions with a short time frame focus on resolving an immediate crisis, while longer ones work on transformation, conflict prevention, sustainable development, equitable social structures, and the creation of respectful relationships among diverse groups (Lederach, 1997, pp. 63–71). In fact, many highly visible interventions occur only after a crisis has developed. They are geared to fixing that crisis rather than to any long-term social transformation. In contrast, Mennonite peacebuilding views conflicts as having long histories of development and transformation. Many of the neighborhood and family conflicts I studied in New England towns also had this long time dimension, but the mediation interventions I observed, run by local mediation programs, typically focused on one-shot solutions to the problem (Merry, 1990). In contrast, Mennonite mediators and peacebuilders enter into long-term situations by integrating their actions with those of previous peace practitioners in that situation.

The second aspect of long-term involvement is the idea that a peacemaker must invest years in understanding a situation, building up contacts, and learning about the history and context of a conflict in order to be helpful. At the same time, this peacemaker need not produce immediate results to justify further support, since resolution is slow. This long-term investment facilitates cultural sensitivity, the acquisition of local languages, and a broad vision of the solution. Most of the peacemakers described in this book invested several years in the place they were working and spent much of this time acquiring knowledge about the place and its people. Such interventions are quite different from those of visiting experts, who are mentioned by several authors as arriving on a short-term basis in the middle of conflict situations. The Christian Peacemaker Teams differ from this model since they intervene on a short-term basis, although as Kern's chapter indicates, there is recognition that this is a deviation from general Mennonite practice.

## Working from the Edge

Another key strategy is working with ordinary, often poor, and powerless people as a route to peace rather than working with top negotiators or government officials. *Working from the edge*, as I call this approach, is connected to the biblical injunction to have special concern for the needs of the poor and vulnerable. The cases in this book show Mennonite peacebuilders locating themselves in rural communities in South Africa, in small villages in Central America, with elders and women in Somalia, rather than with top diplomats and negotiators. There are two aspects to this practice. In addition to the emphasis on working with relatively powerless people, there is an acceptance of small steps forward, incremental change, micro movements toward peace and reconciliation, rather than only seeking out major new accords or cease-fires. These steps may involve creating spaces for peace to emerge, for dialogue to take place, for ordinary people to feel less anger and prejudice toward one another and less hostility toward those who have harmed them and their communities.

Underlying this practice is a particular understanding of peacebuilding. In this view, peacebuilding does not occur only at the top but also comes from micro readjustments of power in the small spaces of everyday social life, accomplished one at a time in the lives of people in situations of conflict. Without local transformations, successful negotiations by top leaders will not produce peace. Peace cannot be imposed from the top down without these long-term, incremental changes in local communities. The activities of the local peace commissions in Nicaragua, for example, provide a good example of this approach to peacebuilding (Chupp, Lederach). From his experience in Nicaragua, Lederach argues that the peace process takes place in many different places and ways at the same time and that high-level negotiations among too few actors may not produce a sustainable peace (1997). Chupp describes the peacebuilding process as walking with those who are making peace a reality, while others sign the peace accords in the capital city. Such incremental change can also lead to major transformation, as occurred in South Africa. Ultimately, it is this kind of major conflict transformation that Mennonite peacebuilders envision.

## Confronting Social Inequality

Mennonite mediation differs from many North American models of mediation in its attention to social inequalities and its commitment to helping the weakest. Indeed, I think that a key dimension of Mennonite mediation is the class analysis behind it, although I do not think Mennonites would use this language. There is a keen attention to differences in social power and the forces that produce these differences. There is concern that professional, educated elites do not take on solving the problems of "lower" social classes.

During the 1970s and early 1980s, community mediation in the United States shared a similar political vision and social analysis, but with its success—its expansion and institutionalization in the late 1980s and 1990s—the commitments to community empowerment, to local conflict managers, and to a deprofessionalized conflict resolution process were largely abandoned. This interest survives only on the margins of a movement increasingly focused on service delivery by professional mediators (Harrington and Merry 1988; Merry and Milner, 1993). Yet, there are constant efforts to retain this commitment within the alternative dispute resolution movement, as there are within the Mennonite mediation tradition.

### Entry through Building Relationships

A key dilemma for any peacebuilder is how to enter a situation of conflict. A central tenet of Mennonite peacebuilding is that entry depends upon forming relationships of trust with the parties in conflict as the basis for negotiations or other interventions. Often, existing Mennonite institutions, churches, or schools will facilitate entry, but in some cases other Christian groups may as well. Creating these relationships takes time and underlies the emphasis on long-term intervention, discussed above. Among the most important partners with whom Mennonite peacebuilders seek to build relationships are those local actors who are in some way engaged in processes of reconciliation or peacebuilding in the area. Often, the Mennonite workers conceptualize their role as supporting local initiatives and local peace activists.

## Key Peacebuilding Activities

What do Mennonite peacemakers actually do, if they are not taking charge and running things? I have identified six key activities based on what writers said they did in their case studies. The first is networking and building relationships within which significant conversations and change can occur. As Chupp puts it, "Conflict transformation involves creating space for dialogue to take place." The second is witnessing or standing with, as discussed above. Part of this activity involves creating a long-term Mennonite presence, which remains despite conflict and danger. The third is training, primarily in conflict resolution but also in trauma healing. A fourth activity is facilitating meetings, as Lederach did in Central America and Bergey in Somalia. Again, this is a supporting rather than a starring role. Fifth, a common activity of these peacebuilders is providing funds: for meetings, for bringing in other Mennonite workers, for sending front-line local peacemakers to the United States for sabbaticals, for providing materials, and for making small grants for local initiatives. This activity should not be minimized, since it appears over and over as an important part of the peacebuilding activity. These activities are supplemented by other development initiatives, as well as by some more focused projects, such as building a network of support for conscientious objectors (Esquivia and Stucky). Sixth, Mennonite peacebuilders engage in more general theory building about the peace and conflict transformation process through the comparison and analysis of peace processes in various social contexts. This activity emanates mainly from centers for the study of peace in Mennonite colleges and universities. This book, as well as a wealth of other publications, testifies to the contribution of Mennonite experience and analysis to the development of theory in the peacebuilding process.

## Dilemmas and Contradictions

Despite the coherence of the underlying social and religious philosophy of Mennonite peacebuilding and the practices I have described, there are inherent dilemmas and contradictions in the body of work represented in this volume. These dilemmas appear most dramatically in the case of Christian Peacemaker Teams, since the CPT philosophy is articulated most explicitly here, and therefore the contradictions are most apparent. I will list four dilemmas and contradictions that confront Mennonite peacebuilders and give some idea of how Mennonite peacebuilders have dealt with these dilemmas.

### Standing with the Oppressed versus Neutrality

Mennonite peacebuilding is primarily dedicated to making bridges and connections among the sides of a conflict rather than advocating for one side or another. At the same time, it is also committed to solidarity with the disenfranchised. In many conflicts, it is difficult to do both. The peacemakers in this book constantly confront this difficulty as they work with South Africans in the homelands rather than with Afrikaners, or with the elders in Somalia rather than with the military leaders of the warring factions. The CPT team in Haiti struggles over whether or not they should talk to the U.S. military, and in Hebron they find it difficult to relate to the settlers and to the local Israeli police. Even though CPT seeks to treat oppressors as the children of God, in practice it is difficult to give equal sympathy and support to all sides. If one side in a conflict has the preponderance of military power and is inclined to use violence to support its side, maintaining neutrality becomes hard. It is theoretically possible to talk to the "sinners," and many Mennonite peacebuilders try, but this conversation is difficult to begin and harder to keep going, particularly with those who seem deeply unjust or unrepentantly violent.

Mennonite mediation does not seek neutrality, however. Instead, it actively advocates for the peace process itself and for those engaged in it. Thus, peacebuilders seek solidarity with those engaged in reconciliation rather than with one side or the other. Moreover, because of the deep concern for the powerless, the vulnerable, the poor, and the oppressed, it advocates for these groups. But, there is an inevitable tension in bringing peace and justice together: Peace in the sense of a cessation of conflict achieved through mutual agreement among the warring parties may be far more readily achieved if it is not accompanied by a rearrangement of the power configuration in a way that the weaker party considers just. This is also a tension inherent in the practice of mediation as it is carried out in many secular settings, particularly following the Fisher and Ury model (1981). Since the goal of the process is to produce an agreement voluntarily accepted by both parties, mediators have difficulty producing an agreement they consider fair if the parties are unequal in power. In practice, mediated agreements are typically the best the weaker party can argue for, but they usually benefit the stronger more. They tend to reflect the difference of power between the parties.

Community mediation faced the dilemma of advocacy versus neutrality in the 1970s and 1980s, as it developed out of a tradition of community advocacy. The experience of the San Francisco Community Boards is particularly relevant, since it tried to empower community people, improve the quality of neighborhood life, and provide neutral mediation services. Although this approach worked well when neighbors were in conflict, it did not replace advocacy for tenants dealing with landlords, women battered by their husbands, or people fighting off the encroachment of small businesses in residential neighborhoods (Merry and Milner, 1993). The community mediation movement coped with this contradiction by abandoning advocacy in favor of neutrality; Mennonite peacebuilding makes the opposite choice by sacrificing neutrality for advocacy.

But this raises another problem. Who are the oppressors, and who are the oppressed? It is not always as clear on the ground as it is in theory. In the current global economy, local merchants, landlords, and political leaders may well be cogs in far larger systems, which they are virtually powerless to change. The small Afrikaner farmer may well be racist, but he did not create apartheid on his own. The Somali leaders fighting bitterly for control are using vast quantities of weapons obtained from the United States and Soviet Union during the Cold War. On the other hand, local people are sometimes more concerned with their position in the larger structure of power than with the interests of other local people. As Fanon pointed out in his study of colonial Algeria, the elites among a colonized people are often deeply complicitous with the metropole and not at all interested in the lot of the poor (1963).

And those who seem powerful and oppressive may themselves be vulnerable in significant ways. The slumlord may be an upwardly mobile second-generation immigrant who is providing substandard housing to more recent immigrants in order to make ends meet for his own family, as I found was often the case in the New England neighborhoods I studied (Merry, 1990). There are some with power and resources who are committed to making a difference by, for example, supporting Mennonite initiatives. Obviously, the social world is complicated, and people do not sort neatly into categories such as oppressor and oppressed. One way of dealing with this complexity is to seek solidarity with those in local contexts who are seeking reconciliation, as Liechty has done in Northern Ireland.

## "Standing With" and the North American Identity

The importance of presence, or standing with, or even standing between, is, as I understand the principle, allowing oneself to be vulnerable along with the disenfranchised person. It may mean placing oneself between that person and a bullet, as Kern says was part of the inspiration for the CPT. But as Mennonite peacemakers move through the world, they carry with them identities in addition to Mennonite. Those who are Americans represent, whether they wish to or not, an economically and militarily powerful nation. When a Mennonite stands with a vulnerable person in another country, he is usually a white, educated, and middle-class person with the privileges of that social position, as well as an outsider from a powerful nation. These are identities that contribute in some ways, possibly significant, to the power of *standing between* in the current political world. The complicity with military power is not easily escaped. It is an inevitable part of being there as a peacemaker in international contexts. Peacebuilders deliberately use their status as North Americans to draw international attention to the abuses of a nation against its citizens.

## Cultural Sensitivity and the Peace Mission

As we have seen, Mennonite peacebuilders are deeply committed to cultural sensitivity and always work to adapt to the cultural practices of the place where they work. But they are also deeply committed to their faith and often describe their work as a peace mission or peacemaking ministry. Singing and Bible study are important to their work and to some training programs, such as the trauma-healing workshops in Liberia. To some extent, the peacebuilding enterprise parallels conversion-oriented missionary endeavors. Like missionary work, peacebuilding builds on notions of service and servanthood that are inculcated in schools and congregations. Peacemakers, like missionaries, are commissioned, sent out, and prayed for by their home congregations. They often build on previous work, particularly in education, by Mennonite missionaries, for example, in the cases of Colombia, South Africa, and Somalia. Such a deep commitment to a particular religious tradition has the potential to contradict the commitment to cultural sensitivity.

## Outsider/Insider Relationships

Mennonites work in international conflict situations as outsiders and search out insiders on site to spearhead the peacebuilding process. As Liechty concludes, this outsider status may provide the best springboard for peacebuilding initiatives. Yet, Mennonites come from a close-knit faith community, which was historically very insular. As Miller observes, Mennonites have a long tradition of separatism based on the belief that it is necessary to disengage from the world to lead a religious life. This idea persisted until World War II,

when the alternative service assignments of Mennonite conscientious objectors exposed them to forms of injustice in the larger society. The notion of a
peace mission grew out of this experience.

Mennonites embarking on international peacebuilding projects are, then,
leaving a small, supportive, fairly homogeneous community in which they are
insiders for a very different setting, where they work as outsiders. Many authors
comment on the support they derived from the Mennonite faith communities
where they worked. Thus, Mennonite peacebuilders are both insiders in a
separate and distinctive Mennonite community located at home and abroad
*and* outsiders to the larger world in which they are working. They move between insider and outsider roles that in some ways are contradictory. These
border crossings are both transgressive and creative, as peacebuilders shift
between a historically insulated community and a secular and morally challenging outside world. Yet, Liechty notes, there are also surprising joinings, as
people with other kinds of close community experiences find common ground
with Mennonite peacebuilders.

## Conclusions

Through these stories of Mennonite peacebuilders, I see the shape of a distinctive approach to peacebuilding. The critical philosophical aspects of this
approach are the connection with the poor, the vulnerable, and the powerless
and the desire to allow local leaders to emerge rather than exporting North
American experts and conflict resolution skills. The approach is founded, of
course, on a spiritual commitment to nonviolent strategies of handling conflicts. The key attributes of this practice are a long investment of time, careful
listening, being inside and outside at the same time, understanding the situation but not taking charge, taking a nondirective stance but walking with or
being there, and working with a profound spirituality and sense of witnessing
for God, which diminishes the need for immediate outcomes.

The differences between Mennonite peacebuilding and other forms of conflict resolution demonstrate the importance of drawing analytical distinctions
within the field of conflict resolution, and they underscore the extent to which
fundamentally different visions of social justice and peace produce different
practices and procedures of handling conflict. In particular, this window into
Mennonite peacebuilding highlights the significant differences that exist between some forms of religiously motivated and secular conflict resolution practices. Whatever the level of success or accomplishment Mennonite peacebuilders achieve, they work within a religious framework that supersedes
secular measures of success, in whatever terms that might be defined. This is
a conflict resolution practice animated by very different sources of inspiration
and vision than most North American community mediation.

Mennonite peacebuilding is defined by a powerful tradition of religious faith
and community life. The Mennonite practice of peacebuilding is deeply influenced by the spiritual and social history of the Mennonites, as the chapters

in this book indicate, joined with newer ideas from the outside, such as civil rights, social activism, and conflict resolution methodologies. Along with the historical emphasis on mission work, community, and pacifism, these cultural traditions have produced a distinctive style of peacebuilding that emphasizes community, servanthood, and witness. It builds on a tradition of Mennonite missionary activity but differs from non-Mennonite mission work, which may lack the traditions of community life, such as the practice of discernment, which define and shape the Mennonite peacebuilding mission.

I think this approach is in many ways opposite to characteristic American modes of intervention based on mastery and accomplishment. It is instead based on sacrifice of self, listening and learning, being with, taking on the suffering and persecution of others, and putting the self in danger. This is a process that could not easily be replicated outside the religious and community traditions of the Mennonites, the spiritual life that is built up through the everyday practices of community. Yet, there is much that can be learned by other practitioners of peacebuilding and mediation. Mennonite peacebuilding offers approaches and perspectives that could be valuable to the broader con-flict resolution field, in particular the emphases on long-term engagement, empowering local leaders, building relationships of trust, and working through local conflict resolution practices.

# Fourteen

## Mennonite Approaches to Peace
and Conflict Resolution

CHRISTOPHER MITCHELL

UNOFFICIAL EFFORTS TO MAKE PEACE between warring adversaries have a longer history than is sometimes supposed. In some cases, peacemakers, both intra- and international, have been secular, but in many others the protagonists in such efforts have come from religious backgrounds or represented religious institutions.

Some religiously inspired peacemaking practices have taken the form of direct involvement as intermediaries, as when the Vatican successfully undertook a mediating role in the Beagle Channel dispute between Chile and Argentina. Others have involved limiting on the destructive effects of conflict and war by attempting to provide sanctuaries, safe havens, and zones (or times) of peace. Probably the best known of these were the thirteenth-century efforts by Pope Gregory IX to have certain categories of individuals—including pilgrims, merchants, and peasants tilling the soil—be given "full security against the ravages of war" by incorporating such immunities into Christian canon law.[1] Still other activities have involved the elaboration of complex schemes for societies that would be inherently peaceful; they were often regional or even "universal." Among many such efforts are the writings of Quakers William Penn and John Bellers, respectively, who within two decades of one another, produced works on *Essays towards the Present and Future Peace of Europe* (1693) and *Some Reasons for an European State* (1710).

In more recent times, a number of religious organizations have become closely and justifiably identified with the practical search for peace and justice among states and within societies. In the twentieth century, the Society of Friends has continued its long-established peace mission of "speaking truth to power" and acting as conciliator and intermediary in conflicts as different as those in Sri Lanka and Northern Ireland. They have even acted in the Cold War itself. In perhaps the most recent example of religious involvement in peacemaking, the Roman Catholic church has begun to expand its activities beyond the traditional role of the Vatican as a mediator, so that bishops in Burundi, Liberia, and Mozambique and the lay Catholic community of Sant'Egidio in Rome have become directly involved as mediators in efforts to end civil wars. Similarly, ecclesiastical coalitions, such as the World Council of Churches or the All Africa Conference of Churches, have involved themselves in efforts to deal with violent conflicts such as those in Sudan and—with less success—in Liberia.

As illustrated in the chapters of this book, another religious group that is consciously and deliberately taking up a public peacemaking role are the Mennonites, whose move from a philosophy of separation and quietism to one of active involvement in many of the most violent and conflict-ridden societies in the period since World War II constitutes something of a revolution in religious practice, although the ideas and traditions on which this activity are based go back to Anabaptist principles first formulated in sixteenth-century Europe. In this chapter, I consider the Mennonite engagement in peacemaking in relation to a parallel development: the growth of theories about and practice in nonofficial conflict resolution during the period from the 1960s through the 1990s. In doing so, I wish to compare and contrast the way in which the two peacemaking movements have developed and the way in which they carry out their perceived role as third parties in protracted, intractable, and frequently violent conflicts. My object is to discover what both approaches have in common and what each might learn from the other about effective processes for long-term conflict resolution and peacemaking.

## Mennonite Engagement and the Field of Conflict Research

As mentioned above, the recent development of a Mennonite calling to become deliberately involved in the practice of public peacemaking, admirably described in Joseph Miller's introductory chapter in this volume, can be seen as one aspect of a deep-rooted and increasingly noticeable trend of religious involvement in the search for solutions to the continuing and massive violence throughout the "postwar" world. Increasing Mennonite involvement, first, as Miller writes, in "helping the larger society find reconciliation in . . . 'social disasters' " and then as "instruments of conciliation, mediation, and transformation" occurred from the 1960s onward. Part of the background to that development was the temporally parallel growth of the academic conflict research movement in North America and Europe, with its insistence upon the need for applied research and for conflict researchers to involve themselves in the practical tasks of resolving conflicts, quite apart from analyzing and understanding their sources, dynamics, and solutions.

To give any impression that the emergence of conflict research or, as it later became better known, "conflict analysis and resolution," was a coherent and straightforward process would be entirely misleading. As with all new fields of study, its boundaries were ill formed and debatable. Was it part of sociology, international relations, social psychology, political science, or what? Was its main focus on interpersonal, intrasocietal, or international conflicts? What remedies did its researchers recommend, in terms of appropriate and acceptable processes: mediation instead of adjudication, conciliation rather than negotiation, facilitation in preference to coercion? Was the objective of applying scholarly findings to conflict situations to help bring about a peaceful society or to bring about a just society—and were these always compatible?

Moreover, the field also experienced much confusion over terminology. Originally, *mediation, conciliation,* and *negotiation* were seen as rather traditional but specific activities carried out as part of the overall process of peacemaking. In contrast, *conflict resolution* covered all activities involved in bringing about a final ending of the conflict, with the adversaries themselves enjoying a wholly different (and usually more egalitarian) relationship. Later, writers started to use the term *conflict transformation* rather than resolution, and the latter term began to carry an implication of superficial tinkering with a conflict, usually with the basic aim of reducing or ending violence. (I continue to use the term in its original sense and do so in this chapter.)

In the 1970s, the situation was further complicated by the increased use of a range of alternative methods of dispute resolution (ADR) in the "real world" outside of academia—the world of labor-management conflicts, of intracommunity conflicts, and of conflicts within businesses and many other types of organizations. In this case, the new approaches to bringing about industrial, organizational, or community peace tended to be alternatives to an increasingly overloaded legal system, which gave rise to a series of debates about the relative merits and weaknesses of litigation compared with various types of ADR.

From this ferment of ideas and debates, a variety of prescriptions emerged for resolving conflicts at various social levels and thus restoring social peace. Most intractable to any of these approaches were the (usually violent) conflicts among large collectivities, which the growing literature characterized as deep-rooted and protracted civil strife and which increasingly appeared to have their origins in situations involving competing ethnic identity groups and issues of secession or integration and control of the state apparatus. Increasingly, and particularly since the demise of the Cold War, it became clear that the major problems confronting potential peacemakers of whatever persuasion at the end of the century would be cases of widespread, violent civil strife, such as Bosnia, Sri Lanka, Sudan, and El Salvador. It also became clear that new approaches to seeking a resolution of such complex and deep-rooted conflicts would have to involve equally complex processes of peacekeeping, peacemaking, and peacebuilding (Ghali, 1992).

In response to the growing number of cases of violent and protracted civil strife, the academic field of conflict analysis and resolution proposed a variety of ideas about alternative processes to those traditionally used to cope with intractable conflicts. Proposals were put forward for problem-solving approaches, for facilitated dialogues, and for interactive conflict resolution as means of helping to resolve long-term, violent conflicts. A number of practitioners began to act as informal and unofficial third parties themselves and to use very similar approaches to bring conflicting adversaries together to analyze their shared predicament jointly and to explore together the potential availability of "win-win" solutions. Although different in detail, the approaches shared a number of common features, most notably:

1. They utilized small, informal groups of key individuals involved in the conflict to analyze the conflict situation in which the parties were enmeshed and to visualize possible solutions.
2. They attempted to apply existing theories about the sources and dynamics of conflict in the search for solutions.
3. They developed a variety of processes to avoid conventionally antagonistic procedures of posturing, bluffing, and bargaining within the meetings (usually termed *workshops*), instead aiming at an open and honest exchange of information regarding the adversaries' interests, values, and dilemmas.

About this time, a former U.S. Department of State diplomat coined the phrase "track two" processes to distinguish such informal, facilitated approaches from those employed officially at the level of track one by diplomats and officials of intergovernmental organizations, such as the United Nations or the Organization of American States (Montville, 1987). During the 1980s and 1990s, track two processes were employed—with varied success—in conflicts as different as those in the Middle East (Kelman, 1982; Rothman, 1992), in Lebanon (Azar, 1990), in Northern Ireland (Arthur, 1992), and over the Falklands/Malvinas Islands (Little and Mitchell, 1989). Undoubtedly, the most widely known example of a successful track two process is now that initiated by Norwegian social scientists working for FAFO (the Norwegian Institute for Social Analysis), which led to the accord between the Israeli government and the leaders of the Palestine Liberation Organization (PLO) in the peace process in the Middle East (Corbin, 1994).

A quick review of the cases discussed in this book will, of course, reveal that protracted and deep-rooted conflicts in various regions of the world were precisely those situations into which Mennonite peacemakers had been drawn and in which they were developing their own peacemaking philosophy and practices. In Central and South America, South Africa, Somalia, Liberia, and Northern Ireland and on the West Bank, Mennonite peacemakers have been confronting the need to develop their own practical approaches to fulfilling the role of peacemaker, sustained by their core beliefs, which are outlined by Joseph Miller in the opening chapter, discussed in chapter 15 by Marc Gopin, and mentioned by all of the other writers as part of their accounts of their individual work in the field.

Like the emergence of analytical track two approaches, Mennonite peacemaking philosophy and practice emerged from the interaction of two sets of factors: experience in the field and reflections on that experience, which resulted in the formulation of some flexible principles for future work. Like track two approaches, the working principles of Mennonite conflict resolution remain flexible and open to revision—both approaches are in a state of "becoming" rather than being fully formed and final. They seem to me to share a number of similarities, and they have some slightly more obvious differences. Hence, I argue that they could and should be used in parallel and be regarded as complementary rather than as competing approaches to finding solutions to protracted and deep-rooted conflicts, such as Somalia, the West Bank, Northern Ireland, Nicaragua, and South Africa.

## Philosophies and Practicalities of Peacebuilding

With this parallel development in mind, the remainder of this chapter will briefly describe the two approaches—track two and Mennonite models—and will indicate what both models have in common, while also acknowledging some important differences. To me, the latter argue for the need to employ elements of both approaches in seeking long-term resolutions for the increasing number of protracted cases of civil strife that are likely to continue to afflict the world as it enters the twenty-first century. I will return to this theme at the end of the chapter.

### Mennonite Approaches to Peacebuilding

The other chapters in this book present a varied and complex picture of Mennonite engagement in peacemaking and peacebuilding activities, but closer examination of the apparently disconnected accounts of Mennonite endeavors in countries as different as Palestine, Northern Ireland, and Nicaragua reveals a clear pattern of ideas and activities connected to those ideas.

This is not to say that what Mennonites actually do in their varied peacemaking efforts yet constitutes a coherent body of practice. Mennonite projects take a variety of forms, develop against different backgrounds, and frequently are initiated by different groups (insiders, as well as outsiders) with a multitude of aims and aspirations. Nonetheless, similar ideas and assumptions do underlie Mennonite work, even in the case of the shorter-term, high-profile, and apparently partisan work of Christian Peacemaker Teams (CPT).

One indication of this intellectual unity is simply the way in which particular words or themes emerge time and again in the authors' accounts of their activities and commitments. Perhaps most strikingly, almost all of the contributors to this volume employ the two words *support* and *service* when describing both Mennonite activities and the philosophies that lie behind them. Many of our authors talk freely about Mennonite activities aimed at *complementing* or *supporting* local endeavors. Kathleen Kern, for example, describes her group's activities in accompanying local people from St. Helene as being intended to share in the latters' experiences but mainly to encourage them *in what they are doing* (ch. 12). Similarly, Barry Hart's account of the trauma-healing work undertaken with such effort in Liberia clearly indicates the extent to which it was built on the local endeavors of the Christian Health Association of Liberia (ch. 11). The theme underlying such expressions and activities is clearly based upon the philosophy of assisting that which is currently taking place, as long as it fits in with Mennonite visions of a peacebuilding activity carried out in a nonviolent manner.

Clearly, then, one basic theme of Mennonite peacebuilding is to engage *with* existing local institutions that contribute to the growth and maintenance of peace and to offer support and help to local endeavors on their own terms, rather than seeking to impose either a vision of what a final peace should look like or to press for a particular process for arriving at that desired outcome. Another important aspect of this central theme is that of simply *offering* such support or waiting until it is *asked for* by local people. On occasions, this implies that the Mennonite engagement in peacemaking, like that of FAFO in Gaza, arises out of a prior engagement in some other valued activity—relief or reconstruction work, for example—which provides both an entrée into the conflict and what Bonnie Bergey (ch. 10) describes as an "earned integrity," perhaps better known among conflict researchers as intermediary credibility.

A second theme that emerges clearly from the authors' accounts is the importance of relationships and the necessity for building positive relationships if lasting peace is to be attained in any society, even the most conflict prone. Interestingly, the theme of relationships has two important aspects in Mennonite engagement. First, Mennonite writings emphasize the importance of building positive and fruitful relationships among local peacebuilding institutes and individuals and the members of the Mennonite mission themselves. These, it is argued, are essential preliminaries to any successful peacemaking or peacebuilding activities by Mennonite missions and, as Kern points out, these relationships extend to all parties involved in a conflict, including security forces and armed settlers (ch. 12). Moreover, it is generally recognized that the building of such prior relationships is a gradual and fragile process, usually involving considerable time and effort. Hence, another major theme emerging from accounts of Mennonite peacemaking is that of *commitment*—and not just intellectual or religious commitment to the task in hand, important though these are, but the practical commitment of both effort and time. Mennonite peacebuilding is very much posited on the principle of continuing involvement over a long period, usually on site and physically in the middle, in much the same way that the Quakers have established permanent houses, centers, and couples between warring factions and in the midst of communities in conflict. Implicitly, Mennonite philosophy seems to be based upon a generalized version of the belief about Somali society well expressed by John Paul Lederach: "It may take as long to climb back out of a conflict as it did for the conflict to build up to its worst, most divided moment" (ch. 3).

The other aspect of relationship building, as it emerges from the accounts in this book, refers to the Mennonite awareness of the need to restore or establish positive relationships among erstwhile adversaries if there is to be a deep and lasting future peace, as opposed to a temporary truce—what Israeli ambassador Shimon Shamir has characterized as a "cold peace," or what early conflict researchers described as a *settlement* rather than a *resolution* of the conflict. Again, this emphasis on the importance of relationship building is something that Mennonite engagement has contributed to one important recent change in the overall field of conflict research: The emphasis can no longer be simply on the process of getting parties to talk fruitfully together so that they can devise their own compacts and agreements. Long-term, sustainable peace is, in the Mennonite view, as much about long-term relationship building as it is about short-term agreements and treaties, a view that finds an echo in the call of former U.N. secretary-general Boutros Ghali for new approaches to building long-term peace. Clearly, Mennonite thinking about this aspect of conflict resolution has struck a chord in the overall field and contributed to a broadening of what are increasingly viewed as essential activities, especially in the post accord phase of a conflict.

Interestingly, there has been considerable debate about this issue of a third-party obligation to engage in long-term relationship restoration and development in recent conflict research literature, and there remains a minority view that, at least at certain social levels, relationship building is an over-ambitious activity, one not to be undertaken by most intermediaries. Tony Marshall, for example, writing about intermediary work at the individual and community levels, is firmly of the view that mediators should "be concerned with relationships insofar as they may contribute to more constructive communication. The improvement of relationships is not, however, to be seen as an end of mediation" (Marshall, 1989).

A third theme that emerges from the practical writings in this book might best be summarized as the idea of *withinness*. Many of the writers use both the word and the concept in discussing their own contribution to peacebuilding, linking it to arguments about the importance of the social, political, and cultural context within which Mennonite engagement occurs; to the need to engage in capacity building rather than in training (the former implying that knowledge, skills, and, above all, local capabilities are there, in the society, awaiting opportunities for use and development); and to the necessity for helping local people to "give themselves permission," in Ron Kraybill's words, to develop their own methods and models.

Inevitably, there is something of a paradox here for Mennonite engagement. On the one hand, there is a clear theme underlying their activities that militates against the idea and practice of being outsiders and of bringing something into the conflicted society, be it ideas, resources, possible procedures, training materials, models of community building, generalized expertise (which can often bring some degree of hope with it), or experience from other situations. Mennonite philosophy involves being there to listen and learn and to act as a "companion in discovery" for locals. On the other hand, as the experiences of Kathleen Kern (ch. 12), Bonnie Bergey (ch. 10), Robert and Judy Zimmerman Herr (ch. 4), and even Joseph Liechty in Northern Ireland (ch. 5) indicate, Mennonites involved in peacebuilding *do* remain outsiders, although rather unusual outsiders, who at some stage make efforts to transfer some things that are not, strictly speaking, local. This problem, of course, does not arise when the Mennonite initiative comes from insiders, that is, arises through the efforts of local people, as in the case of the work of Justapaz in Colombia, described by Ricardo Esquivia and Paul Stucky (ch. 8).

In most other cases, however, the dilemma remains of what to make available and when. The Mennonite answer could be characterized as "not too much, and it has to be culturally sensitized and only when asked for by local people and deemed to be in line with Mennonite values." In this, the Mennonite answer seems different in degree rather than kind from that which might be given by a track two intervenor, who might suggest it appropriate to transfer "what experience (or theory) and careful listening tells you is relevant, carefully tailored to the parties and the circumstances, and offered as a tentative idea to be explored and—possibly—rejected outright."

Two other major themes of Mennonite engagement in peacebuilding emerge from the accounts presented in this volume. The first of these could be summarized as the idea that part of a Mennonite philosophy of engagement in a conflicted society is that a Mennonite presence should have the function of witness and revelation. I am not here using the word *revelation* in any theological sense but rather using it to describe situations where what is going on is seldom revealed accurately to a wider audience, or where only sanitized versions of the conflict are permitted to reach the wider world. Several of our writers talk about their task of accompanying and being present as witnesses to what is going on in a conflict, especially at local levels; of writing reports and of publicizing events that would otherwise go unnoticed; or of simply being there and, through the warning of potentially damaging revelations, deterring the violent and repressive behavior of the more powerful parties to the dispute. This function clearly ties in with the Mennonite practice of insisting that their role in peacebuilding can only be carried out successfully by their living with or standing with one or both parties to the conflict, of maintaining a long-term presence within the conflict and the community.

This theme returns us to the paradox discussed above, as this revelation function can only be carried out successfully because Mennonites *are* outsiders and have important linkages to the outside world. The whole paradox might be summarized by saying that Mennonite peacebuilding works because those involved strive to become as near to insiders as they can while maintaining a relevant deterrent role as outsiders.

The last theme emerging from the descriptions of Mennonite peacebuilding is a rather obvious one, but it needs mentioning because it is such a central part of the whole endeavor. If it were possible to summarize this theme in a single word, the word would be *localism*, in the sense that much of Mennonite peacebuilding is aimed at grassroots communities and individuals, with the underlying assumption that broader peace can be developed from the ground up by working with local people. It hardly needs pointing out that such an approach fits into traditional Mennonite distrust of governments and of national-level politics, so that local peacebuilding was a natural social niche for Mennonite engagement. What might not be quite so obvious is the manner in which this level of involvement also fits in with another major theme in Mennonite thinking, namely the search for justice and the manner in which this is linked to the development of long-term sustainable peace. Increasingly, at the end of the twentieth century, the kinds of conflict that cry out for some form of effective peacemaking and peacebuilding are no longer traditional wars *between* states but high levels of civil strife *within* ostensibly viable, sovereign, and independent states. Many of the latter type of conflict are structured as contests between a dominant state or a government controlled by one community (usually a majority), and a dominated and discriminated-against community (usually a minority).[2] In other words, Sri Lanka, South Africa, Northern Ireland, and Georgia are examples of highly *asymmetric* conflicts, where one adversary has a much greater capacity and opportunity for inflicting injustices and violence than has the other.

In such asymmetric conflicts, it is all too often the case that the dominated community is the one initially requiring protective and peacebuilding services, so Mennonite engagement takes the form of living and standing with a grassroots community and supporting and complementing that community's efforts to deal with a much more powerful (and potentially destructive) adversary. Hence, the theme of local, grassroots action that comes across strongly in this book. Mennonite engagement seems to be characterized as local involvement often supporting and at the service of the dominated party in an intrastate conflict, although it is hoped that it bears in mind Liechty's stricture that "those who practice violence must not be demonized and ignored. . . . how will there be peace if no one talks to the violent?" (ch. 5). Again, these sentiments echo both the Quaker belief that there is an element of God in everyone, including the Slobodevics, Tudjmans, and Radics of this world; and one of the fundamental principles of track two approaches: It is necessary to involve all the parties in a lasting resolution, including the dominant, the powerful, and the initiators of violence. Other parallels reveal themselves in the next section, which examines some of the themes and principles of track two approaches to peacemaking.

## Track Two: Search for a Resolution

In recent years, a large number of track two practitioners have written about their experience of conflict resolution, and works by Kelman (1990), Burton (1969), Fisher (1997), and Mitchell and Banks (1996) have all attempted to summarize and clarify almost thirty years of experience with the approach. In spite of such writings (more often quoted than read, apparently), a widespread—and somewhat negative—image of the approach has become prevalent. This image—caricature, almost—involves intermediaries with only a short-term, self-interested commitment to a conflict situation and those embroiled in it; the flaunting of an irrelevant expertise accompanied by a lack of sensitivity to local norms, customs, and cultures; a spurious neutrality or objectivity that masks a set of values often foreign to the local conflict situation; and an elitism that consists partly of a concentration on the leadership levels of parties in conflict and partly in a distancing of the intermediary from those directly involved in the conflict and a separation of the third party as observer from the observed adversaries, an image that sits ill with current postmodern ideologies. The extreme picture is that of an intruding outsider, peddling peacemaking nostrums brewed far away with suspect ingredients. As Sally Engle Merry notes, it focuses on an image of the outside "hero making things different" (ch. 13) or, in Richard Rubenstein's characterization, on a modern missionary with a light in her eye and a copy of an (expensive) training workbook in her hand (1992).

Regrettably, as with all caricatures, there has come to be some truth in this image. Ron Kraybill has given warning of the dangers of what he correctly calls the "competitive professional" (ch. 2), while Merry talks about "the ethics . . . of modern competitive professionalism, which seeks to develop and sell a service" (ch. 13). It is clearly the case that much so-called conflict resolution work has become commercialized, and the result has been an increased effort to exploit what is becoming known as the "North American Export Model" (NAEM) of commercial peacemaking.

Moreover, it is true that this commercial model continues to bear some relation to the original—or what might be termed the classical—model of analytical, track two conflict resolution, but the connection is increasingly remote. Some idea of the contrast can be gained by considering the process used by Norwegian academics and diplomats in bringing together representatives of the PLO and Israeli academics and officials in Oslo during 1993. In this case, an almost purist conflict resolution model was used, involving interested but impartial third parties, a long-term commitment to the conflict resolution process, nondirective procedures in the hands of the parties themselves, and a sensitivity to the needs of the actual participants and their parent institutions during the process of helping in the development of a mutually acceptable agreement.

Originally, I would argue, track two approaches were established on a number of principles that make them at once different from NAEM and (in some respects) similar to approaches used in Mennonite peacemaking, which were developing during the same time period. It is, of course, true that the whole original approach was elite rather than grassroots oriented. The original track two approach used the idea of a small, interactive group, consisting of representatives from the parties in conflict, facilitated by a panel of intermediaries, who would supply process skills derived from their knowledge of group dynamics and theoretical ideas derived from a study of the general features of protracted and deep-rooted conflicts. As the workshop group needed to be kept small in order to maximize the informality of the exchange and to enhance group creativity, the question of who should be invited to represent the views of each party was initially answered by seeking those with maximum flexibility to explore tentative options accompanied by a high degree of access to and credibility with key leaders. In this way, the impact of any new thinking could be maximized among parties with hierarchical decision-making structures. (Of course, the issue of representation became more problematic if a reasonably clear hierarchy did not exist, or if it had simply collapsed.)

Original track two approaches were, therefore, inevitably elite oriented, with the precise nature of the elite—and hence the participants—depending on the level of the conflict (national, regional, or local). It was only a short time, however, before track two workshops were being used by practitioners at non-elite levels, and workshop series were being conducted with journalists, opinion leaders, teachers, and others (Kelman, 1982; Fisher and Keashley, 1988). As early as 1977, Folz wrote about the need for a distinction between elite-level problem-solving workshops and middle-rank process-promoting workshops (Folz, 1977).

It is equally true that the classical track two model did emphasize ideas and theories that, during an analysis of the conflict in question, would be introduced into the discussion by the panel of intermediaries—the outsiders— although always with due caution and sensitivity. The fundamental idea underlying this early version of track two was to supply participants directly (and their principals indirectly) with a range of useful ideas, concepts, processes, and possibilities to be examined with, rather than in isolation from, members of the suspect and mistrusted adversary. The conception fell somewhere between Merry's principle of "not taking charge" in order to avoid "telling social subordinates how to do things" (ch. 13) and Chupp's of "holding back" so as not to impose an outsider's ideas and agenda (ch. 7), the principle being that others' ideas and experiences might even, on occasion, prove useful.

Hence, one of the major principles underlying the holding of intensive workshop discussions with participants involved in intractable and violent conflict was that of *inquiry* rather than *instruction*. As one of the pioneers of the approach once remarked, there was no better way of testing out ideas and theories about conflict structures, dynamics, and (possible) solutions than by presenting these to people intensely and directly involved in a conflict and seeing whether the ideas made sense or were of any use to them. Experience soon showed that ideas that were not relevant would rapidly be discarded by embattled elites or advisers, while those deemed even remotely useful would be subjected to an informed scrutiny amounting to high suspicion by workshop participants, who would have to return with them to even more skeptical leaders. My own experience of working with track two at this level is that claims to expertise by intermediaries are given remarkably short shrift by participants, who know about their conflict because they have lived through it.

Another principle underlying early conflict resolution approaches again echoed one of the characteristics of Mennonite practice, namely, the commitment to long-term involvement. Contrary to the current image of the third party as parachutist or visiting (expert) fireman, the original proponents of conflict resolution approaches envisaged a problem-solving initiative as being a long-term commitment, involving initial, exploratory visits to establish contacts and credibility and to inform the third party about the nuances of the situation; a series of facilitated meetings or workshops, lasting as long as they were of use to the parties; careful follow-up subsequent to each meeting, both to continue the process and to evaluate the effects (if any) of such meetings; and a willingness to hand on the process to the parties themselves or to other, local institutions when circumstances seemed appropriate. None of this was short term. The series of workshops, visits, and publications that focused on the Falklands/Malvinas conflict following the 1982 war and that were arranged by Edward Azar and John Burton at the University of Maryland lasted for more than eight years. Herbert Kelman's series of workshops and contacts between Israelis and Palestinians took place for well over a decade. Early on, the principle became established of planning for a series of meetings (unless participants indicated they wished the process to conclude) rather than a one-time discussion.

Moreover, part of the total process usually involved establishing a long-term, working relationship with local institutions involved in the conflict or in the practice of conflict resolution. On occasion, this principle involved contacts with local universities or a local peace research center, especially when the track two initiative was itself based at a university. The partnership among the Gernika Peace Research Center, the Institute for Conflict Analysis and Resolution at George Mason University, and Eastern Mennonite University that was formed to work on the Basque/Spanish conflict is only one example of this principle in operation. On other occasions, the relationship involved helping to create new institutions with which to partner, so that the track two process could continue over the requisite time period. An example of this principle in operation is the establishment of the South Atlantic Council in London, which cooperated with the Consejo Argentino de Relaciones Internacionales in Buenos Aires and the Center for International Development and Conflict Management at the University of Maryland to continue contacts and thinking about the Falklands/Malvinas problem (Little and Mitchell, 1989; Mitchell, forthcoming).

Another parallel that can be drawn between the classical model of track two conflict resolution and the developing Mennonite practice is that, increasingly, track two practitioners became convinced of the need to be sensitive to local norms and customs in the actual design of the workshop process itself. This particular aspect of the development of track two practice seems to have gone through three stages, although treating practitioners' experiences as though they fit neatly into a three-stage model is inevitably an oversimplification. Initially, when workshop approaches were being tentatively developed from ideas about group dynamics, integrative bargaining sessions in industrial conflicts, T-group theory, and social work principles, the processes used in facilitated discussions or workshops were tentative and highly flexible. Later, as experience accumulated, practitioners felt that they understood the dynamics of workshop procedure and could guide the process into its most productive format. (From this period dates the slogan that the participants own the content and the outcome of the workshop, but the practitioners own the process.) More recently, track two practitioners have again become more tentative about procedures and take into account local norms and practices when designing a discussion. In the classical analytical model, the agenda was always broad and flexible; now, as a first step in any workshop, panelists tend to devise an agenda and an agreeable set of procedures with the participants.

## Distinctions and Complementarities

In summary, then, the classical model of a track two process focused on facilitated discussion or joint problem solving within a series of workshops and involved a philosophy based upon principles that seem to have much in common with the themes underlying Mennonite engagement. In summary the process is:

- *Voluntary.* Continued participation is entirely in the hands of the conflicting parties, who can abandon the process (and frequently have) when it no longer seems useful or productive.
- *Nondirective.* The procedure and the content of the discussions are ultimately in the hands of the parties through their representatives.
- *Self-determined.* The search for acceptable solutions remains in the hands of the parties themselves.
- *Inclusive.* It attempts to involve all the relevant parties to the dispute and excludes none on any grounds, including the lack of formally recognized status or the use of violence or behavior that would otherwise be deemed criminal.
- *Analytical.* The process involves joint inquiry and an interactive search for solutions and procedures that will lead toward a self-sustaining and acceptable peace. (Mitchell, 1981a)

On the other hand, there are some clear differences between the track two model and the Mennonite engagement model. The first and most obvious of these involves the levels at which the two models operate, with track two processes being concentrated on the upper decision-making levels of communities and governments, which are assumed to possess intact, hierarchical decision-making structures. This model is therefore founded upon the conception that the initial steps in peacemaking best involve a top-down procedure, which, in turn, assumes that those involved in track two initiatives are close to, or even part of, an intact decision-making hierarchy that still possesses some acknowledged authority over rank-and-file followers and that can expect some conformity with its decisions regarding peace agreements.

In contrast, Mennonite engagement, following the church's traditional distrust of elites and authority, works mainly at grassroots levels on the assumption that, for any peace agreement to have a chance of surviving, becoming accepted, and altering long-term, adversarial relationships, full and long-term involvement in the peace process by followers as well as leaders is essential. As Merry summarizes the idea, "peacebuilding does not occur only at the top but also comes from micro readjustments of power in the small spaces of everyday social life" (ch. 13).

As Lederach has suggested, where the two approaches overlap is at a third, intermediate level of societies, involving notables, opinion leaders, and local elites. At this level, both classical track two and Mennonite practices converge in the idea that peacebuilding will depend crucially on the understanding, acceptance, and support of this stratum of any conflict-torn society (Lederach, 1997). However, the convergence only goes as far as agreement about the key role played by people at this middle level. The two models adopt different practices regarding how such people are to be involved in a peacemaking or peacebuilding process, although both clearly involve elements of what Quaker Adam Curle refers to as befriending (Curle, 1986).

A final, interesting distinction (which needs much closer investigation than I have space for in this short chapter), involves the clear stand of Mennonite peacemakers on the issue of justice and peace compared with the apparent ethical confusion of the academic field of conflict research and analytical practice on the relationship between those two concepts. While the Mennonite view of there being a necessary connection between the existence of a just social order and the achievement of true peace is clear and is given expression in several chapters of this work (see, for example, Chupp and Esquivia), the track two practitioners' view is far more ambiguous. Much early conflict research insisted that track two peacemaking approaches had to be noncondemnatory, impartial, and supportive of all the parties in conflict, on the grounds that selecting right and wrong sides usually grossly oversimplified a complex political and ethical situation, as well as played into the perceptions of adversaries, who inevitably saw their situation as involving moral and immoral parties. (Who, for example, was the wronged party in the Israeli/Palestinian dispute or in the Cyprus conflict?) Rapidly surfacing doubts about this overly simple stance of neutrality toward adversaries and about the ethics of seeking to resolve conflicts between dominated and dominant parties have led to a debate about practice in the field that continues unresolved.

One result of this distinction appears clearly in both the writings and the practice of Mennonite peacebuilders and academic conflict resolvers. Mennonite commentators usually assume that they are describing and will be dealing with highly asymmetric conflicts, in which there exists a clear choice between the dominant and subordinated classes or categories in the conflict-torn society. Proponents of track two approaches, in contrast, tend to describe what they are doing as always being between (roughly) equal adversaries or, at least, adversaries who are sufficiently symmetric to be treated as equals.[3]

Practically speaking, this raises another distinction between Mennonite engagement and classical conflict resolution practice, as revealed in previous chapters. Clearly, on many occasions, Mennonites see themselves at least as starting peacemaking *with* one of the parties in conflict—usually the disadvantaged and dominated party—by helping to reduce the degree of asymmetry in existing relationships between top dogs and bottom dogs. Equally clearly, proponents of track two usually see themselves as starting to help resolve conflicts *between* adversaries, which places them in a radically different position of being with neither, which, hopefully, as the process proceeds, changes to being with both.

Whatever the distinctions and differences, I conclude by arguing that, properly used, both Mennonite engagement and analytical conflict resolution processes can play important roles in helping to bring sustainable, long-term peace to conflict-torn societies. It seems clear that the approaches are complementary rather than rival. Most conflict researchers of my acquaintance would agree that it is of vital importance to operate at all three major strata of parties in conflict—grassroots, intermediate, and elite—and that neglect of the first and second levels can result in the continuation of long-term suspicion and hostility, at best, and to the breakdown, rejection, or nonimplementation of elite-negotiated agreements, at worst (for example, Ireland in 1922 and again in 1996, or Liberia in 1993–1996). Most Mennonite peacemakers of my acquaintance would agree that elite agreements, as in South Africa in 1994 or between Israel and the PLO in 1993, can establish a helpful initial framework for long-term peacebuilding efforts, which remains crucial to the achievement of a real and lasting peace.

Much remains to be done, however, both analytically and practically. One ongoing task for both groups of searchers for peace is to discover appropriate processes for matching and interconnecting peace efforts at all three levels. Another is to find successful ways of building peace upward in societies where hierarchy no longer exists, where state structures and governments have collapsed, and where local peacemaking, while being a triumph where successfully established, has to be translated into broader, national peacebuilding. Neither Mennonite peacemakers nor scholarly conflict resolvers are likely to find themselves without challenges as both groups leave the twentieth century.

## Fifteen

## The Religious Component of Mennonite Peacemaking and Its Global Implications

MARC GOPIN

IN ORDER TO UNDERSTAND THE RELIGIOUS foundations and unique character of Mennonite peacemaking, it is necessary to explore briefly the origins of the community and how this affects the nature of their peace work. But first, a word is in order about the definition of terms. *Conflict resolution* has the implication for some of a type of mediation or intervention, usually in the form of a dialogue workshop or some alternative arrangement to the courts, all within a fairly limited span of time. I mean conflict resolution in its broadest sense: the varied approaches to understanding and intervening in intractable conflicts. I also use it to refer to the entire field of conflict analysis and practice as a professional endeavor. In a Mennonite context, however, it is important to add the terms *conflict transformation, peacemaking,* and *peace-building,* which all mean something more far reaching. These are difficult to define briefly, and in a certain way, their definition is the subject of this entire volume. For purposes of this chapter, I use these terms to describe a Mennonite commitment to the creation of deep relationships over time that, with proper care, lead both oneself and those with whom one is engaged in the direction of a profound transformation of conflictual and unjust human relationships. I use these three terms interchangeably, although certain Mennonite theorists do not.

When I refer to *Old Order Mennonites* in this essay, I mean, roughly, those groups that have emphasized in the modern period a continuation of the separatist tradition. By *modern Mennonites,* I mean primarily those Mennonites who demonstrate a strong affinity for engagement with the world, either through mission work or peace and justice work.

### Key Concepts

I will now outline some key concepts that are critical to a deeper understanding of Mennonite peacemaking on a psycho-cultural level.

## Separatism and the Evolution of Peacemaking

The foundations of the Anabaptist tradition, to which the Mennonite communities belong, are most clearly seen in the Schleitheim Statement of Brotherly Union of 1527 (Driedger and Kraybill, 1994, pp. 22, 54). There are two key components of that statement that explain a great deal about the character of the Mennonite community and its peace work. Ironically, in terms of peace and conflict resolution, perhaps the most important feature of the statement is the commitment to separatism. The second characteristic is the commitment to meekness, in emulation of the "lamb of God," namely, Jesus.

The separatist imperative is quite familiar to students of religion. The world, in this formulation, is divided into the realm of light and the realm of darkness, those who are "outside the perfection of Christ" and those who are part of the fellowship (Yoder, 1973, pp. 39–40, as quoted in Driedger and Kraybill, 1994, p. 22). Menno Simons, after whom Mennonites are named, said in one sermon that they are the "Lord's people, separated from the world, and hated unto death" (1956, p. 1045, as quoted in Driedger and Kraybill, 1994, p. 54). There are those who are "called out of this world unto God," and they must not mix with the abominations of the world. This dualist worldview has deep roots in the origins of Christianity, rabbinic Judaism, and the respective mysticisms of the two faiths (see Pagels, 1981; on Judaism, see Scholem, 1977, pp. 40–79). It is the resonance with these old theological roots that makes separatist religious communities so intriguing. They are also an important part of the history of European utopian communities (Manuel, 1979).

Many modern Mennonites who do peace work globally, the main subject of this study, would be, as far as I have observed, rather uncomfortable with this separatist strain in its premodern sense or as it may be practiced even today by the Amish, Old Order Mennonites, or perhaps even conservative conference members of their church. The degree of separation from the world still appears to be a key defining difference among the many Mennonite communities. In fact, the Amish and the Old Order Mennonites rejected until recently active proselytizing, something central to other forms of Christianity. They will aid the poor or someone in distress, no matter who they may be, after the model of Jesus. But they have tended not to proselytize. This is in contrast with the Mennonites of this century, many of whom have engaged in proselytizing. This is a complicating factor in evaluating the issue of conflict prevention and conflict resolution, as we shall see later.

## Persecution and Pacifism

The Old Order Mennonite and Amish rejection of proselytizing is based not only on the separatist strain in Mennonite spirituality but also on a combination of the deeply rooted pacifist strain of Mennonite Christianity together with the historical Mennonite experience of persecution. One of the most central Mennonite teachings is that Jesus as a pacifist is deeply concerned to never interact with others in an aggressive fashion, even with his enemies.

This has its roots in Romans 12:14–21, "Bless them that persecute you . . . recompense no man evil for evil . . . avenge not yourselves . . . if thine enemy is hungry, feed him . . . be not overcome of evil, but overcome evil with good."[1] This is the essence of Christian pacifism with roots going back as far as the Hebrew Bible.[2] Proselytizing and encouraging others to convert has a checkered history in the annals of religious traditions, especially the biblical ones. Sometimes, it has been benign; at other times, it has been deadly. But all efforts to convert others involve a degree of assertiveness, which has easily spilled over into aggression whenever the people being proselytized actually want to adhere to their own faith, which is quite often.

There is also a deep strain in Old Order Mennonite religion of identification with the persecuted, the defenseless (*wehrlos*) (Driedger and Kraybill, 1994, p. 23). This, too, goes back to the biblical texts that Mennonites have studied so carefully over the centuries: "What occurs has happened before, and what will occur has already occurred, and God seeks those who are pursued" (Eccles. 3:15).[3]

Mennonites remember their persecution well, and it is here that the several aforementioned strains come together to illustrate my thesis. It must be kept in mind that the original impulse of Mennonite separatism was in the context of a hostile, even murderous *Christian* environment, which persecuted Anabaptists for their commitment to several distinctive practices that they believed to be at the heart of Christianity, including adult baptism, an emphasis on direct study of the New Testament by laypeople, an unswerving commitment to the life of Jesus as a model, separation of church and government, and pacifism.

The *Martyrs Mirror*, a key text that documents the bloody torture and execution of thousands of Mennonites at the hands of fellow Christians, was one of the most important volumes on the Mennonite bookshelf for centuries. Their murders were no doubt preceded by attempts by other Christians to cajole them back to the "true faith" and away from their heresy. In other words, they were missionized by fellow Christians in order to save their souls and bring them back to Christ. The result, finally, was massive persecution upon refusal to come back.

This kind of persecution is, tragically, an easy leap for an evangelical belief system that combines with a dualist view of the world, that sees the world in terms of those who are in the fellowship of God and those who are not. Mennonite belief is based on this dualist view and could easily have turned aggressive, for it is easy to go from mildly aggressive efforts to missionize those who are not part of the saved realm to the demonization of the outgroup that refuses to repent or convert. The outgroup becomes the other half of the dualistic world, and its elimination becomes a necessity in order for good to triumph over evil. This is precisely why Mennonites were determined to prevent the dualist view from devolving into an aggressive or violent posture vis-à-vis the world of unbelievers.

I would argue that the separatism of original Mennonitism, the commitment to separation of church and state (which eliminates coercive power from the religious domain), and the reluctance to proselytize by at least a significant group of Mennonites all stem from the deep roots of their emulation of Jesus' pacifism and the painful memories of their own experience of religious violence.[4] In other words, in the wake of their own persecution, they maintained strictly the dualist worldview, the division of the people of God from the world's abominations. But they also ensured that this very dualism would not and could not result in an aggressive posture vis-à-vis others, not even through proselytizing. They understood Christian history and understood that the idea of a separate realm of those who follow Jesus' model was vital for their faith, but they were determined to eliminate its violent potential. This they did through pacifism and their reluctance to proselytize. Old Order Mennonite religion, in my opinion, questions whether active efforts to convert can truly coexist with pacifism in its deepest sense. To this day, it seems a commonplace assumption, even among modern Mennonite peacemakers, that Constantine's conversion to Christianity and the unification of the Roman Empire with Christianity was a tragedy in terms of Christianity's religious integrity, precisely because the aggressive and imperial nature of Rome infected religious institutional life.

## The Modern Mennonite Dilemma and Conflict Transformation

Many Mennonite institutions in the modern period, by contrast, seem deeply committed to actively seeking converts to Christianity and the Mennonite faith. American evangelism has had a deep impact on the Mennonite community. Many Mennonite activists, especially those who work internationally, have either done missionary work themselves or are the children of missionaries. It must be emphasized, however, that *mission* is a difficult topic to define in the Christian world, especially today, because there is such a varied interpretation of what it means. Furthermore, there are no data available on how many of the peace activists have been involved in mission work nor on what kind of mission work they may have done.

In the Mennonite circles that I have studied, it appears that a number of people who engage in peace work are uncomfortable at the very least with the most aggressive interpretation of mission, namely, the active process of converting as many people to Mennonitism or Christianity as possible. Some are uncomfortable with proselytizing altogether, while others are committed to mission in the sense of a religious calling and are looking to define "peace work as mission."[5] This would make sense as a development of the Mennonite focus on the life of Jesus. They would see Jesus' principal endeavors as involving direct service, aid to and healing of those in need, and the teaching of nonresistance,[6] not the construction of an empire of followers. The latter they might see as a by-product of his work but not as its focus. This does not necessarily mean that they would be displeased by more Christians in the world. It is unclear, and that appears to be a sensitive issue.

Mission means something quite significant to Old Order Mennonites. It means standing for a certain faith and a certain way of behaving in the world, as Jesus did. It seems to me that the modern Mennonite peacemakers, while far more actively engaged in the world than Old Order Mennonites, seem to share with them a more nuanced understanding of mission than the way this is aggressively expressed by some other Christians.

In the course of our discussions, it became clear that many of this volume's Mennonite authors who are peace activists seem reluctant to proselytize because of the arrogance associated with that posture. I was struck by how rarely they advocated, expressed pride in, or pressured me in any way to see the beauty of Christianity or Mennonite belief. They rarely used words to describe what they loved about their faith, at least not in public. They seemed to see the term *Christian* as referring to someone who lives like Jesus did, not someone who declares himself regularly to be a believer. Christian is therefore a deeply moral and spiritual term, and it borders on arrogance to refer to oneself, for example, as a fully successful Christian in the sense of being "born again." Rather, being called born again is an honor bestowed by others if one earns that title by the way one lives in relationship to others. They tell the story of a man who is asked by someone, "Are you born again?" to which he replies, "Here is a list of people—my wife, my banker, my grocer, all my associates. Ask them if I am born again."

It seems to me, based on my own analysis, that modern Mennonites who engage in peacemaking and conflict resolution and who are deeply committed to tolerance and pluralism are caught in a bind that is rarely articulated—and not directly addressed in the case studies, although I would argue that it is right beneath the surface. Mission, as they understand it, has propelled them into the world. They see conflict resolution, which by definition is a rather invasive process of entering into someone else's culture and problems, as a necessary means to follow Jesus' role model as peacemaker and as justice seeker for those who are injured. They also need to fulfill what they see as an important Christian precept or tenet of faith, namely, mission and witness. For their ancestors and present-day cousins, witnessing could be seen as a religious task done by example of one's personal and communal life, not by engaging the realm of sin.[7]

Clearly, the spirituality of the Mennonites represented in this volume is moving away from this separatist take on mission and witness. On the other hand, every aspect of Mennonite life and formation of character reinforces values, personality traits, and modes of engagement that express humility, a studied effort to emulate Jesus, and a level of benign engagement with others that emphasizes listening, care, and gentle patterns of interaction. In other words, one can trace the roots of their peacemaking methods, especially the elicitive method, to the commitment to adhere to Mennonite values, even as these peacemakers now enter, cautiously, the unredeemed world, which so many of their ancestors had rejected. Hart exemplifies this method in his efforts to elicit the elders' old methods of peacemaking.[8]

Furthermore, Lederach's concept of conflict transformation, with its emphasis on deep resolution of conflict and its involvement of social justice as a component of peacemaking, emerges out of an attempt to address the evil of the worldly realm that Menno Simons rejected. It is a determination to bring into the harsh realities of a violent world the elements of ideal community, which for Mennonites are found in the example of Jesus, namely, a community dedicated to humility, compassion for and service to those who suffer, justice for the persecuted, and a standing with the defenseless.

Conflict resolution, a deeply activist and engaged method of affecting human relations, is being used by modern Mennonites but is also transformed by them. It has transformed them into actively engaged Christians, but they, in turn, have transformed conflict resolution and transformed the Christian concept of mission. The hermeneutic circle of receptivity and two-way transformation here is clear (see Gadamer, 1994, pp. 265ff). For the Mennonites represented in this volume, conflict resolution as a method of engagement in the world has given them a vehicle for both maintaining the deepest pacifist values of their community and combining it with a reworked concept of mission.

The idea of mission pushes them into the field and so does a commitment to actively engage issues of justice and injustice in such a way that they can never again be accused of quietism and selfishness in the face of evil, as they were accused by some in World War II. On the other hand, the commitment to listening, patience, eliciting from others their needs and strategies for change, the self-doubt and self-criticism that permeate their work all reflect the character of deeply committed pacifists who know how dangerous it is to presume to change someone else's life, no matter how much that person is crying out for help. They seem to know intuitively, based on their religious pacifist training, how slippery a slope this engagement is and how dangerous is the power that one feels in changing other lives, especially when those others are in a vulnerable position economically and emotionally. They express the intuition that aggression of the subtlest forms is always a possibility for the social change activist who enters into wartorn, impoverished situations. Rarely have I seen such close attention and self-scrutiny among international development activists and peacemakers to the dilemma of intervention and to the subtleties of aggression by intervenors who may have the best of intentions. Hart, in particular, seems aware of the prejudices that he brought to his encounter with other cultures.

Perhaps it is the very ambiguity of modern Mennonite entry into mission, their memory of brutalizing efforts to invade their lives by others centuries before, and the ever-present model of Old Order Mennonites preserving a strict notion of nonaggression that give the modern Mennonites the creative drive to forge a radically new way of engaging the troubled part of the world, the world of sin and violence.[9] They seek a way of intervention that is radically nonviolent. In such a world, they know that always "sin coucheth at the door"[10] and that a group can easily become part of the very illness of violence that it seeks to heal. Mennonite sensibility reflects this constant attention to the thin line between good and evil intervention in the world.

There is also a subtle awareness, out of respect for their roots perhaps, that quietism has an undeserved negative reputation, that quietism, when taken to extremes, perhaps is passivity and even selfishness or indifference to evil. But quietism in small doses is a key to a nonaggressive approach to the world, and one can learn as much from not doing, not speaking, and not invading the world as one can by intervention and failure. This nonaggressive religious strain is present in many religious cultures that value not doing or the refraining from doing in order to achieve high ethical ends, as much as or even more than positive ritual or proactive interaction with the world. This presents a sharply contrasting model to Western patterns of intervention in the world's problems.

This awareness has generated a creative tension that, in turn, has created an unusual spiritual philosophy of intervention, which is deliberately benign in its execution and mode of interaction with others. It propels the adherents into conflict resolution and social transformation and then restrains them from the natural human urge—and the urge of institutions, both religious and secular—to refashion the world, violently if necessary, in one's own image. This tension requires constant self-scrutiny and a spiritual community that restrains itself and its members from slipping into aggression.

### The Stranger, Peacemaking, and the Existential Awareness of Otherness

The other element in this creative tension turns once again to the separatist roots of the community. The conflict resolvers that we studied hardly consider themselves separatists today. But some benefit has come to them from their separatist roots. A separatist community is deeply aware of the experience of Otherness and of being outsiders. Both Liechty and Chupp exemplify this extraordinary awareness of being an outsider.[11] The history of persecution as outsiders leads, I believe, to a deep respect for Otherness, for the stranger. This also has deep biblical roots in love of the stranger (*ger*) as one of the highest forms of love described by the Hebrew Bible (Deut. 10:19), and this is also one of the chief preoccupations of Jesus' life as recounted in the New Testament.

The stranger in biblical tradition is never to be oppressed, "for you know the feelings of the stranger, having been strangers in the land of Egypt" (Exod. 23:9). This awareness of Otherness is also an awareness of the multiplicity of identities around us. Ironically, it is typical of conflict-generating thinking to formulate one's identity in opposition to another's identity, with the formation of self as a part of an ingroup in opposition to the outgroup (see Volkan, 1988; and Gopin, 1997, p. 22). The natural response to counteract this is to assume that the best form of identity is universal identity, namely, a self-conscious identification with all humankind or some consciousness that is akin to this.

The irony, as Derrida, among others, has alerted us, is that there is no easy escape from the process of creating identity in opposition to the Other, and what appears to be universal or inclusive of the universal is not that at all and may, in fact, consciously or unconsciously, be a vehicle of oppression of the identity of the Other.[12] This is one reason why Emanual Levinas's ethics are predicated not on universal codes but on the phenomenology of the face-to-face encounter between one human being and the Other. It is the encounter with the image of the Other, the awareness of Otherness, that generates the ethical response of care, compassion, or pity (see, for example, Levinas, 1985, 1987).

It is deeply important in this regard that Gandhi did not argue that "we are all human beings, and, therefore, let us care for one another." He said, in so many words, as well as through his embrace of religious and cultural ideas from around the world, that his identity was multiple in nature, that he was a Hindu but also a Muslim and also a Christian.[13] I have argued elsewhere that this awareness of multiple identities is a key characteristic of successful peacemakers, particularly in the sphere of interreligious conflict. It is clearly interwoven in its psychological foundation with the characteristics of compassion and humility in that it involves not the suppression of personal identity but the enlarging of that identity in some way that one sees Others and then internalizes their reality.

I would argue that it is vitally important, perhaps central, that a conflict resolver, in the largest sense as peacemaker, needs to be someone who understands Otherness in a deep, existential way. That Otherness need not be based on her ethnicity or religion, but it must be a self-conscious awareness of that which makes all human beings, beginning with oneself, Other in some way to other beings. Without that understanding, it will be difficult to comprehend the alienation caused by and fear of Otherness that drives so much interhuman conflict.

Mennonite Otherness is key not only to their own distinctive contribution to peacemaking but also as an example to the field of conflict resolution as a whole in terms of what is necessary in the existential awareness of the third party to understand parties to a conflict and to be a vehicle of reconciliation among them.

The text from Exodus cited above, "for you know the feelings of the stranger, having been strangers in the land of Egypt," reads like a description of the evolution of Mennonites from a banished outgroup, like the Israelites in Egypt, to a group that works on caring for the downtrodden in distant cultures in remembrance of their old experience. This is crucial to their peacemaking method, namely, a deep and abiding respect for identity affirmation, or what I have termed Otherness, of each party to a conflict, as well as of their own.

The peacemakers among the Mennonites travel the globe in search of the defenseless, keenly aware of their own history as defenseless strangers. In a certain sense, each time they work toward securing the legitimacy of Otherness and the identity of a threatened group, they reaffirm the spiritual depth of their own experience. It involves caring for the Other, respecting his Otherness, and making a commitment not to invade his culture.

This is also, once again, an emulation of Jesus in the sense that it means being in the world of another but not of that world. It means that each time one enters into another culture, one enters as a healer but not as an invading army. One is in the world of the other culture but self-consciously not of it. One acknowledges and respects boundaries between peoples as a religious experience not as a barrier to that experience. At the same time, there is a feeling of deep identity with the suffering group.

This method of awareness of Otherness is crucial for the third party in conflict resolution and, ultimately as well, for each of the conflicting parties, for they often cannot accept the identity of Others because of their own doubts about identity, as Hart observes. The third party often sets the tone and creates a model of intervention that either perpetuates the inability to recognize Otherness or that, alternatively, engenders it in the conflicting parties.

### Community and Peacemaking

How Mennonites manage to respect Otherness is intimately related to how they create and sustain their own community while engaging in peacemaking. This brings us to the topic of spiritual community. It must be remembered just how much the maintenance of community, Mennonite community, is key to the stories in our volume. There are several ways in which the communal impulse is maintained, in altered form to be sure, across thousands of miles and many cultures. This is a vital component of who they are and also something the field of conflict resolution in general may be able to learn from them (see Kraybill, 1996, ch. 7).

Several of the case studies suggest the central importance of the creation and maintenance of community. Liechty, in particular, shares with us how much time he spent simply maintaining Mennonite community. Bergey, among the most isolated in her assignment, shares with us how she compensated for the lack of community by her intimate association with an international group of women, mostly Mennonites, who prayed for and helped one another through their challenges. In one of our authors' meetings, we learned of prayer calendars, through which Mennonites facing difficult situations all over the world are prayed for by their fellow Mennonites, many of whom they have never met. This has roots in communal missionary customs, as does the widespread practice of a communal "commissioning" by the home congregation of a person, or family, who is embarking on a service or mission assignment.

These methods, adopted from early support of international missionaries, have some crucial lessons for conflict resolution theory and practice. Peace and justice advocacy, conflict prevention, intervention, mediation, resolution, and post-trauma healing involve such profound challenges to the inner emotional life of the peacemaker that it is no wonder that many people burn out from this work. Isolated, often attempting to cope with witnessing the worst human degradation, the intervenor cannot live with this work alone for long.

The Mennonite creation of community gives peacemakers the tools to endure great psychological stress. Communal support allows them to engage in peacemaking for extended terms, which they believe in spiritually and which also may be far more effective than short-term engagements. Since many conflicts are protracted and deeply rooted, it is considered arrogant to believe that intervention can be quick and invasive. Their belief is that only through building relationships and local capacities over years can true transformation take place. This long-term building of a relationship of trust also seems to be a healthier response to the pain of local people than coming in for ten days and leaving with a combination of relief and guilt. Such relationship building also gives non-Mennonite local people the psychological fortitude to persist in this difficult work. Furthermore, listening and understanding the peoples of other cultures is central to the Mennonite religious value system, and thus the peacemakers' work is felt to be the fulfillment of the highest spiritual calling.

This emerges out of their commitment to humility, but it has also evolved into a kind of cultural ethos, which Lederach formalizes, in my opinion, in the elicitive approach. This way of interacting takes time. Time means isolation of the individual peacemaker, unless he has community. It may be that one of the reasons for the Western tendency to quickly intervene and then leave conflict situations transcends budgetary constraints on international agencies or political constraints placed by the voting public. There may be an implicit awareness of the problematic isolation of intervenors. That is surely one reason why Mennonite international peace activists have been so intertwined with the Mennonite missions around the world. It is often the missions upon whose long-term presence, network of relationships, formation of trust, and secure sense of home the peacemakers initially build. In time, the peacebuilders establish those attributes for themselves.

### Moral Character and Peacemaking

Some key moral characteristics give Mennonite peacemaking such a distinctive character. It cannot be emphasized how important to our subject is the imperative to be "meek and lowly of heart" in emulation of Jesus (Driedger and Kraybill, 1994, p. 22). In almost all of the case studies, there are statements professing ignorance, a sense of inadequacy, self-deprecation, and a deep sense of trepidation in invading the space of other peoples and cultures. These Mennonite peacemakers often see this exhibition of underconfidence as a flaw. I see it as a strength. It leads to the extraordinary level of cross-cultural sensitivity that emanates from the authors, both in writing and in person. It also leads to a deep commitment to listening and receptivity, which has a prominent and early place in MCC methods of listening and learning as a part of peacemaking, which, in turn, is an important foundation of Lederach's theoretical development of the elicitive method.

The characteristics of listening, relationship building, and cross-cultural sensitivity have been the key missing ingredients of Western engagement in peace and justice work, as well as in poverty relief.[14] A high level of brutal, if unintentional, deafness and arrogance is quite common in international affairs, and the Mennonite method of intervention, a way of humble listening, may be not only a more moral path of intervention. It also seems to be a more rational and less wasteful path than that which is followed by many players on the international scene today.

This method of engagement of radical humility, more than an ethical act or a strategy of intervention for Mennonites, appears to be a part of their being, a cultural characteristic that is at the heart of their religious experience of divine closeness and emulation. Every feeling of pain before the suffering of others is a living embrace of the life and person of Jesus. The community prayers, songs, and sermons often revolve around this theme.

How does one replicate such humility among other religious peacemakers if there is not a high premium placed on a humble character? How does one replicate it in the secular community of international agencies where output and efficiency may be more important as standards of evaluation than a particular trait of character? Furthermore, how does one operationalize humility when there is no deep metaphysical imperative for such behavior in the secular community?

I think humility can be and should be inserted into general conflict resolution training in some fashion. Faith in God is not the only deep motivator of ethical character, and I believe that there could be ways to justify this training. For example, human needs theory, a school of conflict resolution theory, is built upon a humanist conception of a wide variety of basic human needs that must be fulfilled in order to prevent violence. Some of those needs are "higher" needs, such as the need for freedom or meaning. There is quite a bit of disagreement on what needs are universal to all people, or whether it is fair to even posit universal needs rather than operating with a basic assumption that there are needs that vary from group to group.[15]

One topic that seems to me to be neglected by this school of thought is the needs of the third-party intervenor. In general, there has been a tendency to assume this intervenor to be a value-free, godlike figure capable of neutrality and infinite professionalism. This is somewhat of a myth or, at best, an extremely difficult goal to achieve. It seems clear to me that the conflict resolver's needs and, correspondingly, her character are crucial. The Mennonite model seems quite pertinent here. In a number of the case studies, it was clear that the experience of peacemaking was spoken of as one of learning and transformation for the intervenors; this required great humility from them to admit. Furthermore, in the context of describing difficult experiences, numerous authors, including Hart, Kern, Bergey, and Chupp, refer to how crucial to their needs was the prayer and sharing of community. This community, in turn, reinforced the moral values and character traits necessary to do their work. Humility was primary in that process of communal sharing.

I would suggest that a nongovernmental organization (NGO) or any agency could constitute or express itself as a community with certain key values and make characteristics such as humility a fulfillment of what it is to be part of that conflict-resolving community. Thus, as the individual—religious or not— trains himself in these character traits, he fulfills the need to be good at what he does, the need to be a good peacemaker, and the need to be a good member of the conflict-resolving community. The community of the NGO or other agency strengthens and encourages this self-definition.

Humility in international work could also be reinforced by an environmental ethic that calls on the human being to recognize her place within the totality of nature, along the lines of much Native American thinking. Work that combines environmental justice and conflict resolution could express itself in this fashion.

It seems clear for peace and development work in many parts of the world that this quality of humility is critical to serious work with poor people, people in conflict, or both. Thus, replication of this spiritual quality, even in some secular variant, would have a powerful impact on large-scale efforts at conflict resolution and development for the poor.

## Critical Issues

I want to raise two critical issues in Mennonite peacemaking that have broad implications for conflict resolution: the nature of the relationship to those in conflict and the struggle to balance conflict resolution as a moral imperative and justice as a moral imperative. Finally, we will look at the problem of replicability.

### Instrumentalism versus Mennonite Peacemaking

The inherent moral value of building relationships is another key ethical component of Mennonite peacemaking. It is founded on what I would define as a noninstrumentalist approach to human relations in the conflict scenario. Mennonite spirituality guides the peacemaker to build relationships in the conflict situation but not only as an instrument that produces an outcome. The standard emphasis of process-oriented workshops or conflict resolution activities is that of a third party facilitating, mediating, and perhaps even making initial contacts and gestures, all with the purpose of getting the parties to the table and achieving resolution of the issues in conflict. This is encapsulated in the phraseology of evaluation, such as, "outcome-based" evaluation. While the idea of evaluating one's work and one's effectiveness would not be strange at all to the ears of Mennonites (they tend to engage automatically in self-criticism), the idea of delimiting relationship building to an instrumentalist focus on outcome would sound rather strange. Evaluation is not the problem here. It is the reduction of the human moment of relation to its instrumentality that is problematic for Mennonite peacemakers and, undoubtedly, many other peacemakers as well.

We see here an often overlooked but real clash of civilizations. Emanating out of certain religious traditions and ethical schools of thought is a rebellion against the treatment of a human being—or, in some traditions, even an animal—as an object that is instrumental in one's efforts to achieve some social, economic, or military goal. For Immanuel Kant, a person must always be considered an end in himself. Kant's principal ethical imperative, which he spent much of his life proving, is "Act so as to treat man, in your own person as well as in that of anyone else, always as an end, never merely as a means" (1977, p. 178). The moral sense theorists also posited, not in Kant's categorical, imperative fashion but in terms of a direct observation of nature, that the beneficent qualities of love or compassion are innate and that there are moral acts that we engage in that are not motivated solely by the instrumental furthering of self-interest but by compassionate or loving human qualities.[16]

Martin Buber deepens the Kantian move and makes this into an existential response to others of deep religious significance. I–It is instrumentalist, the relation of subject to object, whereas I–You is relational, the relation of subject to subject, and it expresses the greatest end of spiritual relation:

> The basic word I–You can only be spoken with one's whole being. The basic word I–It can never be spoken with one's whole being. . . . Whoever says You does not have something; he has nothing. But he stands in relation. (1970, pp. 54, 55)

This is the essence of human relations that Mennonite peacemaking at its best tries to foster. As opposed to Hobbes, Machiavelli, and the political realist school, it is a worldview that celebrates the opportunity to meet the Other in relation and believes that this is a possibility in human life that demonstrates by its very reality that war and violence are not the only options in human relationships.

The Mennonite religious response is different also from the utilitarian perspective, best represented by John Stuart Mill. The latter is so pervasive in modern bureaucratic culture that it is practically unconscious. It entails the constant attention to outcome and the instrumentalizing of one human moment for the purposes of the next human moment, all leading to some abstract social goal. It is a laudable method of governing society and appears to be especially necessary in the unprecedented human task of governing and fulfilling the basic needs of hundreds of millions of human beings who may inhabit one society. Perhaps moral and political utilitarianism is an inevitable and necessary by-product of overpopulation. But its level of abstraction and inattention to the subtleties of human relationships can also have a devastating impact on society, especially in situations of bitter conflict where extensive human interaction is vital to heal the hatreds and anger.

Conflict resolution methods have been dominated by consequentialist methods of process and outcome evaluation. This is understandable and vital in many instances. But Mennonite intervention offers a different vision. The moment of relation becomes a moment of religious fulfillment, of *imitatio dei*, in their case, emulating Jesus. The person in relation becomes an end in herself. The cultivation of relationship between human beings and the careful attention to the style of interaction and the character that one brings to that relationship are the essential elements of their peacemaking activity, because they are the primary moment of religious experience and discovery of the Other in the world. The outcome of the relationship is, one hopes, the creation of peace and the reduction of conflict. But that is not the sole purpose of every activity.

People the world over crave authentic relationship in a time of violent crisis, and they often do not receive this at the hands of professional but cold and instrumentalist intervention by outsiders.[17] Surely, many Western conflict resolvers intervening in other cultures have often entered into deep relationships with the parties to the conflict. But was it incidental or central? Could they report this in their evaluations as a major success to foundations and agencies, or was it irrelevant to project evaluation by their sponsoring agencies? This is where the Mennonite model might have something to teach in terms of what becomes the focus of our entry into situations of conflict and what we call success or failure in the field. The creation of human bonds across cultural lines, the opening up of relationships among groups through the agency of intermediaries, the solidarity expressed with those who suffer should be highly valued by agencies, whether or not a settlement of a particular conflict is achieved in the short term. These relationships should be considered a success in and of themselves. Evaluation would then involve the question of how well the group did at creating and living out those relationships, in addition to an assessment of any specific conflict resolution outcome.

This is not to say that Mennonites do not care about outcomes. On the contrary, their prayers, songs, and the evidence that we see in the case studies all testify to a deep yearning to create real change in the lives of those who are affected by war and poverty. There is little evidence here of certain religious schools of thought, which minister to the poor and downtrodden without any genuine efforts to improve their lives. Clearly, Mennonites are working at conflict resolution methods that, on the contrary, go to the root of conflict; they argue that real resolution involves social transformation.

But a solely instrumentalist, outcome-based, process-oriented approach to conflict resolution runs two risks. First, exclusively outcome-based approaches invite burn-out on the part of the third party or peace activist. Many conflicts are intractable, requiring years or decades of work. That poses a major question of how to sustain motivation and commitment for an individual or even an agency, especially one that evaluates its work solely based on outcome. There must be other motivations and rewards that accrue from the actual work itself and that therefore make the work self-sustaining, even when the measurable outcomes are not achieved. Most people in the field and most analysts who sustain this work over years develop this additional set of motivations. But since it is rarely articulated and validated by their agency, institution, or community, it seems to me to place an unnecessary burden on those who do this work.

Moreover, instrumentalist, goal-oriented approaches to conflict (or to other intractable problems globally) pose the danger that all means to reach the goal become justified. This includes the abuse that some NGOs perpetrate on their own workers in the name of sacrificing for "the cause." It also often descends into petty rivalries between organizations, which cause harm on the ground. Furthermore, the pursuit of narrow bureaucratic outcomes leads often to astounding levels of duplication in the field, which only confuse many situations.

Gandhi demonstrated that there must be no difference between means and ends in the struggle for social change and that the means really are the ends. This, it seems to me, is deeply resonant with Kant's kingdom of ends and Buber's I–You relations. It means that building human relations *among* peacemakers, inside organizations and communities of peacemakers, is an end in itself, with the conviction that it is also the best means to achieve the goal of peacemaking in its deepest sense. This creates a sustainable group of peacemakers, because they are constantly reinforced by the deep awareness that everything that they are doing is inherently valuable, even if subject to periodic evaluations on how to do it better. It means that the community of peacemakers can count on the fact that the ends desired for conflicting parties are also the guiding standard for their own community's treatment of its peacemakers. The ends of peace, justice, fairness, honesty, and compassion become the means by which the community of peacemakers functions. This creates trust, eliminates destructive feelings of hypocrisy, and creates a model for those conflicting parties who come into contact with such peacemakers.

It is surely not the case that all Mennonites behave in this fashion, nor am I suggesting that they are the perfect paragons for every conflict resolution practitioner. My point is structural and relational. Making the act of building human relations itself into an ethical or sacred task unifies, in principle at least, means and ends. This should be considered by all conflict resolution activists as a powerful model for sustainable conflict resolution work. John Burton and others have suggested that, in order for conflict resolution to really work on a global scale, it is going to have to become part of the political ethos of modern civilization (Rubenstein, 1990, p. 325). I suggest that, in order for it to really work on a global scale, it is going to have to become part of the *ethical* ethos of civilization, not just an end but part of the means, both interpersonal and institutional, by which conflict resolution and peacemaking are pursued by individuals and institutions.

One final word on instrumentalism. It should be noted that mission and building up of the church is instrumentalism of a sort. The conversion of people to one's religion, the most aggressive form of mission, may be internally perceived as a process of "spreading the Good News," but it is definitely perceived by Others as the instrumental use of people to strengthen a church or religious structure. It complicates the relationship with aid recipients or parties to a conflict. While it is clear to me how much the peacemakers in this volume studiously avoided using their peacemaking as a vehicle of conversion, it must be acknowledged that mission activity in many parts of the world today, particularly where Christianity and Islam meet, is often conflict generating. Furthermore, for some other Christians in the field, proselytizing is so central a tenet of faith that both the evangelist and the evangelized become largely an instrument of church building. That would be an inaccurate description of the style and character of the peacemakers we are studying here. Nevertheless, any consideration of mission and peacemaking activities creates complications of inner motivations and perceptions from the outside.

This is clearly both a basic theological issue and a dilemma for modern Mennonites, as I noted earlier. But I would argue that the creative process—sometimes stated, sometimes unstated—that I observed regarding future religious definitions of mission as it relates to peacemaking should be accelerated. This could help to clarify for themselves and others what mission really means to them.

### Peacemaking versus Justice

A critical issue that has long preoccupied Mennonite thinking on peace and pacifism is the relationship of peace and justice. This has become an increasingly central, though unresolved, issue as the modern wing of Mennonitism becomes more engaged in the world. World War II and the shame suffered by many due to their pacifist position (see ch. 1) spurred a great deal of rethinking and critical evaluation of the quietist and separatist aspects of Mennonite pacifism. The call for a theology of involvement encouraged greater commitment to active engagement in major social issues (Driedger and Kraybill, 1994, p. 53), but this also posed a challenge to a strict two-kingdom theology of separation of the worldly and spiritual spheres.

The starkest example of this shift from quietism to activism is the recent development of the Christian Peacemaker Teams. The methods and religious characteristics of CPT seem at first glance to set it in opposition to the character and style of Mennonite conflict resolution, the elicitive method, and conflict transformation. First, CPT missions have so far been decidedly partisan. The teams go where they are invited by one side to stand with them in their suffering (although the ideal CPT intervention would come about as a result of invitations from both sides in the conflict). Mennonites have been doing this for a long time, but CPT is far more aggressive in its pursuit of visible forms of protest against injustice and of publicity. As opposed to other expressions of Mennonite peacemaking, which stress a bringing together of both sides and a reduction of conflict, there appears to be a commitment, as Miller records, of "interventions for truth" that involve travel, talk, and "trouble." The military language used to describe the teams is also uncharacteristic of Mennonite peacemaking in other situations. There seems to be an effort to invite trouble in order to witness or to highlight the injustice of the situation.

This is clearly a situation in which the religious value of peace is at odds with the religious value of justice. This dilemma has old roots in biblical tradition, where God is portrayed as a God of justice punishing the wicked but also as a merciful God who loves repentance and forgiveness. Furthermore, God has a set of ideal characteristics for human beings to emulate, which include both peace and justice. "Execute the justice of truth and peace in your gates" (Zech. 8:16).[18] This is a decidedly difficult set of traits to combine, yet God is set up as the ideal being who does successfully combine them. It seems to me that conflict transformation as a method and the case studies in this volume express a deliberate process of attempting, as much as humanly possible, to combine a commitment to peacemaking and to social justice.

The CPT method makes the choice for justice stark. This has an honorable history, as in the nonviolent forms of confrontation and protest that Gandhi championed. In the Christian case, there is also a martyrological element, with some deep resonance in Mennonite history, of preparing to be assaulted for the sake of those who are defenseless. That is why, in Kern's essay, the "attack" plays such a prominent role. It is the most feared event but truly is the one that fulfills the self-image of CPT. This kind of witnessing has strong roots in various Christian denominations, and it clearly has some roots in Jesus' life. Thus, it must resonate with that side of the Mennonite community that is particularly outraged by injustice to those who do not have guns.

It is unclear to me, however, how or whether it makes sense to think of this approach in terms of conflict resolution. On the contrary, it appears to purposely generate conflict for the sake of witnessing and calling attention to injustice and for the sake of standing with the defenseless in such a way that one invites injury. The invitations to intervene come from one side of a conflict, and, therefore, the team is immediately entering as partisans. This makes perfect sense in pursuing justice but not conflict resolution, nor do I believe it serves the ultimate purposes or strategies of conflict transformation, as Lederach defines it. Nevertheless, there is some effort of the CPTs to teach by example the principle of nonviolent resistance, and it would be valuable to see follow-up on how many of the people they have stood with have adopted those methods.

CPT entry into hot political situations is done more quickly and for much shorter periods of time than is characteristic of other Mennonite peacebuilding activities. It also exposes some problems with the process of choosing one side for the sake of justice. Mennonites tend to side with whoever is not brandishing guns and to view with suspicion those who do. There are obvious historical and theological motivations for their choice. But it is fraught with danger. In the immediate sense, whoever is not holding the guns is much more likely to be the persecuted group. But looks can be deceiving, and it is also easy to fall prey to popular and prevailing political perceptions of who the victims are.

As an example, I understand why CPT wanted to send a team to Iraq when it was being attacked by the U.S.–led forces. But why not send a team to

Kuwait to witness the brutality of the Iraqi forces there? Could it be that they would have been welcomed by Saddam in Iraq as a public relations ploy but killed by Saddam in Kuwait? As another example, I could not sympathize more with CPT in Hebron bearing witness to the terrible treatment of Arabs at the hands of some of the settlers. But would CPT don Jewish clothing and drive unarmed through West Bank towns with Israeli license plates in order to accept the violence of Hamas upon themselves and in order to bear witness to the evil of terrorism against unarmed men, women, and children? I understand that pursuing justice involves deciding who has suffered the most harm and siding with them. But it seems to me that this involves one in some problematic choices from the point of view of peacemaking, and it makes it difficult to understand how justice and injustice are viewed by all sides of a conflict.

One also runs the risk of being used, when playing a partisan role, by people who have no commitment to peacemaking now or in the future. The conflict resolver who builds relationships on both sides may, in a worst case scenario, be manipulated by people who have no interest in peace, but she has never lent her name to a partisan effort that turned out to be an adjunct to or a cover for violence. At worst, the peacemaking effort did not succeed, but the integrity of the commitment to peacemaking remains.

Another problem with this kind of intervention from the point of view of both conflict analysis and religious ethics is that today's victims are tomorrow's killers. You can side with those who do not have guns, but their relatives in the next town may be using guns against the other side, even as you protect them. Or, a child that you stand with today may in a year or two become a terrorist. This is where a method focused on relationship building with all sides of a conflict protects you from gross manipulation and becoming embroiled in a conflict rather than becoming a part of its resolution.

In private conversations, Kern has lamented the fact that Quakers and Mennonites are perceived by many Israelis as anti-Semitic (see, for example, Soloway and Weiss, 1971), and she has tried personally to combat anti-Semitism (Kern, 1995). It must be disconcerting for members of a peace church to be perceived in this way. The activity of the peace churches in Israel for the past forty years, however, with a few individual exceptions, has been in solidarity with the suffering of Palestinians, not in mediation efforts or relationship building on both sides, nor in identification with the suffering that both sides have endured historically and more recently due to wars. As Christians, it should be obvious to them how this would be perceived by the bulk of Jews, who came to Israel in the first half of the century in order to escape from pogroms and genocide in Christian lands. The entire ethos of Zionism, for better or worse, is founded upon a response to the centuries of persecution of Jews in Europe. This must be confronted and taken into account by Christian peacemakers. The only sympathetic Christians that most Israelis ever really see are waiting for the return of all Jews to Israel, for Armageddon, the destruction of two-thirds of the Jewish people, the second coming of Christ, and the conversion of the Jewish remnant to Christianity.

Right-wing Israelis have welcomed the financial support of these Christians who, incidentally, believe that war with Muslims is inevitable. But peace-loving Israelis and the million and a half citizens who voted for the Oslo Accords, with a few exceptions, feel mostly isolated from and suspicious of the Christian world. This is a perfect example of why partisan approaches to conflicts may satisfy the call of justice but do little for true conflict resolution.

The tragedy is that the work of the peace churches, especially the grassroots work more typical of the Mennonites, is precisely the kind of activity that could have averted the setback to the peace process of the 1996 Israeli elections, a difference of just 20,000 votes. The elite side of the Middle East peace process, namely, the business partnerships and negotiations among political leaders, were and still are in motion. But the deep levels of fear and anger of the masses of people on both sides were not and are still not being addressed. These elite strategies of conflict resolution were set in motion years ago by key representatives of conflict resolution theory. The challenge at the time was the intractable nature of the government-to-government conflict. But it is rage at the popular level, especially religious rage, that has threatened the peace process to its core. It is this level of conflict at which Mennonites have excelled elsewhere, and this is precisely where young idealistic women and men, such as Kern and her CPT colleagues, could have made and could still make a decided difference. It is also where training on both sides in conflict resolution could be effective, especially in Lederach's methods, which emphasize, both scientifically and theologically, the suspension of judgment of others as one tries to transform a conflict into a sustainable process of reconciliation.

The Middle East also could benefit from an elicitive approach to the religious communities involved in the conflict. Eliciting conflict resolution and peacemaking methods from religious cultures will be crucial to the future of the Middle East, especially since so much of the violence and opposition to the peace process has come from religious communities: Hamas and Islamic Jihad on one side and the Israeli religious parties and the settlers on the other side. But that requires deep entry into both cultures and long-term trust building, especially because of old issues of both Jewish and Islamic distrust of Christian intentions as third parties. But, in my opinion, it could be done over time.

There is no clear answer for the religious dilemma of justice seeking versus peace seeking or for the dilemma of peace seeking with all parties versus keeping oneself distant from the military powers that be. They do seem to come into conflict often, and one has to acknowledge that within complex moral situations, choices for justice will be made by some and not by others. But one should be clear that justice seeking is not always peacemaking. As a South African religious peacemaker, Khuzwayo Mbonambi, told me, "Justice preserves the peace, but it never makes peace. Only reconciliation and forgiveness do that" (1997).

It may be that in the future CPT and the authors of Mennonite conflict transformation theory will engage in more dialogue or community *discernment,* an important spiritual means by which Mennonite communities work on their goals. Out of that may emerge a CPT structure that engages in both witnessing in violent situations and serious conflict resolution techniques. Otherwise, I see these as two diverging spiritual trends within Mennonite activism. Conflict transformation, as it is being articulated and practiced by the Mennonites in this volume, appears to hold peace and justice in dramatic tension. There is a strong commitment to pursue peace but only together with justice, no matter how many extra complications this creates. Yet, these complications are the key to authentic peace or conflict transformation, as opposed to mere conflict settlement, which could easily be dismissed as pacification in situations of severe power imbalance.[19]

Conflict transformation is not just the process of enabling change to take place in the conflicting parties. We see from Chupp especially the way in which the Mennonite intervenor is prepared to go through a personal spiritual transformation. There is an openness to learning and a sense of gratitude for the opportunity to do that. This creates a much more symbiotic relationship between the conflicting parties and the peacemakers. There is a sense that they share a destiny of change and growth that empowers all of them, rather than maintaining one as the recipient of the good graces of the other. This is one reason why Chupp feels so gratified to be able to enable leadership to develop in the others, while he remains quiet. It is the give and take of moral and spiritual learning that allows for this kind of generosity.

Conflict resolution as a field of inquiry needs to think much more about how and whether the third party truly enables others to change and whether that is possible without the third parties being transformed themselves. Furthermore, it seems quite clear that ethical traits, such as gratitude, an eagerness to learn from others, an openness to positive change, and generosity, are all critical to Mennonite conflict transformation. Their replication would require, in my opinion, training people in the development of ethical character. This is a radical idea for the field of conflict resolution, but it bears consideration.

Another issue of peace and justice is the attitude toward those in power. The Herrs and Bergey demonstrate the strong Mennonite tendency to identify with the powerless. Often this is quite understandable, but it also reflects the Mennonites' strong antimilitary orientation. This preoccupation seems to me to be at some odds with a mode of peacemaking with all sides. One can notice, however, that the same activists in our study who express this distaste for power also engage in extensive efforts at peacemaking with the powers that be. Bergey was particularly adept at this in a uniquely quiet way. There is, nonetheless, a clear theological/cultural tension here with extending these listening and peacemaking skills to those who hold guns. That having been said, the level of empathy shown by Mennonites for everyone is remarkable, such as Kern's identification, even in the worst of circumstances, with the Israeli soldiers (albeit far less than with those who do not possess weapons).

The Colombian Mennonite experience also highlights this tension but seems to present a more balanced approach. In Colombia, Mennonite efforts have been weighted heavily toward the seeking of justice, human rights, and conscientious objection to military service—all emanating out of deep theological conviction. Unlike the CPT model, however, there appears to be an authentic effort to integrate peacemaking and justice seeking through Lederach's model of conflict transformation. This seems especially the case as time has gone on and the severity of the justice issues has been somewhat ameliorated. The descriptions of the several Mennonite organizational efforts provide good examples of the practical complexities of combining peacemaking and justice seeking, in addition to the ways in which this is negotiated theologically. This is not a neat process, but as with other Mennonite peacebuilding activities, it seems that the network of relationships together with the experience of collective discernment determines the give and take of negotiating these often-conflicting moral/spiritual values and political goals. This is precisely the kind of struggle that the theology held by most Mennonite peacemakers welcomes as an indispensable part of the process of transforming conflict and broken societal relationships into lasting peace and reconciliation.

## Women and Peacemaking

An encouraging development, in terms of religious peacemaking, is the place of women in Mennonite peacemaking. Zimmerman-Herr, Bergey, and Kern all display extraordinary gifts of empathy and listening, especially to those who are not regularly heard. Bergey's experience shows the harsh realities of being isolated in terms of her religion and gender in a violent situation. She learned to listen to the women's segment of society in ways that provided crucial insight into the true nature of the conflict situation. She also expressed an extraordinary level of connection with those who were suffering. This clearly challenged her emotionally, but her spiritual connection to women around the world was critical to her coping with what she saw, heard, and felt.

## Christian Foundations and Replicability

One issue that emerged from many of the case studies is the role of Christian prayer and song as a frame for dialogue between enemies. This was especially true for Chupp and Hart. More thinking must go into what such a frame actually accomplishes. Suggestions from Chupp and Hart include the idea that the frame is a unifying force in an otherwise deeply divided situation. I would suggest that it also deepens the experience, makes it more momentous, and, perhaps, even sacred. Such moments generally evoke in people their highest aspirations for themselves and for others, and this provides a useful counterbalance to the primal fears and anger that would otherwise naturally dominate one's consciousness in meetings with enemies.

I believe that biblical study is also key here. Especially when portions are chosen with some relevant ethical content, biblical study inserts into a deeply political and even military situation the fundamental questions of interpersonal ethics. It makes justice, peace, empathy with suffering, and mourning over suffering into topics of intellectual study. Generally, in tough negotiations, such as those described by Chupp, the only areas of intellectual inquiry or reasoned discussion are tough exchanges on substantive issues regarding cease-fires, distribution of scarce resources, reconstruction, elections, and so on. Bible study makes the issues of justice and peace into an intellectual inquiry on a par with the other pragmatic issues. It makes values into pragmatic reality. That is a useful frame for discussions, and it makes it more likely that, in the process of negotiations, the minds of the participants will associate with the questions of how to pursue justice, peace, or reconciliation. The association may lead to more creative problem solving that interweaves pragmatic needs and ethical goals.

The one cautionary note is to acknowledge that the frame is highly culturally specific, in this case, to the culture of Christianity. Clearly, in any context that has more than one religion represented, the ideal would be an artful combination or alternating frames that refer to the traditions of everyone involved. In the context of indigenous peoples, I would assume that in most contexts it would be vital to include indigenous religions and tribal customs, unless the groups in question have converted to one religion and unless they all strictly adhere only to their new religion. Certainly, if it is a mixed group of religious and nonreligious people, this would have to be accommodated as well. The last thing that a frame for discussions should do is encourage exclusion or ideological coercion. Then, it tends to appeal to the worst instincts in the participants rather than the best ones.

The same is true of some of the reconciliation methods mentioned by Hart. Forgiveness is particularly important in Christian tradition and will play an important role in conflict resolution for Christian contexts. But it is not a universally accepted method of reconciliation, especially in its unilateral form. At the very least, it is not as highly positioned theologically and should not be expected to be the *only* means to create peace among enemies, even religious enemies. I am still undecided about its universal usefulness, and I believe it requires further study.[20] In other traditions, such as Judaism and Islam, for example, a shared commitment among enemies to justice may work better as a vehicle of peacemaking, although I have witnessed the powerful effect of unilateral apologies in Jewish-Islamic relations. But each religious community has different sets of traditions and high ideals, and it is out of those ideals that conflict resolution methods must emerge. Forgiveness is important in all these traditions, but how important it is, how it is done, and under what circumstances is clearly conditioned theologically and culturally.

## Conclusion

In sum, Mennonite peacemaking methods are integrally related to their religious values. These, in turn, are formed by their historical experience, their close reading of biblical tradition, and their evolving spiritual response to the world around them. In many ways, their methods are unique to their religion and culture. But, as I have suggested, their methods pose powerful challenges to the general field of conflict resolution. Because of the immense power of the United States and Europe in the affairs of people, especially poor people, the world over, Western modes of interaction with the rest of the world are in need of perpetual self-scrutiny and creative growth. Mennonite conflict resolution and peacemaking offers a powerful model of human interaction that, to be replicated, would have to be appropriately adapted to fit other worldviews and institutions. Nevertheless, the forms of peacemaking analyzed here have within them enormous transformative potential for the future interactions of the global community.

# Sixteen

## Local Assessments of
## Mennonite Peacebuilding

CYNTHIA SAMPSON

W<small>E HAVE BEFORE US ACCOUNTS OF</small> peacebuilding told by Mennon-ite practitioners and analyses of their work by scholars writing from the perspectives of their respective disciplines. What remains for this chapter is to provide some local assessment of Mennonite peacebuilding from those who have had direct experience of some of those initiatives.

This will not be an exhaustive undertaking. It has not been possible to dispatch independent researchers to four continents to provide a comprehen-sive evaluation of the efficacy and impact of Mennonite peacebuilding. Nor has it been possible to provide equal coverage in this chapter for all of the volume's case studies. We were able to select but two locations, Colombia and Northern Ireland, for site visits, which were made in October and November 1996. We felt these cases offered a contrast: Colombia presents the work of Justapaz, an initiative of the Colombian Mennonite church, whereas Northern Ireland, more typical of the other case studies in the book, presents the work of North American Mennonites who have served as resources in the devel-opment of indigenous peacebuilding capacities. A list of all individuals for-mally interviewed is included at the conclusion of the chapter.

I have also, however, been able to draw upon a larger pool of data. In my other travels, I have often encountered individuals whose work has been touched by exposure to Mennonite ideas and practice, particularly in the area of training. As a non-Mennonite associate of the Institute for Justice and Peacebuilding (IJP) of Eastern Mennonite University (EMU), I have partic-ipated in the development of training programs delivered by a number of the authors or individuals mentioned in this book, and I have met and interacted with dozens of training participants, as well as students in EMU's Conflict Transformation Program. I have had in-depth conversations with people from each of the other countries represented in the case studies in this volume. So I draw upon a broad range of assessments in writing this chapter, not all of them represented by the formal interviews listed here.

A final introductory word—about terminology. My use of terminology is consistent with that of Lederach (1995c, 1997) and IJP colleagues (Conflict

Transformation Program, 1997, pp. 38–39). I use the term *conflict transformation* to signify the full range of activity that might be employed to change a conflict from destructive, often violent manifestations to constructive and just outcomes. *Peacebuilding* refers to activities occurring at any time in a conflict transformation process that are proactively constructive of the relationships and conditions that can achieve and sustain peace. I use *conflict resolution* and *peacemaking* to refer to intermediary efforts employed to bring conflicting parties together.

## Colombia

Although the chapter by Ricardo Esquivia and Paul Stucky documents a longer history of Mennonite involvement in Colombia, I shall focus here on the work of Justapaz as the central coordinating peacebuilding structure of the Colombian Mennonite church. It is also the primary link to Mennonite international peacebuilding, through its networking across international borders and the financial support and resourcing it receives from the Mennonite Central Committee (MCC).

*La violencia* was the starting point of the majority of conversations I had in Colombia. Colombian officials, academics, pastors, teachers, and community workers were all keenly aware of the pervasiveness of violence in their society. None of them appeared to question the appropriateness of Justapaz programs that brought together peacebuilders from different sectors of Colombian society and from grassroots organizations to the highest levels of the national government. There seemed to be an implicit recognition that violence needed to be dealt with in all of its expressions in society, and therefore peacebuilders in all sectors and at all levels had common cause. As one person put it, "The family is where peace is born."

The mainstay of the Justapaz program is service to grassroots communities, mainly but not exclusively through structures of the church. Justapaz serves as a resource and provides training in conflict resolution and transformation, human rights, and related topics and skill areas to local churches, schools, youth groups, and community-based mediation centers. Through its Seminary for the Training of Peacemakers, it provides a program of religious formation for young men seeking deferment from military duty.

Justapaz also plays an active peacebuilding role, however, in the broader arena of civil society, in the development of government programs, and in bridging peacebuilding activity across the sectors and levels of Colombian society. Thus, although deeply committed to serving its grassroots base, to a considerable and growing extent Justapaz functions as a middle-range actor (see ch. 3 and Lederach, 1997). It is actively linked through multiple networks and direct cooperation with constituencies at all levels of peacebuilding process and, as such, is strategically situated to foster the development of an infrastructure for peace.

The Justapaz contribution to peacebuilding in Colombia falls into three broad, interlinked categories: framework setting, capacity building, and program development and implementation.

### Framework Setting

Three of the people I interviewed, all of them formally schooled in conflict resolution, chose to describe the Justapaz contribution by contrasting it with the prevailing, more technical approach to conflict resolution, sometimes referred to generically as the "Harvard model." These people did not reject the various multistep "efficiency" models of mediation being promoted by government agencies and chambers of commerce. They recognized that such approaches have their place in providing citizens access to the judicial system and in helping disputants settle their differences.[1]

Further, one of the three maintained that, although Colombian writers, intellectuals, and politicians have thoroughly analyzed the Colombian reality and the antecedents of the conflict, they have not generated much by way of proposals for transforming it. Another suggested that the attention given to conflict resolution in Colombia has often been driven by anguish over the violence in that society, and this has led to too much focus on ending armed conflict and finding formulas for reaching agreement, while forgetting the aspect of social justice. He noted that most models in the conflict resolution field in Colombia are from abroad and are skills oriented, with little conceptualization of what peace means.

The Justapaz approach, on the other hand, was seen as clearly distinctive and original in its focus on the more long-range undertaking of construction of peace,[2] over and above what might be happening in a particular conflict. Justapaz, in conjunction with John Paul Lederach, who has served as a primary resource to its work,[3] is credited with having introduced the peacebuilding perspective into the Colombian conflict resolution field and with introducing ideas that, although framed theoretically, are accessible to all kinds of people and are applicable to the day-to-day work of constructing peace. It was clear, for example, that the concept of a strategic infrastructure for peace had found widespread currency in peacebuilding circles from the numerous references made by interviewees working in different arenas.

The other voice and orientation that Justapaz has consistently brought to higher-level peacebuilding circles is that of grassroots people and communities and the validation of local and indigenous mechanisms of conflict resolution.

### Capacity Building

Justapaz has not only popularized the concept of an infrastructure for peace, it is broadly and significantly engaged in developing such an infrastructure through capacity building, mainly in the form of training programs in conflict resolution, human and civic rights, and peacebuilding more broadly; and in the development of concrete peacebuilding programs (see next section).

*Schools.* I visited two of the schools that were receiving conflict resolution training through the Program for Peacebuilding in School Settings, begun in 1994. Although operated by Mennonites, the majority of the pupils at these primary schools in Cachipay and La Mesa were non-Mennonite. Initially focused mainly on mediation skills for teachers and the older children, the training was later expanded to include work on self-esteem, sharing, negotiation, values, and human rights and to include children of all ages.

The teachers and administrators I spoke with at both schools praised Justapaz instructors for teaching by example. They said that teachers and students alike have felt valued and affirmed by the instructors and are now better able to value, understand, and get along with one another. Listening skills were cited as being especially helpful in this regard.

Teachers reported that the words *mediation* and *nonviolence* had entered the vocabularies of their pupils, many of whom come from violent family and interfamily contexts. Children have shown a new willingness to try to work out their differences peacefully, and discipline has improved.

Parents' surveys at La Mesa have revealed widespread support for the school's emphasis on peace and its attention to the formation of the children. Although the school had previously worked with the Mennonite concepts of peace and nonviolence, these concepts had become more sharply defined and operationalized through the work with Justapaz. Families at both schools have commented on changes in the children, some of whom have intervened in family conflicts. One such story was recounted by a school official, whose young son mediated a conflict between her and her husband in a moving and transforming experience for the whole family. Teachers have also begun to recognize and change some violent aspects of their own behavior. Said one, "We have to control our reactions."

In La Mesa, interest in conflict resolution spread through some of the students' families into the public school system, and Justapaz was enlisted to train all of the public high school's seventy teachers and 1,200 or so students. The school formed mediation teams, and the high school program also led to a Catholic-Protestant ecumenical project for peace in the park in La Mesa.

*Church structures.* Justapaz has provided various kinds of training for Mennonite congregations and youth. The Mennonite church in Girardot, for example, has received training in conflict resolution and the exercise of human rights and democracy, most recently to prepare members of the congregation and nearby communities for the opening of a community mediation center.

One Mennonite pastor interviewed had received training through Justapaz's Permanent Course (discussed below). She has actively applied new conflict resolution skills in neighborhood and family conflicts, with tangible results. She, too, identified listening as a particularly effective new skill, because people are not used to being listened to: "The very fact of listening to them leads to a solution." Her goal is to open a mediation center affiliated with Justapaz.

*Conscientious objection.* I had a lively discussion with a group of earnest young men, seven of the hundred or so who at the time were pursuing conscientious objection through studies at the Seminary for the Training of Peacemakers. These men felt that the education they were receiving and the alternative service in their communities were life-changing experiences. They described the program as nurturing, as a leadership formation experience, as giving them alternatives to pursuing their wishes violently, as opening a new space and creating new opportunities for them.

They were aware of no other comparable program in Colombia. "School and academia are deficient in this kind of formation," said one. "Before I entered this service," said another, "I was looking for something to work for and express myself. Justapaz gave me that opportunity. I was able to discover goals and create a life project." Several felt their families and friendships had also been touched by what they had learned and that their interactions had become more peaceful. They believed that they themselves would be better parents as a result of it.

*Permanent Course (Curso Permanente).* Begun in 1993, Justapaz's Permanent Course provides a continuing program of training in conflict transformation for representatives from key sectors of peacebuilding activity throughout Colombia. By mid-1997, eight workshops had been held on a range of topics growing out of the work and needs of the participants, including basic tools for conflict analysis, analysis and transformation of conflict among social groups, developing an infrastructure for peace, interview techniques in mediation and conciliation, and the legal basis for conflict mediation and conciliation. Instruction had been provided by Justapaz staff (Esquivia, Stucky, Lina Maria Obando) and by staff and associates of the IJP of Eastern Mennonite University (Lederach, Vernon Jantzi, Mark Chupp).

Originally intended for a group of twenty-five to thirty, the popularity and timeliness of the course had driven attendance at some segments to as high as eighty or more. Participants came from a variety of nongovernmental organizations (NGOs), community groups, churches, universities, national and local governments, the Organization of American States, and, recently, from several Central American states.

My interviews with participants revealed an appreciation for the broad mix of people gathered in the Permanent Course. A Mennonite pastor who had attended all segments of the course reported that she had found everything she learned to be applicable in her situation. At the same time, she received much encouragement and support for her work from participants working in other sectors, including the top level of national government.

A participant who had studied conflict resolution at the university level found the course gave her instruments for applying the theories and an opportunity to test their usefulness through Justapaz's applied Center for Conflict Analysis and Transformation. Another participant, an academic, portrayed the Permanent Course as a venue for a fertile intermixing of diverse perspectives and the lively engagement of and testing of peacebuilding frameworks.

Another participant saw it as a process that validated the expression of diverse ideas and that was contributing to thinking about new options for peace in Colombia.

### Program Development and Implementation

Justapaz is often sought out in program development precisely for its distinctive approach to peacebuilding. In 1994, for example, during a formative stage in the development of its Program on Community Mediation, the Office on Justice of the National Rehabilitation Plan of the Colombian Presidency reached out to Justapaz for assistance. Under a mandate from the 1991 constitution, the program's purpose was to generate dialogue among counties and NGOs working on community mediation. Justapaz was seen as the organization that could supply the conceptualization and theory of conflict resolution for which the program was searching. That proved to be the case.

Justapaz participated in a small working group of NGO and government representatives. This process led to the creation of a Network for Community Justice and Treatment of Conflicts, involving NGOs from all over Colombia, as well as communities representing religious, black, and indigenous peoples. The network provides NGO participation in governmental projects, such as a major project of the Bogotá mayor's office for the reduction of violence and conflict resolution (see below).

Gradually, Justapaz—in particular, Justapaz Director Ricardo Esquivia—emerged as an institutional leader, and the network's national office was housed at the offices of Justapaz to facilitate its leadership and coordination role. Justapaz's solid track record, seriousness of commitment, and close connection to the people were credited with bringing to the still-young network a higher level of credibility and respect than it would otherwise enjoy and of opening many doors.

A description of Esquivia's leadership style by a network colleague shed light on his personal contribution to the network development. Referring to Esquivia's Mennonite heritage, this colleague said, "One of the fundamental ways of expressing who you are and where you come from is how you are and the example of your life." Esquivia's example, he said, is one of "simplicity [in life], profound patience, listening, and trying to understand people in all their dimensions." He described Esquivia's work with people as "adding rather than subtracting. Rather than saying, well, such and such a person doesn't serve, . . . he tries to draw them in to contribute and add."

A spate of new program ideas involving Justapaz have emerged out of agencies whose staff have participated in the Permanent Course. At the time of this writing, they included:

- The Ministry of Interior's Division of Public Order and Coexistence, which works with state governors, mayors, and other authorities, had enlisted the help of Justapaz and EMU's IJP in a pilot peacebuilding project in an area of worsening violence on the Caribbean coast. Esquivia, Stucky, and Lederach had participated in a program-design meeting of the Strategic Committee, which involved representatives of the Office of the Presidency, Interior Department, Ombudsman's Office, and High Commission for Peace, among others.

- The Justice and Human Rights Office of the Bogotá mayor's office was developing a program to build broad community awareness for addressing conflict nonviolently, and each of the city's twenty boroughs was opening an office with a primary focus on family matters and mediation. The mayor's office was interested in commissioning Justapaz and the IJP to provide training and follow-up on mediation, conflict transformation, and human rights for mayors and other officials.
- The Ombudsman's Office, a semiautonomous state office looking out for citizens' interests and rights at the national, regional, and local levels, had requested Justapaz's assistance in its efforts to resolve a situation involving economic, political, military, social, ethnic, and ecological problems near the Panama-Colombia border. The office had also proposed that Justapaz provide training for staff involved in mediating between organs of the state and civil society. Already, Esquivia was serving as a consultant to the office on human rights.
- The state university's school for Higher Education in Public Administration, which trains government bureaucrats, had discussed a formal relationship with Justapaz and EMU's master's program in conflict transformation.
- With an eye to upcoming Colombian elections, the Interior Ministry had discussed with Justapaz and the IJP possible work with Colombian governors and mayors in designing a plan for creation of an infrastructure for peace in each of the states. The plan in each state would be carried out with the support of the governor, the police, and the army.
- The Organization of Black Communities had proposed a long-term peacebuilding project that would provide training and formation to leaders of the black communities. African-Colombians comprise 30 percent of the Colombian population.

Clearly, Justapaz is making a significant contribution in the private and public sectors toward the development of frameworks, individual and institutional capacities, and programs related to conflict transformation and the construction of peace. The one criticism of Justapaz that surfaced in my interviews in a sense provided further verification of the esteem in which its work is held. The peacebuilding center was faulted for not making more of an effort to systematically document, analyze, and build theory from the lessons learned in peacebuilding practice. Its only book on conflict resolution at the time was a training manual. Theories generated out of such rich practical experience, argued one academic, could serve as guides to action for a much broader circle of peacebuilders.

## Northern Ireland

Writing about Mennonite peacebuilding in Northern Ireland poses a dilemma for this researcher. Well do I know that Mennonite peacebuilding is distinctly community based and built on a premise of local empowerment. Humble in style and modest in pretensions, it avoids drawing attention to itself in general and to individual personalities in particular. In contrast to the case of Justapaz, however, for lack of a local Mennonite structure, all peacebuilding by Mennonites in Northern Ireland has been carried out by individuals, some of whom have broad international experience and a fairly high degree of visibility within peacebuilding circles. So it was natural for the people interviewed to address their comments to the work of specific individuals.

For these few pages, therefore, the spotlight will shine, uncharacteristically, on individual Mennonite peacebuilders. I believe that this is particularly warranted here, for woven throughout the interviews was abundant and eloquent comment on the demeanor and style—the way of being with others—of Mennonite practitioners. This was so consistent that I have included those comments here as a separate category of Mennonite contribution. But, as we shall see, it was also easy for the Irish to generalize in this regard across the Mennonites they had met, such that we clearly have before us the example of practitioners who have made significant individual contributions and yet are also expressions of communal spirituality, culture, values and sensibilities.

The Mennonite contribution in Northern Ireland thus divides into four categories: capacity building, framework setting, support for religious reconciliation, and way of being with others.

### Capacity Building

Mennonite involvement in efforts to develop local peacebuilding capacities dates from 1985, when Ron Kraybill introduced mediation training into Northern Ireland. Kraybill returned for two brief visits in the 1990s, once with his brother Nelson, to provide workshops in conflict transformation and advanced mediation. The people I interviewed recognized Kraybill as having prepared the ground for the mediation movement in Ireland, North and South, and also for the Mennonites who followed. He was also specifically credited with having shared two insights that proved helpful and reassuring to local practitioners: that peacemaking is not a question of having all the answers and, drawing from the South African experience, that peacebuilding takes a long time, and there will be setbacks along the way, but these will not prove insurmountable in the end.

In 1987, Barry Hart went to Dublin for most of a year, during which time he conducted mediation training and training-of-trainer courses for many types of community organizations and also for the Probation Board of Northern Ireland. Hart's stay was well timed, according to a trainer who was active at that time, to coach and increase the confidence of local trainers. He was helpful in shaping the content of training, and he helped encourage more people to become trainers. Of particular usefulness was his emphasis on listening skills, an aspect of training that local trainers had rushed over prior to that time.

Over the decade 1987–1997, Howard Zehr, a specialist on restorative justice with MCC, made four trips to Northern Ireland under various auspices.

Through a broad range of contacts, conferences, and training workshops, he interacted with government officials, academics, criminal policy makers, senior sentencers, and others working in justice-related programs. According to the assessment of an organizer of several of the trips, Zehr has had "a profound impact with a wide range of influential professionals, who are by nature conservative and cautious." As a result, "Restorative justice is very high on the agenda of the people who need to know [and] . . . to accept its crucial relevance to the community." In addition, some former paramilitary people had become interested in the application of restorative justice principles to alternatives to paramilitary violence.

John Paul Lederach made his first visit to the province in 1993 and had returned frequently, sometimes several times a year since then, often in the capacity of resource and trainer with The Mediation Network for Northern Ireland. He had also participated in a number of major conferences (see next section). Lederach's arrival coincided with a growing awareness that the prevailing mediation models, introduced from the outside, were not entirely appropriate to the local culture. He was credited with carrying the message that there is no one right way to do mediation and with giving Irish practitioners the confidence to develop models more appropriate to their context. Lederach also introduced the concept of an insider–partial intermediary, a role that has been actively embraced by a number of individuals from the two religious communities. Finally, Lederach was credited with having the particular gift, as an observer of the Northern Irish scene, of being able to "name, map, and chart" what he understands of the conflict dynamics. "Touching an intuition within us," said a mediator who works closely with him, "[this] gives us a handle [on how to proceed]."

John and Naomi Lederach, the parents of John Paul, in retirement spent three years in Belfast as MCC volunteers with the Mediation Network (1994–1997). During that time, they conducted trainings, usually working with Irish cotrainers, in conflict transformation for churches, social workers, housing executives, mental health staff, and community groups. On a number of occasions, they undertook intraorganizational mediation at the request of the organization involved. Naomi Lederach was particularly active with women's groups, and John Lederach worked with police through the Community Awareness Programme. Both Lederachs were credited with making an influential and strategic contribution to the family program of the Family Caring Trust. The Lederachs also provided considerable operational support to the Mediation Network. In addition to their substantive and process contributions, the Lederachs were credited with developing relationships and with "giving wise counsel and acting as spiritual guides" for those with whom they worked. They were praised for their "willingness to give up years of their lives in a way in which it is so obviously about giving."

In 1996–1997, EMU's IJP became a resource to the Mediation Network in a training program for community workers in five "flashpoint" areas of particularly high intercommunal tensions. Kraybill, Hart, Lederach, and Chupp each paid separate visits to Northern Ireland, and thirteen Northern Irish community workers participated in IJP's 1996 Summer Peacebuilding Institute. One of the project's participants reported that the hands-on mediation training and ideas about peacebuilding had given him the confidence to pursue the development of two conciliation centers.

Finally, the Mennonite contribution to capacity building may also be seen as including to some degree the work of Joseph Campbell as a mediator and trainer with the Mediation Network, for although Campbell is himself a Presbyterian elder, partial support for his work has come from Mennonite agencies.

Extending well beyond training, Mennonite practitioners participate in a broad range of activities, such as briefings and consultations; meetings, seminars, and conferences; prison visits; and off-the-record discussions with key players in the conflict, including political leadership. Mennonite peacebuilders may also find themselves at times in a position to apply the skills of conciliation, mediation, and reconciliation as they move among the Northern Ireland parties. They do this, however, not for the purpose of developing an independent third-party role for themselves but rather in partnership with and in support of the ongoing work of Irish colleagues.

As a group, Mennonites were assessed very favorably by the people who were interviewed. Their denominational base appears not to have hampered their ability to operate effectively in the secular realm, despite admitted initial skepticism on the part of some. They were credited with being the outside group that was most sensitive to the need for indigenization of practice. As one local practitioner put it, "[They] didn't come with answers. The answers were in us. What we needed to do was bring them out. They helped identify the questions."

*Framework Setting*

With strong echoes of the Colombian case, a significant aspect of the Mennonite contribution in Northern Ireland has been the introduction by John Paul Lederach of a strategic peacebuilding framework. Prior to that time, efforts at economic and political reform, community relations, community development, and so on had been largely unconnected and lacked a unifying framework and strategy. Without prescribing answers for Northern Ireland, Lederach's framework, or analytical "sets of lenses," offered a means of understanding the actors and activities appropriate to different time frames, levels, and sectors of peacebuilding process. It helped local practitioners understand where existing initiatives fit into a larger picture and where efforts should most strategically be placed next.

Two major conferences were particularly influential in reaching significant groups of players with whose experience the ideas resonated powerfully. The first, Beyond Violence: The Role of Voluntary and Community Action in Building a Sustainable Peace in Northern Ireland, took place in Belfast in November 1994, just weeks after the republican and loyalist cease-fires were announced. After twenty-five years of violence, the cessation of violence brought confusion for a time among peacebuilders on how to proceed. Lederach's keynote address seemed to meet participants at exactly their point of need. A conference organizer told me that Lederach's keynote address "put into words so much of what people wanted to hear."[4]

The assertion by Lederach that peace and reconciliation do not require that people either forgive and forget or remember and not change—but that they remember and change—inspired two subsequent initiatives. The first was the formation of a working group, the Remember and Change Consortium, comprised of the Northern Ireland Association for Mental Health, University of Ulster, Mediation Network, Corrymeela Community, Victim Support, and Belfast Samaritans. The consortium developed an approach to dealing with trauma and violence based on that thesis, and in 1996 it launched a twelve-part course in listening skills, with Naomi and John Lederach teaching two of the sessions.

Remember and Change also became the title for the second major conference, held in Enniskillen in October 1996 and attended by representatives of all of Northern Ireland's twenty-six District Partnership Boards[5], as well as by academics, politicians, and funders, including a member of the European Commission. By the assessment of one of the organizers, the address was enthusiastically received, even by a number of serious skeptics, and "learning on [the] part of the partnership boards was immense. . . . Quietly but authoritatively [Lederach] explained to people where we're at. We could locate ourselves. . . . He was not selling quick fixes. This is a process."

Perhaps of greatest immediate and strategic value to Irish practitioners has been Lederach's pyramid showing the three levels of peacebuilding activity (see ch. 3). My interviews revealed that levels analysis had become second nature within the practitioner community. Said one, "It was a framework for knowing the kind of work you could do and not be isolated—that everything fit into one process." For a Community Relations Council official, the pyramid graphic became part of every presentation she gave, with illustrations of the levels taken from the agency's work that week. For her, it was instructive in that "if we see something happening at one level, we need to be sure it is happening at other levels too." In particular, community-level practitioners became aware of the need to also focus attention on middle-range and top-level actors.

### Support for Religious Reconciliation

An intriguing aspect of the Mennonite contribution in Northern Ireland has come through the influence of Anabaptist thought within some Protestant evangelical circles in providing a theology for engagement around social issues. The major impetus toward social engagement by evangelicals has come from ECONI, the Evangelical Contribution on Northern Ireland, whose staff and conceptual thinking have been heavily influenced by Anabaptist thought. Citing the writings of Mennonite theologian John Howard Yoder,[6] among others, a leading ECONI thinker explained that the personal is political: "Jesus calls you to cross the boundaries. He touched the untouchables of his day, which was an extremely political act." Believing that the Irish problem was bound up in the nature of church and state, this thinker saw the Anabaptist witness as breaking the monopoly of the Constantinian mindset in Ireland.

Several in the ECONI leadership traced their interest in Anabaptism to a long association with the Mennonite center in London and, in particular, to its director, Nelson Kraybill, and to Alan and Eleanor Kreider, two long-time workers who made annual visits to Northern Ireland. In addition, Campbell and ECONI's Derek Poole had hosted an Anabaptist study group in Belfast.

Actual on-the-ground support for religious reconciliation in Northern Ireland has been carried out primarily by Joseph Liechty, through his work on sectarianism and through his strong and natural connection to the evangelical community, support to the ecumenical movement, and networking more broadly among religious peacebuilders, including the reconciliation communities. Liechty's credibility and influence as an outsider in this work, according to Irish scholars and practitioners, were to a large extent derived from his long investment of time in getting to know the Irish context and from his expertise as a scholar of the history of nineteenth century evangelicalism. Said one colleague, "He comes on secure ground in terms of history. He can break an argument down historically and can help people read their own history." The fact that an American bothered to come and take the time to learn Irish history is remarked upon by all sorts of locals, according to this colleague.

Liechty was praised for having studied at a Catholic university, demonstrating "his willingness to be cross-grained with his own tradition." To an academic colleague, this modeled something important—the possibility of doing research that has integrity by adopting a perspective somewhat different from where one would naturally be: "This builds dialogue into the quest." She also saw his outsider status as a strength: "Outsiders have invaluable perspectives, sometimes even naive questions." She cited the notion of a "second naiveté," one held by more experienced outsiders, who recognize ambiguities and yet still raise the question: Does it have to be like this?

Liechty was recognized as maintaining important lines of connection to the Protestant evangelical community and contributing significantly to ECONI. At the same time, he was seen as at the cutting edge of ecumenism. "He has been able to model the crossing of boundaries," said a member of the Catholic community, "to reach within his own community, understand the differences, and reach across."

Liechty's family base was noted as an important dimension of his life and work in Ireland. The Liechtys, said a friend and colleague:

> have tried to create something special in their lives, living authentically and with sensitivity to meeting people where they are. This is conveyed in the work situation. Joe is very willing to try to hear all sides . . . even when under attack. . . . He tries to live a kind of peace and sensitivity. I've seen him draw people out, with a sensitiveness of approach and lack of presupposition.

She described his conversation style as "questioning, pushing, and reflecting back with the person" until he has a clear picture of what the person is saying and as having "the capacity for disagreeing without being either aggressive or dismissive."

With the work on sectarianism very much still in progress and the nature of this work being "quiet, building trust, and reaching across traditions," a colleague assessed the impact of Liechty's work as being incremental, a broadening base of people working for peace and reconciliation. "There are not too many stars and prima donnas in this work. It is more at a level of being part of a network of communities of peace and reconciliation."

A postscript to this section on religious reconciliation goes to an encounter between John Paul Lederach and ECONI, which took place at an ECONI retreat in April 1996. In the course of a presentation of his peacebuilding framework, Lederach made a comment that proved disproportionate in its impact on the organization's development. ECONI was on the verge of confronting the militant wing of its own Protestant community, the Orange Order, about actions ECONI considered to be objectionable. Turning to a concept he had first heard from Quaker peace scholar and activist Elise Boulding, Lederach suggested that instead of prophetic speaking, they might consider prophetic listening.

"If you go in with judgment," one ECONI member recalled his saying, "you make your point but lose the relationship. Prophetic listening hears people into being, gives them a place to stand, builds trust and relationship. You're listening to them, whether or not it's reciprocal." Describing this challenge as seminal, the member continued, "It changed the way we thought in relation to the Orange Order. We went with an interest in relationship building." Angry with the Orangemen since childhood, she told me this changed her life; she turned back to her own community with more compassion for them than ever before.

They had assumed that they understood their own community, another ECONI member said, so there was no great urgency to build bridges within the community. But "prophetic listening is taking people seriously." Once you start listening to the other side, explained a third, "You realize they have validity. There's some justice and rightness in what they say. You start articulating that to others." He found he had become uncomfortable with the stereotyping of the Orangemen common in most circles. ECONI also realized, he said, that there is a fine line between prophetic speaking—naming and defining issues and standing in contrast to the other side—and deeply despising the other side. Then you become part of the problem, through a new form of sectarianism in the name of prophesy, which lacks compassion or empathy for the other group's fears.

This new understanding brought an awareness of the diversity—the ambiguities and tensions—throughout the pro-union community. Said a fourth ECONI member:

> All of a sudden it all seems much more complicated than previous assumptions that the Orange Order was bad. Now there is this moment that is ambiguous. . . .

That can be quite frightening because it seems overwhelming. But it is also seen as opportunity, because we are not dealing with a monolithic structure, but points of contact with people who are more than willing to think through things with you.

## Way of Being with Others

Many of the people I interviewed had bitter complaints about some types of Americans who had meddled in the Northern Ireland conflict. Three caricatures of unwanted visitors were described to me: Americans who jet in, do experiments, and leave people raw; researchers who come for two weeks, then go home and write a book; preachers who come with all the answers—"simple answers to complex issues, which are usually wrong but are preached with great certainty."

Mennonites were explicitly excepted from these characterizations. Virtually every person interviewed made some comment about the manner of the Mennonites they had known and the quality of the interactions with them. Mennonites were described as unobtrusive and nonintrusive; as quiet, gentle, sincere; as people whose mission was clearly informed by a serving ethic; as committed to people, relationships, and to listening.

One Irish practitioner cited John and Naomi Lederach as good examples of these qualities. Not only were they not selling a particular set of answers but were also not selling their own church. This enabled them to relate to people across the spectrum. Another described them as "a tremendous point of sanity, with a sense of quietness in a conflict-ridden world . . . a source of warmth and facilitation . . . with the capacity to quietly give with wisdom and gentleness." The Lederachs' ability to adapt to Irish life was attributed by one who knew them well to their spirituality, the kind of humility that requires an "inner security and awareness within oneself."

Very much appreciated was the commitment of time on the part of Mennonite volunteers who come and live there long enough to begin to understand life in Northern Ireland. Also appreciated were those who came back again and again, paying repeat visits to even "the most hardened of men." One local practitioner with experience dating from 1987 talked about the Mennonites' "personal approach. . . . We never feel talked down to. They're very respectful. . . . We don't feel exploited. We feel valued. Aside from their expertise, they are models. It's more the experience of being with the person. That's what they leave behind. It's what I know most about the Mennonites." This manner of being with people and valuing them, she said, "frees people up sufficiently to listen."

Liechty was described as exemplifying servanthood, possessing discernment, and modeling prophetic listening in relationships. Said a colleague:

> For an outsider with an American accent, he has the rare quality of having the objectivity of an outsider but has embraced Irish people with real compassion. . . .

He's as close to objectivity as you will get. But it's not written coldly, but with real love for the people.

This colleague praised his "tremendous willingness to actually learn. He is not coming with answers. He does have things to say, but is quick to learn what may be helpful."

John Paul Lederach was described as coming and going quietly and with integrity; as unthreatening and highly respected in many circles; as engaging many different groups, even prisoners and members of the security forces, gently, laying out a few ideas for them to discuss among themselves. "John Paul leaves aside criticism," according to one experienced observer. "He's affirmative, talks about possibilities with the calmness and saneness from the nourishment of his religion." To another who has known the inside of a prison, Lederach is respected because he is not an opportunist, ego driven, or self-seeking. To a third peacebuilder, "He's very intuitive, and he's with the people totally. He can always pitch at the level of the people he's with. He can reach their hearts and minds."

The same is true with Howard Zehr, this practitioner said. And then, summing up, "This is a gift—the lack of ego, the humility. . . . They are making an enormous contribution, quietly."


## Conclusions

To what extent might we consider the local responses from these two cases to be representative of those from other contexts of Mennonite peacebuilding? Here I draw upon the broader set of exposures mentioned at the beginning of this chapter, as well as my own experience as a non-Mennonite working with Mennonites associated with the Institute for Justice and Peacebuilding and the Mennonite Central Committee. My answer would be that three of the categories identified above—capacity building, framework setting, and way of being with others—characterize the Mennonite contribution universally. (The category of program development and implementation is a function of Justapaz's central role as an indigenous peacebuilding center. In other contexts, Mennonite participation in program development through consultation, funding, and even active participation would fit comfortably within the rubric of capacity building.)


### Capacity Building

If there is one concept that comes closest to capturing the essence of Mennonite peacebuilding, it is capacity building. As Mitchell has discerned, capacity building for Mennonites implies that "knowledge, skills, and, above all, local capabilities are there, in the society, awaiting opportunities for use and development" (ch. 14). So much of what the Mennonites bring to international peacebuilding is a function of this predisposition and orientation, not the least of which is the elicitive approach to training and practice, whose very basis rests on this principle. Other themes of Mennonite peacebuilding identified by Mitchell and Merry bear this out further, for example, the practice of not taking charge but rather of giving priority to supporting and complementing existing local endeavors and institutions, and the respect and validation shown local cultures and peoples in making a long-term commitment to engagement with them and, specifically, through the methodology of listening and learning.

How are these orientations and practices received by people on the ground? The voices from Colombia, Northern Ireland, and others I have heard from around the world suggest that local parties do feel respected, valued, supported, empowered, and validated as the central players for peacebuilding in their contexts. In fact, in the eyes of some, if Mennonites err at all in regard to this standard, it is that for some cultures Mennonite practitioners are sometimes too reticent to share the wisdom gained across their many years and contexts of experience, too reluctant to offer formulas, too averse to prescribing, to commanding center stage and holding forth. That Mennonites resist these pressures reveals a profound adherence to religiously and culturally prescribed values and norms of a different sort, a strong congruence of ideology and practice in the service of local empowerment and transformation, rather than the promotion of self as intervenor or high-profile personality.

## Framework Setting

The evidence would suggest that virtually everywhere Lederach's peacebuilding framework has found exposure, it has found application. Derived as it is from practice and the depth and breadth of Lederach's experiences in many contexts, indigenous practitioners have put the framework to the most strategic use in situating their work in the larger picture and charting critical next steps. As in Northern Ireland, Lederach's pyramid has proven to be a simple yet powerful analytical tool in a multitude of contexts, and it is surely the element of the peacebuilding framework that has been most broadly applied and frequently reproduced (see, for example, Perera, 1996, p. 11; and Lutheran World Relief, 1996, p. 22). Associated with the pyramid and also of widespread influence and strategic value, as in Colombia, has been the concept of a strategic infrastructure for peace and the vital role that middle-range actors can play in its construction.

The framework has also found currency in other practitioner circles. It has received global circulation among international humanitarian NGOs, and, as awareness has grown of the impact of relief and development projects on conflict dynamics and the long-term prospects for sustainable peace, the ideas have informed and helped transform the mandates, missions, and program development of several specific NGOs. Though fewer in number, top-level officials working in government, diplomacy, intergovernmental organizations, and the military have also found the framework of value, particularly in understanding the role and interrelationship of their work with other spheres of peacebuilding activity. As one U.N. official said, this is the framework that "ties it all together."

## Way of Being with Others

This last category, with which we close this chapter and our entire exami- nation of Mennonite peacebuilding, is perhaps at its root the explanation for all that has come before and certainly for the previous two categories discussed here. Surely, it is a theologically inscribed humility and a pervasive ethos of service that have made possible a radical commitment to empowerment and to the development of the capacities of others to solve their problems, rather than prescribing solutions and taking charge. Out of a methodology built on listening and a view of practice as the accompaniment in discovery of that which is inherent in people and contexts, a framework has come in which all constructive activity for peace finds a place of understanding, validity, and import.

It is this way of being with others—quietly, gently, respectfully, noncom- petitively—that opens the way for people who are struggling with some of life's deepest challenges and darkest tragedies to discover a more constructive and courageous side of their own natures and to glimpse the beginnings of a way forward. These qualities are not unique to Mennonites, but they are dis- tinctly characteristic of Mennonite peacebuilding. It is this way of being with others that is the starting point of Mennonite practice, and the relationships that grow out of that way are the foundation upon which the activities and programs are built.

## List of Interviews

### Colombia

Edith Acuña, pastor, Mennonite Church of Juan Pablo II, Bogotá

Edgar Ardila, director, Justice Office of the National Rehabilitation Plan of the Presidency of Colombia, and professor, National University, Santefe de Bogotá

Mario Madrid Malo, professor, School for Higher Education in Public Ad- ministration, and Javeriana University, Bogotá; former director for promotion and publicity, Ombudsman's Office of the Colombian government

Peter Stucky, Mennonite pastor and vice president of Colombian Mennonite Conference, Bogotá

Pedro Valenzuela, professor, Javeriana University, Bogotá

Jesús Vargas, executive director, Network for Community Justice and Treat- ment of Conflicts, Bogotá

Maria Lucia Zapata, attorney and consultant to Human Rights and Justice Office of the City of Santefe de Bogotá

Mediation Center of the Mennonite church, Girardot
    Gerardo Mecón, director
    Nelly Ospitia, volunteer
    Raul Vasquez, pastor

Mennonite School, Cachipay
    Maria Elena Aponte, pastor
    Julia Jimeníz, teacher

Mennonite School, La Mesa
    Guillermo Vargas, director
    Otilia Garzón, teacher
    Estela Tiguaque, teacher
    Nubia Urueña, teacher
    Patricia Urueña, teacher
    Jorgé Vargas, teacher

Seminary for the Training of Peacemakers, Bogotá
    Andreiev Alberto Pinzón Franco, student
    John Jairo Alvarado Horta, student
    Wilmer Daniel Castello Juque, student
    Duvan Hernan Lopez Meneses, student
    Juan Carlos Santos Ortegon, student
    Sergio Vargas Pinzón, student
    Ricardo Armando Ramirez Rubiano, student

Interviews were conducted October 8–10, 1996, with interpretation by Paul Stucky.

### Northern Ireland and Republic of Ireland

Joan Broader, director of services, Extern Organisation, Lisburn

Joseph Campbell, assistant director, The Mediation Network for Northern Ireland, Belfast

Cecilia Clegg, research coordinator, Moving beyond Sectarianism Project, Irish School of Ecumenics, Belfast

Alan Ferguson, chief executive, Northern Ireland Association for Mental Health, Belfast (by telephone)

Mari Fitzduff, director, Community Relations Council, Belfast

Billy Hutchinson, director, Springfield Inter-Community Development Project, Belfast (by telephone)

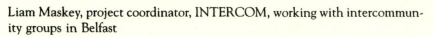

Liam Maskey, project coordinator, INTERCOM, working with intercommunity groups in Belfast

Brendan McAllister, director, The Mediation Network for Northern Ireland, Belfast

Martin McAnallen, probation officer, Probation Board of Northern Ireland, Belfast (e-mail communication, July 19, 1997)

Aideen McGinley, chief executive, Fermanagh District Partnership Board, Enniskillen (by telephone)

Geraldine Smyth, president, Irish School of Ecumenics, Dublin

David Stevens, general secretary, Irish Council of Churches, and member of the Support Body for Mennonite Witness in Ireland, Belfast

Evangelical Contribution on Northern Ireland (ECONI)
    David Porter, director
    Janet Norris, member of Central Coordinating Group
    Derek Poole, development officer
    Alwyn Thomson, research officer

Interviews were conducted October 31–November 6, 1996.

# Appendix A

## *Who Are the Mennonites?*

JOSEPH S. MILLER

THROUGHOUT THE WORLD TODAY, there are more than one million Mennonites, Brethren in Christ, Amish, and Hutterites, who are the progeny of the Reformation radicals known by the epithet Anabaptists. Today, these spiritual children of the Radical Reformation are found on every continent of the globe. They first spoke German and Dutch, but the worldwide family of Mennonites now speaks more than seventy-eight languages, and one of the fastest growing regions for Mennonites today is Africa. When average North Americans or Europeans think of Mennonites, they often conjure up images of the "plain people" who drive a horse and buggy. While this image is an important part of the Mennonite family, it does not capture the diversity of Mennonites in North America or the world.

Mennonites trace their roots to the 1520s Reformed movement in Switzerland. The women and men who began what would become known as the Mennonite church wanted an even more radical commitment to what they viewed as New Testament Christianity than Reformed church leader Ulrich Zwingli would tolerate.

### Rebaptizers → Anabaptists → Mennonites

On a Saturday night, January 21, 1525, Conrad Grebel, a one-time follower of Zwingli, along with a number of other radical Christian reformers, gathered for prayer and Bible study. One of the group asked Grebel to rebaptize him as an adult believer. With that baptism, the Anabaptist, or rebaptizing, church was begun. Rebaptism as an adult meant a formal break with the official state-sanctioned churches, and Mennonites began experiencing persecution, torture, and death at the hands of church and state authorities. In spite of horrific persecution, most Mennonite groups held firmly to the belief that Christians could not use violence, even in self-defense. When they studied the life of Christ and Christ's teachings, they heard a clear call to love one's enemy and an existential mandate to "overcome evil with good."

As the Mennonites were driven across Europe, they witnessed to their new way of Christian faith in life and word. This "third way" of Christianity touched a raw nerve in a society in which common people were experiencing a growing incongruity with the sixteenth-century feudal structures of both the state and the church. Thousands joined or were influenced by the Mennonites, who taught that ordinary women and men could serve as priests. They audaciously claimed that when a group of believers gathered in the name of Christ, studied the Scriptures, prayed together, and asked the Holy Spirit to guide them, they could know and live out the will of God.

The significance of these new Christian circles of believers cannot be over-emphasized in understanding Mennonite history and thought. There were, declared the iconoclastic Mennonites, no holy people, places, or things. What was holy and what could be trusted was God, the Bible, and the community of faith. These small, unpretentious Bible study and prayer circles, guided by God's Holy Spirit, were the locus, said Mennonites, where God's word was revealed and God's will discerned.

One of the most important leaders of this new movement was Menno Simons, a Catholic priest in the Netherlands who broke away to join the new Anabaptist movement. Simons wrote prolifically about the new free church movement, stressing that Christians needed to be faithful to God, study the life of Christ, and diligently follow in Christ's footsteps. Simons's name became so connected to the new movement that many Anabaptists began calling themselves Mennonites.

For Simons and other Anabaptists, the cross of Christ, that evocative Christian symbol, became wedded to two great inseparable truths. First, they agreed with other Christians that Christ's cross made possible the propitiation of the sin and failure of humans. Second, the Mennonites proclaimed that discipleship was found in the cross, not only in Christ's cross but in the cross of the one who sought to follow in Christ's footsteps. The cross of personal discipleship became a touchstone of such potency that, 500 years after Simons's own day, his twentieth-century spiritual children could still be found singing in worship the rhetorical question: "Must Jesus bear the cross alone, and all the world go free? No. There's a cross for everyone, and there's a cross for me" (*Mennonite Hymnal*, 1969, p. 345).

As Mennonites continued their search for tolerant places to practice their faith, many made their way to George III's North America (1683) and to Catherine II's Russia (1762). Both the American and Russian Mennonites prospered in ethnic/religious enclaves that eschewed much contact with their non-Mennonite neighbors.

## Structure of the Mennonite Church in North America

As a result of the streams of history, migration, and theological divergences, there have always been a wide variety of Mennonites. In North America, there are more than a hundred different groups, ranging from the ultratraditionalists, with their horse and buggy, to Mennonites who, for all intents and purposes, have become assimilated into the larger American society.

Mennonites in North America have been structured rather loosely. Most congregations relate to a conference, which is a regional grouping of congregations, and to their larger denominational headquarters. The four main denominations are the Mennonite Church, General Conference Mennonite Church, Mennonite Brethren, and Old Order Mennonites. In the summer of 1998, the General Conference Mennonite Church and the Mennonite Church merged into the Mennonite Church USA.

The variegated Mennonite experience in North America has never been able to agree on style of clothing, mode of transportation, or design of churches. What has held Mennonites together more than anything else has been their commitment to what one Mennonite writer called the "Anabaptist Vision," expressed in a theological triumvirate of a life of discipleship, a voluntary church, and an ethic of love and nonresistance (Bender, 1944).

## Mennonite Missions

The first North American Mennonite mission effort was begun in 1872 by the General Conference Mennonite Church. In the succeeding years, other Mennonite groups began formal mission agencies, with some sponsoring small efforts involving only one or two workers and others sponsoring efforts with many more missionaries. These activities were funded by donations from individuals and congregations. Today, several of the larger mission boards hire full-time staff members whose sole task is to help raise financial support for their mission agencies.

In 1987, more than a century after its founding, the General Conference Mennonite Church mission agency had 162 workers overseas. The Mennonite Brethren Board of Missions, begun in 1878, had 149 workers overseas a hundred years later. The Mennonite Board of Missions, begun by the Mennonite church in 1882, had 130 overseas workers in 1987. In 1914, the Lancaster Conference of the Mennonite Church began its own mission board, known today as Eastern Mennonite Missions.

The mandate of these denominational mission boards is primarily to teach and preach the message of the Good News of Christ. While not as deeply involved in relief and development as their sister service agency, the Mennonite Central Committee (MCC), the various mission boards have strong elements within their programs that relate to peace and justice issues, which are at times similar to MCC's peace and justice efforts.

## Ethos of Service

From their beginnings, Mennonites have had a strong sense of what they called "mutual aid," communal support for members in times of spiritual and financial hardship. It became axiomatic that no member of the Mennonite church family should ever be allowed to become destitute. This concern for what Mennonites called "brotherhood"—more recently, "peoplehood"—was directed primarily toward their own members. More muted, but always quietly present, were examples of Mennonites offering assistance to their non-Mennonite neighbors. An Anabaptist in Switzerland, who was later martyred for his faith, wrote in 1528: "If they know of anyone who is in need, whether or not he is a member of their church, they believe it their duty, out of love to God, to render help" (*Mennonite Encyclopedia*, 1990, p. 858). One such example occurred during the American Revolutionary War. As told by their family, Mennonites Anna Eshelman Baer and her preacher husband, John, died in 1778 of a contagious disease they contracted while ministering to soldiers wounded in the battle of Brandywine.

In the 1890s, North American Mennonites became involved in the first major organized relief effort that was not directed toward their fellow Mennonites. Famine in India, by 1898, was drawing the attention of many North American Protestant churches. A Mennonite agency was organized under the rubric Home and Foreign Relief Commission, which was an inter-Mennonite relief effort that included many of the North American denominations of Mennonites.

## Mennonite Central Committee

Sustained cooperation in relief and development efforts among the various Mennonite groups began in the 1920s as a result of the desperate need of Mennonites in Russia, who were starving as a result of the turmoil and revolution there. North American Mennonites created a new inter-Mennonite agency, the Mennonite Central Committee, to respond to their needs. MCC subsequently became an important vehicle for the shared desire of those same North American groups to offer relief not just to fellow Mennonites but to others throughout the world. MCC has grown expeditiously over the decades of the mid-twentieth century.

The earlier mission groups had tended to be somewhat more concerned with "making people into Christians" and only collaterally involved in relief and development. The reverse has been the case for the Mennonite Central Committee. The organization's mandate has been relief and development and, to a lesser degree, Christian evangelism. By 1995, more than 900 people were serving as full-time volunteers or salaried workers with MCC in fifty-seven countries. The annual MCC budget in 1995 was $43 million. Perhaps most intriguing are the thousands of additional people who regularly volunteer a day or two with MCC in a vast array of projects, such as staffing used clothing shops or packing containers of food, clothing, and medicines to be shipped overseas. Several times a year, most Mennonite churches have an MCC work day in which all members are invited to volunteer a day of manual labor.

Money is provided for MCC by individual and congregational donations. In addition, explains Donald B. Kraybill, money comes through a variegated financial typology, which makes MCC possible:

> Thirty-seven communities hold annual relief sales, which in 1994 totaled $3.5 million. Since their beginnings, some 700 auctions have generated more than $55 million. In 1994 Selfhelp Crafts (now called Ten Thousand Villages) created the equivalent of close to 11,000 full-time jobs for third world artisans. Some 8,000 volunteers operate 84 thrift shops, and 20 communities have built 40 Houses Against Hunger, which generated contributions of $3.5 million. (1995, p. 8)

One particularly winsome project in recent years has been what MCC calls Penny Power. Children in churches are encouraged to collect pennies for MCC projects and are told how pennies help purchase chickens and seeds for Southern hemisphere farmers. Every year, thousands of dollars are raised in Mennonite and Brethren in Christ churches through children's pennies.

Structurally, Mennonites have tended to think in terms of relief and development, with Christian missions somewhat separate. They have at times considered MCC as their avenue for relief and development and have set up separate denominational mission programs to do the more traditional evangelizing of their Christian faith. Yet the lines between relief and Christian missions have never been completely delineated for Mennonites.

There has been a willingness to live with the creative tensions between relief and development work and evangelizing, knowing that in the final analysis the impetus that pushes Mennonites and Brethren in Christ toward relief and development is their Christian commitment. Because MCC functions as something of a consortium and includes the most traditional and the most progressive in the Anabaptist family, the organization has held its evangelizing rather more gently.

In reference to MCC's organizational structure, one writer has said, only half-jokingly:

> Mennonite Central Committee really shouldn't work. It's an organization of paradoxes and ambiguities, one I suspect some management consultant might have shut down long ago. Take, for example, its structure. MCC is controlled by a board of 38. But there's also MCC Canada with its own board of 30—and a US counterpart with an equal number. Add to this five provincial offices in Canada and four regional ones in the US, all with their own boards, plus. . . . But you get the point. (J. Lorne Peachey, 1995, p. 20)

The writer goes on to say that MCC actually does work for three reasons. First, because Anabaptists feel deeply that their faith must be put into action. Second, in spite of what appears to be a complicated structure, MCC works because it is a grassroots-oriented organization that is responsive to its stakeholders' desires and interests. Finally, MCC works because it benefits from the collective efforts in relief and development of a diverse group of Amish, Brethren in Christ, and Mennonites.

MCC's volunteers normally give a minimum of three years for an overseas assignment and two years for a North American assignment. Volunteers receive no salary during their time of service, although MCC does provide their food, housing, medical care, transportation, and a small stipend for personal spending money. MCC chooses its volunteers carefully, looking for men and women who are committed Christians, who are committed to nonviolence, and who are culturally sensitive.

# Notes

## Chapter One

1. This article was written while Yoder was living in Valdoie, France. In it, he writes, "Our nonconformity should consist not in ignorance or withdrawal, but in the exercise of independent judgment and continual application of basic Christian truth" (1954, pp. 1209, 1221).
2. During World War II, 4,665 Mennonites served in Civilian Public Service camps.
3. See also Williams and Mergal (1957, p. 141). Williams records the tale of Anabaptist Michael Sattler. The charge against Sattler was disloyalty, in part because Sattler stated that he would not under any condition defend Austria against a Turkish invasion.
4. See also the extensive collection at Bethel College Historical Library, North Newton, Kansas, of oral history interviews with men who served in CPS.
5. This textbook incorporated information gathered through experiments on CPS men who volunteered to serve as human guinea pigs.
6. The Mennonite Disaster Service was conceived at a Sunday School picnic in Hesston, Kansas. A number of the class members had recently returned home from their CPS assignments and wanted to continue to find ways to serve society. With the helping hand of MCC, community people make themselves available for a day or two to help clean up areas that have experienced natural disasters (Roupp, 1978).
7. I would argue that Mennonites to some degree continue to hold that Christian humility is a necessary part of being faithful to the way of Christ. A healthy Christian humility has allowed Mennonites to enter other cultures as a people ready to genuinely listen and learn from their hosts.
8. Some ten years later, John Paul Lederach would cite the Irish experience as illustrative of how skills and culture must converge. He referred to how the early work of Barry Hart and others was appropriately becoming "Irishized" (1995c, p. 92).

## Chapter Two

1. The U.S. Department of War was renamed the Department of Defense in 1947.
2. The intent in 1942 was to build a massive TNT dump; in 1951 it was to build a $60 million expanded air base. The account here deals only with the 1942 expe-

rience. In 1951, the site was rejected because of the large number of sinkholes found to exist in the limestone soil.

3. Both quotes are from Mary Jean Kraybill, "Bosslers Mennonite Church and the TNT Plant Crisis of 1942: The Making of a Myth" (1974). Kraybill's sources are newspaper articles and the Lancaster County historian, H. M. J. Klein, who described the tearful colonel in a paper entitled "The Army Has a Heart," read before the Lancaster County Historical Society on December 8, 1946.

4. Mary Jean Kraybill notes that the War Department was at an early and fairly tentative stage in their exploration of possible sites and that the lobbying effort by the larger community against the effort was an intensive one.

5. Grandpa Kraybill always said at election time, "I'll vote on my knees." Like most Mennonites today, he believed that God works primarily through the church to accomplish divine purpose, rather than through government. Unlike most Mennonites today, Grandpa and his generation felt this belief ruled out any participation in governing processes.

6. Inconsistencies in stance toward government and the military within the Mennonite community must be acknowledged. While refusing to fight in World War II, for example, most Mennonites in our area supported war rationing and a few even purchased war bonds as a way to support a cause believed by many to be just. The more skeptical view of government described in the text reflects what I believe has been the historical understanding of Mennonites and the understanding of those who significantly shaped me as a youth: my family and many in our congregation, as well as the generation of young Mennonites whose response to the Vietnam war played a key role in moving Mennonites towards a more active expression of our peace convictions.

7. The 1980s and 1990s saw a proliferation and decentralization of Mennonite peace efforts to local peace centers, colleges, and seminaries and also saw a greater prominence of peacebuilding as a theme guiding the larger MCC as well as various Mennonite mission organizations.

8. Adams's experiences are recorded in some detail in his book *At the Heart of the Whirlwind* (1976). Fortunately, Laue lived long enough to enjoy some of the recognition he so richly deserved for his efforts. But his close friend Adams, who pioneered conflict resolution initiatives under Methodist and National Council of Churches auspices throughout the 1970s at places like Wounded Knee, Miami Beach, and Kent State, died in 1983, largely unrecognized for his pioneering efforts.

9. Conflict resolution practitioners differ, of course, as to how far cooperative conflict resolution approaches can go. Nevertheless, I think it safe to generalize that people in the field believe that it is possible to expand the range of situations amenable to nonviolent resolution of conflicts substantially further than their fellow citizens commonly believe. To hold such optimism regarding the possibility of nonviolent resolution of conflicts as to refer to it as a "way of life" (which, of course, not all practitioners do) is to assert that the principle of nonviolent conflict resolution is of more than utilitarian value. It holds deeper status as a moral principal. The point at which this claim is made is where conflict resolution enters the realm of the difficult philosophical issues referred to above.

## Chapter Three

1. The Moravian logo is "Our lamb has conquered, let us follow Him."

## Chapter Four

1. The young man stayed with us for several weeks and then went on to Lesotho, where he was granted refugee status.

## Chapter Five

1. I have given this quote in the form in which it has been passed on many times; it became almost a Troubles slogan and symbol of despair. It is worth noting, however, that Rose immediately added to this quote: "at least no solution recognizable in those more fortunate parts of the Anglo-American world that are governed with consensus." Rose wanted to shock us into seeing the enormous difficulty of creating a workable politics in Northern Ireland, but he was not actually counseling despair.
2. In 1989, I arranged to see Alan Ford, a young historian of the Irish Reformation, whose research interests coincided with mine. Meeting over coffee in a busy Dublin cafe, Ford asked what I was doing in Ireland. Opting for candor, I explained that I had come to Ireland in 1980, that I worked for the Mennonite church, that Mennonites had supported me to do a Ph.D. in Irish history, and that my job description was to use what I had learned to further Catholic-Protestant reconciliation and church renewal. Ford threw himself back in his chair and exclaimed, "What an enlightened church!" Not language I would ordinarily use, I thought, but yes, maybe it's true.

## Chapter Seven

1. For a more complete history of MCC involvement in Central America, see Robert S. Kreider and Rachel Waltner Goosen, "A Young Church Awakens to Crisis: Honduras," in *Hungry, Thirsty, a Stranger* (1988).
2. For a more complete account of the peacemaking efforts between the Sandinista government and the East Coast leaders, see Nichols (1994).
3. The Alternatives to Violence Project began in 1975 as a Quaker initiative in New York state prisons, training inmates in self-esteem, group building, nonviolence, and conflict resolution.
4. For a broader discussion, see Chupp (1991).

## Chapter Ten

1. General Aideed died August 1, 1996, after being wounded in battle in Mogadishu; he was succeeded by his son, Hussein Aideed.
2. Somalis have an oral culture, second to none, which transmits information, rumor or truth, with incredible speed. In poetry, Somalis record history, clan feuds, major events—and in poetry, they can make peace. Poetry plays a major part in communication and is still being practiced and shared among Somalis today. A poet is highly esteemed among Somalis. In Somalia, one does not seek the truth as much as one observes how people perceive the rumors and how they react to them. To be able to argue well, to tell elaborate stories, and to be clever in understanding and playing games with words are admirable characteristics among the Somali people.

Chapter Eleven

1. From a 1993 survey conducted by the author of ninth graders at Gray D. Allison Elementary and Junior High School in Monrovia, Liberia. This survey is detailed further in Hart (1995).
2. Of course, there were numerous factors leading up to the war that were not happy for many members of these ethnic groups, especially related to the 1983 and 1985 coup attempts to overthrow the Doe government.
3. The terms *tribe* or *tribal* are generally regarded as pejorative, but Liberians still use these terms to describe or explain their ethnic groups.
4. Americo-Liberians are descendants of freed African-American slaves, who settled on what was then known as Africa's Grain Coast beginning in 1821. With their sponsors, the American Colonization Society (ACS), an organization made up of American politicals, religious leaders, and slave-holding plantation owners, freed American blacks sought a location where they could be completely free. The ACS and the settlers also wanted to introduce Protestant Christianity in the region and to begin a "civilizing process" among the indigenous population. Americo-Liberians governed the region until 1980.
5. One clear example of this difference was the use of land. Indigenous Liberians had no concept of the sale of land. The American officers of the ACS, who were negotiating for the early settlers, viewed land as a commodity, the importance of which was in the "ownership" of land and the establishment of a permanent and secure place of residence. The indigenous groups' perspective was that land was sacred, and it was used within the framework of lineage associations, customs, and traditions. The sale of land had no meaning in an indigenous society that used land communally.
6. In Liberia, as well as in other contexts, there is first a political manipulation. Then, a certain segment of society, usually the military, which is under the greatest pressure from above and receiving the strongest propaganda, accepts this rhetoric as its own. Political and military leaders know this and keep the pressure on until it is achieved. But they may—and often do—lose control of the engine they have constructed. This can cause fractionalization of the military, which usually prolongs war and affects the civilian population even more negatively.
7. CHAL's prewar programs were Environmental Health Care, Curative and Preventative Health Care, and Information and Communication. It then added a psychosocial component.
8. Mulbah, Subah, and Isaacson brought strong beliefs in biblical faith and healing to this work. But they also called for the application of psychological processes to our trauma-healing and reconciliation workshops.
9. In 1987, I had been sent to the Republic of Ireland and Northern Ireland for four months by MCC. This led to an interest in ethnic-related conflict, which I pursued in graduate school. My initial doctoral dissertation proposal was on ethnic tension and threats to ethnic identity in the Northern Ireland context.
10. In the Schumm report to CHAL, the CHAL Support Group, and MCC, these understandings were first presented.
11. CHAL had used the Training for Transformation elicitive approach for some time. This was also the heart of the community-based mediation model of the Mennonites.
12. Also during this time, I worked with UNICEF to develop a three-month psychosocial program that was to be connected to a local training college in Monrovia

and a university in central Liberia. The implementation of this project was delayed because of renewed fighting, but it finally began in early 1993. Nurses, social workers, pastors, and others working or living in Monrovia (the fighting prevented it being implemented in central Liberia) attended morning courses on trauma healing and reconciliation, workshop design, drama as an educational and conciliation methodology, conflict resolution, etc. I taught two three-month sections on trauma awareness and healing and reconciliation across ethnic divides. I drew on the CHAL workshop experiences and invited traditional leaders and healers into the course to explain their understandings and methods of conflict resolution and community healing. This psychosocial program continues at the time of this writing, and some 170 persons have graduated from it.

13. Monrovia was attacked in late October 1992. I was determined to stay and support my CHAL colleagues, despite the fact that representatives of the American embassy were calling for the evacuation of all U.S. citizens. But my determination to stay was cut short both by the danger presented by the incoming rockets and by the fact that my CHAL colleagues encouraged me to leave. They did not need the extra burden of looking after me while they were trying to survive. I understood this but nevertheless felt guilty for leaving and temporarily settling in Côte d'Ivoire. I attempted to assuage some of this guilt by providing help to Liberian refugees fleeing to border towns in Côte d'Ivoire. I also stayed in daily touch by radio with the CHAL office in Monrovia. I returned to Monrovia in January l993.

14. As Mennonites, we hold Scripture and the works, death, and resurrection of Jesus as central to our faith. Our biblical understanding of community is also central to this faith, since it is about the importance of interdependence for spiritual and practical support. Community for Mennonites is key to our attempt to identify with the early church and its sense of communal worship, with sharing and encouragement, as well as a strong recognition that we need this base from which to work in a world of pain and often extreme need.

15. Hodges's contention is that not everyone in Liberia had or would have psychological problems. But he speaks to the duration of conflict resulting in "greater prevalence and persistence of disorders" (1991, p. 3). This latter point is of key importance. When fighting goes on and on and persons see no end in sight, as was the situation in Liberia after October 1992 until the cease-fire in 1996, psychological problems are compounded, and stress and traumatic reactions will begin to emerge, even in those persons who previously had not been traumatized.

16. Ethnicity is often manipulated by those in power or wanting to achieve power, and "ethnic conflict" is the name they give to the conflicts that are generated. The term is also frequently used by the media or governments outside the context to describe (incorrectly) a conflict that is actually much more multi-faceted and complex.

## Chapter Twelve

1. In Mennonite circles, the term *peacemaking* includes a broad range of activities, including relief and development work, education, pursuit of social justice, advocacy-oriented nonviolent direct action, and intermediary work in mediation and reconciliation.

2. The CPT mandate, as printed in the organization's brochure, is as follows:
   1. We believe the mandate to proclaim the Gospel of repentance, salvation and reconciliation includes a strengthened Biblical peace witness.

2. We believe that faithfulness to what Jesus taught and modeled calls us to more active peacemaking.

3. We believe a renewed commitment to the gospel of peace calls us to new forms of public witness which may include nonviolent direct action.

4. We believe the establishment of Christian Peacemaker Teams is an important new dimension for our ongoing peace and justice ministries. . . .
   To be authentic, such peacemaking should be rooted in and supported by congregations and churchwide agencies.

3. Because of the number of ongoing projects, CPT, at the time of this writing, is still without a pool of volunteers who can drop everything and move into a new project as needed.

4. These have included a prayer and fasting campaign for Haiti, annual Christmas campaigns against violent toys, and the Campaign for Secure Dwellings, which matches North American churches with Palestinian families facing the demolition of their homes because of Israeli settlement expansion.

5. Conventional wisdom attributed this to Clinton's 1993 embarrassment in Somalia, where eighteen U.S. soldiers were killed in intense street fighting. Revelations in 1995 by Emmanuel Constant, leader of the paramilitary group Front for Haitian Progress and Resistance indicate that the CIA may have supplied Clinton with false information, leading him to believe the armed paramilitaries were more dangerous than they actually were (see Weiner, 1995, p. 6).

6. The other participating groups included Pax Christi, Peace Brigades International, Witness for Peace, and the Washington Office on Haiti.

7. Devotions usually included prayer, readings, silence, and singing—the proportions of each depending on the person leading them.

8. It is worth mentioning that the project in Jeremie did not represent the totality of CPT's Haitian experience. Our contacts in Port-au-Prince forwarded our reports to the press and connected these reports to the larger picture of what was happening in Haiti. CPT also sent short-term delegations to Haiti to learn about the situation there, do public witnesses, and report back to their congregations about what they had seen. In the United States, CPT staff spent hours getting out articles and alerting churches to prayer-action campaigns.

9. Front for Haitian Progress and Resistance. Ostensibly, FRAPH was the political wing of the military. However, most of the violent attacks we witnessed or heard about in Jeremie were perpetrated by FRAPH members.

10. The Israeli settlers in town call it the Cave of Machpelah (see Gen. 23). Muslims, Jews, and the Christian crusaders have all identified it as a holy site for the last millennium. As is true in other cases, one's terminology defines one's political stance.

11. They may have fled alongside Muslims also targeted by the Inquisition. Several places in Hebron, such as Qurtuba (Cordoba) school and the Al Andalus mall, retain traces of the Muslim heritage in Spain.

12. The Hebronite version of the massacre says that the Arab mob was composed of riffraff brought from the outside by the British, because they had been unable to play Jews and Arabs in Hebron against each other as they had in the rest of Palestine. I spoke to an old man who had been a *Shabbos goy* for a Jewish family (i.e., he would turn off their lights during the Sabbath). As a young adolescent, he said, he witnessed British soldiers opening the gates of the Jewish Quarter and telling the mob to go inside and "get" the Jews. The names of the Jews saved by their neighbors may be found in *Sefer Hebron* (Auissar, 1970, pp. 424–426).

13. Bloc of the Faithful.

14. This is the official figure released by the Israeli government. Palestinian sources put the figure higher. Several eyewitnesses claimed there was a second gunman involved. IDF soldiers claimed they fired in the air as the worshipers fled the mosque in panic, but several witnesses claimed that the soldiers fired into the crowd as the people fled.

15. Initially, we chose to do so because we simply needed a quiet place. Later, we came to feel that there was some significance in our choice. People had murdered and others had died because two religions were fighting over the supposed burial place of Abraham and his family. By worshiping in the park, we demonstrated our conviction that one did not need to be in a certain place to be close to God.

16. Dubboya Street connects the settlements of Tel Rumeida and Beit Hadassah. Historically, there have been many violent encounters on this street between settlers (or right-wing visitors to Hebron) and the Palestinian residents and shopkeepers on the street. It is also the location from which Palestinian commandos launched the attack on the yeshiva students in 1980 (discussed above).

17. The names have been changed.

18. This particular team member wore an Amish-style beard, similar to those worn by religious Muslims.

19. At the request of those who invited us, the inviting body or bodies shall remain anonymous.

20. This was untrue, according to our sources at the university. Administrators had never come to the Civil Administration to ask for the doors to be opened. "It is not for them to give permission. It is our right," a friend said.

21. We wore the *keffiyahs* (checkered head coverings that some Palestinian men wear) on our backpacks so that Palestinians would not mistake us for settlers. Many of the settlers had strong reactions to them. One woman said it was the equivalent of wearing gang colors. Even one of our Israeli peace activist friends told us he felt uncomfortable with us when we displayed them. He told us it showed we had definitely "sided" with the Palestinians.

22. On November 4, 1995, the same day Yitzhak Rabin was assassinated, a woman who had come to join the team after I left was knocked to the ground by young Israeli men, and the Palestinian teenage girl to whom she had been speaking was dragged along the ground by her hair braid. The young men kicked her as she screamed. The *New York Times* later conflated the two attacks in an article about Yigal Amir, the young man who assassinated Prime Minister Rabin:

> Such trips to Hebron were one of the [Amir] brothers' frequent activities. Several weeks ago, witnesses say, the two swaggered in the lead of such a group, some of whom broke ranks and attacked a line of Christian women peace activists who regularly placed themselves between the Jews and Palestinians, knocking two of them down and dragging them by their hair. (Kifner, 1995, p. 12)

Since the article refers to this attack as happening some weeks before Rabin's assassination, it is probably referring to the one involving my teammate and myself.

23. In 1995, CPT received an invitation from Chechen women's groups and from an organization composed of the mothers of Russian soldiers. It was the first invitation received from representatives on both sides of a conflict.

24. One of the Washington team members, however, had a bicycle wheel stolen by teenagers who later told him, "That's what you get for being an Orange Hat." (The Orange Hats are local citizen patrols in D.C. neighborhoods.)

25. Among Israelis, for example, one finds Orthodox Zionist Israelis, Orthodox anti-

Zionist Israelis, the secular Zionist left, the secular anti-Zionist left, the religious Zionist left—all with different attitudes toward the peace process. Likewise, among Palestinians, there are Fatah supporters in favor of the Oslo Accords, Fatah supporters against the Oslo Accords, Hamas, Communists, etc.

26. I spoke with the Hebron Solidarity Committee about this. Their position is that Israelis living in Hebron—even if they are sympathetic to Palestinians—are essentially settlers. They also said that it was not their place to serve as a co-inviting body, since Hebron was a Palestinian city.

27. I found this out after about the third time that a soldier said, "You don't like us very much, do you?"

28. In Hebron, the police are responsible for protecting both Palestinians and settlers. The soldiers have orders to protect the settlers only. For this reason, while Palestinians view the police as ineffective, they do not resent them in quite the same way that they resent the IDF.

29. In Washington, D.C., we faced a similar dilemma when neighborhood Orange Hat patrols invited armed police officers to walk with them.

30. Almost everyone we knew in the West Bank and Israel spoke a little English.

31. A nun who worked in Port-au-Prince once told a friend of mine that she thought maybe the best thing for Haiti would be for all the aid and mission organizations to pull out, because she believed that these agencies had relieved just enough misery over the years to keep the pot from boiling over.

32. The four CPC objectives are (1) to advance the cause of lasting peace by giving skilled, courageous support to peacemakers working locally in situations of conflict; (2) to provide congregations with firsthand information and resources for responding to worldwide situations of conflict and to urge their active involvement; (3) to interpret a nonviolent perspective to the media; and (4) to inspire people and governments to discard violence as a means of settling differences in favor of nonviolent action.

33. One of my coworkers in Haiti asked whether "cultural worriedness" was a better term than "cultural sensitivity" to describe the place it had in our deliberations.

34. Elsewhere, there are dialogue efforts, such as those of the Center for Rapprochement in Beit Sahour. There are even dialogue efforts taking place in the settlement of Efrat. There is a fundamental recognition in these groups, however, that the other side has a right to be where it is.

*Chapter Thirteen*

I am grateful for the insights of all the contributors to this volume. I particularly appreciate the suggestions of several who read and commented on my chapter: Mark Chupp, Ron Kraybill, John Paul Lederach, Joseph Liechty, and Cynthia Sampson.

*Chapter Fourteen*

1. A full list of those deemed immune, as included in Gregory's papal bull *De Treuga et Pace* (Of Truces and Peace) consisted of "clerics, monks, friars, other religious, pilgrims, travelers, merchants and peasants cultivating the soil" (see Meron, 1993, p. 91).

2. In some cases, such as Somalia or Liberia, the level of conflict and violence has led to such a complete collapse of the political system and the division of the country

into warring fiefdoms accompanied by generalized banditry that the term *collapsed state* has been coined to indicate an extreme arena of conflict.

3. I have tried to deal with the theoretical neglect of important structural asymmetries between unequal adversaries elsewhere but have avoided the attendant ethical issues. This probably reflects my own moral ambiguity in the peace and justice debate. Is one always ethically correct to support the underdog?

*Chapter Fifteen*

1. Ron Kraybill (1997) rightly points out my bias toward "proof texts" in religious life. He suggests that, more deeply than text, *Nachfolge Christi*, following the way of Jesus in his dealings with enemies, was a key resource for Anabaptist justification for this behavior. I agree and assume the centrality of *imitatio dei* here, but I suggest simply that the text is the only way for believers to learn what the way of Jesus was.

2. Several Pauline texts demonstrate the hermeneutic interaction of Paul and his Hebrew biblical sources: "If someone returns evil for good, evil will not depart from his house"; "If your enemy is hungry, give him bread to eat"; "Do not rejoice at the fall of your enemy"; "If you see the donkey of your enemy struggling under its burden, you shall surely lift it up with him" (Prov. 17:13, 25:21, 24:17; Exod. 23:5).

3. The Hebrew term for "pursued" is *nirdaf*, and it is questionable from the context whether this is, in fact, a moral statement about God protecting the persecuted. Early rabbinic interpretation from the first centuries C.E., however, confirms that God sides with anyone being persecuted or pursued, no matter how "wicked" they may be. In other words, there is a divine preference in all circumstances for the persecuted (see *Leviticus Rabbah* 27:5). This interpretation of the verse is probably familiar to Mennonites, although I have not found a source for this.

4. It should also be noted that this combination of faith and group experience with persecution, which leads to resistance to violence, is evident among those European Christians who risked their lives to save Jews during the Holocaust. Resistance to evil and saving lives is a slightly different religious and ethical activity than peacemaking among Mennonites. They share a common commitment, however, to engage the world nonviolently and to resist violence, and they also seem to share a willingness to be different from or go against the dominant cultural trends around them that are violent. Furthermore, they seem to share a high level of empathy for the persecuted (see Hallie [1979] on the character of the residents of Le Chambon). Most of the research on altruism in these circumstances stresses the importance of loving family environments, education in moral values, and a general prosocial orientation, which seem to give rise to this kind of behavior (see Oliner et al., 1992). But I would argue that not enough attention has been given to the awareness of being separated, different, and/or persecuted as key motivators of human empathy, which leads individuals and groups to nonviolent interaction, altruism, and peacemaking. The theological worldview of these groups builds itself around the cognitive and emotional orientation that is unique to their historical experience. This is the only way that I see to explain how deeply embedded this posture is as a Christian faith for some Christian groups or families, while at the same time, Christian faith is being used by others, in the very same period a few miles away, to justify theologically the most brutal racist violence of the twentieth

century (see Heschel [1995] on the theological program of de-Judaizing Christianity). The Confessing Church declared in May 1939:

> In the realm of faith there exists the sharp opposition between the message of Jesus Christ and the Jewish religion. . . . In the realm of volkish life an earnest and responsible racial politics is required for the preservation of the purity of our people. (Heschel, 1995, p. 4)

This subject deserves a separate study. Philippe Lasserre, who as a little boy in northern France played a key role in his family's scheme to lead to safety approximately thirty Jews over a period of several years, at considerable risk to their lives, suggested to me recently that his family's experience of and awareness of being different as Protestants and the history associated with that in France gave them a special level of concern for the persecuted that combined seamlessly with their religious faith (1997). On the evolution of Christian wars, persecution, and pacifism, see Bainton (1960).

5. It must be acknowledged, however, that Mennonites, few in number, are growing only because of their converts. Mennonites today speak more than seventy-eight languages, whereas originally they only spoke German and Dutch, and the fastest growing segment of the community is in Africa. This is clearly the result of serious mission activity for conversion to Christianity or Mennonitism. There are only a couple of million Mennonites in the world, and this mission activity may be vital to their survival, unlike other Christian denominations. It should also be noted that the need to create new members seems to be going hand in hand with oral reports that I have received of Mennonite converts who are actually unaware of the pacifist element of the Anabaptist tradition, which is the central spiritual foundation for the Mennonites that we are studying in this volume. What this means for the future character of Mennonite belief and practice remains to be seen.

   It should be noted that many of the authors responded to my initially rather unexamined use of the word *mission*. Clearly, the concept of mission is deeply important to them. Furthermore, one of them, Joseph Liechty, is committed to *evangelism*. Here we see an intense commitment to a nonaggressive understanding of evangelism. Liechty writes: "I see evangelism as involving proclamation, invitation, and inclusion, none of which is necessarily problematic, all of which can be" (1997). He defines *mission* as

   > including all activity that seeks to make known, live out, embody, or give expression to God's will for the world. Thus peace work is an essential part of mission, which can be in tension with evangelism, but does not necessarily need to be. (1997)

6. From its earliest roots, American Mennonite missionizing appears to have focused on the teaching of pacifism (see Driedger and Kraybill, 1994, p. 29).

7. There is yet another interesting parallel here to Jewish values rooted in the Old Testament conception of the people as a "kingdom of priests and a holy nation," which is based on Exodus 19:6, with *holy* interpreted in its original meaning as "separated" or "consecrated." It suggests a special destiny in the world but a separated one. Other sources, however, such as Genesis 18:19 and Isaiah 42:6, convey the notion of a people with a mission, "a light unto the nations [*or la-goyim*]," teaching the "path of God [*derekh YHVH*]." One mandate suggests active integration in the world, while the other implies separation. Traditional Orthodoxy of the last 2,000 years tended to see the separation as key, with the mission being expressed by example, by distant example. Modern liberal Judaism has tended to

emphasize the mission, though not to convert the world to Judaism but to teach prophetic social values, while also maintaining a distinct religious identity. This seems to me to be an interesting hermeneutic parallel to Amish and modern Mennonite divisions on this subject.

8. I want to highlight Hart's suggestion that we embrace the "positive" suggestions for peacemaking of elders. Religiously based conflict resolution, in its natural sympathy to what is premodern, should not assume that what comes culturally and religiously before colonialism is always good. It seems to be that the elders in Hart's case study have ways of coping with conflict that are far more attuned to their culture than anything we could imagine and that this resource has been grossly neglected by the international community. It is also possible that there were in the premodern period traditional outgroups who suffered at the hands of an unjust social order. Thus we might, in our humility, want to listen to and learn from native traditions, but that is not the same as completely surrendering our sense of what is just and unjust. This is a constant dilemma in international aid, development, and social reconstruction, which has not been examined sufficiently by members of the development community, including the progressives among them. In point of fact, it should remain a dilemma, where the individual intervenor should always keep in tension his need to listen and elicit, on one side, and on the other, his need, or obligation, to maintain his own ethical judgment.

9. It also occurs to me that Mennonites have certain advantages for healing and learning from their pain that other abused groups have lacked. They emphasized to me that their worst suffering, on the whole, occurred centuries ago, and time does heal wounded groups to a degree. Second, their separated and rather safe rural existence has given them the nurturing space in which to heal themselves, and from that safe space they have been able to reflect on the ethical and spiritual implications of their ancestors' suffering and what it implies for all human beings. This is a luxury unavailable to most minorities around the world, who are in the throes of abuse presently or who only recently emerged from this; they have not been given the time or the space to heal. Often they find themselves in a tense, antagonistic relationship with competing groups, either in the city or in the countryside. This hardly gives them the time or the place to work through the trauma that they have suffered. Thus, sustained injury easily turns into outer-directed violence. If my hypothesis is correct, conflict resolution strategies would need to address this and creatively seek ways for the minorities who both suffer persecution and persecute—Hutus, Tutsi, Serbians, etc.—to find or be given the time and the space to heal themselves. The Mennonite experience would be impossible to recreate, but it may provide a model for approximating measures. Ury and Fisher have already expressed the legitimacy of approximating the best possibility in negotiation, BATNA. Perhaps we need to think in terms of the best alternative to psychological healing for groups that cannot easily extract themselves from intractable problems. We know, furthermore, that there are always—even in the most damaged groups engaging in massive violence—those individuals for whom the violence is not passed on but experienced as clear testimony to the futility and evil of violence itself. We should be thinking of how we can creatively conceive of ways to support this nucleus of people, who could be at the vanguard of healing their community. Some comparative studies on the relationship between a major trauma suffered by minorities at a discreet point in time, such as a genocide, and the character of their subsequent reaction to either hostile or healing circumstances would be very useful.

10. Genesis 4:7 expresses this idea as it describes Cain's jealousy during an episode that is the prelude to the first murder in biblical literature.

11. Hart's sensitivity to "frames of different worlds," a conflict theory associated with Oscar Nudler, emerges out of the same awareness of otherness (see Nudler, 1990, pp. 177–201).

12. See the discussion in Laurence Silberstein (1994, pp. 1–34). Silberstein also confronts a related issue regarding "antiessentialist" definitions of cultural identity. Essentialists argue for a singular definition of a particular cultural identity, whereas antiessentialists, influenced by postmodern thinking, argue that cultural identity, while having some essential characteristics, is evolving all the time and is dependent upon the interaction and mutual influencing of many identities. With regard to conflict analysis, the latter approach is often to be found among those actors who are comfortable with their identities but unafraid of the creative process of interaction with other group identities and their accompanying values. This approach seems to apply well to the Mennonite peacemakers whom I have encountered. Conversely, rigidly essentialist positions are often to be found among those actors who express deep suspicion of intergroup interactions. One possible way of accounting for this difference is that the very artificiality of essentialist postures, e.g., only Christians truly understand love, only Jews are truly compassionate, only Germans understand culture, make them highly vulnerable to deniability if subjected to extensive intergroup relations, which fundamentally threaten this thin essentialist identity and the psychological life that it buttresses.

13. "I believe in the fundamental truth of all great religions of the world" (Gandhi, 1980, p. 55, and, generally, pp. 54–56).

14. I had occasion to make some small contribution to disaster relief in the wake of the Rwandan genocide. Thousands of people were on the edge of starvation in the refugee camps, and hundreds of international agencies had descended upon these camps to save lives. Yet, apparently, only two agencies bothered to ask the refugees if there were any doctors or nurses among them. All of the other agencies imported their own. One would think that rationality would be enough to encourage agencies in emergency situations to utilize local talent and to engage whatever cultural resources could be helpful in dealing with a crisis. But rational self-interest may also argue for agencies to utilize their own experts, to demonstrate expenditures to donors, or some other rational calculation. If a moral quality such as humility were to become part of the culture and modus operandi of an agency, such abuses of the dignity of aid recipients could be avoided and conflict with them minimized. In fairness, it may be the case that aid agencies choose sometimes to *not* utilize local resources in order to *avoid* conflict. But that should not be done summarily without first humbly engaging a community that is in need.

   In Liberia, the international community has brought the warring parties to the conference table thirty-two times, and scores of initiatives have been funded by foundations and agencies. Virtually ignored have been indigenous traditional peacemaking methods and the tribal elders who used to enact those peacemaking traditions. Nor were women, the guardians of Liberian peacemaking rituals, ever involved until the warlords themselves came one day to a woman, the then-head of state, and asked her to stop the war for them. Almost half of those who held guns in militias in Liberia were under the age of fifteen (Doe, 1997), and almost all of them were orphans. Yet few in the West have thought that these desperate, damaged children might respond more to the deep need for parents and the guidance of elders than they might to a piece of paper signed in Geneva.

15. See Burton, *Conflict: Human Needs Theory* (1990). For a critique of the theory, see Avruch and Black (1987, pp. 87–96).

16. Francis Hutcheson, for example, argues that if our motives in care were purely instrumental and self-interested, we would never express any admiration for those who love or give to others, and we would love equally those who give to us while also giving to others and those who give to us and brutalize others. But this is plainly not the case with our feelings, says Hutcheson (1937, p. 404). In general, the moral sense theorists posit that basic feelings of compassion and love that are plainly observable in nature should form the basis of one's ethical response to the world and that education is the key to the strengthening of those moral senses. This was written, of course, before the Freudian critique of conscious motivations, but a rejoinder to the Freudian critique, while important, is beyond the scope of this chapter.

17. Of course, I recognize the irony that my desire to study the net effects reflects an instrumentalist orientation. My analysis in no way disparages other modes of peacemaking. But each has its weaknesses to guard against, and the comparison would be instructive in this regard for all methods.

18. See, generally, Psalm 85.

19. Liechty adds that he sees the ideal approach as "solidarity with the reconcilers (reconciliation being understood to include justice) . . . with those who are trying to move beyond the binary oppositions that are part of the problem" (1997).

20. This is also complicated by the fact that *forgiveness* seems to include or mean many different things in some Christian contexts, such as unilateral apology, mutual apology, unilateral or mutual verbal expressions of forgiving, gestures of friendship, repentance, or expressions of love and acceptance. See the various ways in which it has been engaged historically in Henderson (1996). Depending on what is meant, there will be more or less in common with other cultures and religions, which often have parallel moral values or spiritual states, but then embrace these conditionally, depending on how they are carried out.

*Chapter Sixteen*

1. This is known in the United States as alternative dispute resolution.

2. The Spanish translation of the recently coined English word *peacebuilding* is "construction of peace."

3. Lederach's monograph *Building Peace: Sustainable Reconciliation in Divided Societies* (1997) was published in Spanish by Justapaz.

4. Lederach's address, "Beyond Violence: Building Sustainable Peace," subsequently appeared in print (1995a).

5. These boards were established early in 1996 to adminster peace and reconciliation funding from the European Union. The members were nominated by political parties, voluntary and private sector organizations, trade unions, and statutory agencies.

6. In particular, Yoder's *The Politics of Jesus* (1972).

# Works Cited

Adams, John. 1976. *At the Heart of the Whirlwind*. New York: Harper and Row.

Anderson, Jon. 1994. Jan. 7. "Faith in Peace: An a Army of Christians Has Mobilized to Stop the Violence." In *Chicago Tribune*.

Arthur, Paul. 1992. "Negotiating the Northern Ireland Problem: Track 1 or Track 2 Diplomacy." In *Government and Opposition* 25:4, pp. 403–418.

Avissar, Oded. 1970. *Sefer Hebron*. Jerusalem: Keter.

Avruch, Kevin, and Peter Black. 1987. "A Generic Theory of Conflict Resolution: A Critique." In *Negotiation Journal* 3, pp. 87–96.

Azar, Edward E. 1990. *The Management of Protracted Social Conflict: Theory and Cases*. Aldershot, U.K.: Dartmouth Publishing.

Bainton, Roland. 1960. *Christian Attitudes to War and Peace*. Nashville: Abingdon.

Bartsch, Karl, and Evelyn Bartsch. 1997. *Stress and Trauma Healing: A Manual for Caregivers*. Botha's Hill, S. Africa: Vuleka Trust.

Beechy, Atlee, and Winnie Beechy. 1986. Report to MBM and MCC.

Bender, Harold S. 1944. Apr. "The Anabaptist Vision." In *Mennonite Quarterly Review* 25, pp. 67–88.

———. 1950. Apr. "Mennonite Peace Action throughout the World." In *Mennonite Quarterly Review* 24, pp. 149–155.

Bontrager, Herman. 1979. Aug.–Sept. "Relief, Development, and Justice: Synthesis or Tension?" In *Peace Section Newsletter* 9:10, pp. 4–8.

———. 1989. Sept. 22. Letter to Ray Brubacher. MCS 1989 International File, MCC Records, Akron, Pa.

Braden, Murray. 1965. Apr. "Fire on the Mountain." In *Christian Living* 12, pp. 22–24.

Brubacher, Ray. 1978. Nov. 15–18. "Case Study of Southern Africa." Unpublished paper prepared for the Mennonite Peace Theology Colloquium II: Theology of Justice.

Buber, Martin. 1970. *I and Thou*. Translation and notes by Walter Kaufmann. New York: Charles Scribner's Sons.

Burrell, Jr., Curtis E. 1965. Sept. 7. "Our Mennonite Oppressors." In *Gospel Herald* 58: 35, pp. 783–784.

Burton, John W. 1969. *Conflict and Communication*. London: Macmillan.

Burton, John W., ed. 1990. *Conflict: Human Needs Theory*. New York: St. Martin's.

Caucus Members. n.d. [1991]. Eleven caucus members to John Lapp. MCS 1990–1991 File, MCC Records, Akron, Pa.

Chapa, Jr., Teodoro, Lupe DeLeon, Jr., and Neftali Torres, Jr. 1974. July. "Task Force Report to the Spanish Concilio of the Mennonite Church on the Farmworkers Issue in California." MCC 1974 Folder 3, Farm Workers (1973–1976), Archives of the Mennonite Church, Goshen, Ind.

Chupp, Mark. 1990. Personal journal.

———. 1991. Summer. "When Mediation Is Not Enough." In *Conciliation Quarterly* 10:3, pp. 2–3, 12–13.

Classen, Susan. 1992. *Vultures and Butterflies: Living the Contradictions.* Scottdale, Pa.: Herald.

Conflict Transformation Program. 1997. *Conflict Transformation Program 1994–97 Report.* Harrisonburg, Va.: Eastern Mennonite University.

Corbin, Jane. 1994. *The Norway Channel.* New York: Atlantic Monthly Press.

CPT. 1993. Oct. 10. "Considerations for CPT Decision Making for Entering Crisis Situations." From the web page of Christian Peacemaker Teams, cpt@igc.apc.org.

Curle, Adam. 1986. *In the Middle: Non-Official Mediation in Violent Situations.* New York and Hamburg: Berg.

———. 1990. *Tools for Transformation.* Wallbridge, U.K.: Hawthorn.

Darby, John. 1976. *Conflict in Northern Ireland: The Development of a Polarized Community.* Dublin: Gill and Macmillan.

Darrow, Ken, and Mike Sarenian. 1993. *Appropriate Technology Sourcebook.* Stanford, Calif.: Volunteers in Asia.

Derstine, C. F. 1946. June. "Postwar Readjustments." In *Christian Monitor* 38, pp. 190–191.

Doe, Samuel. 1997. July 10. Letter to Marc Gopin.

Driedger, Leo, and Donald B. Kraybill. 1994. *Mennonite Peacemaking: From Quietism to Activism.* Scottdale, Pa.: Herald.

Dunn, Elwood D., and Svend Holsoe. 1995. *Historical Directory of Liberia.* London: Scarecrow.

Ediger, Elmer. 1977. Summer. Personal interview by Ron Kraybill. Prairie View Mental Health Center. Notes by Kraybill, MCS 1977 File 1, Archives of the Mennonite Church, Goshen, Ind.

Epp, Frank H. 1963. May 10. "Civil Disobedience." In *Canadian Mennonite* 11:19, p. 6.

Fanon, Frantz. 1963. *The Wretched of the Earth.* New York: Grove.

Fisher, Roger, and William Ury. 1981. *Getting to Yes.* Boston: Houghton-Mifflin.

Fisher, Ronald J. 1997. *Interactive Conflict Resolution; Pioneers, Potential and Prospects.* Syracuse, N.Y.: Syracuse University Press.

Fisher, Ronald J., and Loraleigh Keashley. 1988. "Distinguishing Third Party Intervention in Intergroup Conflict: Consultation Is Not Negotiation." In *Negotiation Journal* 4, pp. 381–393.

Flackes, W. D., and Sydney Elliott. 1989. *Northern Ireland: A Political Directory, 1968–88,* 3d ed. Belfast: Blackstaff.

Folz, William J. 1977. "Two Forms of Unofficial Intervention." In *Unofficial Diplomats,* edited by M. R. Berman and J. E. Johnson, pp. 201–221. New York: Columbia University Press.

Freire, Paolo. 1970. *Pedagogy of the Oppressed.* New York: Seabury.

Gadamer, Hans. 1994. *Truth and Method.* Translated by J. Weinsheimer and D. Marshall. New York: Continuum.

Gandhi, Mohandas. 1980. *All Men Are Brothers,* edited by Krishna Kripalani. New York: Continuum.

Ghali, Boutros. 1992. *An Agenda for Peace: Preventive Diplomacy, Peacemaking and Peacekeeping.* New York: United Nations.

Gopin, Marc. 1997. Jan. "Religion, Violence and Conflict Resolution." In *Peace and Change* 22, pp. 1–22.

———. 2000. *Between Eden and Armageddon: The Future of World Religions, Violence, and Peacemaking.* New York: Oxford University Press.

Halcon, Comandante. 1990. Mar. 6. Prepared statement for a meeting with the Zonal Peace Commission.

Hallie, Phillip. 1979. *Lest Innocent Blood Be Shed.* New York: Harper and Row.

Harding, Vincent G. 1958. Sept. 30. "To My Fellow Christians: An Open Letter to Mennonites." In *Mennonite* 73:38, pp. 597–598.

Harrington, Christine, and Sally Engle Merry. 1988. "Ideological Production: The Making of Community Mediation." In *Law and Society Review* 22, 709–737.

Hart, Barrett S. 1995. "Repairing the Effects of Threats to Ethnic Identity: Trauma-Healing and Reconciliation Workshops in Liberia during the Civil War." Ph.D. diss., George Mason University.

Hauerwas, Stanley. 1984. Dec. 25. "The Faithful Are Not Always Effective." In *Gospel Herald* 77:52, p. 902.

Henderson, Michael. 1996. *The Forgiveness Factor.* Salem, Oreg., and London: Grosvenor.

Herr, Bob, and Judy Zimmerman Herr. 1994. Jan. 17. "Function and Organization of ICS." Mennonite Conciliation Service International Folder, July–Dec., 1993, MCC Records, Akron, Pa.

Hershberger, Guy F. 1945. "The Mennonite Community: A Syllabus." A course in the Farm and Community School of CPS Camp No. 138, Unit 2, Malcolm, Nebr.

———. 1946. *War, Peace and Nonresistance.* Scottdale, Pa.: Herald.

———. 1974. "Supplement to Ted Koontz's Report to the MCC Peace Section." MCS 1974–1976 Folder 4, Archives of the Mennonite Church, Goshen, Ind.

Hertzler, Daniel. 1986. June 3. "Is This an Idea Whose Time Has Come?" In *Gospel Herald* 79:22, p. 396.

Heschel, Susannah. 1995. Apr. "Transforming Jesus from Jew to Aryan: Protestant Theologians in Nazi Germany." The Albert Bilgray Lecture. Tucson: University of Arizona.

Hess, James. 1984. Dec. 25. "Pacifism: Politics or Religion?" In *Gospel Herald* 77:52, p. 902.

Hodges, Reginald K. 1991. *A View of Psychological Problems Resulting from the Liberian Civil Conflict and Recommendations for Counselling and Other Corrective Activities.* Monrovia, Liberia: Opportunities Industrialization Centers International.

Hope, A., and S. Timmel. 1984. *Training for Transformation: A Handbook for Community Workers,* books 1, 2, and 3. Zimbabwe: Mambo.

Hutcheson, Francis. 1937. "Concerning Good and Evil." In *The Classical Moralists,* compiled by Benjamin Rand. Boston: Houghton-Mifflin.

Jeffrey, Paul. 1989. Sept–Oct. "Peacemaking at the Grassroots." In *CEPAD Report,* pp. 1–6.

Johnston, Douglas, and Cynthia Sampson, eds. 1994. *Religion: The Missing Dimension of Statecraft.* New York: Oxford University Press.

Juhnke, James. 1972a. "Bibles and Bullets: Military Conscription in South Africa." In *A Collection of Writings by Mennonites on Southern Africa,* edited by Vernon Preheim, pp. 1–4. Akron, Pa.: Mennonite Central Committee.

———. 1972b. June 15. "Mennonites in South Africa—Dilemmas and Prospects." In

*A Collection of Writings by Mennonites on Southern Africa*, edited by Vernon Preheim, pp. 49–53. Akron, Pa.: Mennonite Central Committee.

———. 1989. *Vision, Doctrine, War: Mennonite Identity and Organization in America 1890–1930*. Scottdale, Pa.: Herald.

Kant, Immanuel. 1977. "The Metaphysical Foundations of Morals." In *The Philosophy of Kant: Immanuel Kant's Moral and Political Writings*, edited by Carl Friedrich, pp. 140–208. New York: Modern Library.

Keeney, William. 1976. "Mennonite Conciliation Service: A Theological Rationale (Justification)." MCS 1974–1976 File 4, Archives of the Mennonite Church, Goshen, Ind.

———. 1995a. June 26. Personal interview by Joseph S. Miller. Wichita, Kans.

———. 1995b. Nov. 3. Personal interview by Joseph S. Miller. Akron, Pa.

Kehler, Larry. 1981. May 25. "MCC and the Volunteer." Unpublished paper. Vertical file, MCC Library, Akron, Pa.

Kelman, Herbert C. 1982. "Creating Conditions for Israeli-Palestinian Negotiations." In *Journal of Conflict Resolution* 26:2, pp. 39–75.

———. 1990. "Interactive Problem-solving: A Social-Psychological Approach to Conflict Resolution." In *Conflict: Readings in Management and Resolution*, edited by John W. Burton and Frank Dukes, pp. 199–215. London: Macmillan.

Kern, Kathleen. 1994. *When It Hurts to Live*. Newton, Ks.: Faith and Life.

———. 1995. *We Are the Pharisees*. Scottdale, Pa.: Herald.

Keys, Ancel, et al. 1950. *The Biology of Human Starvation*, 2 vols. Minneapolis: University of Minnesota Press.

Kifner, John. 1995. Nov. 12. "The Zeal of Rabin's Assassin Springs from Rabbis of Religious Right." In *New York Times International Edition*, p. 12.

Klein, H. M. J 1946. "The Army Has a Heart." In *Lancaster County Historical Journal* 50:6, pp. 129–140.

Kolucki, Barbara. 1996. *Different and Equal: A Review of Peace Education Projects from Mozambique, Liberia, Sri Lanka and Lebanon*. N.Y.: UNESCO.

Koontz, Ted. 1974. "Report to the MCC Peace Section on Conversations in California Regarding the Farm Labor Situation." MCS 1974–1976 Folder 4, Archives of the Mennonite Church, Goshen, Ind.

———. 1976. Apr. 8. Letter to William Keeney. MCS 1976 Folder 4, Archives of the Mennonite Church, Goshen, Ind.

Kraus, C. Norman. 1968. June 18. "A Theology of Action." In *Gospel Herald* 61:24, pp. 538–540.

Kraybill, Donald B. 1995. Nov. 14. "How MCC Serves the Church: The Highest Common Denominator." In *Gospel Herald* 88:45, pp. 8–11.

Kraybill, Mary Jane. 1974. "Bosslers Mennonite Church and the TNT Plant Crisis of 1942: The Making of a Myth." Eastern Mennonite College history seminar paper. Menno Simons Historical Library, Eastern Mennonite University, Harrisonburg, Va.

Kraybill, Ron. 1977a. "A Paraphrase of the Meeting Held April 18, 1977, in New York on the Involvement of Religious Bodies in Community Dispute Intervention." MCS 1977 File 1, Archives of the Mennonite Church, Goshen, Ind.

———. 1977b. Summer. "Report to MCC Peace Section on the Mennonite Conciliation Service." MCS 1977 File 1, Archives of the Mennonite Church, Goshen, Ind.

———. 1977c. Aug. 5. Letter to John Adams. MCS 1977 File 2, Archives of the Mennonite Church, Goshen, Ind.

————. 1977d. Aug. 29. Letter to Bill Keeney. MCS 1977 File 2, Archives of the Mennonite Church, Goshen, Ind.

————. 1982. June. "MCS 'Chapters'." In *Conciliation Service: An Occasional Quarterly* 1:1, p. 3.

————. 1983a. "MCS Plans to Expand." In *Conciliation Service: An Occasional Quarterly* 2:2, pp. 4–5.

————. 1983b. July 20. Letter to Urbane Peachey. Personal papers of Ron Kraybill, Harrisonburg, Va.

————. 1985. "Journey to Belfast, Dublin, and London, March, 1985." MCS 1985 International File, MCC Records, Akron, Pa.

————. 1986. July 17. Letter to Tilman Metzger. MCS 1986 International File, MCC Records, Akron, Pa.

————. 1987. Jan. 28. Letter to John A. Lapp. MCS 1987 International File, MCC Records, Akron, Pa.

————. 1988. Summer. "Looking for the Holy Grail." In *Conciliation Quarterly* 7:3, p. 5.

————. 1995a. Nov. 24. Personal interview by Joseph S. Miller. Lancaster, Pa.

————. 1995b. June. Personal conversation with Robert Herr and Judy Zimmerman Herr. Lancaster, Pa.

————. 1996. "An Anabaptist Paradigm for Conflict Transformation: Critical Reflections on Peacemaking in Zimbabwe." Ph.D. diss., University of Cape Town.

————. 1997. Jan. 15. Letter to Marc Gopin.

Kreider, Alan. 1976. Jan. 12. Letter to MBM administrator Wilbert Shenk.

Kreider, Robert S. 1975. Letter to Ted Koontz, June 9, 1975. MCS 1974–1976 Folder 4, Archives of the Mennonite Church, Goshen, Ind.

————. 1995. June 7. Personal interview by Joseph S. Miller. Akron, Pa.

Kreider, Robert S., and Rachel Waltner Goosen. 1988. *Hungry, Thirsty, and a Stranger.* Scottdale, Pa.: Herald.

Lancaster, John. 1995. July 15. "Hebron Daunting for Ex-DC Activist: Advocate's Efforts Result in Israeli Detention." In *Washington Post,* A16.

Lasserre, Philippe. 1997. Mar. 24. Letter to Marc Gopin.

Lederach, John Paul. 1987. Nov. 6. MCC Peace Portfolio Staff Report. MCC Records, Akron, Pa.

————. 1988a. Spring. "Learnings from the Nicaraguan/YATAMA Negotiation." In *Conciliation Quarterly* 7:2, p. 6.

————. 1988b. Summer. " 'Yes, But Are They Talking?': Some Thoughts on the Trainer as Student." In *Conciliation Quarterly* 7:3, pp. 10–11.

————. 1988c. "Of Nets, Nails and Problems: The Folk Vision of Conflict in Central America." Ph.D. diss., University of Colorado.

————. 1989a. May 3. Letter to Herman Bontrager and John Lapp. MCS 1989 International File, MCC Records, Akron, Pa.

————. 1989b. Dec. 7. Letter to Ray Brubacher, John Lapp, Herman Bontrager. MCS 1989 International File, MCC Records, Akron, Pa.

————. 1990. June. "International Conciliation: A 10-Year Perspective, June, 1990." In ICS 1990 File, MCC Records, Akron, Pa.

————. 1992. Jan. "Missionaries Facing Conflict and Violence." In *Missiology* 20:1, pp. 11–19.

————. 1994. "The Conflict in Nicaragua's Atlantic Coast: An Inside View of War and Peacemaking." In *War and Peacemaking,* edited by Ed Garcia, pp. 101–102. Quezon City, Philippines: Claretian.

———. 1995a. "Beyond Violence: Building Sustainable Peace." In *Beyond Violence: The Role of Voluntary and Community Action in Building a Sustainable Peace in Northern Ireland*, edited by Arthur Williamson, pp. 11–22. Belfast and Coleraine, Northern Ireland: Community Relations Council and University of Ulster.

———. 1995b. Sept. 27. Personal interview by Joseph S. Miller. Harrisonburg, Va.

———. 1995c. *Preparing for Peace: Conflict Transformation across Cultures.* Syracuse, N.Y.: Syracuse University Press.

———. 1997. *Building Peace: Sustainable Reconciliation in Divided Societies.* Washington, D.C.: USIP Press. Originally published in Tokyo: United Nations University, 1995.

Levinas, Emanuel. 1985. *Ethics and Infinity.* Translated by Richard A. Cohen. Pittsburgh, Pa.: Duquesne University Press.

———. 1987. *Time and the Other.* Translated by Richard A. Cohen. Pittsburgh, Pa.: Duquesne University Press.

Liebenow, J. Gus. 1987. *Liberia: The Quest for Democracy.* Bloomington: Indiana University Press.

Liechty, Joseph. 1980. Jan. "Humility: The Foundation of Mennonite Religious Outlook in the 1860s." In *Mennonite Quarterly Review* 54, pp. 5–31.

———. 1987. "Irish Evangelicalism, Trinity College Dublin, and the Mission of the Church of Ireland at the End of the Eighteenth Century." Ph.D. diss., St. Patrick's College, Maynooth, Dublin, Ireland.

———. 1997. Jan. 13. Letter to Marc Gopin.

Liechty, Joseph, and Mike Garde. 1986. Sept. 23. Letter to Wilbert Shenk.

Little, Walter, and Christopher Mitchell, eds. 1989. *In the Aftermath: Anglo-Argentine Relations since the War for the Falklands/Malvinas.* College Park, Md.: CIDCM.

Lutheran World Relief. 1996. "Peace and Reconciliation: A Case Study of the Ogwedhi-Sigawa Development Project." Nairobi: East and Southern Africa Regional Office.

Manuel, Frank. 1979. *Utopian Thought in the Western World.* Oxford: Blackwell.

Marshall, Tony. 1989. Editorial. In *Mediation* 6:1, p. 3.

Mbonambi, Khuzwayo. 1997. Personal converation with Marc Gopin. Harrisonburg, Va.

MCC News Service. 1977. Apr. 22. "Peacemaking Task Enlarged." MCS 1977 File 2, Archives of the Mennonite Church, Goshen, Ind.

McGarry, John, and Brendan O'Leary. 1995. *Explaining Northern Ireland.* Oxford: Blackwell.

Mcoteli, G. T. 1983. Personal conversation with Robert Herr. Umtata, South Africa.

MCS. 1985. Jan. 4. "Discussion of the MCS Future: Overseas and Structural Questions." MCS 1985 International File, MCC Records, Akron, Pa.

*Mennonite Encyclopedia.* 1955. "Civilian Public Service." In *The Mennonite Encyclopedia: A Comprehensive Reference Work on the Anabaptist-Mennonite Movement* 1, p. 604. Scottdale, Pa.: Herald.

———. 1990. "Stewardship." In *The Mennonite Encyclopedia: A Comprehensive Reference Work on the Anabaptist-Mennonite Movement* 5, p. 858. Scottdale, Pa.: Herald.

*Mennonite Hymnal.* 1969. Scottdale, Pa.: Herald.

Meron, Theodor. 1993. *Henry's Wars and Shakespeare's Laws.* Oxford: Clarendon.

Merry, Sally Engle, 1990. *Getting Justice and Getting Even: Legal Consciousness among Working-Class Americans.* Chicago, Ill.: University of Chicago Press.

Merry, Sally Engle, and Neal Milner, eds. 1993. *The Possibility of Popular Justice: A Case Study of American Community Mediation.* Ann Arbor: University of Michigan Press.

Metzler, Edgar. 1987. July–Aug. "What Brings Us Together." In *Peace Section Newsletter* 17:4, p. 2.

Mitchell, Christopher R. 1981a. *Peacemaking and the Consultants' Role*. Aldershot, U.K.: Gower.

———. 1981b. *The Structure of International Conflict*. New York: St. Martin's.

———. Forthcoming. "In the Aftermath: The Falklands/Malvinas War and the Utility of Problem solving Workshops." Fairfax, Va.: Institute for Conflict Analysis and Resolution.

Mitchell, Christopher, and Michael Banks. 1996. *Handbook of Conflict Resolution*. London: Cassells.

Montville, Joseph V. 1987. "The Arrow and the Olive Branch: The Case for Track Two Diplomacy." In *Conflict Resolution: Track Two Diplomacy*, edited by John W. McDonald, Jr., and Diane B. Bendahmane, 5–20. Washington, D.C.: Foreign Service Institute.

Morrow, Duncan, Derek Birrell, John Greer, and Terry O'Keeffe. 1991. *The Churches and Inter-Community Relationships*. Coleraine, Northern Ireland: Centre for the Study of Conflict.

Ngcobo, Samuel Bongani. 1985. Personal conversation with Robert Herr and Judy Zimmerman Herr. Umtata, South Africa.

Nichols, Bruce. 1994. "Religious Conciliation between the Sandinistas and East Coast Indians of Nicaragua." In *Religion: The Missing Dimension of Statecraft*, edited by Douglas Johnston and Cynthia Sampson, 64–87. New York: Oxford University Press.

Niebuhr, Reinhold. 1937. Nov. 10. "Japan and the Christian Conscience." In *Christian Century*, pp. 1390–1391.

Nudler, Oscar. 1990. "On Conflicts and Metaphors: Toward an Extended Rationality." In *Conflict: Human Needs Theory*, edited by John Burton, pp. 177–201. New York: St. Martin's.

Oliner, Pearl, et al., eds. 1992. *Embracing the Other: Philosophical, Psychological and Historical Perspectives on Altruism*. New York: New York University Press.

O'Malley, Padraig. 1983. *The Uncivil Wars: Ireland Today*. Belfast: Blackstaff.

Pagels, Elaine. 1981. *The Gnostic Gospels*. New York: Vintage.

Peachey, J. Lorne. 1995, Nov. 14. "Something Keeps Us in There with MCC." In *Gospel Herald* 88:45, p. 20.

Peachey, Paul L. 1958. Oct. "Dare We Work for Peace?" In *Japan Christian Quarterly* 24, pp. 283–289.

———. 1976. "The Peace Churches as Ecumenical Witness." In *Kingdom, Cross, and Community*, edited by John R. Burkholder and Calvin Redekop, pp. 247–258. Scottdale, Pa.: Herald.

Peachey, Urbane. 1976. July 30. Letter to William Keeney. MCS 1974–1976 File 4, Archives of the Mennonite Church, Goshen, Ind.

———. 1977a. Feb. 21. Letter to Lynn Roth. MCS 1977 File 2, Archives of the Mennonite Church, Goshen, Ind.

———. 1977b. Apr. 14. Letter to Ron Kraybill. MCS 1977 File 2, Archives of the Mennonite Church, Goshen, Ind.

———. 1978. Apr. 27. Letter to Brice H. Balmer. Personal files of Urbane Peachey, Akron, Pa.

———. 1995. Dec. 13. Personal interview by Joseph S. Miller. Akron, Pa.

———. 1996. Nov. 2. Personal interview by Joseph S. Miller. Lancaster, Pa.

Penner, Leona. 1994. Apr. 19. Letter to MCC Headquarters. MCC Records, Akron, Pa.

Perera, Jehan. 1996. Aug. "War or Peace?" In *Lanka Monthly Digest* 3:1, pp. 5, 7, 11.

Pilarte, Doralisa. 1989. Sept. 20. "Carter Arranges Deal for Miskitos' Return." In *Detroit Free Press*, p. 7A.

Polkinghorn, D. 1983. *Methodology for the Human Sciences System of Inquiry*. Albany: State University of New York Press.

Price, Alice. 1990a. July 17. "Future Directions for MCS Network." MCS 1990 File, MCC Records, Akron, Pa.

———. 1990b. Oct. 26. Letter to MCS affiliates and colleagues. MCS 1990 File, MCC Records, Akron, Pa.

———. 1991. Sept. 16. "Follow-up and On-going Dialogue." Letter to attendees at L.A. consultation of September 16, 1991. MCS 1991 File, MCC Records, Akron, Pa.

———. 1996. Mar. 4. Telephone interview by Joseph S. Miller. Akron, Pa.

Purves, John H. 1972. June 15. "Report. Part II: South Africa." In *A Collection of Writings by Mennonites on Southern Africa*, edited by Vernon Preheim, pp. 73–82. Akron, Pa.: Mennonite Central Committee.

Rempel, Henry. 1978. Nov. "Response to the South African Case Study." Paper presented at Peace Theology Colloquium, Mennonite Central Committee, Akron, Pa.

Rosado, Caleb. 1994. Aug. 15. "America the Brutal." In *Christianity Today* 38:9, pp. 20–25.

Rose, Richard. 1976. *Northern Ireland: A Time of Choice*. London and Basingstoke: Macmillan.

Roth, Lynn. 1977. Mar. 11–12. Letter to MCC U.S. Ministries members. MCS 1977 File 1, Archives of the Mennonite Church, Goshen, Ind.

Rothman, Jay. 1992. *From Confrontation to Cooperation: Resolving Ethnic and Regional Conflict*. Beverly Hills: Sage.

Roupp, Milford. 1978. Personal interview by Joseph S. Miller. Bethel College Oral History Collection.

Rubenstein, Richard E. 1990. "Unanticipated Conflict and the Crisis of Social Theory." In *Conflict: Readings in Management and Resolution*, edited by John Burton and Frank Dukes, pp. 316–327. New York: St. Martin's.

———. 1992. July. "Dispute Resolution on the Eastern Frontier: Some Questions for Modern Missionaries." In *Negotiation Journal* 8:2, pp. 205–213.

Sareyan, Alex. 1994. *The Turning Point*. Scottdale, Pa.: Herald.

Sawyer, Amos. 1992. *The Emergence of Autocracy in Liberia*. San Francisco: Institute for Contemporary Studies Press.

Schlabach, Gerald. 1984. Sept. "MCC Central American Peace Portfolio 1985 Annual Plan." MCC Records, Akron, Pa.

Scholem, Gershom. 1977 [1941]. *Major Trends in Jewish Mysticism*. New York: Schocken.

Schumm, Dale. 1991. May. "Mennonite Board of Missions Liberia Report." Mennonite Board of Missions, Elkhart, Ind.

Seremane, Joe. 1989. June. Personal conversation with Judy Zimmerman Herr. Consultation for South African church leaders, Maseru, Lesotho.

Shenk, Sara Wenger. 1984. Dec. 25. "A Lot of Nerve!" In *Gospel Herald* 77:52, p. 902.

Sider, Ronald J. 1984a. "God's People Reconciling." In *Proceedings: Mennonite World Conference XI Assembly, Strasbourg, July 24–29, 1984*. Lombard, Ill., p. 224.

————. 1984b. Dec. 25. "Are We Willing to Die for Peace?" In *Gospel Herald* 77:52, p. 900.

————. 1989. *Non-Violence: The Invincible Weapon?* Dallas: Word. Originally published as *Exploring the Limits of Non-Violence*. London: Hodder and Stoughton, 1988.

Silberstein, Laurence, ed. 1994. *The Other in Jewish Thought and History*. New York: New York University Press.

Simons, Menno. 1956. *The Complete Writings of Menno Simons*. Translated by Leonard Verduin and edited by John C. Wenger. Scottdale, Pa.: Herald.

Soloway, Arnold, and Edwin Weiss. 1971. *Truth and Peace in the Middle East: A Critical Analysis of the Quaker Report*. New York: Friendly House.

Stauffer, Carl. n.d. [1995. Oct.] "Change from the Inside Out: Shifting Attitudes in the New South Africa." Unpublished report to MCC. MCC Records, Akron. Pa.

Stoltzfus, Gene. 1996a. Jan. 16. Personal correspondence with Kathleen Kern.

————. 1996b. Jan. 18. Personal correspondence with Kathleen Kern.

Stoner, John. 1976. July 22. Letter to William Keeney and Urbane Peachey. MCS 1977 File 1, Archives of the Mennonite Church, Goshen, Ind.

————. 1990. Apr. 18. Letter to John Paul Lederach. ICS 1990 File, MCC Records, Akron, Pa.

————. 1992. Nov. "CPT to Develop Peace Reserve." In *Signs of the Times*, pp. 1–2.

————. 1993. *Interventions of Truth: Christian Peacemaker Teams*. Chicago: Christian Peacemaker Teams.

————. 1995a. Dec. 15. Personal interview by Joseph S. Miller. Akron, Pa.

————. 1995b. Dec. 29. Personal interview by Joseph S. Miller. Akron, Pa.

Tapscott, Christopher. 1983. Personal conversation with Robert Herr. Umtata, South Africa.

Vivas, Antonio. 1990. June 29. Personal conversation. Nueva Guinea, Nicaragua.

Volkan, Vamik. 1988. *The Need to Have Enemies and Allies*. Northvale, N.J.: Jason Aronson.

Warry, Wayne. 1992. Summer. "The Eleventh Thesis: Applied Anthropology as Praxis." In *Human Organizations* 51:2.

Wehr, Paul. 1979. *Conflict Resolution*. Boulder, Co.: Westview.

Weiner, Tim. 1995. Dec. 3. "Haitian Ex-Paramilitary Leader Confirms CIA Relationship." In *New York Times*, p. 6.

Wenger, Andrea Schrock. 1988. Mar. 1. "Mennonite Mediator Helps with Nicaraguan Peace Agreement." In *Gospel Herald*. 81:9, pp. 152.

White, Dale. 1991. March. Personal conversation with Robert Herr and Judy Zimmerman Herr. Meeting of MCC and Wilgespruit Fellowship Centre Staff, Roodepoort, South Africa.

Whyte, John. 1991. *Interpreting Northern Ireland*. Oxford: Clarendon.

Williams, George H., and Angel M. Mergal, eds. 1957. *Spiritual and Anabaptist Writers: Documents Illustrative of the Radical Reformation*. Philadelphia: Westminster.

Wright, Frank. 1987. *Northern Ireland: A Comparative Analysis*. Dublin: Gill and Macmillan.

————. 1988. "Reconciling the Histories: Protestant and Catholic in Northern Ireland." In *Reconciling Memories*, edited by Alan D. Falconer, pp. 68–83. Blackrock, County Dublin: Columba.

Yoder, John Howard. 1954. Dec. 21. "The Subtle Worldliness." In *Gospel Herald* 47: 51, pp. 1209, 1221.

————. 1961. *As You Go: The Old Mission in a New Day*. Scottdale, Pa.: Herald.

————. 1972. *The Politics of Jesus*. Grand Rapids, Mich.: William B. Eerdmans.

————. 1973. Translator and editor. *The Legacy of Michael Sattler*. Scottdale, Pa.: Herald.

Yoder, Ronald E. 1993. Sept. "Visioning Future Structure for Mennonite International Conciliation Work." MCS Folder, July–Dec. 1993, MCC Records, Akron, Pa.

Zonal Peace Commission. 1990. Jan. 15. Unpublished 1989 annual evaluation. Nueva Guinea, Nicaragua. CEPAD Records, Managua, Nicaragua.

# Index